The internationalization of Japan

The Internationalization of Japan provides the English-speaking reader with the opportunity to read what some of Japan's leading social scientists and other commentators have to say about the internationalization of their country as well as its impact overseas. The topic of internationalization is of extreme importance now that the international community's demands on Japan call for a greater contribution to international society as well as changes in the domestic structure to facilitate foreign access.

The book discusses the internationalization of politics, economy and society. Topics of special interest include the internationalization of Japanese capital and automobile manufacturing, the response of Japanese society to foreign workers, local level initiatives for internationalization, and the internationalization of education. To place the internationalization of Japan in comparative perspective there are chapters on Britain and the United States from two leading political scientists of both countries.

The volume should appeal not only to students and scholars of Japanese studies, but also to political scientists and specialists in international affairs who are interested in the rise and fall of great powers. A distinctive feature of the volume is that most of the contributors are highly regarded Japanese scholars or commentators. Thus readers will be able to study at first hand what the Japanese themselves are thinking about internationalization from a wide variety of perspectives.

Glenn D. Hook is Professor of Japanese Studies at the University of Sheffield. Prior to taking up this position he was a Research Fellow at the University of Tokyo (1975–9) and a Lecturer at Okayama University (1979–88). He has published extensively in both Japanese and English. **Michael A. Weiner** is Lecturer in Japanese Studies at the University of Sheffield. His publications include work on the treatment of the Korean minority in Japan.

Sheffield Centre for Japanese Studies/Routledge Series

Series editor: Glenn D. Hook, Professor of Japanese Studies, University of Sheffield

This new series, published by Routledge in association with the Centre for Japanese Studies at the University of Sheffield, will make available both original research on a wide range of subjects dealing with Japan and will provide introductory overviews of key topics in Japanese studies.

Forthcoming titles:

An Introduction to Japanese Literature
Miriam Jelinek and Irena Powell

The Korean Minority in Wartime Japan
Michael A. Weiner

Social Welfare in Japan
Martin Collick

The internationalization of Japan

Edited by
Glenn D. Hook and Michael A. Weiner

London and New York

First published 1992
by Routledge
11 New Fetter Lane, London EC4P 4EE

Simultaneously published in the USA and Canada
by Routledge
a division of Routledge, Chapman and Hall, Inc.
29 West 35th Street, New York, NY 10001

Typeset in Scantext Times by
Leaper & Gard Limited, Bristol
Printed and bound in Great Britain
by Mackays of Chatham PLC, Chatham, Kent

British Library Cataloguing in Publication Data
A catalogue record for this book is available
from the British Library

0–415–07138–0

Library of Congress Cataloging in Publication Data

The Internationalization of Japan/Edited by Glenn D. Hook and
    Michael A. Weiner
    (Sheffield Centre for Japanese Studies/Routledge series)
    Selection of papers originally presented at the two-day Silver
    Jubilee Conference of the Centre for Japanese Studies at the
    University of Sheffield, held in September 1989.
    Includes bibliographical references and index.
    ISBN 0–415–07138–0
    1. Japan–Foreign economic relations–Congresses 2. Japan–
    Relations, Foreign countries, Congresses 3. International
    cooperation, Congresses I. Hook, Glenn D. II. Weiner, Michael A.
    III. University of Sheffield, Centre of Japanese Studies
    Conference (1979) IV. Series
    HF1601.I56   1992
    337.52–dc20

To the memory of
Maekawa Haruo and Bamba Nobuya

Contents

Figures

Tables

Contributors

Ehara Takekazu Associate Professor of Comparative Education, Kyoto University, and recently Senior Associate Member, St Antony's College, University of Oxford. His research interests include the Japanese and American education systems.

Richard Falk Albert G. Milbank Professor of International Law and Practice, Professor of Politics and International Affairs and Faculty Associate of the Center of International Studies, Princeton University; Senior Fellow of the World Policy Institute. His research interests include international law, world order and peace issues.

Andrew Gamble Professor of Politics at the University of Sheffield. His research interests include political theory, political economy and public policy, and British politics.

Hatsuse Ryūhei Professor of International Relations, Kobe University. His research interests include right-wing thought in Japan, internationalization and peace and nuclear issues.

Glenn D. Hook Professor and former Director of the Centre for Japanese Studies, School of East Asian studies, the University of Sheffield. His research interests include the internationalization of Japan and Japanese security and defence policy.

Horibe Masao Professor of Comparative Law at Hitotsubashi University and Director of the Law and Computers Association of Japan. His research interests include legal problems relating to broadcasting, telecommunications, data protection, and related matters.

Katō Shūichi Professor of Japanese culture at Ritsumeikan University, and Director-General of the Tokyo Metropolitan Central Library. His research interests include the literature, art and politics of Japan.

Nagai Michio Senior Adviser to the Rector, The United Nations University. Chairman of the Board of Directors, the International House of Japan, Inc. His research interests include educational sociology.

Nimura Kazuo   Professor and Director of the Ōhara Institute for Social Research, Hōsei University. His research interests include Japanese labour history.

Ogata Sadako   UN High Commissioner for Refugees and formerly Dean of the Faculty of Foreign Studies and Professor in the Institute of International Relations, Sophia University. Her research interests include Japanese foreign policy and the United Nations.

Sakamoto Katsuzō   Formerly Chief Economist and Chief Representative of Daiwa Securities Research Institute, London. Now secretary to the Chairman of the Board, Daiwa Securities, Tokyo. His research interests are in the Japanese bond market.

Shimokawa Kōichi   Professor and former Vice-President of Hosei University. His research interests include American and Japanese business and the Japanese automobile industry.

Sugiyama Yasushi   Former Professor of Political Science, Aoyama Gakuin University. Sadly, Professor Sugiyama passed away in May 1990.

Takahashi Susumu   Professor of International History, University of Tokyo. His research interests include German foreign policy.

Tanaka Hiroshi   Professor of Political Thought, Daitobunka University, Professor Emeritus, Hitotsubashi University. His research interests include European and Japanese political thought.

Michael A. Weiner   Lecturer, Centre for Japanese Studies, School of East Asian Studies, the University of Sheffield. His research interests include ethnic and racial minorities in Japan, human rights, and labour migration.

Yakushiji Taizō   Formerly Professor of Technology and International Relations at the Graduate School of Policy Science, Saitama University, now at Keio University. His research interests include automobile industries, science and technology policies, international co-operation, dual-use technologies, and telecommunication policies.

Yamazawa Ippei   Professor of Economics, Hitotsubashi University. His research interests include international economics (especially trade policy) and investment and industrial adjustment.

Yoko Sellek   Lecturer, Centre for Japanese Studies, School of East Asian Studies, the University of Sheffield. Her research interests include labour economics (particularly migrant workers in Japan).

Preface

The chapters in this volume have been selected from amongst the twenty-eight papers presented at the two-day Silver Jubilee Conference of the Centre for Japanese Studies at the University of Sheffield. The Conference was held in September 1989 on the theme, 'The Internationalization of Japan in Comparative Perspective'. The Conference provided a multi-disciplinary forum for Japanese, European and North American scholars, (the non-Japanese mostly not specialists on Japan, to address) Japan's internationalization in a comparative perspective. Among the participants were more than forty of Japan's leading social scientists as well as nearly 200 European academics, government officials, and members of the business community. Never before, at least in Europe, had such a large number of Japanese scholars been gathered together for a conference on Japan's role in the contemporary world. This in itself is evidence of the extent to which 'internationalization' has come to dominate the national agenda in Japan. Equally, the fact that a 'Japan Conference' attracted such a large number of non-Japanologists demonstrates the degree to which Europeans are interested in Japan. This interest can be seen to result from Japan's 'internationalization'.

With the exception of one chapter and the introduction, written especially for this collection, the sixteen chapters were revised and edited after their initial presentation at the conference. The sessions were in principle organized so that the Japanese scholars presented the papers, in sessions chaired by European or North American specialists on Japan, with comments by British social scientists, politicians or representatives of the business community. The sessions, conducted in English, were organized in this way in order to place the central theme of Japan's internationalization in a comparative setting, and to promote a dialogue between the English-speaking Japanese and non-Japanese-speaking European participants, with the session chairs facilitating these interactions.

The plenary sessions considered internationalization at the global level, at the local level, in labour markets and in domestic perspective. Other sessions addressed themes arising out of the internationalization of Japanese politics, economics, society and education. The papers, selected from each of these sessions, have been organized here into the following sections: (1) Comparison: Britain and the United States; (2) Meanings and implications; (3) Japan and the world economy; (4) National and local politics; (5) Labour markets and migrant workers; (6) Education and the individual; and (7) The future. The editors would like to take this opportunity to express their thanks to the Japanese participants, all of whose papers were written and presented in English. Their co-operation in the editing of this volume has also been appreciated.

Dedicatory note

Internationalization results from the efforts of people. During the conference and shortly thereafter two people who had contributed to the internationalization of Japan passed away. One is widely known as the namesake for the 'Maekawa Report'; the other was a friend or colleague of many at the conference. Maekawa Haruo, former Governor of the Bank of Japan, died on 22 September 1989 aged 78. Bamba Nobuya, then Professor of International Behaviour at Osaka University, died on 6 October 1989 aged 52. The different ways in which each contributed to Japan's internationalization, and the close timing of their deaths, prompted this dedication.

Maekawa Haruo's contribution to Japan's internationalization was in the area of finance and economics. This comes first from his work at the Bank of Japan, especially during his term as Governor, a position he gained after having carved out a career for himself as a specialist in international finance. In the early postwar years he played a role in Japan's reintegration into the international financial community. Later, at meetings of the International Monetary Fund and other international bodies, he participated in major decisions relating to international finance. As Governor, he strove to maintain price stability during the second oil shock, and contributed to the stabilization of the international currency market. He did this by breaking what had been until then regarded as a taboo: changing Japan's base rate at the time of the budget debate in the Diet. In this way, Maekawa helped to bring Japan to the forefront in international finance.

It was against this background that, after his retirement, Maekawa came to play a major role in the internationalization of the Japanese economy. Then Prime Minister Nakasone Yasuhiro selected him as chairman of a committee set up to investigate the steps Japan should take to make structural adjustments in the economy in order to promote international harmony. The early 1980s were a time when the Japanese economy was undergoing rapid internationalization. The committee's report, which became known as the Maekawa Report after it was issued in 1986 (and as the new Maekawa Report when issued in 1987) called for domestic changes in order to promote international harmony and reduce friction with Japan's trade partners. In particular, the report called for Japan to move away from being an export-dependent economy, which had led to its surplus and the resultant economic frictions, to one led by domestic demand. The committee called for an expansion in domestic demand, liberalization, and the relaxation of restrictions in a wide range of sectors. In essence, the proposal aimed to internationalize the Japanese economy and open Japan to the world.

In contrast to Maekawa's contribution to the internationalization of finance and economy through the shaping of Japanese policy, Bamba Nobuya's contribution was to the internationalization of education and society through teaching and research. His personal experience of teaching and research abroad, as well as his contribution to international and national academic conferences, was such as to make him a force for the internationalization of the educational and academic environment in Japan. He was an internationalist (a 'globalist'), a teacher who provided his students with a breadth of vision not common even among those with foreign experience. As a researcher, he brought a fresh breeze to academic societies in Japan (such as the Peace Studies Association of Japan, of which he was President at the time of his death) by trying to internationalize the agenda, increase the number of foreign participants, and develop an international network crossing the boundaries of north and south as well as east and west.

His research, too, was infused with a concern for issues related to internationalization. An interest in international issues arises naturally from his discipline, but, unlike mainstream research, where the state is the central focus of attention, Bamba was largely concerned with subnational actors – local governments, non-governmental organizations, and the citizen. These he saw as playing an essential role in the internationalization of Japanese society. Again, instead of focusing his attention on 'national interest', which is rooted in a state-centric view of the world, he developed the concept of 'human interest' – the theme of the paper he presented at the Sheffield conference. To Bamba, 'human interest' was to establish peace, economic security, harmony with nature, respect for the individual, and absolute equality. Yet 'human interest' was more than an academic concept for Bamba, who believed in struggling to realize these values in everyday life. This was reflected in his own life by, for instance, his active involvement in non-governmental organizations like Amnesty International.

In this way, Maekawa Haruo and Bamba Nobuya contributed to the internationalization of Japan – in finance and economy, education and society. While Maekawa's main contribution was in influencing Japanese policy, Bamba's was in influencing Japanese attitudes. In the further internationalization of Japan, both are essential.

Glenn D. Hook

Acknowledgements

I first wish to thank all those who contributed to the success of the conference, especially the Japanese speakers and commentators, without whom the conference would not have been possible. For financial support of the conference I would like to thank the Foundation for Advanced Information and Research (Tokyo), Hitotsubashi Josuikai (London Branch), Japan Foundation, Japan Foundation Endowment Committee, Nichimen Europe Limited and the Nisshō Iwai Foundation. These organizations helped to make both the conference and this book possible. Finally, thanks are due to Michael A. Weiner for agreeing to jointly edit this volume.

Glenn D. Hook

NOTE

Throughout the text, the names of the Japanese contributors follow the convention of surname first with given name following.

Introduction

Glenn D. Hook and Michael A. Weiner

The *Concise Oxford Dictionary* defines 'internationalize' as 'make international, esp. bring (territory etc.) under combined protection etc. of different nations'. The term, however, is seldom encountered, except in legal treatises. In contrast, the Japanese expression *kokusaika suru* (internationalize) or *kokusaika* (internationalization) frequently appears in journalistic, academic and political commentaries. The saliency of the *kokusai* theme in the 1980s can be seen from former Prime Minister Nakasone Yasuhiro's pledge to transform Japan into a *kokusai kokka* (international state) – a commitment hardly met by similar exhortations among the leaders of other industrialized states. Indeed, to many, the term is a contradiction: it is precisely as a result of the existence of individual nation states that international society exists. Or, again, the very notion of 'internationalization' may contradict the existence of the nation state as now constituted. Nevertheless, increasing interdependence, which has led to a greater reliance on international or even supranational organizations and laws in the resolution of conflicts arising between nation states, makes it essential that *kokusaika* is not simply regarded as a 'buzz word'.

Analytically, internationalization can be understood to involve a multidimensional process – of one nation penetrating another; of a nation being penetrated; of policy adjustment on the national level in response to international pressures; and of subnational actors influencing the international system. The impact of these processes on a country differs depending on its position in the international system. Today, Japan is trying to cope with the consequences of these processes as it redefines its role in the world.

First, Japan's present position in the world economy results precisely from its penetration of other nations and its own increasing interdependence. This has been manifest during the period of Japan's 'modernization' in a variety of forms; most recently, by the high level of its economic presence in both the industrially developed and developing countries. One salient aspect of this has been direct investment and the outflow of capital, particularly to the developed economies of Europe and North America. In the developing economies, particularly in South East Asia, technology transfer has played a significant role in industrialization. The export of Japanese-finished products, which was for much of the postwar period accepted as a manifestation of 'free trade' and Japan's reintegration into the international economic system, is to some now more a threat to the stability of that very system. At its crudest, this fear has taken the form of 'Japan bashing' in Europe and the United States. In certain parts of South East Asia this asymmetrical process of penetration has also engendered fears of a recrudescence of Japanese ultra-nationalism, and images of a Greater East Asia Co-Prosperity Sphere first envisaged prior to 1945. Similar sentiments have been expressed in Japan. Paralleling the proliferation of Japanese goods in the world market, as a result of the success of its export-led industries, has come the increasing outflow of people. This is not only the ubiquitous Japanese tourist on a brief visit to foreign lands, but involves business people and their families who spend extended periods abroad and then return home. One of the consequences of this has been the establishment of Japanese schools overseas, which provide a Japanese curriculum for the children of businessmen, diplomats, and so forth. For those who attend local schools, however, return to Japan and reintegration into the highly competitive school system presents considerable difficulties.

Similarly, the penetration of Japan by the outside world has been a constant feature of Japan's modernization since the country was opened to foreign trade in the middle of the nineteenth century. Indeed, the degree to which Japan has assimilated foreign technology and ideas has generated a stereotypical view of a mimetic Japan. Although such charges, at least to some extent, reflect the European and American obsession with 'race', little doubt exists as to the Western impact on Japan. The influence of Western political thought and institutions on the evolution of politics in Japan, both in the prewar and postwar periods, is a case in point. The American Occupation is often cited as the pre-eminent example of this type of penetration. More recently, economic concerns have taken centre stage in the form of demands for liberalization of Japan's markets and in the migration of thousands of workers from the developing countries of Asia to Japan.

Thus the problem of racial discrimination, previously considered in the context of Burakumin, Ainu, Koreans and other long-term Asian residents, now encompasses these migrant workers from other parts of Asia. Here Japanese policies have been adjusted in response to the norms incorporated in the growing body of international laws. While Japan's ratification of a number of international covenants has significantly ameliorated the situation for Japan's foreign residents, discriminatory practices persist. Again, educational policies and the content of school curricula have had to be adjusted as a consequence of international pressures. The best-known recent example is the 'textbook controversy', where the governments of the

Republic of Korea, the Democratic People's Republic of Korea and the People's Republic of China bitterly criticized the government's attempt to obfuscate Japan's aggression in Asia. Clearly, xenophobia continues to exert an influence on Japanese perceptions of the outside world and of themselves. This clash in Japanese society between xenophobic and ethnocentric attitudes (which have been integral to Japanese national identity) on the one hand, and nascent pluralism, on the other, represent the cutting edge of 'internal' internationalization. This is particularly evident in the position taken by most Japanese trade unions, where the interests of indigenous workers are in apparent conflict with their traditional commitment to international solidarity.

Finally, at the subnational level, local governments and citizen groups in Japan and elsewhere have assumed an increasingly important role in shaping international society. This takes the form of agenda-setting, alternative policy proposals, and actions on issues with international implications. The voices raised have often been in conflict with central government policies, as seen in the case of the promulgation of 'anti-nuclear' statements and the creation of 'nuclear-free zones' by local authorities. In Japan, the existence of discrimination against ethnic minorities has clearly influenced, and in turn been influenced by, relations with other countries, particularly the Republic of Korea. The stance local governments have taken against central government policies, particularly on the issue of fingerprinting of foreigners, means foreign and local governments have shared a common cause. On other occasions, as in the case of laws to protect privacy in the collection, storage and transmission of data on individuals, both within and across national boundaries, local-level initiatives have preceded legislation at the national level.

These dimensions of internationalization, as touched on above, are not unique to Japan nor to the present international system. What is striking about the contemporary world, however, is the extent to which Japan, along with other countries, is integrally tied into these processes. Thus, even hegemonic powers need to take into account the international dimension in the formulation of many national policies. The adjustment of currency exchange rates, changes in the industrial structure, and the revision of nationality laws, are all areas in which domestic policies may be influenced by international considerations.

It is against this background that the chapters in this book address issues generated by the internationalization of Japan. Much of the initial discussion at the Sheffield Conference was given over to an attempt to delineate the parameters of internationalization. While the participants agreed that internationalization involves the transmission of information, technology and resources, both human and material, they focused on different aspects of this process. What emerged from the discussions was first, that the question of Japan's internationalization should be taken up in the context of the current transformation of the international system; second, that Japan remains ill-prepared for a more active role in global affairs; and third, that domestic resistance to internationalization, at both the institutional and individual level, remains salient. These points will become clearer from the chapters that follow.

In Part I of this volume, Andrew Gamble and Richard Falk examine the internationalization of Britain and the United States respectively. Gamble focuses on Britain as the classic example of the developmental cycle a hegemonic power experiences: its rise and decline as an economic, political and military hegemon in the world system. For Britain, this involved a short-lived period of hegemony, coterminous with the creation of an overseas empire, followed by a more lengthy decline through the erosion of its hegemonic base of power. As John Westergaard pointed out at the conference, the recent social history of Britain has been shaped by the search for an explanation of Britain's hegemonic decline. While Gamble focuses on external factors, both the right and left wings in British politics tend to focus on the internal: the right associates the decline with the restraints imposed by union power; the left, in contrast, lays the blame at the door of the ruling elites, which have failed to invest at home.

Sakamoto Yoshikazu, in commenting on Gamble's paper, highlighted the need to take account of the non-European experience of 'internationalization'. For many of the countries in the developing world, this process was a product of imperial penetration and colonial domination – an asymmetric form of internationalization. To Sakamoto, Gamble's internationalization is akin to global economic liberalization, as seen from the perspective of a dominant power in the international system. While Gamble accepted the need to distinguish between different forms of internationalization, he saw the historical context of that internationalization as crucial. Thus, the asymmetric process referred to by Sakamoto has been but one stage in Britain's internationalization.

Gamble addresses Britain's decline in economic importance, the subsequent transfer of the hegemonic mantle to the United States, and, most recently, Britain's reluctant integration into the European Community. In Sakamoto's view, Britain's hegemonic legacy is most apparent in its 'imperial insularity' – that is, attempting to influence international society while limiting its impact at home. As a result, the internationalization of British society was not a concomitant of imperial expansion in the nineteenth century. This legacy helps to explain the parochial attitudes towards internationalization in the twentieth century, as recently seen in Britain's resistance to the creation of a European polity.

Gamble enumerates three principal differences between British and American hegemonies – economic power base, formal/informal empire and military expenditures – but grounds his analysis in the economic dimensions of hegemony. Along with Britain's imperial expansion came a greater dependence on the world economy, and increased responsibility to maintain the international system from which the hegemon is the chief beneficiary. While agreeing with Gamble on the importance of these principles, Kamo Takehiko, in his comments, raised the question of whether multiple hegemonic powers may exist, with economics playing the crucial role. The relative importance of the economic dimension of hegemony was returned to in the comments by Brian McCormack in the conference's economy section. For McCormack it is trade, not military expenditure, that comprise the key indices in explaining the decline of hegemonic powers. Kamo expressed similar sentiments. For him, the lesson to be learned from the British experience is that, in pursuing policies promoting internationalization, Japan should resist the temptation to boost military spending and strengthen strategic and military power. Kamo recommended policies shaped by 'enlightened national interest' as the most appropriate for Japan.

In Richard Falk's view, American internationalization has largely been an asymmetric process of America influencing other nations. In the postwar context, the salient feature of this has been the 'Americanization' of the world. This he equates with the expansion of America's global military, economic and cultural power. The latter, especially American consumerism, is viewed as particularly important. From this broad perspective, the Soviet challenge to American hegemony was always more imaginary than real. While agreeing on the important impact Americanization has had on the world, particularly the transmission of universal values such as human rights and democracy, Sakamoto Yoshikazu questioned the centrality of the US as a purveyor of consumerism.

Falk points to an apparent contradiction in the United States between isolationism, on the one hand, and the deeply held conviction that others can only benefit from contact with superior American culture, on the other. Japan, clearly regarded as a beneficiary of this American proclivity, is now also widely viewed in the United States as a competitor, especially in economic activity. Pressed by the Japanese challenge, the United States still seeks ways of sustaining the global ascendancy it has enjoyed since 1945. Sakamoto reminded us that the United States has not been reluctant to make use of international concepts in an attempt to rationalize and justify its own global interests.

The three chapters in Part II focus on the meanings and implications of Japan's internationalization. For Ogata Sadako, internationalization, which involves the transformation of attitudes and values, needs to be distinguished from interdependence, a phenomenon resulting from increased economic, political and human links between nations. In her view, Japan's asymmetric external relations are mirrored in the internal structures of society, and for internal internationalization to proceed, problems such as discrimination against ethnic minorities, returnee children, and foreign workers need to be resolved. She expresses disappointment that both government and business have been slow to respond effectively to the challenges generated by internal and external internationalization. Ogata supports the further internationalization of Japan – a type of 'cultural liberalism', as Barry Buzan commented – as a means of making Japan more open. This is in contrast to what Buzan termed 'cultural mercantilism', that is, a closing in of a society as it attempts to limit external influences. Buzan drew attention to the fact that, outside the parameters of internationalization touched on by Ogata, which focused on the internal dimension, there is also the external dimension – that is, the influence of Japanese culture on global society in, for example, the arts. For Ogata, however, crucial to external internationalization is a more proactive role for Japan in the security field, managing the global economy, development assistance or disaster relief; or, in general, placing issues of global concern on the national agenda.

Sugiyama Yasushi shares Ogata's concern with the attitudes and values associated with internationalization. The public opinion surveys he examines clearly indicate that, on the one hand, the Japanese people attach a positive value to internationalization, but, on the other, regard themselves as members of a tightly knit, closed society. His chapter is particularly relevant to an understanding of the two interrelated dimensions of internationalization – internal and external. Sugiyama's diagnosis includes an expansion of existing cultural and student-exchange programmes, revision of the school curriculum, and the utilization of returnee children as an educational resource for the creation of a more internationally oriented society.

In his commentary on Sugiyama's paper, Westergaard argued that the existence of divisions within society throws doubt on the extent to which any society constitutes a single normative system, at least one reflected in public opinion surveys. He thereby questioned a fundamental premise underlying much writing on Japan: that a high degree of homogeneity in terms of race, ethnicity and social classes exists. For Westergaard, any attempt to analyse attitudes towards internationalization should take into account class-based differences. For societies are beset with competing images not only of other states, but of their own. It is this, more than anything else, which militates against the understanding of 'other' people.

By examining a number of Japanese political thinkers, Tanaka Hiroshi shows how, in the nineteenth and early twentieth centuries, a wide spectrum of Western political ideas was introduced into Japan, but the underlying values of liberal democracy, such as the right to individual freedom, were not fully assimilated. By setting his topic in historical perspective, Tanaka is able to show how the uneven grafting of key democratic principles has inhibited the role of the individual in Japanese society. He remains convinced that the assimilation of universalistic values imported from the West can contribute to the creation of a more democratic and humanistic society in Japan.

This was a point pursued by Steven George, who questioned the extent to which the absence of universalistic values is characteristic of Japanese political culture. For Tanaka this is very much the case, as illustrated by the uneven absorption of universalistic concepts from the West. Therefore, for Japan to become a truly internationalized society, Tanaka sees the need for the universalistic values and principles derived from the West to be fully incorporated into the political culture of Japan.

The three chapters in Part III consider the internationalization of the Japanese economy. Yamazawa Ippei examines Japanese government policies geared to liberalization of markets and industrial restructuring. These he sees as stemming from both Japan's overseas economic expansion and the criticisms thereby generated. In his comments, McCormack, however, argued that the expansion of imports should be regarded not only as a response to external pressure to liberalize domestic markets in Japan, but also as a means to maintain the level of exports. He drew parallels with Britain in the mid-nineteenth century, when the abolition of the Corn Laws, which had limited imports, facilitated the expansion of exports. In addressing industrial restructuring, Yamazawa emphasizes the pace at which this has taken place in the service sector in Japan. This type of rapid growth in the service sector, McCormack reminded us, was even more apparent in Britain prior to the discovery of North Sea oil in the 1960s.

The chapter by Sakamoto Katsuzō and Richard Conquest addresses the internationalization of Japanese capital by charting Japan's rise as both a creditor and an investor nation. In their view, the recent massive accumulation of capital in Japan has further fuelled the process of internationalization by enabling Japanese firms to expand their overseas investments at an unprecedented rate. This has also stimulated growth in the world economy. The authors document how, despite Japan's undeniable importance in global economic affairs, the yen does not yet play a substantive role as an international currency, and they argue that it is not likely to displace the US dollar as the prime international currency in the foreseeable future. In their view, Japan should continue to support US economic leadership and open its markets to more imports.

While agreeing that the Japanese yen is not yet fully accepted as an international currency, McCormack questioned whether Japan should be unduly influenced by the economic priorities of the United States. He reminded us of the problems that have arisen in the past as a consequence of America's economic leadership. For instance, under a system of fixed exchange rates in the 1960s, the US increased the supply of dollars and this led to worldwide inflation; more recently, the US has increased its borrowing and this has led to an increase in interest rates, precipitating the debt crisis in the Third World.

The final chapter in Part III is a case study by Shimokawa Kōichi of one of the most visible signs of Japan's external internationalization – the basing of automobile plants abroad. The author examines the different approaches taken by Japan's principal auto-manufacturers in locating their factories in North America and Asia as the first phase in the international-ization of their industry. After examining the range of difficulties they have encountered in basing overseas, he discusses the future prospects for the emergence of an international division of labour in the production of automobiles. McCormack here drew attention to the fact that responses to this form of direct investment are largely determined by the nature of the relationship between the recipient nation and Japan in the world economy. This helps to explain why Japanese automakers have been encouraged to base their operations in the United States and Britain, whereas, in South Korea, for instance, restrictions have been imposed on Japanese firms to protect domestic producers. Shimokawa maintains, however, that the need to import more sophisticated technology will in time force the abandon-ment of this kind of protectionism.

The longevity of Liberal Democratic Party (LDP) rule in Japan is now well known in the West, the LDP having been in power continuously since 1955. The extent to which Japanese politics is internationalized, however, has only recently become the focus of scholarly interest. In Part IV this issue is examined on national and local levels. In his chapter, Yakushiji Taizō summarizes the development of political institutions in Japan showing that, from the Meiji period onwards, these have been influenced by both Western and indigenous elements. He stresses that Japan's postwar political culture is an amalgam of American democratic institutions, intro-duced during the Occupation, and prewar patterns of political behaviour. This 'grafted democracy' has, on the one hand, provided the institutional framework for Japan's postwar economic growth; but, on the other, has failed to create an internationally oriented type of politician in Japan. This, as Steven George pointed out in his comments, contrasts sharply with the situation in Britain, where the elite political culture has been dominated by a global perspective. This he viewed as a product of the determination to maintain a global economic and political order which redounded to the benefit of Britain, or at least certain groups in British society. Whereas Japanese voters appear to be aware of the degree to which Japan's prosperity is dependent upon the rest of the world, George maintained that the British electorate is less aware of this interdependence.

On the local level, Takahashi Susumu analyses the policies to promote internationalization pursued by the Kanagawa Prefectural Government. He addresses not only the external aspects of internationalization, in the form of cultural and economic exchange programmes with foreign countries, but also the internal aspects. In Kanagawa the latter has taken the form of policies to promote interaction between Japanese and long-term foreign residents, with a view to creating a new internationalized sense of local community. Kanagawa's commitment to the protection of the human rights of all residents, irrespective of nationality, has brought it into conflict with the central government on more than one occasion. This is best exemplified by Kanagawa's refusal to accept central government policies uncritically, as seen in its anti-nuclear stance and its opposition to laws requiring the fingerprinting of foreigners. Here Takahashi highlights the crucial role that Governor Nagasu has played in creating a regional agenda for the internationalization of Kanagawa. The issue of local-level internationalization was commented on by David Blunkett, who identified several areas of common concern for Britain and Japan. One area was the challenge to central government policies represented by the anti-nuclear stance taken by some local authorities in Britain, typified by the declaration of nuclear-free zones. In his comments, Nicolas Wolfers noted that the involvement of local governments in international issues should be regarded as a significant aspect of current internationalization.

The three chapters comprising Part V all focus on a theme of major concern for the 1990s – the impact upon society in general, and the economy in particular, of the migration of Asian workers to Japan. In their commissioned chapter, Michael Weiner and Yoko Sellek point out that this is not a new phenomenon, but only one phase in the internationalization of labour. Indeed, Japan experienced a much larger influx of foreign workers earlier in this century, and all three chapters consider the current debate within the context of discrimination against Korean and other foreign residents. Utilizing the concepts of 'disparity' and 'network', Weiner and Sellek provide a comparative setting for the analysis of the recent arrival of migrant workers to Japan.

For Hatsuse Ryūhei, the history of this earlier migration not only influences the formulation and implementation of immigration laws and policies, but also reinforces a stereotypical image of Asians. Like other authors in this volume, Hatsuse regards the persistence of racial ideologies as a major obstacle to internationalization. After presenting the arguments for and against the acceptance of 'guest workers', he proposes that, at least as an interim measure, a programme for the employment of Asian workers on a reciprocal basis should be implemented.

The response of the Japanese trade union movement to the arrival of a new wave of foreign workers is taken up in the chapter by Nimura Kazuo. In his analysis, Nimura identifies major differences in the positions adopted by Japanese labour federations as well as individual unions. Nimura addresses the perennial problem confronting labour organizations when their duty to safeguard the interests of their members comes into conflict with their ideological commitment to international labour solidarity. In Nimura's view, this conflict of interest is largely the reason why the trade union movement has only been willing to provide minimal support for foreign workers, whose interests are not necessarily shared by its members.

In commenting on the contributions by Hatsuse Ryūhei and Nimura Kazuo, Colin Holmes emphasized the comparative aspects of labour migration. He reminded us that, as in Japan, postwar immigration to Britain has prewar antecedents. These migrants were met with similar responses to those now occurring in Japan. For instance, the response of Japanese trade unions to Asian migrant workers is similar to the response of British workers to the Irish migrations of the nineteenth century and other more recent immigrants. Holmes also questioned Hatsuse's concern with controlling the number of migrant workers as a means of resolving the current controversy. Robert Miles, the other commentator, argued that any analysis of labour migration should not be restricted to assessing the characteristics of the migrants; rather, analyses should focus upon the nature of the receiving society. For Miles, the problem of labour migration to Japan should be placed within the much broader context of the internationalization of labour in a capitalist world economy.

The two chapters in Part VI address issues of critical importance in determining the future shape of Japanese society: education, which has been a focus of controversy throughout the postwar period; and the position of the citizen in society, as expressed in the tension between individual rights and collective duties. Ehara Takekazu evaluates the government's understanding of the 'internationalization of education' as reflected in reports issued by the Ministry of Education and the Prime Minister's Office. As these show, the government has responded, however reluctantly, to internal and external criticisms of both the content and objectives of Japanese education. In commenting on Ehara's paper, Bryan Coates noted how, under Britain's present government, education is becoming less international in outlook, as evidenced by the stress placed on British history in the new national curriculum. An area which Ehara singles out as being particularly significant for internationalization is contact between Japanese students and their counterparts overseas. He argues that exchange programmes would facilitate the internationalization of education, which he defines as a process through which the young are exposed to global values and attitudes in a setting accessible to students of all backgrounds. At the same time, Ehara recognizes the importance of programmes involving the greater participation of foreigners in the education system, such as the employment of non-Japanese at the secondary and tertiary levels. Coates drew attention to how, under the Japan Exchange and Teaching (JET) programme, young British graduates were contributing to the internationalization of Japanese education by teaching in Japanese schools. Although these and other measures implemented by the Ministry of Education are evaluated positively by Ehara, he still finds scope for improvement, particularly in regard to the reintegration of returnee children into Japanese society.

Horibe Masao's chapter deals with the issue of individual rights by focusing upon the right to privacy in Japanese law, with particular reference to the collection, storage and transfer of information by computers. Horibe notes that the concept of privacy, like many of the legal and political terms in current usage in Japan, has its origins in the West. But, whereas individualism (*kojinshugi*) has been translated into Japanese, the legal notion of 'privacy' only exists in a katakana rendering, *puraibashii*, which entered usage from the late 1950s. This aside, Japan has been a pioneer in areas related to technology and individual freedom, and the term 'information society' is itself a translation of the Japanese, *jōhōshakai*. Horibe highlights how local governments have played a major role in the formulation of laws on data protection and the rights of the individual. In contrast to the United States, where the federal government has played a dominant role, in Japan it is on the local level where the right to privacy has received the most attention. It was not until 1988 that comprehensive legislation to protect privacy was introduced at the national level.

In commenting, Westergaard outlined how attempts to protect the individual's right to privacy are subject to numerous limitations. These involve not only legal enforcement in the private and public sectors, but also questions of definitions. For the conventional boundary between public and private is blurred and changes over time, as seen in Britain during the 1980s. He also expressed concern that the recent legislation on data protection in Japan and elsewhere is wholly or largely confined to computer-stored information, while privacy-threatening information stored by more primitive techniques has been largely ignored. A further limitation is the range of legal exemptions permitted for so-called legitimate purposes. This begs the question, Westergaard stressed, of 'whose legitimacy'?

The concluding Part VII of this volume is given over to future considerations of Japan's role in the world by Nagai Michio and Katō Shūichi. In this respect, Nagai emphasizes that Japan's position as an economic superpower brings with it new responsibilities. This, he argues, may require a redefinition of Japan's postwar relationship with the United States in particular. Leaving questions of security aside, Nagai sees an important role for Japan in the revitalization of the US economy, which is vital to global stability and prosperity. He is also concerned with the future relationship between 'technology' and 'society'. While Japan's postwar prosperity has been brought about by harnessing the powers of science and technology, Nagai recognizes that they have also engendered a threat to security as symbolized by nuclear weapons. In commenting, Fred Warner accepted Nagai's assessment of the integral relationship between technology and society, but warned against a Luddite response to the continuing search for new technologies. He shared with Nagai the hope that Japan will continue to harness technology to the needs of international society.

The second chapter, by Katō Shūichi, views Japan's relationship with the United States in a more critical light. Thus, what others in Japan widely regard as fulfilling 'international' responsibilities he views as the subordination of Japanese interests to those of the United States. The decline of American power in the 1980s, together with Japan's economic success, has created a new-found sense of self-confidence amongst the Japanese people. This, he suggests, has provided fertile ground for a rebirth of Japanese nationalism. Indeed, under the Nakasone government, nationalistic sentiments were encouraged by state policies. The emergence of 'neo-nationalism' Katō views with alarm – a sentiment not shared by Warner. For him, present-day neo-nationalism is unlikely to lead to a recrudescence of the ultra-nationalism of prewar days.

In this way, the chapters in *The Internationalization of Japan* give the reader access to the current debate on internationalization. The Japanese contributors, all of whom have participated in this debate in some form or other, have themselves also contributed to 'internationalization'. In some instances, this has been through critical analyses; in others, through policy recommendations; and finally, through policy formulation. Given the views expressed it is clear that, as the internationalization of Japan proceeds through the 1990s, both internally and externally, many of the underlying assumptions about Japan and its place in the world will need to be reassessed. The chapters in this volume provide a starting point for just such a reassessment.

Part I

Comparison: Britain and the United States

Chapter 1

Internationalization and the national economy
The British case

Andrew Gamble

HEGEMONY AND INTERNATIONALIZATION

The capitalist world system that has emerged since the sixteenth century has been responsible for an unprecedented rise in output and productivity, as well as a progressive increase in the interdependence of all regions and nations. This process is reflected in repeated pressures towards the widening and deepening of the global division of labour, and the increasing complexity of the networks of production, trade and finance.

This world system, however, is a political system as well as an economic system. Its most important political agents are the nation states. The differing capacities of these states and the competition between them are a major source of the dynamism and unpredictability of the system. As Immanuel Wallerstein describes it: 'Its life is made up of conflicting forces which hold it together by tension, and tear it apart as each group seeks eternally to remould it to its advantage'.[1]

As a world economy, the world system displays a trend towards ever greater cohesion and interdependence. As a world polity, it remains highly fragmented. The world system has never been transformed into a political empire. Its unity has been economic rather than political. The technological dynamism of this world system has ensured that no state has been able to stand outside indefinitely. Every state has tried to influence the terms of its participation by competing with other states for territory, resources and population. States seek to maintain whatever comparative advantages their national economies enjoy, and where they cannot, they seek to protect their citizens from the consequences.

Competition between states in the world system has aided its expansion and led to a highly unequal distribution of resources and income within it. The hierarchy of states has not remained constant, however. States have risen and fallen. Those states that achieve dominance in one period frequently lose it in the next as rivals emerge to challenge them.

The integration and complexity of the world system has increased, in particular as a result of industrialization. But nation states remain the seat of decision-making and the focus of legitimacy. International institutions have been slow to develop, and have never kept pace with economic integration. This lack of balance has frequently been a source of instability. The need for political institutions to create and maintain the conditions for international economic order has come to be widely recognized. The world market, no less than a national market, requires a central public authority. The establishment of international rules, institutions and norms of behaviour have slowly evolved. Progress has been swiftest when one of the leading states in the world system has become so dominant that it has been able to exercise 'hegemony' over the other leading states, without ever being in a position to absorb them politically.

Hegemony arises when one state achieves clear economic supremacy over all others. No second power or combination of powers is able to challenge its economic supremacy effectively. This supremacy is manifested in production (technological lead), in commerce (share of world trade) and in finance (international credit). The leading power enjoys supremacy in all three areas and it attempts to consolidate this transient advantage by political, military and ideological means. As the hegemonic power, a state is able not merely to secure its own interests more effectively, but also comes to assume state functions for the whole world system, acting as though it were the central public authority for the world economy.

Yet hegemony is immensely fragile. The position of the hegemonic state is quickly undermined, in part because of the possession of hegemony itself. The economic supremacy of one state, and the stable conditions in the world market which this ensures, spurs the development of rivals from among the other leading states, or stimulates the emergence of new states from the periphery. These challengers may try to create protected spheres of interest and dare the hegemonic power to use military force to prevent them.

A second problem is the effect which the possession of hegemony has upon the hegemonic power. There are some major costs to be borne. The source of these extra burdens is the difficulty of simultaneously maintaining a world role and preserving relative economic efficiency. The hegemonic power typically experiences a significant diversion of the energies of its citizens into non-productive activities; the pressure for internal redistribution results in wage levels considerably above its competitors; consumption receives a higher priority than investment; and a high value for the national currency is sought in order to minimize the cost of funding the military and diplomatic commitments inherent in world role and foreign investment. What are neglected are the supply side conditions for achieving rapid economic growth.

This theme has been recently explored by Paul Kennedy.[2] He argues that states which have become 'great powers' exhibit similar patterns in their development. There is a trade-off between military security and economic security. Great powers repeatedly fail to maintain a balance between the two and are eventually eclipsed by rising powers which are more single-minded in the pursuit of economic success.

Kennedy argues that in the long run political and military power depend on economic strength. The dilemma for the governments of great powers is that they must simultaneously provide three things: arms spending to maintain military security; goods and services to satisfy the needs and demands of their citizens; and a policy framework which promotes the investment necessary to ensure sustained growth. If growth is not rapid enough, the government cannot pay for the levels of military and personal consumption that are politically necessary, and even more seriously, it risks a relative decline which will undermine both military and economic security in the future.

As a result, periods of hegemony in the world system tend to be short-lived. More common are periods of conflict, in which a former hegemonic power may be declining or a new hegemonic power rising, or in which there is no clear pattern at all. The absence of a hegemonic power does not mean, however, that there is any less need for the political functions that such a hegemonic power typically undertakes.

One of the problems in using the concept of hegemony in the world system is that the theory has been constructed on very few historical cases. Only three periods of hegemony are normally identified: Holland, 1620–72; Britain, 1815–73; and the United States, 1945–73. These three periods of hegemony occurred at very different stages in the development of the world system. The contrasts between them are likely to be as instructive as the similarities. Yet even though the occurrence of hegemony is rare, the study of these periods can give insights into the way the world system has evolved and how it might evolve in the future.

Britain is the classic example of a state which first achieved and then lost its position of hegemony.[3] The interaction between the domestic and global aspects of internationalization is particularly evident. Britain was the first country to accept fully the logic of internationalization both for its foreign economic policy and for internal social organization. In the period of its decline, Britain sought to use its powers to resist that logic and defend its privileged position. In the transition since the 1960s to the post-imperial phase of its development, the British state has begun to accept that logic once more and increasingly seeks to modernize within its constraints.

BRITAIN AS A HEGEMONIC POWER

Britain emerged as the hegemonic power in the world system after 1815. It had established a clear dominance over all its rivals in finance, commerce and industry. London was now the undisputed centre of the world's financial and commercial system, and this supremacy was further enhanced during the period of British hegemony. By 1870 the London capital market was twice as large as all the capital markets of its rivals combined. Sterling was established as the leading international currency and this brought further prosperity to the flourishing financial and commercial sector.

The view that Britain first enjoyed an export surplus on its manufacturing trade in the first half of the nineteenth century which it then used to finance foreign investments and develop a powerful financial sector has been discredited.[4] British commercial supremacy did not depend on a surplus of manufacturing exports. The invisible service exports provided the surplus from the outset. Despite the advent of modern industry, Britain remained above all a commercial power. The new wealth and opportunities which industry provided were fully exploited, but within the framework of the network of relations which Britain had already established in the world system.

The development of industry did make one major change. It allowed much greater specialization in the division of labour within the world system. The chance was seized and self-sufficiency in agriculture was abandoned between 1820 and 1850. The number of Britons fed on foreign wheat rose from 611,437 between 1811–20 to 3,451,608 between 1841–50.[5]

The commitment to free trade followed a commercial rather than an industrial logic. British prosperity and the feeding of its growing population came to depend on the maintenance of the network of trading relationships which now covered the whole world: its centre was London. Britain's interest in preserving the free movement of goods, capital and labour in this world economy emerged when British manufacturing industries had a clear technological lead over all others. But it did not diminish when this lead began to vanish. The maintenance of an open world economy remained a vital British interest.

Britain's position in the world system was, as a result, significantly different from that of the United States or Germany. Both the United States and Germany aspired to world power on the strength of their industrial manufacturing base. They pursued a policy of building up an export surplus, but trade was never a necessity for them in the way it was for Britain. For them, a policy of autarky in many sectors and strictly regulated trade was also feasible. Britain's hegemony required a permanent deficit on its visible trade which both stimulated economic development in other parts of the world economy and gave rise to increasing demand for British services – banking, shipping and insurance. This made the British national interest ever more closely involved with maintaining the openness of the world system.

The hegemony of the United States, by contrast, required some means to offset the huge American export surplus, which reflected the overwhelming industrial and technological dominance the American economy had acquired by 1945. The solution was found through the granting of credits and by increases in American foreign investment and overseas military spending.

Two further contrasts between Britain and the United States as hegemonic powers should be noted. Both exercised great power in the world system because of their dominant market position. But in addition to this informal empire, Britain had also acquired a large formal empire during its rise to hegemony, and greatly added to it between 1815 and 1918. British commitment to universalism and to the preservation of the open world economy was qualified by the alternative attractions of protecting a sphere of interest within the world economy. These attractions grew once Britain was faced with rivals claiming spheres of interest of their own. The existence of the British empire made Britain's world position last much longer than it would otherwise have done, but it also made Britain less credible as an advocate of the conditions for international economic order. The United States was never inhibited in quite the same way.

The two powers were also very different in respect of the military underpinning of their hegemony. The Pax Britannica required a naval budget of only £8 million.[6] The Pax Americana has seen the construction of an extensive system of overseas military bases, made necessary by the failure to incorporate the Soviet Union within the framework of the new world economy after 1945. It has meant that American hegemony has been exercised through political and military means to a greater extent than was the case with Britain.

In the various challenges to British hegemony, the industrial and commercial challenges were the first to develop. The challenge to Britain's financial supremacy came later. The commercial challenge was the one which worried political opinion in Britain the most. The open-door policy allowed foreign exporters to invade the British market, while British exporters had to sell over high tariff barriers in an increasing number of countries. The rising tide of protectionism was accompanied by a wave of new colonization.

Since Britain was unable to restore the conditions for an open world economy, it took steps to safeguard its position by enlarging its own direct sphere of interest. As Halford Mackinder explained:

> Under a condition of universal free trade, the dream of the sixties of the last century, industrial life and empire might be dissociated, but when competing countries seek to monopolise markets by means of customs tariffs, even democracies are compelled to annex empires. In the last two generations ... the object of vast British annexations has been to support a trade open to all the world.[7]

Britain at the turn of the century experienced a major debate on foreign economic policy centred on the rival attractions of the formal and informal empire. At the height of Britain's hegemony in the 1840s, the claims of the formal empire were much diminished. The case for free-trade imperialism was succinctly stated in the debate on the repeal of the Corn Laws by one MP who argued for free trade because it meant that 'foreign nations would become valuable colonies to us, without imposing on us the responsibility of governing them'.[8]

Britain's case for free trade could also be put in terms more fitting for a hegemonic power. In a memorandum written in 1907, Sir Eyre Crowe argued:

> Second only to the ideal of independence, nations have always cherished the right of free intercourse and trade in the world's markets, and in proportion as England champions the principle of the largest measure of general freedom of commerce, she undoubtedly strengthens her hold on the interested friendship of other nations, at least to the extent of making them feel less apprehensive of naval supremacy in the hands of a free trade England than they would in the face of a predominant protectionist power.[9]

This policy came under fierce attack from those who wanted to see Britain develop the empire as its priority, whatever the consequence for the open world economy. They wanted naval supremacy in the hands of a protectionist England. Chamberlain and Milner spearheaded the assault on the policy of free trade. Milner declared:

> Let us free ourselves from the insane delusion that a nation grows richer by buying outside its borders what it can produce within them. It is not a blessing when, in the blind worship of cheapness, we undermine our own industries. Now is the time to strike a blow to free ourselves from the shackles of an antique creed, to open the door which has been banged and barred against our fellow-countrymen in the Dominions.[10]

The conflict between free trade and tariff reform reflected the extent to which British governments had come to pursue incompatible aims. Protecting the British empire and preserving a balance of power in Europe meant preparing for war. Safeguarding the open world economy meant maintaining the peace. Only peace would ensure that world lines of communication were kept open, international contracts honoured and foreign investments secured. A Foreign Office memorandum of 1927 stated: 'We have got all we want – perhaps more. Our sole object is to keep what we have and to live in peace'.[11] Such a policy implied that those powers who were not content with what they had would have to be appeased.

After 1918 there was increasing awareness that Britain itself could no longer sustain the conditions for economic order in the world system. Yet there was reluctance to abandon either the overextended British empire or

Britain's central role within the open world economy. In these circumstances, the attraction of closer collaboration with the United States grew. The idea of an Atlantic Union began to be discussed.

BRITAIN AND AMERICA

In 1940 Churchill declared:

> These two great organisations of the English-speaking democracies, the British Empire and the United States, will have to be somewhat mixed up together in some of their affairs for mutual and general advantage. For my own part, looking out upon the future, I do not view the process with any misgivings. I could not stop it if I wished: no-one can stop it. Like the Mississippi, it just keeps rolling along. Let it roll. Let it roll on full flood, inexorable, irresistible, benignant, to broader lands and better days.[12]

Britain's hegemony had lasted from 1815 to 1870. In the last decades of the nineteenth century, Britain faced a rising industrial and military challenge from new rivals, particularly from Germany and the United States. Both resorted to policies to protect their new industries from British competition and both contested the inclusion of so much of the world in Britain's sphere of interest, whether as colonies or through the commercial and financial links Britain has established with them. Both also tried (with increasing success) to exploit the British policy of allowing open access to its markets. The British press became greatly alarmed by the success of American and German competition. The first great bout of introspection about economic decline was soon under way.[13]

The challenge to British power meant that either Britain had to come to terms with its new rivals or it had to fight them. If appeasement was chosen, a significant surrender of British power would be necessary. A negotiated balance of power and division of the world between spheres of interest would be very different from an undisputed hegemony, arising from supremacy in the world market. Using force, however, to resist the challenge and the re-ordering of world power would carry heavy risks and might ultimately weaken rather than strengthen Britain's position, even if Britain emerged as victor in the short run.

The arguments for appeasement of the new industrial and military rivals Britain faced by 1900 were persuasive. Yet appeasement could only be viable if the rivals in their turn were prepared to moderate the demands they were making on Britain, and bury, or at least postpone, their own aspirations for world power. The failure to reach an accommodation with Germany precipitated two world wars. Britain twice abandoned its policy of appeasement towards Germany, but at no time did it abandon its policy of appeasement towards the United States. Indeed, war with Germany made appeasement of the United States all the more necessary.

The struggles between the European powers made the rise of the United States swifter than it might otherwise have been. It also meant that the military contest between Britain and the United States, which many Bolsheviks confidently forecast as the next round of imperialist struggle after 1918,[14] never took place. Instead the United States emerged as the undisputed hegemonic power in the world system after 1945 with, on balance, more collaboration than resistance from the power it was displacing.

This collaboration was most visible in the military sphere. The German challenge to Britain was only defeated with American help. But equally significant was the collaboration over the construction of a new world order, the re-establishment of an open world economy, and the attempt to remove existing exclusive spheres of interest in favour of multilateral trade and a unified international monetary system.

The transfer of hegemony went through three main phases. In the first phase Britain acquiesced in the organization of an American sphere of interest. At this stage it was envisaged that British and American interests might be complementary, each dominating its own sphere of interest and co-operating to maintain international economic order. The second phase, during the 1940s, saw the development of the idea of a special relationship between Britain and the United States.

This notion was only intermittently accepted by the United States government, but it enjoyed much support in Britain. From the British standpoint, the purpose of the special relationship was to allow Britain to act as broker between the United States and Europe. By this means, Britain expected, while ceding the leading role in the world system to the Americans, to remain a powerful and independent voice with its own power base. In the third phase, the United States moved to a new conception of an Atlantic partnership in which a united Western Europe, under the leadership of a revitalized West Germany, became the central objective. Britain was now relegated to a subordinate and dependent role within the alliance.

The decision to appease rather than confront the United States was crucial for later developments. In 1895–6 Washington intervened in a boundary dispute between Venezuela and British Guiana. The American right to do so was conceded. It led to further steps. Britain abandoned its half share in the future Isthmian canal and withdrew its navy from the Western Hemisphere. No formal treaty was signed, but the unilateral declaration by the United States that this region fell within its sphere of influence was tacitly recognized. In 1901 the Admiralty was asked to advise on the feasibility of a war against the United States. It told the Cabinet that in order to place Great Britain in a position to acquire the command of the seas on the coast of America, it was essential for the neutrality of the European powers to be assured.[15] The Admiralty's assessment underlined the weakness of Britain's position and the need to maintain friendly relations with the United States.

The arguments against fighting the United States, even if the neutrality of the rest of Europe could be assured, were many and compelling. Given the interdependence of the two economies it would have been a major economic disaster. There were vast British investments in the United States, and a huge volume of trade between the two countries. A war would have given great opportunities to Britain's other leading rivals to divide up the British empire among themselves. Apart from these practical considerations, there was strong ideological distaste for a clash with America. The ideology of Anglo-Saxon unity was already potent, and was to become still more influential in subsequent decades, propagated by groups like the Rhodes Trust and the Round Table, and by intellectuals like Walter Lippmann.

The growing understanding between the two powers prepared the way for wartime collaboration in 1917–18. Germany was defeated, but the balance of power between Britain and the United States was decisively shifted. The Americans consolidated their advantage after the war at the Washington Naval Conference by insisting on naval parity with Britain. As a result of the war, they had overtaken Britain as the world's leading creditor nation, and were now without dispute the leading industrial power.

Despite the evidence of America's new dominance and Woodrow Wilson's commitment to the building of a new international political and economic order, the United States was not yet ready to take a leading role in the world system, and relapsed into isolationism. The interwar years demonstrated, however, that an international order could not be rebuilt without the United States. The collapse of the gold standard in 1931 underlined this. The consequent fragmentation of the world economy into currency blocs and protected spheres of interest reduced trade and output, and contributed to the rise of regimes committed to the redistribution of territory in the world system by force.

The second phase, the phase of the special relationship, began with the conclusion of the Lend-Lease Agreement. The establishment of the Coalition government in Britain and the decision to wage total war, brought a sharp break with both the domestic and the foreign policies of British governments in the 1930s.[16] The dependence of the British on the Americans was much more marked than in the earlier conflict, and from the outset the Americans demanded a high price for their support. The 1941 Atlantic Charter set out plans for a reconstruction of the international economic order on universal principles. Spearheaded by the State Department under Cordell Hull, the United States as the emergent hegemonic power in the world system had begun to redefine its interests.

A particular target was the exclusive spheres of interest which had been organized in the 1930s. Cordell Hull described the Ottawa agreements which established imperial preference within the British empire as 'the greatest injury, in a commercial way, that has been inflicted on this country since I have been in public life'.[17] During the 1930s, the Americans had been content to accept the existing division of the world market and had toyed with the idea of organizing a new informal empire – the Grand Area – to include the Western Hemisphere, Britain and the British Empire, the Dutch East Indies, China and Japan. This bloc was intended to counterbalance Germany and the Soviet Union.[18]

The outbreak of the Second World War allowed more ambitious schemes to be floated. The Grand Area could be expanded to include both Western Europe and the Soviet Union. Britain and Japan could be forced to surrender their exclusive spheres of interest. The Americans were determined to remove imperial preference and to force the European powers to give up their colonies. The British, however, viewed their alliance with the Americans as a partnership and saw no need to abandon the arrangements which had perpetuated Britain's world power long after Britain's hegemony had disappeared.

Opinion in the American government was split between those who favoured maintaining a special relationship with Britain in the interests of building a stable international economic order, and those who were against making any concessions to Britain that were not made to all other countries. Negotiations over the shape of the postwar order were protracted and many of the more ambitious plans were never realized. In particular, the hopes for an early resumption of multilateral trade and convertibility which underlay the 1944 Bretton Woods Conference were disappointed.

The British and the Americans put forward rival plans at Bretton Woods, and the final compromise owed more to the White plan than to the Keynes plan. The compromise was attacked in the United States and in Britain. In America it was feared that the proposals departed too much from the canons of sound finance, and that America's interests would be best served by adhering to the principles of the gold standard, which would not permit discretionary rules aimed at maintaining activity in the world economy and easing the position of persistent deficit countries. In Britain, by contrast, painful memories of the collapse of the international financial system in the interwar years had to be erased, and political opinion had to be convinced that abandoning the new security which a protected sphere of interest policy had given to Britain was justified. Keynes himself had been an advocate of bilateralism in the 1930s, but by 1944 he was once again a defender of the traditional liberal British policy, suitably modified. He defended the Bretton Woods compromise in the House of Lords:

To suppose that a system of bilateral and barter arrangements ... is the best way of encouraging the Dominions to centre their financial systems on London, seems to me pretty near frenzy. As a technique of Little Englandism, adopted as a last resort when all else has failed us, with this small country driven to autarky, keeping to itself in a harsh and unfriendly world, it might make more sense. But those who talk this way, in the expectation that the rest of the Commonwealth will throw in their lot on these lines and cut their free commercial relations with the rest of the world, can have very little idea of how this Empire has grown or by what means it can be sustained.[19]

The Americans pressed hard for as full and as complete a liberalization of international economic relations as possible. The British held out for a period of transition, and important currents of British opinion, in both major parties, resisted what they saw as the forced liquidation of Britain's sphere of interest and, with it, its aspirations to global power, as well as the placing of severe constraints on the ability of British governments to pursue national economic management.

The policies of multilateralism and convertibility had failed by 1947, and the United States launched Marshall Aid in order to reconstruct the Western economy and help to underpin the new military alliance against the Soviet Union. Only much later were the objectives of Bretton Woods to be realized. From the outset, American hegemony was marked both by universalism in respect of the international economic order and by a sphere of interest policy aimed at containing the Soviet Union. Britain had an interest in both, but British attempts to maintain an independent position within the world system which could continue to give it special privileges in dealing with the Americans eventually failed. Although interested at times in the special relationship, the Americans were still more interested in seeing the liquidation of what alone could give the special relationship credibility – the British empire. Britain's failure at Suez in 1956 demonstrated clearly the impossibility of Britain pursuing a major policy independently of the Americans while remaining firmly within the American world order. Britain's peculiar postwar problem was that it failed to maintain the special relationship and therefore the basis for a continuing world role; but it also failed to reorganize its domestic economy and society to compete effectively within the new expanding world economy. Hegemony was transferred, international economic order was eventually rebuilt, but the former hegemonic power was incapable of benefiting from it. Instead, the relative decline became more pronounced.

BRITAIN AND EUROPE

The perception that Britain was performing less well than comparable economies became a dominant issue in British domestic politics in the 1960s and 1970s and produced new programmes aimed at modernizing the

British economy and society, remedying its deficiencies so as to enable it to catch up with comparable economies. When the hopes that were placed in these programmes were disappointed, more radical questioning both of Britain's place in the world economy and of its domestic social organization began to be voiced.

These debates took place against the background of a changing world system. Challenges to American leadership, the end of the long boom in the world economy, the increasing pace of internationalization, and the belated entry of Britain into the European Community provided a new context for domestic political debate.

The domestic compromise between labour and capital which had sustained the British polity for more than forty years broke down and its disappearance called into question the social democratic order which had been grafted on to Britain's old constitutional state. The failure of successive governments to modernize the British economy and arrest the relative economic decline had an increasingly severe impact on inflation and unemployment, and led to a crisis of confidence in British institutions and political leadership.

Positions quickly polarized. A national protectionist strategy emerged on the left, which was hostile to Britain's links with the European Community and with the United States, arguing that the British economy could only be rescued if it transformed its links with the world economy, insulated itself from world competition, and gave priority to a major programme of domestic investment.[20] On the right, the Conservative Party under Margaret Thatcher became committed to a strategy for freeing the economy and strengthening the authority of the state to restore and defend a market order from those groups such as trade unionists who were undermining it.[21] It planned to open the British economy to external competition and inward investment, while dismantling the collectivist institutions that had accumulated in the previous fifty years. It aimed to do this while re-affirming Britain's ties with the United States. Centre opinion, which included many in the Conservative and the Labour Parties, by contrast emphasized the importance of making the European Community the linchpin of Britain's new foreign economic policy, and urged the necessity of wide-ranging institutional reform, including constitutional reform, to create a new developmental state in Britain that could successfully carry through modernization.[22]

The election of a Conservative government in 1979 and its further victories in 1983 and 1987 ensured that the free economy strategy would get an extended trial. The Thatcher government was determined to expose British industry and British workers to the full force of international competition, by withdrawing subsidies, abolishing exchange controls, and refusing to bail out companies that got into difficulties. Its tight monetary policies during the recession of 1979–81 helped increase the pressure on British industry and led to a very large increase in bankruptcies and unemployment. The government justified its policies as the harsh medicine necessary to make British industry competitive again.

At the same time, the Thatcher government gave a much higher priority to its links with the United States than to its links with the European Community. Since joining the Community in 1973, Britain had been a lukewarm member. Under the Thatcher government, Britain became notorious as the most obstructive and difficult member state, particularly in disputes over Britain's contribution to the budget.[23]

Since 1983, however, the Europeanization of British politics has notably accelerated. The budget issue was settled in 1984 and a new momentum for European economic and political integration developed. The most important sign of this was the Single European Act of 1985, which committed the member states to create a single market by 1992 and extended majority voting to speed agreement on the 280 pieces of legislation required to give effect to it.

Since the signing of the Act, major disagreements have once again surfaced about the direction in which the Community is moving. The Thatcher government favoured measures that created a single market by deregulating markets throughout the Community. But it never favoured the goal of complete economic integration, fearing that it would lead to political integration as well, and the loss of British sovereignty over such matters as tax rates and border controls. Thatcher in particular steadfastly opposed the wider implications of 1992 and the desire of other European states to move to full economic and political union. In September 1988, in a speech in Bruges, she denounced the moves towards economic and monetary union and the plans for a social charter, and reasserted the importance of maintaining national sovereignty as the basis of the Community. Her stance created serious divisions inside the Conservative Party and the Conservative Cabinet.

The new momentum behind Europeanization has been a catalyst for a major change of attitudes in the Labour Party and the trade unions. By 1988 both had abandoned their former opposition to membership of the Community, seeing in the social charter a means of winning domestic political arguments. The Community was now recognized as the indispensable framework for Britain's future economic development, and the issue shifted to what kind of Community it was to be.

By the end of the 1980s a significant section of British political opinion had come to support the wider programme of economic and social integration of the Community advocated by Jacques Delors and the European Commission, while the Thatcher government seemed determined to perpetuate for as long as it could the idea of Britain as an independent sovereign state. It still appeared to favour transatlantic ties over European ones, since these were the link to Britain's former power and status within the world system.

The pace of economic integration in Europe, however, and the extent of the economic interdependence which has already emerged (more than 50 per cent of Britain's trade is now with the Community) ties Britain's future firmly to the Community. Full integration in Europe would signal the end of Britain's post-imperial phase, which in a number of ways the Thatcher government tried to perpetuate rather than leave behind. Paradoxically, the internal shocks administered by the Thatcher government seem to have persuaded many in Britain that the centralized national state is an obstacle to finding solutions to Britain's problems, and that modernization is more likely to be achieved if sovereignty is devolved down to local regions and up to European institutions.

Whatever the party label of the government that succeeds Margaret Thatcher's, it is likely to embrace a foreign economic policy that emphasizes Britain's role in the European Community, and abandons the attempt to preserve economic sovereignty and the special relationship with the United States. If Britain moved in this direction it would entail a new phase in the internationalization of the British economy, quite different from the earlier phases when Britain was the hegemonic power, and then sought to transfer hegemony to the United States. It would mean accepting in full the consequences of being a part of the European economy, and assisting in the creation of an adequate European polity to oversee it.

CONCLUSION

Periods of hegemony are rare and transient phenomena in the life of the world system, and their rarity reflects the rudimentary stage of development of a world polity. A few state functions have come to be discharged at the international level but most remain firmly in the hands of national state structures. Hegemonic states have been mostly concerned with the process of circulation, with maintaining the flows of capital and commodities. They have been most active in promoting conditions for international monetary stability, improving global communications, securing property rights and enforcing contracts.

Politics in the world system remain at a very early stage of development. They are concerned with formal exchange equality and with conditions of exchange.[24] Since there is no central authority, there is no focus for most political demands at the international level; no body which could grant political rights or take binding decisions. Above all, there is no authority to take decisions to stabilize the whole world system, to redistribute income and wealth, or to undertake expenditures to promote balanced development or limit environmental damage. There is no counterpart for the modern nation state at the international level.

The absence of such a central authority is felt most keenly during periods of recession and heightened political conflict. In such times there is no hegemonic state to remove spatial and credit barriers which hold back the pace of economic growth, and the problems of investment and profit-ability receive no remedies at all on a global scale. Hegemonic states find it impossible to retain hegemony for very long: once it is lost it seems im-possible to regain. But the existence of periods of hegemony and their association with periods of expansion and stability in the world system prompt investigation of whether they offer any clues as to how a more permanent and broad apparatus of central authority for the world system could emerge.

Some social scientists working within a world system perspective have devoted much energy and ingenuity to identifying short- and long-run cycles. But the very concept of a world system as a singular and cumulative process means that there can be no invariant patterns and that the search for constants is likely to mislead. The danger inherent in the world system perspective, as Theda Skocpol has pointed out,[25] is that too often it is reductionist and does not give sufficient weight to the impact of national state structures.

The transfer of hegemony between Britain and the United States increased awareness of the political conditions for international economic order – in particular, the need for restraints to be placed on the behaviour of all nation states in order for the system to function smoothly. It is in the states that have enjoyed hegemony most recently that this consciousness is most clearly developed. The emergence of elites that think in world system terms, identifying the requirements for international political and economic stability, is a marked feature of both Britain and the United States.

It is therefore not surprising to find that many of the most influential perspectives in geopolitics have originated within these two states.[26] It was theorists like Mahan and Mackinder who began to develop the ideas for a strategic partnership between Britain and the United States. Mahan argued in 1904 that 'the United States has certainty of a very high order that the British Empire will stand substantially on the same lines of world privileges as ourselves; that its strength will be our strength, and its weakening an injury to us'.[27]

As collaboration between the two powers developed, so an influential strand of British political opinion came to designate the United States not just as Britain's partner, but as its natural successor to the leading role in the world system. These groups helped to create a climate which, when the opportunity came, disposed many active in the British state to accept close collaboration with the Americans as not only inevitable but desirable. Many British civil servants, politicians and military personnel came to conceive their task as tutoring the Americans in the difficult job of under-taking international responsibilities. The Americans naturally viewed it rather differently and were always much less willing for close collaboration.

Apart from the influence of such political elites which worked for understanding between the two countries, the factor that was most important in promoting collaboration was the shared interest in promoting the conditions for a genuine international order. There were important differences of emphasis, and the bulk of the sacrifices were made by Britain. What permitted the transfer of hegemony between these two powers to emerge from collaboration rather than from conflict was the continuing importance Britain placed on an open world economy and its appreciation of the political conditions necessary to sustain that: conditions which Britain was no longer able to provide. Ultimately the importance of remaining part of an expanding world economy proved more important and more feasible than the preservation of a local sphere of interest.

A key question for the future of the world system is whether there are likely to be further periods of hegemony. Some analysts of the world system have argued that the degree of pluralization among the core states has tended to increase, which makes the emergence of a new hegemony of the kind exercised by Britain or the United States less likely.[28] But that will increase the pressure for new international institutions to regulate the world system and restrain any tendency for fragmentation into blocs and spheres of interest.

The emergence of Japan as the leading world economy, and the new momentum behind economic integration in Europe are two indications of the extent to which the old transatlantic hegemony based first on Britain and then on the United States has begun to crumble. The forms that internationalization will take in the future will be powerfully influenced by how far economic and political integration in the European Community proceeds, and by the relationships which are established between the United States, the European Community and Japan. Enormous financial imbalances exist within the world system, not least between these three major economies, and mounting ecological problems threaten future economic development. The need for political co-operation to maintain a stable world order is matched only by the difficulty of securing it.

NOTES

1   I. Wallerstein (1974) *The Modern World System*, New York: Academic Press, p. 347.
2   See P. Kennedy (1988) *The Rise and Fall of the Great Powers*, London: Unwin Hyman.
3   See A. Gamble (1990) *Britain in Decline*, London: Macmillan.
4   See A. Imlah (1958) *Economic Elements in the Pax Britannica*, New York: Russell.
5   See B. Semmel (1987) *The Rise of Free Trade Imperialism*, Cambridge: Cambridge University Press.
6   See P. Kennedy (1983) *The Strategy of Diplomacy 1870–1945*, London: Allen & Unwin.

 7 H. Mackinder (1902) *Britain and the British Seas*, London: Heinemann,
    p. 343.
 8 B. Semmel, *The Rise of Free Trade Imperialism*, p. 8.
 9 R.N. Gardner (1956) *Sterling-Dollar Diplomacy*, Oxford: Oxford University
    Press, p. 27.
10 Lord Milner, Speech at Huddersfield, 17 February 1910, pp. 193–4.
11 P. Kennedy *The Strategy of Diplomacy 1870–1945*.
12 See W.S. Churchill (1946) *War Speeches 1940–1945*, London: Cassell, p. 35.
13 See R. Heindel (1968) *The American Impact on Great Britain 1898–1914*,
    New York: Octagon.
14 See L. Trotsky (1974) *Collected Writings and Speeches on Britain*, London:
    New Park.
15 See D. Watt (1965) *Personalities and Policies*, London: Longman, p. 27 and
    D. Watt (1984) *Succeeding John Bull*, Cambridge: Cambridge University
    Press.
16 See M. Cowling (1976) The Impact of Hitler, Cambridge: Cambridge
    University Press.
17 R.N. Gardner *Sterling-Dollar Diplomacy*, p. 19.
18 See K. van der Pijl (1984) *The Making of an Atlantic Ruling Class*, London:
    Verso.
19 R.N. Gardner *Sterling-Dollar Diplomacy*, p. 125.
20 See S. Holland (1974) *The Socialist Challenge*, London: Quartet.
21 See J. Kreiger (1986) *Reagan, Thatcher and the Politics of Decline*, Cambridge:
    Polity Press; K. Hoover and R. Plant (1989) *Conservative Capitalism*, London:
    Routledge; A. Gamble (1988) *The Free Economy and the Strong State*,
    London: Macmillan.
22 See D. Marquand (1988) *The Unprincipled Society*, London: Cape.
23 See S. George (1990) *An Awkward Partner: Britain and the European
    Community*, Oxford: Oxford University Press.
24 See J. Urry (1981) *The Anatomy of Capitalist Societies*, London: Macmillan.
25 See T. Skocpol (1977) 'Wallerstein's world capitalist system: a theoretical and
    historical critique', American Journal of Sociology 82(5), pp. 1,075–90.
26 See G. Parker (1985) *Western Geopolitical Thought in the Twentieth Century*,
    London: Croom Helm.
27 K. van der Pijl *The Making of an Atlantic Ruling Class*, p. 53.
28 J. Boli-Bennett (1980) 'Global integration and the universal increase of state
    dominance', in A. Bergesen (ed.) *Studies of the Modern World System*, New
    York: Academic Press.

Chapter 2

American hegemony and the Japanese challenge

Richard Falk

INTRODUCTION

There is in prevailing global circumstances a contradictory set of tendencies that makes interpretation of the shape of international relations even more confusing than usual. It can be crystallized around our concern with the shifting tectonics of geopolitics, especially with regard to the United States, Europe, Japan and the Soviet Union. On the one side, the United States continues to experience the objective and subjective aspects of cumulative, if relative, economic decline. If the lead runner maintains a steady pace, but his/her rivals continuously accelerate, it seems as if the leader is losing ground all the time. This sense of American 'dependence' was amusingly caught by a recent *New Yorker* cartoon showing a couple seated across from one another at a restaurant, sipping wine. The man proposes marriage, with the caption as follows: 'Will you marry me, if Japan doesn't collapse?'

But at the same time, there are relevant developments that confuse and complicate this sense of international rank-ordering. Primary among these, of course, is the collapse of the Cold War by way of virtual Soviet surrender, including unilateral withdrawal from most points of geopolitical and ideological encounter. To the extent that the United States was straining to stay ahead of the Soviet Union in the bipolar imagery of global rivalry, the race has been narrowed to a single entrant: the Soviet Union has dropped out. This outcome, completely unanticipated as recently as a few years ago, has generated a triumphal mood that in some respects surpasses the sense of US achievement at the close of the Second World War. The ideological interpretation of this dramatic cluster of developments was most vividly set forth in Francis Fukuyama's widely discussed article, 'The End of History?'[1] As an uncontested military presence on a global scale, the United States has recovered a sense of its own supremacy even as it cuts back on its military capability in response to fiscal pressures.

From a still different outlook, the globalization of international life has occurred primarily under US auspices. There is on one side the corporate symbols of globalization associated with Coca Cola, Hertz Rent-a-Car and Hilton hotels. On the other side, the popular cultural points of lights that have spread across the world, ranging from Madonna through jeans and rock music, to the intonations and imagery of CNN (The Cable News Network). From this standpoint, the United States has provided a context for the world, which others, variously situated, decided how to participate in, absorb or protect against. Japan is a spectacular instance of sustaining the integrity of its own cultural space, while exhibiting an extraordinary capacity to take in and take advantage of this phenomenon of Americanization.

Against such a background, the idea of the internationalization of Japan takes on greater depth and substance. The historical circumstance that we explore is the situation of American hegemony that arose out of the Second World War, and assumed its own form in a quite different global setting than the earlier experience of British hegemony depicted in chapter 1 by Andrew Gamble. It is interesting to bear in mind the parallel aspects of hegemony and displacement, recalling that it was the United States that came to displace Britain, climaxing in the decade after 1945, as the global hegemon, and that now, after an interlude of co-hegemonic geopolitical governance, generally called bipolarity or identified as the bloc system, that the main new source of hegemonic challenge comes from still further west, from the economic superpower, Japan, risen from the ashes of its devastation in the Second World War. Perhaps one should also acknowledge a consolidated Europe as a second potential challenger, but more remotely so, as the process of consolidation is likely to be conditioned by interstate rivalry and anxiety, especially between France and Germany. Whether or not these new emergent challenges to the United States are for reasons analogous to the collapse of Soviet ascendancy, a pseudo-challenge remains to be considered. The Soviet Union all along lacked the economic and cultural clout to back up its military and ideological prowess, whereas Japan appears to lack the military capability and political will to reinforce its formidable economic and cultural capacity in such a manner as to challenge the structure of international relations. Arguably, Japan's reluctance to pursue hegemonic ambitions may represent, in part, the continuing trauma of its terrible ordeal in the 1940s. The postwar adjustment over time involved an active economic presence, but a very passive diplomatic style, an approach designed to reassure the power-centres that Japan's economic success did not imply an intention to project power and control beyond its territory.

Without the combination of elements, including a far greater assertiveness *vis-à-vis* the United States and wider sense of mission, it is not possible to establish a hegemonic presence at a global level, and so the progressive dissolution of the American hegemonic capacities should not be regarded as automatically heralding its replacement by an economically predominant Japan, or even by a Japanese predominance linked to European integration, possibly in coalition with Japan. In this respect, it seems most likely that the sequel to the relatively successful hegemonic stability of the postwar world will not be reconstructed under Japanese auspices in the upcoming new era of global politics. What is far more likely is the emergence of complex, many dimensional forms of multipolarity, exhibiting strategic tensions, but also achieving high degrees of policy co-ordination, even co-operation, as the leading states seek to manage the world economy in their shared interest, protect the global environment, and operate in a homogeneous ideological atmosphere in which only 'market-oriented democracies' are treated as legitimate governments. In this regard, the global governance structure of the future may be better prefigured by the annual summits among the seven leading advanced industrial countries than by the irregularly convened summits between the two superpowers, events that had previously generated great excitement and, sometimes, disappointment, providing a kind of centre-stage background during the Cold War period.

The argument here concerns the character of United States hegemony, and the degree to which Japan's rise to economic pre-eminence represents a fundamental challenge to the American position in the world. Certainly, Japan's economic prowess, its superior competitiveness in a series of industries and sectors, and its fiscal strength represent a challenge of a definite sort. But is it a challenge directed at American hegemony, a challenge that seeks to displace the US leadership position? Even economically, the scale of Japanese investment in the United States and of trade, suggests a mutuality of interest – indeed, a strong Japanese incentive commitment to sustaining a robust and expanding US economy. In this key regard, the Japanese challenge is totally different to that associated with the Soviet challenge.

The Soviet challenge was, ideological and military, threatening the very survival of the United States and its allies, and questioning the legitimacy of its political and economic approach to the administration and organization of society. Even if such a challenge were exaggerated by ideological fervour in the West, the stakes of geopolitical rivalry seemed to be of a pre-dominantly antagonistic variety, qualified to some degree by a mutual concern to avoid nuclear warfare, but conflictual in essence. In contrast, the post-Cold War rivalries between the United States, Japan and Europe are underpinned by a commonality of beliefs, a positive experience of alliance, and a perception and reality of shared interests in expanding the orbit of co-operative relations.

The US–Japan relationship has gone through a series of stages: bitter enemies during the late 1930s and the war years, climaxed by the Pearl Harbor attack and culminating in the atomic attacks of 1945; gross disparity in the immediate postwar years of Occupation and US-guided political and economic reconstruction: subsequent full Japanese recovery and gradual emergence as an economic superpower, simultaneous with relative American decline and overextension. From this last phase, uncertainties about the future abound. Japan remains a security ward of the United States as it continues to move toward economic ascendancy. Will the postwar partnership reformulate itself under these altered conditions or generate deepening fissures?

It is important not to confuse the US–Japan relationship with that of the superpowers. Indeed, at this point, it represents a peculiar, distinctive kind of rivalry, which continues to be structured around its opposite – namely, alliance and co-operation. Leaders of both countries appear to envision their economic relations as subordinate to their basic partnership, and in any event, to view diplomatic co-operation as defining the relationship. True, the problematic aspects of the economic relations between the United States and Japan have spilled over, to some extent, to produce some hostile feelings among the citizenry in both countries; moreover there is a future risk that if world economic conditions deteriorate, or the competitive gap widens and the American economy experiences serious further deterioration, then a dangerous conflict spiral could be generated. In the background, then, is the importance at this time of appreciating these risks, and interpreting the relationship of challenge and response between the two countries in such a way as to encourage perceptions of net and cumulative benefits associated with the co-operative sides of the relationship.

INTERNATIONALIZATION

To approach the theme of 'internationalization' requires some preliminary clarification. There are three dimensions of internationalization that bear on Japan's altered participation in international society. The most salient dimension of internationalization, stressed in Andrew Gamble's chapter, involves the projection of power beyond the boundaries of one's own country. Such a projection occurs in economic, political, ideological and cultural spheres. This sort of internationalization also relates to the perceived dependence of a country on international trade and international security arrangements: that is, basic structures of reliance on interaction with economic and political actors that are located beyond the reach of territorial sovereignty. It is these geopolitical forms of internationalization that have mainly shaped international relations thinking. Such internationalization is both an extension of territorial capabilities and a qualification of the autonomy of the sovereign state as independent political actor. As such, internationalization can either serve a state well by increasing its prosperity and security, or it can accentuate the vulnerability of a state to economic and political forces beyond its control.

The story of postwar Japan is a narrative of the transition from a condition of unconditional vulnerability to the gradual attainment of an autonomy so well grounded in economic capabilities and fiscal resources as to threaten others. This transition for Japan has been facilitated both by the emergence of the Cold War, and then by its particular form of end-game involving the Soviet geopolitical collapse. The onset of the Cold War accelerated the process by which Japan was reintegrated into international life, becoming perceived as a major strategic asset in the Pacific region. As a result, Japan progressively moved from the status of badly defeated ex-enemy to, by the late 1940s, that of potential ally, making it immediately desirable to promote the recovery of Japanese strength. This process of reintegration of Japan into the world political system culminated in the US–Japan security treaty of 1951. The Korean War created both a sense of credible threat, and solidified the US role as guarantor of Japanese security in the Cold War years. Japan's role as a rear base area and major transhipment point, especially during the periods of warfare in Korea and Vietnam, also contributed significantly to the pace of economic reconstruction.

Geopolitical developments in the late 1980s have also been helpful to Japan. The ending of the Cold War, with its attendant removal of any serious Soviet threat, makes Japan's security dependence on the United States less pronounced. As such, it provides Japan with more room for manoeuvre within which to uphold its economic interests. It also puts economic concerns at the centre of international political life. The United States, aware of its deficiencies, yet continuing to cast itself in the role of hegemon, is in the 1990s positing some extraordinarily intrusive demands with respect to Japan's internal affairs – for instance, that Japan dispose of its trade surplus by higher levels of public sector investment at home. It remains to be seen whether such demands will be met, and if not, what consequences will ensue. In this regard, the post-1945 primary form of Japanese internationalization – that is, its subjection to US influence in certain critical areas of policy – remains formally, but can no longer be consistently implemented.

At the same time, Japan has reinternationalized its own presence in the Pacific, achieving by trade and investment the kind of Asian co-prosperity sphere it earlier tried to establish by wars of conquest followed by regimes of colonial occupation. Thus, Japan is a player on the global level when it comes to world economic policy (a ranking member of the G-7 group of leading industrial countries), but a hegemonic actor, to a significant degree, within its own region.

There is a second dimension of internationalization that bears significantly on the United States–Japan relationship. It is the nature of receptivity that a society has to ideas and practices that come from beyond its borders. In effect, the degree of openness, or closedness – degrees of receptivity measured along a spectrum. This sort of receptivity takes on a different character depending on the substantive setting, whether it be the degree of tolerance, the extent of curiosity towards things foreign; attitudes towards immigration, emigration and refugees; the extent to which the citizenry is multilingual and sophisticated about foreign cultures; the extent to which the main educational and socialization process encourages the study of historical and cultural traditions other than one's own; the extent to which it attaches a positive value to the diversity of cultural experiences and traditions that exist in the world.

There are popular beliefs that colour these perceptions of this second form of internationalization. The United States purports to be exceedingly open to diversity, priding itself on being a land of immigrants and a place of asylum for those suffering privation elsewhere. This image of receptivity is best expressed, perhaps, by the Statue of Liberty, a welcoming of the outside world to partake of American 'blessings of liberty'. In contrast, Japan is viewed as closed and hostile, proud of its ethnic homogeneity and threatened by and hostile towards outsiders. Japan borrows technique, but operates within a framework of traditions and behavioural patterns that is now the object of admiration throughout the world.

The actual record is more complex and confusing. America is quite provincial, lacking deep cultural traditions of its own and quite inept about projecting its influence elsewhere. Its hegemonic pretensions run deep, recalling its earliest claims to be 'a city on the hill', a beacon to others; these pretensions are often intertwined with a distinctive sort of moral vision that was part of its founding mythology. The United States, from its earliest period as a distinct country, conceived itself as morally superior to the European powers, and it has recurrently insisted that it has generated the ideas for organizing itself and others based on the twin embrace of constitutional democracy and a market-oriented economy. The one-sided outcome of the Cold War has been interpreted by American leaders and by the public as a dramatic confirmation of the essential rightness of the American view of organized political life.

In an important sense, Japan was a test case of the export of the American way. To a significant degree, the nature of the Japanese defeat in the Second World War made it an occupied country in which the ideas and approaches of its own elite had been decisively discredited through experience, and yet these ideas remained deeply embedded in Japanese culture and in the sensibility of its people. As a consequence, the dynamics of Americanization reoriented the governing process in Japan, and appeared to involve a complete acceptance of US political and economic conceptions. A closer look suggests a fascinating mixture of acceptance and rejection. Japan's economy continued to be dominated by concentrations of capital working in close concert with the government; the Emperor system was never dislodged and provides a quasi-religious justification for Japanese traditions; and the adoption of multiparty constitutionalism has been more apparent than real, having been quickly reshaped by a consensus party that has held control of the Japanese government throughout almost the entire postwar period.

At the same time, Japan has mastered the sort of modern consumerism that evolved in the United States and that gives a surface character to contemporary life. Japan has indeed been so receptive that it is now itself the citadel of consumer styling and product quality. As has been widely noted, it is now the United States that is struggling to learn how the Japanese do it. There are throughout the United States a myriad of books and management seminars on Japanese corporate style, and the American innovators are acutely envious of the Japanese capacity to sustain worker loyalty and productivity. At present, the average Japanese worker is increasing his/her productivity three times as rapidly on average as an American counterpart. The perception of American 'decline' is connected with this lesser ability to handle the economic challenges of the current period of capitalist evolution. This perception, also, leads to rethinking a variety of other matters in Japan's favour, such as the relative strength of family, early education and cultural traditions.

On an idealistic level, the contrast between American 'internationaliza-tion' in this second sense and Japanese reclusiveness persists. The United States remains relatively generous, if selective, about opening its borders to those who suffer persecution and privation elsewhere. Japan remains extremely reluctant to accept refugees and immigrants in large numbers, despite labour shortages that could be usefully reduced by reliance on immigrant guest workers. There is a definite conviction, given voice at various times by Japanese leaders, that the Japanese ethnic stock is superior to that of others, and that homogeneity is a definite advantage when it comes to societal organization. Japan's extraordinary economic surge has strengthened this cultural disposition.

The United States, until experiencing defeat in Vietnam and a loss of competitiveness in relation to Japan (and Northern Europe), has had an imperial outlook with respect to ideas and beliefs. It possessed a message of modernity to spread for the sake of others, but little, if anything, to learn. This confidence, reaching its height in the years just after the Second World War, has been restored, at least temporarily, by the Soviet surrender in the Cold War. But in the current atmosphere, the geopolitical victory has not been accompanied by economic ascendancy or diplomatic prowess. As a consequence, both leaders and citizens appreciate that they have much to learn from others, and especially from Japan, if the United States is to succeed in the decades ahead. And in some dramatic sense, there has been a role reversal between the two countries with respect to this second form of internationalization. What had started out as one-directional penetration through the mandate of physical occupation has been supplanted by a much more mutual relationship. If anything, in the 1990s, Americans fear a gradual Japanese takeover of their economy (and society) by way of the marketplace. Such symbolic Japanese acquisitions as the Rockefeller Center and Columbia Pictures have stirred these fears. And this is accentuated by the difficulties of access to the Japanese market, a contention that the playing field between the two countries is not level, and that the American approach to internationalization has become a definite liability in relation to the Japanese challenge.

The third dimension of internationalization arises from the increasing porousness of even strong states. The whole basis of world order has traditionally rested upon the capability of the state to extend its writ effectively throughout its territory. This notion of territorial supremacy was closely associated with the implicit social contract between civil society and the state that legitimized the modern state. Such a conception of meaningful, defensible borders is being undermined by two main sets of tendencies: the global scale of technology and markets, and the shift in economic and political emphasis from tangibles to intangibles, from productive sources of wealth to services and finance.

We grasp the vulnerability of the statist conception most easily by considering the case of a weak state. Cambodia or Lebanon in recent decades has not been able to protect its territorial integrity against antagonistic regional and global forces. As a consequence, such countries have been ravaged by the interventionary violence of outsiders that has upset the internal balance of social forces in an explosive manner, generating devastating cycles of chaos and destruction. This sense of geopolitical weakness, of loss of control of internal destiny, was also the experience of Japan as a defeated country after the Second World War, coerced as it was into surrendering everything except its Emperor system, which was, admittedly, a vital focal point of Japanese identity. The United States imposed its ideas and assessments (including the criminal prosecution of Japan's wartime leaders, again excepting the Emperor) upon Japan as weak state with formal sovereignty, but little other control over its territorial integrity and political independence. The government of Japan even waived the claims of its citizens arising out of the atomic bombings of Hiroshima and Nagasaki.

As we now fully appreciate, the United States for reasons of state interests and foreign policy, as well as its imperial vision of 'a good society', rapidly facilitated Japan's recovery of strength. Japan has always been particularly protective of its territorial supremacy, resisting economic and cultural penetration during the colonial era to a far greater extent than most other Asian countries. The so-called 'opening' of Japan in the mid-nineteenth century never encroached upon Japanese territorial supremacy. And the Japanese rise to economic ascendancy in the postwar era has been accompanied by the closing of Japan, especially in relation to the entry of non-Japanese as real participants. The inability of foreigners to be treated fairly in Japanese business or professional settings is pronounced. More telling, possibly, as disclosing Japanese extremism on this point, is the problem that Japanese schooled overseas currently experience upon returning to Japan to assume a permanent residency. Even this form of cultural contamination can result in lifelong prejudice and discrimination.

But there is a deeper reality present. Increasingly, even strong states resolved to stay 'closed' are losing control over their borders, and cannot regulate territorial space with any success. The globalization of capital and information flow mean that it is impossible to maintain autonomy in relation to the world economy or to insulate culture from alien ideas and influences. The modern state is inherently porous, being situated in a world system that is increasingly tightly integrated. The effects of atmospheric pollution, deforestation and climate change give this sense of porousness a primary environmental referent. The safety of even strong states against external attack is contingent on the restraint and rationality of others rather than on the capacity to *defend* territory – and this seems accurate at both ends of the force spectrum, as much so for terrorism as for nuclearism. Japan as victim of the only atomic attacks in history remains more aware of this type of porousness than most other countries, and even after more than four decades, despite its new geopolitical weight and pressure from the United States to share security burdens, continues to adhere, more or less, to the 1 per cent of GNP ceiling on military expenditures. Indeed, it is this acquiescence in military porousness that sets Japan apart from other major states at this point. As has been noticed, this low military budget frees up public sector resources for more productive use, including facilitating trade expansion and commercially relevant research and development.

This new reality of the porous state as inherent in the reality of statehood has not yet been fully assimilated into the political imagination, and does not figure as prominently as it should in political commentary. Some reactions to this condition of porousness are becoming evident. The European moves towards economic unity for the NATO countries is principally driven by world market and capital accumulation forces. The state, as such, in Western Europe, which gave rise to modern conceptions of the territorial state and of the state system, is losing out functionally to larger conceptions of integrative relations; yet, paradoxically, at the same time also losing out to smaller conceptions. From Punjab to Quebec the inflamed interplay of economic and ethnic considerations are eroding the viability of established multinational political units. The breakup of the Soviet Union into its constituent republics is perhaps the most prominent, and troublesome, instance of this phenomenon.

The United States is deeply and diversely affected by each of these dimensions of internationalization. The effects of internationalization change in their relative intensity over time, and are perceived in a wide

variety of ways by insiders and outsiders. Generalizations are suspect, and
if made, are controversial. Nevertheless, some dominant tendencies can be
noted. First of all, there is no doubt that the United States has measured its
success in the world by its capability to project overseas its preferences and
beliefs, and by its ability to exclude those perceived as hostile. The Cold
War involved at its core the collision between two *military* superpowers,
each intent on extending the domain of its ideological orientation. In this
primary understanding of internationalization, Japan participated as a
subordinate member of the US camp, not only aligned ideologically, but
reliant upon US military support in the event of a breakdown of international order. Such subordination can be expected to persist, although its
relevance will diminish if indeed the Soviet threat remains muted.

With regard to the second and third types of internationalization, the
United States has complex and contradictory connections. In certain
respects, the US takes in ideas, persons and beliefs from outside its borders.
Its endorsement of freedom of expression and religion also implies an
affirmation of diversity. Its modes of borrowing from outside are eclectic
and spontaneous, involving the seizure of opportunities and the preferences and projects of subgroups.

Japan is differently constituted with respect to these forms of internationalization. Its recovery from the Second World War helped to restore
Japanese priorities involving a hyperfunctional approach to economic
policy and a related set of efforts to erect a regime of cultural exclusiveness
(that had, as a side-effect, a degree of economic protectionism). This
divergence from US style has generated a new type of conflict and misunderstanding between these two countries, giving rise to US perceptions
of Japan as intent on taking unfair advantage of the new situation,
including its failure to recognize that its success is both attributable to US
help and guidance in the early period and to the greater American disposition towards openness. Both the United States and Japan based their
security in the pre-Second World War period on geographically rooted
traditions of isolationism, centred around what is now called non-align-
ment. The United States postwar leadership role, and network of global
commitments, moved such a tradition to the margins of its political activity.
At times of trouble and policy disappointment, as after the Vietnam War,
there was a kind of isolationist mood present (George McGovern in his
failed 1972 presidential campaign accented this note with his slogan 'Come
Home America'). Also, at a time of relative global serenity, as during this
post-Cold War period, the fiscal attractiveness of reduced overseas
commitments generates what might be called an isolationist temptation. So
far, these mood swings have not seriously altered the US embrace of the
primary, willed form of internationalization: at most, some downward
adjustments at the margins of internationalization have occurred, reflecting
such factors as the style of political leadership, public and Congressional

opinion, the nature of interventionary 'opportunities', and the general condition of international relations.

Japan has been far more cautious about moving in a deliberately internationalist direction, especially so far as diplomatic initiative is concerned. Japan has nurtured its low profile and passivity; yet an ineluctable process of internationalization is at work. Japan as of 1990 is the world's biggest donor country when it comes to the quantity of foreign aid and foreign investment. What is unlikely for a long time to come is any *direct* attempt by Japan to protect its interests and ideas by interventionary diplomacy. To this extent, the long shadow of the Second World War remains.

AMERICANIZATION OF THE WORLD: FOR BETTER AND FOR WORSE

My focus is upon the projection of American influence in the world, a phenomenon I identify by the somewhat hyperbolic phrase, 'the Americanization of the world'. This influence has positive and negative features; first, however, let me clarify what I mean by this phrase. 'Americanization of the world' is intended to be a provocative acknowledgement of the prominence of the role of the United States in international political and economic life, together with its potent political culture which exerts a magnetic pull on aspirations and tastes of people everywhere. The dissemination of this popular culture is facilitated by the global scale of mass media and by a deliberate promotional campaign most manifest in relation to consumer products and a sense of the lifestyle appropriate to materialist success. The power of this popular culture is not purely a reflection of advertising campaigns: in many respects, the American way appears to correspond to the actual distribution of desires held by the peoples of the world, especially the urban young.

The contours of Americanization are necessarily vague and in constant flux. Perhaps, the core of Americanization can be identified by reference to images and personalities that were specifically generated in the United States – Coca Cola, Madonna and jeans. Underneath these images exists a coherent political culture based on worldwide products, on the energies of youth and sexuality, and on a casualness of style that is also associated with the sensuous pleasures of 'the good life'. Of course, Americanization does not seek directly to displace the totality of indigenous culture of foreign countries. The emergence of various forms of fundamentalism represents, to a significant degree, a backlash against Americanization, which is sometimes more generically associated with Westernization and even with modernization. This broader way of designating the phenomenon was relied upon by the post-revolutionary leadership in Iran despite directing its onslaught more concretely against the United States as 'the Great Satan'.

Americanization is a specific representation of Westernism that became ascendant in the period after the Second World War, undoubtedly reflecting US success in the military, economic and diplomatic domains. To some extent, Americanization was imposed on Japan as an incident of military occupation. Undoubtedly, underneath Americanization lies a set of ideas associated with the making of the modern world, especially reliance on technology and rationality as the basis for human progress and satisfaction.

My use of the term 'Americanization' is not meant to be judgemental, but rather to describe a measurable set of tendencies that bear upon how people live and wish to live. This pattern of Americanization has established a set of conditions that shape the manner by which others participate in the world. Japan, for instance, despite the distinctiveness of its cultural traditions, has been adept at appropriating 'Americanization', especially in relation to commercial development and trade expansion. But the impact of Americanization is broader than popular cultural attitudes. It associates the good life, more generally, at an individual and collective level, with the approach taken by the United States, although the actual impact is filtered through a diversity of perceptions. The main political consequence of Americanization is to endorse moderation and constitutional democracy, at least as a privileged alternative to more extreme approaches to state and government.

The path to greater Americanization is not without obstacles. There is now surfacing a variety of theories of US decline, ranging from Paul Kennedy's emphasis on cyclical tendencies to the critique of American economic practices now being made by conservative Japanese observers who call attention to the falling relative rates of productivity and competitiveness. There are also the various expressions of cultural resistance, already mentioned in relation to fundamentalism.

APPRAISING AMERICANIZATION

Generally, Americanization is dismissed, at least by intellectuals, as leading to the vulgarization of social and cultural life, as a form of corporate-inspired globalization that is epitomized by the McDonald emblem or by the lifeless music and culinary appeals of a worldwide hotel chain. Certainly, there is this dimension to Americanization, but there is also something more positive.

Americanization also means self-expression and individuality. There is a rebellious spirit at the core of rock music, which in many respects reaches the youth of the world more directly than any other element of Americanization. And with this rebelliousness comes a political message – support for constitutionalism and diversity, and ultimately for moderation and tolerance. Countries such as Japan (and to a lesser extent Germany) have culturally tamed the American version of constitutional democracy, but on some level they have also acknowledged the premise of consent by the governed and its corollary, the right of dissent from, and even organized opposition to, constituted authority. Such political realities seem to place some limits on governmental authority and to avoid the destructiveness of extreme postures. In the end, despite its unrestricted hedonism when it comes to materialist indulgence, Americanization has stood firmly in support of moderation when it comes to politics.

On an international level, the United States introduced in a serious manner the 'realistic' expectation of a better world brought about by adherence to international law, through the creation of a network of international institutions, the fulcrum of which is the United Nations. There existed a genuine and consequential idealism that was definitely part of the Americanizing influence in the early years after the Second World War. True, as changes have occurred in the global political climate, the United States government has wavered in these normative commitments, and since the Reagan presidency it has frequently relied on military force in foreign policy, becoming the leading unilateralist state in the world. Nevertheless, the United States earlier planted the normative seeds, and several have taken root. The 1990s, at the initiative of the Non-Aligned Movement, has been declared by the General Assembly to be the Decade of International Law. Of course, such commitments are often nominal, mere diversions from the actual currents of international politics. This must be conceded. Yet the achievement remains: the growth of law and institutions continues to provide the best alternative we have to unbridled geopolitics; states can be challenged both from below (civil society) and from without (international public opinion) by an appeal to ideas of legal accountability. The materializing of this possibility is a legacy of the early phases of Americanization.

The inspirational aspect of Americanization persists despite the evident failure of the United States to sustain its own level of commitment. On a more pragmatic basis, the United States has maintained an equilibrium between state, society and the market that has generated a sustainable prosperity for itself, and has provided the model for other states in the industrialized sector of the world. This balance may have contributed to the evolution of an American-led postwar security system that resisted the expansion of Soviet power without provoking a third world war. This contribution is contested by those who argue that the costs of militarization were unduly high; that the risks of nuclear war were unwarranted and reckless, especially during international crises; and that the effects of this approach on the Third World were generally cruel, and often disastrous. Yet the basic orientation of American policy *vis-à-vis* much of the world, especially Japan, was to provide the longest period of uninterrupted European peace among leading states in modern times. Indeed, this

American willingness to organize the security of the entire non-communist world enabled Japan to become an economic superpower without the tensions, fissures and diversion of resources that would have accompanied a commensurate militarization, especially in light of the unhealed wounds left by the era of Japanese militarism that produced a crushing defeat and surrender in 1945.

The negative sides of Americanization are largely implicit in the foregoing description. On a cultural level, the American influence disseminated a materialist ethos and encouraged a consumerist direction of development, an orientation of policy that was perfected and carried to extremes by Japanese abilities and cultural resolve. The most problematic aspect of Americanization is its *apparent* non-applicability to the poorer, more populous countries of the world, no matter what organizational skills and technological prowess may be acquired in years to come. There is in the word 'apparent' an acknowledgement of a tiny possibility that technological solutions will be found to the challenge of enlarging productive capacities in such a manner as to satisfy the basic human needs of all the peoples on the planet without wrecking the environment. From the perspective of the early 1990s, such an eventuality can almost be dismissed as technofantasy. The most plausible interpretation of the cumulative environmental impact of Americanization is a lethal mixture of eco-decay and eco-imperialism: of continuing environmental deterioration of basic resources of land, water and air and of the wasteful, destructive and inequitable appropriation of these resources by a tiny minority of humankind, leaving the majority of the human population at or below the level of subsistence and posing severe risks of ecological collapse that could diminish the life circumstances for the species as a whole, or at least for large segments of it. Even without any efforts at a more equitable distribution of resource uses, the challenge of environmental adjustment seems overwhelming in a world of territorially sovereign states of grossly disparate capabilities and environmental impacts. Japan has been basically led down this non-sustainable path of growth (which is calculated without environmental costs being subtracted) by the influence of Americanization, although conceivably it could have come about in some other, possibly more destructive form. The Eastern European environmental catastrophe establishes that Americanization is not the worst of all ecological scenarios for the planet. Indeed, what has moderated Americanization in its environmental impact are the 'checks' on the growth ethos exerted by social forces of criticism and resistance in civil society, a countervailing political trend absent or feeble in every authoritarian state/society structure.

The relative economic, political and ecological success of Americanization, as compared to Sovietization, does, at least temporarily, make it difficult to correct the flaws. These flaws are societal, as well as environmental. The high crime, drug, divorce and suicide rates in the United States disclose a culture in acute anguish. Such an impression is deepened by reference to the inequities of 'cruel capitalism', with homelessness accepted as a visible expression of human distress for which neither the market nor the state offers a remedy. In these regards, Americanization appears less successful in practice than several variants of European capitalism that seem to have institutionalized in a permanent way a welfare system of entitlements that reaches virtually the whole of society. Japan appears to have avoided the literal implementation of Americanization with respect to 'losers' in the struggle for individual success, and seems committed to a more encompassing variant of welfare capitalism.

Americanization has twice exerted a decisive influence over the shape of world order since 1945. First of all, it managed the recovery from the Second World War, including the security of the entire non-communist world, and it did this for several decades without generating severe war or economic collapse at the level of the global system. Secondly, by holding firm and by stimulating democratic forces of resistance within the communist world, the United States has helped to provide the global setting for the spread of democratization to Eastern Europe and the Soviet Union. Americanization has moved East, and most of the new leaders in Eastern Europe acknowledge the support from above and below that facilitated the collapse of autocracy. In this regard, Americanization could provide the ground for a new era of co-operative geopolitics. The Soviet Union can be helped to avoid regression. Japan has been a beneficiary of the first phase of Americanization, and stands to gain from the second phase. At the same time, the underlying logic and ethos of Americanization endangers human survival; Japan not only is swept up by these forces, but for decades has itself been an active contributor.

In fact, the failure of postwar democratizing forces to produce a strong civil society in Japan has produced a greater state/society imbalance than exists in the United States. The retention of the Emperor system and its vigorous hold on popular beliefs erode governmental accountability, making it particularly difficult for popular forces to correct abuses of state power. Here, too, the causal complexity is great. Undoubtedly, the successful maintenance of the Emperor system weakens democratic sentiments and strengthens mass disposition towards deference, a persisting feature that is also congruent with a deeply entrenched Confucianism. Further, the efforts of General MacArthur during the Occupation to create a robust democratic reality in Japan was abruptly halted by the onset of the Cold War, and the felt need to integrate rightist elements into the Japanese postwar order. As a consequence, the pre-1941 Japanese economic, social and political structures and attitudes have persisted, despite formal commitment to constitutionalism. Whether this persistence is dangerous to the future of Japanese-style democracy remains controversial.

THE REVERSAL OF AMERICANIZATION: JAPANIZATION AS CHALLENGE, THREAT AND MODEL

Perhaps, starting in 1971 with the Nixon 'shocks', which unilaterally altered economic relations with Japan, there has been a sense in the United States that some facets of Americanization have gone too far. Japan as defeated enemy in the Second World War became a compulsory ally in the Cold War, and then helped to glorify the reality of US influence by its remarkable recovery and development in the 1960s and 1970s. None the less, although rarely articulated by US officials, there was a belief that Japan, as beneficiary of enlightened US postwar policies, had a duty to pull back, to refrain from emerging as a serious economic rival, as this was beginning to reveal some embarrassing deficiencies in the US economy. But forces of restraint in Japan were either too weak, or lacking the apparatus to slow sufficiently the momentum of Japanese competitive operations on a global scale. And, indeed, the whole conception of slowing down a favourable economic dynamic for reasons other than averting inflation and overheating are quite alien to the capitalist (or for that matter, to the materialist) mindset. What is wrong with taking advantage of superior economic performance? From Adam Smith onward the maximal pursuit of comparative advantage in the marketplace has been unquestioned, and ultimately of mutual benefit. Capitalism has no room for geopolitical deference.

Yet, cultural and political factors dilute the force of economistic arguments. Japan has been blamed for not playing fair, for penetrating foreign markets while defending its own domestic market and by imposing a high rate of savings on the population. Japanese corporate and financial operations have been attacked for their alleged overseas amorality, including engaging in bribery and whatever corrupt business practices prevail under local conditions, and for being supported in so doing by the Japanese government. Some have complained that the Japanese state has unfairly fostered and subsidized the development of frontier technologies in an allegedly anti-capitalist manner that is uncongenial to the US conception of arm's length, business–government relations. In other words, Japan is blamed for its success, thereby creating a conflictual attitude, whether expressed generally as anti-Japanese hostility or more concretely in terms of protectionism, or even the advocacy of limited forms of economic warfare.[2]

Such enmity often coincides, almost unabashedly, with admiration, even a frantic effort to find the way to Japanize US economic policies. In this regard, even Japanese foreign investment in the United States is sometimes perceived as the equivalent of a benign occupation, a way to bring the Japanese miracle home to America. The many books on Japanese management technique are a further expression of American discipleship. Even

Japanese culture is studied with unquestioning admiration, envied especially for its relative success in sustaining civic life and domestic stability
despite the many years of steady economic growth, and more recently, of
affluence. More and more Americans envy Japan, and believe sincerely
that Japanese culture is superior in its formation of character and citizen
behaviour.

For many Americans this mix of hostility and admiration is left un-
resolved. There is, more generally, a mood of uncertainty in the United
States as to whether to be angry with Japan or to try harder. What is
evident, despite the triumphal ending of the Cold War, is the ascendancy of
Japan as economic superpower and the new defensiveness of the United
States as debtor country operating with chronic budget and trade deficits.
Of course, this new circumstance does not amount to anything like a role
reversal, but with the decline in East–West tensions and the disappearance
of the Soviet threat, security issues loom less large on the global agenda.
Commentators at the 1990 economic summit, held in Houston, associated
a new degree of Japanese assertiveness with this new, post-Cold War,
geopolitical atmosphere. Japan remains subordinate in matters of international security and global diplomatic presence. The United States continues to be a truly global actor and diplomatically ascendant, and the
openness and vitality of its society keeps it the central cultural arena for the
peoples of the world. Most of the new images of transnational mass culture
continue to derive from the United States, or at least from a Euro-
American cultural reality. In this regard, Japan remains marginal and
exotic, as well as lacking the geopolitical basis to become a major player in
the militarized world political system. Such marginality is also a consequence of Japan's conviction that its successful 'co-prosperity sphere'
depends on keeping as low a regional profile as possible. In this respect, the
American assumption of security responsibilities in the Western Pacific
continues to suit Japan, and undoubtedly discourages any serious hegemonic ambitions on the part of even the more conservative factions among
Japanese elites. Japan, for well-rooted and fully grasped historical reasons,
is in no position to fulfil its geopolitical potential if assessed from a purely
economic perspective; although outside the Pacific, it could expand greatly
its participation in the regional affairs of the world. As a result of this
overall circumstance, there exists a very strange set of disjunctions between
policy and performance on the part of both the United States and Japan as
we move toward the next century. To some degree, these factors also bear
on Germany's situation, but less dramatically, because of the larger European reality that is unfolding. In this regard, one could more readily envisage Germany under the banner of Europe evolving as a full-fledged
geopolitical challenger to the United States, yet here too formidable
counter-pressures persist, especially in Europe itself.

THE EMERGENT NEW GEOPOLITICS

It seems we are confronted by the persistence of a non-geopolitical, yet politically very important variant of US influence. And this dissemination goes on at a time when there is simultaneously taking place a very confusing crisis of transition from the postwar world, from the world that we have known since 1945 through 1989. The large question that is posed by this transition is whether it represents one more phase in a historical sequence of changes in great power management of international political life that has occurred throughout the history of the state system, and whether the United States can adapt to a post-Cold War setting and re-establish under altered conditions some appropriate form of global leadership. The most likely alternative geopolitical scenario is a mixture of multipolarity at the global level and greater regional autonomy; a less cohesive, more complex and more integrated variant of world order. One question is whether such a multipolar international system can yield the collective mechanisms that will be needed in an increasingly crowded and fragile world. The prevailing view of most specialists is guardedly optimistic, stressing the continuity of international political life and claiming that the problems we confront today are of the same general order as the problems that have been confronted in international society in the past. I am less hopeful. I believe we must take seriously the challenges implicit in what might be described as an unprecedented crisis of internationalization. A more structural view of these challenges leads me in a pessimistic direction. I doubt whether the regulative mechanisms of the past that have often produced acceptable, if not satisfactory, forms of international stability and order, are any longer reproducible. The nature of the environmental and economic challenges seems to be of a radically different character that draws into question the viability of territorial allocations of authority and of military conceptions of security. The prospect of this new international situation makes such ideas as the balance of power seem quite obsolete in relation to handling the multiple challenges of environmental decay and of tightly interlinked world financial, information and trade systems.

There are other considerations too. The moderate demographic projections for the year 2030 tell us that the planet will have 9 billion people living on it, using at the minimum 75 per cent more fossil fuels than in 1989, and requiring a much greater increase in energy and water supplies than currently exist in the reserves of the world. The poverty of the Third World can only be overcome by new forms of political radicalism, the emergence of which would undoubtedly be perceived as a threat to the post-Cold War stability that the US seeks to maintain. The almost assured effect then of significant attempts to redress North–South disparities or poverty in Asia, Latin America and Africa, would likely provoke another cycle of US intervention. Fundamental adjustments in population levels and lifestyle will be brought about by coercion and in an arbitrary manner if global initiatives are not commenced soon.

Time magazine, which is not noted for environmental radicalism, featured the endangered planet as its 'person of the year' in 1988, high-lighting its editorial sense of the magnitude of the environmental agenda. For once, no person was a sufficiently dominant historical force, and so the planet itself was cast in this role. The cover story explaining this selection read as if written by an environmental alarmist, in a rhetoric that *Time* itself scorned a few years earlier, then dismissing environmentalism as marginal, regarding environmental problems as fully manageable within existing frameworks, and treating most environmentalists as either sinister or naïve enemies of modernism, of progress, and of the proven path of market-driven economic growth. There has, in other words, now emerged an ecological consciousness that has become especially prominent in civil society and among social movements, including those of a transnational character.

The effect of this rise in consciousness has been to change the political climate. Even governments are now 'green' in their political language, reacting both to pressure from below and to their own assessment of deteriorating conditions. It is encouraging that this surge of awareness has occurred in the past several years, and that acting in response is surely facilitated by the moderation of East–West tensions and the demilitariza-tion of geopolitics on a global scale. It has even been suggested, provoca-tively by Mary Kaldor, that it might be possible in the next phase of international relations to supplant military Keynesianism by ecological Keynesianism.[3] Such a 'conversion', however enticing, might be especially difficult for the United States (and possibly the Soviet Union), given the continuing influence of their respective military-industrial-academic es-tablishments, a variety of other claims on funds, and also considering the weak public sector in both economies. It is here, too, that a reconfigured world system might take shape. One possibility would be for Japan and Germany, among others, to take the lead in financing this conversion on a global scale and to subsidize those societies least able to bear the adjust-ment burdens.

Whatever the modality, it seems evident that unprecedented forms of peacetime co-operation are indispensable to maintain stability and prosperity at anything like present levels, and to foster some progress towards decency on the planet as a whole. If that progress towards decency is not sustained, it will lead to a crisis of governability throughout large portions of Asia, Africa and Latin America. In other words, the claim of decency is not just an altruistic search, it relates directly to the danger that the poorer parts of the world will come to resemble Lebanon, Cambodia and Sri Lanka. In effect, Lebanon, Cambodia and Sri Lanka are not just isolated misfortunes, but represent prophetic examples and warnings of the profound ruptures of basic order that are threatening to occur throughout Africa, Latin America and large parts of Asia. The Third World will not be forgotten in this process of transition, but the form of its presence is uncertain, potentially threatening and troublesome.

One of the dangers of the refocusing of American attention on the Japanese challenge is that it reinforces a pre-existing tendency to ignore the Third World, to neglect the southern part of the world, and especially to forget the hopes of a decent life on the part of the majorities of peoples of Asia, Africa and Latin America. The United States entered the postwar period with a conviction that it could help itself by helping the Third World in the post-colonial period. What the United States wanted to encourage was a style of modernization of the sort that did eventually catch on in such Asian countries as South Korea, Taiwan, Hong Kong and Singapore. Such an evolution would bring improvements in the standard of living, while integrating the society into the world economy in a manner resistant to political radicalism. Obviously, this pattern did not take hold very generally, and in many Third World countries either capitalist ineptitude or antagonistic nationalism tended to disillusion US policymakers and public opinion about either its capacity to help or even its ability to control indigenous patterns of change. The nuclear stalemate tended to shift the sharpest East–West encounters to the Third World, at a great cost in suffering and devastation. On the American side, interventionary diplomacy climaxed and was strongly tested during a decade of warfare in Indo-China. The outcome was defeat, disillusionment and an unresolved domestic debate about the nature of the struggle and why it was lost.

To some extent, President Reagan's foreign policy rehabilitated an interventionary option, at least in small countries that had traditionally fallen within the sphere of US influence and were located in the Caribbean or Central America. But even Reagan quickly retreated from Lebanon in 1983 after a massive terrorist attack on US marine barracks, making it evident that a US military presence would be politically inconclusive, yet costly in lives and prestige.

With the Soviet withdrawal in frustration and defeat from Afghanistan, and more generally from the Third World, the strategic rationale derived from the Cold War is a spent ideological force as a source of justification for either assistance or intervention. Reinforcing this development is the increasing unavailability of government resources for either foreign aid or an assertive foreign policy. The idealistic rationale for help has been eroded through a variety of disillusioning experiences, possibly highlighted in the Kennedy years by the initial promise and subsequent disappointment related to the Alliance for Progress as a means to promote social reform and economic development in Latin America. And, finally, the continuing offscale commitments to Israel and Egypt (the US financial payback for Camp David), as well as political backing for assistance to Eastern Europe, make it very difficult for the US government to contemplate at present any constructive initiatives taken for the benefit of the Third World. At most, there is some focus on modest forms of debt relief, and this mainly to avoid destabilizing world banking and trading systems.

Such a set of circumstances makes it very tempting to overlook large portions of the Third World, and to ignore the warnings of deepening and spreading troubles. One signal of this danger is the growing appeal of fundamentalism in the Third World, particularly in the Islamic world which is so strategically relevant. Fundamentalist politics have succeeded only where despair and desperation have obtained a hold on mass levels. Putting Third World grievances on hold seems likely to ensure the spread of fundamentalist challenges. It is this post-Cold War set of attitudes that has so easily produced the false consciousness that a new geopolitics of stability can best be achieved by working out the economic relationships among the leading industrial states – hence, the symbolic significance attached to the annual G-7 summits and the virtual neglect of the UN General Assembly or the initiatives of the mid-1970s to establish a framework for more mutual North–South economic relations under the rubric of a New International Economic Order.

Japan, it is true, has emerged in the early 1990s as the leading foreign aid donor, and this has enhanced its reputation without undermining its relationship with the United States. It may be possible here to nurture a creative division of labour between the United States and Japan, with the US continuing to provide 'security' and Japan providing development assistance, as well as financing Third World environmental adjustments, and even providing the venture capital needed to reconstruct America's flagging economy (i.e. Japanese investment in the United States creates the self-interested basis for revitalization of the American economy, and complicates the view of the two countries as economic rivals).

THE UPHEAVAL IN INTERNATIONAL RELATIONS: REDEFINING THE ROLE OF THE UNITED STATES

The story of US participation in the world has always been confusing, even to Americans. There are two peculiarly contradictory traditions that are reconciled, if at all, only by a rarely articulated allocation of emphasis based on geography, and now, on historical tradition. The tension over role arises, however, from a clash of attitudes: on the one side, a condescending repudiation of geopolitics that can be evaded by isolationism, and on the other, a vaulting ambition to expand and control. If more closely explored, the isolationist rationale was always intended as a regional policy of non-involvement in the European struggles for ascendancy. The United States, at the inception of the republic, correctly regarded its own interests as being far better protected during its early decades of independence by letting European countries work out their own relations without getting drawn into wars on the continent of no real consequence to the territorial independence or economic well-being of the United States. The confusion arose because of Eurocentrism that led most commentators to formulate the policy of isolationism in a generalized language that seemed to apply to the whole world. It never did. Always, American statecraft aimed to achieve continental and hemispheric ambitions by way of a policy of military and commercial expansion, and this led the United States from its earliest period as an independent country to consider its vital interests as extending both throughout the Western hemisphere and to the far reaches of the Western Pacific.

What remains true, and is to some extent relevant to the unfolding debate about the post-Cold War future of NATO, is a belief that the United States has become overextended geopolitically, and that this has had adverse economic consequences over the long haul. It has been expressed more in an economic vocabulary of burden-sharing than in the earlier preoccupation with irrelevant warfare. With the experiences of both world wars, and the uncertainty about whether European states could resist communism, there is no longer any doubt about the US interest in European affairs. This view has been reinforced since 1945 by the perceived importance in the nuclear age of preventing warfare rather than reacting after the outbreak of war. Now, arguably, with Europe moving towards regional unity as never before, the United States could face a problem not previously encountered – namely, exclusion. Of course, such a prospect is a long way off, but should the world system be dominated by trading blocs, it seems quite likely that a Europe not faced with a security threat might well begin acting to recover its full political autonomy. The Cold War, with its formation of blocs, led to some encroachment upon traditional sovereign domains, especially with respect to security issues of allies, including decisions about strategic doctrine that deeply affected war risks and likely consequences. Such a relationship of dominance was evident on the Soviet side, less so on the Western side. The possible reassertion of territorial sovereignty in the aftermath of the Cold War in both Western Europe and Japan might well occur, and could easily strengthen the complementary US impulse to cut back its overseas commitments at this stage.

The world situation remains exceedingly uncertain, especially given the turmoil within the Soviet Union itself. As long as this uncertainty persists, it is unlikely that the United States will alter its relationship in any fundamental way to the Pacific region. It may make tactical adjustments in response to regional developments, as might be required if it loses basing rights in the Philippines or if Korean unification talks bear fruit, but the basic role of a hegemonic security presence in the region is likely to persist and to be quite widely welcomed by the established governments, including that of Japan. Partly, the US role is perceived as an alternative to an intensification of regional rivalry, including anxiety that Japan might be led to project its power militarily in the region if the US presence diminished. In this regard, the Japanese themselves remain exceedingly reluctant to redefine their geopolitical identity in the unfolding new situation.

Finally, the underlying dynamics of economic and environmental internationalization may come to dominate the foreign policy agenda of major countries in a manner that makes the older debate between 'internationalism' and 'isolationism' seem extremely dated and irrelevant. In this regard, the demilitarization of geopolitics, if it proceeds, may lead to an era of international relations in which world order bargains and functional arrangements reduce the importance of statist images of security and relationships. Such prospects, it needs to be stressed, remain highly speculative.

But there is one aspect of this setting that could bear interestingly on the future US–Japan relationship. Part of the US self-image with deep historical roots, is that of a teacher of nations, a new Jerusalem, an exemplary society, the city on the hill, that contributes to a continuing sense of American exceptionalism. This orientation has infused even the recent period of imperial geopolitics with ideas of the United States as benefactor, even when the US is in an interventionary or occupying relation to another country. It is an extraordinary form of arrogance, but there is just enough plausibility to sustain the belief. It assumes two characteristic modes: realistic (even target societies should be grateful for being occupied, or destroyed, provided American influence prevails) and idealistic (by assuming a position of global leadership in international politics, the world can be transformed in ways that are beneficial for all). In both modes the United States is 'the teacher' and Japan 'the pupil' – possibly a useful way to compensate for the reversal in economic and societal relations in which Japan has become the teacher and the United States the pupil.

The postwar experience with Germany and Japan is taken as exemplifying this faith in American geopolitical pedagogy. The lesson is reinforced that there is nothing better that can happen to a society than to be occupied by the United States after a defeat in war. It guarantees political democracy and economic recovery, even prosperity beyond that of the occupying power, so generous is the United States as an occupier and so powerful is its pedagogical impact. There persists an extraordinary sense of US detachment which plays into these other feelings of exceptionalism and interventionism. The turning point for the United States in its attitude towards geopolitics was occasioned in this century by the two world wars, and especially the controversies between these two tendencies as applicable to Europe that emerged out of the First World War. The basic American conviction that it should remain neutral in relation to European armed struggle was overcome. Woodrow Wilson succeeded in challenging the earlier consensus that the appropriate US style of internationalization was to ignore geopolitics, which was conceived in exclusively Eurocentric terms. The US had believed that its vital interests were not affected by the outcome of wars in Europe, and this seemed basically correct until this century.

When the United States entered the war it did so with false consciousness. Woodrow Wilson promised to provide a new world order beyond the European geopolitics of balances and alliances. He mobilized support for intervention by appealing to this idealistic interest of Americans that included spreading their particular gospel of global reform. Wilson and British propaganda manipulated American public opinion to believe that Germany was more evil than its adversaries, and second, that it was being very provocative towards the United States by waging submarine warfare against the ocean commerce of neutrals. This is not the place to consider the controversy about the First World War, but the great loss of life and the gradual realization that nothing more than power relations was at stake lay behind a legacy that the United States was best off at home; that it was not worth the cost in blood and treasure to influence the outcome of a European war; that the Europeans could not be saved from themselves; that Wilson's good intentions were naïve and rested on inadequate understanding of world politics; and, finally, that European diplomats were cynical realists, not a receptive audience for American good intentions and global reformist ideas. Besides, no domestic consensus existed in the United States itself for any permanent globalization of the US role. The US role after the First World War was again to be one of detachment from Eurocentric geopolitics. The League of Nations, a prime product of Wilson's idealism, but an organization that the US government refused in the end to join, was seen in retrospect as an idealistic fig leaf affixed to traditional geopolitics. The failure of the League was anticipated by the isolationist forces that repudiated Wilson's efforts to give the United States a permanent role in managing the central security relations of the world.

Despite efforts by Franklin Roosevelt to edge the country towards involvement in the Second World War, isolationist sentiment remained strong until the Pearl Harbor attack. Indeed, it was this event more than any other occurrence that gave the internationalists the upper hand in the postwar world. Pearl Harbor decisively shattered the illusion that the United States possessed an isolationist option with respect to central geopolitical conflicts, whether centred in Europe or the Pacific. Also, the Second World War, unlike the First World War, engaged American values and sense of moral purpose. The defeat of fascism and militarism seemed worthwhile to the public, and this conviction was widely confirmed by the documentation of Nazi atrocities that occurred at the Nuremberg trial proceedings, and to a far lesser degree at the parallel proceedings against Japanese military and civilian leaders held in Tokyo. And, of course, since 1945 the global scope of the Cold War, as well as the emergence of a more interdependent world economy, solidified the hold of the internationalists in the United States on the foreign policy process. At this point, the invocation of isolationist approaches is pure nostalgia, although one can find isolationist elements in the neo-conservatism of the Reagan-Bush years. For instance, the rejection of the Law of the Seas Treaty, the withdrawal from UNESCO, the termination of US acceptance of the compulsory jurisdiction of the World Court, and the generally scornful attitude towards international law were all policy initiatives that were intended to reject the liberal side of internationalism, especially the commitment of liberals to an expanded role for law and institutions in international life. But neo-conservative foreign policy never challenged the internationalism of US business and banking operations. Recalling the earlier discussion of Americanization, it is helpful to realize that this neo-conservative posture is quite compatible with a missionary attitude towards the spread of the American way, whether it be consumerist lifestyle or the acceptance of a market-based economy and a degree of constitutionalism as the foundation of political legitimacy.

What did emerge from the Second World War in a permanent way was a bipartisan consensus on a continuing direct US involvement in the affairs of Europe, the Pacific and the Middle East, as well as in relation to the basic arrangements for maintaining global peace and security. It was understood by the political leadership that the United States had to build upon its role in the Second World War, and take the initiative in organizing the postwar maintenance of international order. Despite immediate steps towards demobilization, it was soon agreed that Europe could not be left on its own, that it was impossible to approach the prospect of a third world war in the manner that the First and Second World Wars had been addressed. Anticipatory war prevention was essential. This meant the basic shift from defence to deterrence, a shift understood as a reaction to the possession of nuclear weapons, but likely to reflect a wider appreciation of the growing destructiveness of major warfare. The rivalry with the Soviet Union provided a persuasive and credible pretext for the indefinite occupation and division of Europe and for the indefinite and acceptable division of Germany, two sets of realities mutually agreed upon in the 1975 Helsinki Accords. Without the Cold War and the success of Western European economic reconstruction, that kind of punitive peace would not have been politically acceptable, especially not to the Germans. Now with the Soviet withdrawal from East Europe, the end of the Cold War, and German reunification, there is a belated acknowledgement by some United States policymakers that, yes, the Cold War was helpful as a basis for stability in Europe. This acknowledgement of the utility of the Cold War, though not surprising to me personally, has been widely taken as an unexpected development.

It is difficult for today's leaders to decide what to do in a world where the Soviet Union no longer provides an organizing focus for foreign policy and for the justification of high defence expenditures and the militarization of security. We are now facing the consequences, in a certain sense, of American postwar success, success in all three of these forms of internationalization mentioned at the outset. The consequences of this success pose several new types of challenges that seem to give some clarity to the present moment. One of these challenges concerns whether significant resources can be reallocated from military to non-military purposes to enable the kind of emphasis on environmental and economic priorities that seems essential in the present world situation. Whether this reallocation (the so-called 'peace dividend') can occur is partly a domestic question of whether the power of the military is so great that it can continue to command current levels of resources. Whether or not the military and industrial complex will prove to be a paper tiger depends on what occurs in the Soviet Union and elsewhere in the world. It will still be quite plausible to perceive threats to US interests around the world. The social forces that will weaken the national security hold on the policy process are not well organized enough to mount a political challenge at the present time.

In the background a further rarely discussed anxiety about moving beyond the Cold War exists. There is a concern that military Keynesianism has been responsible for sparing the United States and the world from any deep recession since 1945. Even more hidden from view is the fear that capitalism cannot sustain growth without a war economy, and that only the onset of the Second World War rescued the United States and Europe from the Great Recession. Thus, in effect, the quick embrace of the Cold War, and the rather minimal diplomatic effort to identify alternatives, reflected an unvoiced and, possibly, unconscious attraction to an international situation that could justify a war economy for the indefinite future. The Cold War was a kind of wonder drug for the economy as it reaped the benefits of wartime without the death and destruction of war (in fact, of course, the Cold War generated a series of bloody wars in the Third World). Throughout the postwar period there has existed this background fear about the economic consequences of moving away from a war-based conception of security. In effect, Gorbachev's unilateralism gave the West no choice but to move towards an acknowledgement that the Cold War was winding down, even if not definitely over. Even right-wing intellectuals such as Jeane Kirkpatrick and Richard Perle, possibly oblivious to the apparent dependence of the economy on a high state of East–West tensions, now endorse the view that a post-Cold War world is emerging, and with it a new security agenda, possibly with reduced budgetary demands. There is, of course, the Japanese model of sustained economic growth that has been coupled with exceedingly low military expenditures. In the present setting of US concern about falling behind in the struggle for shares of the world market, the Japanese model could induce business and government pressure for a large peace dividend, particularly in light of ecological and fiscal demands on budgetary resources. That is, there are at least two more constructive policy alternatives to a mindless adherence to military Keynesianism: first, a move towards the Japanese pattern of budgetary allocation; second, a shift towards another sector as the basis for Keynesian deficit spending, i.e. ecological Keynesianism, or even a revival of welfare Keynesianism.

There are some other obstacles on the path towards deep military cuts, especially if involving the career military or national security establishment. The reassimilation of such individuals into civilian life may prove difficult: they may forge dangerous proto-fascist linkages if released into the private sector. The disclosures involving Oliver North's effort to circumvent Congressional restrictions on Contra funding gave a disturbing insight into this underworld of former national security bureaucrats who privatized their operations after leaving government. Privatization meant illicit arms dealing, contacts with organized crime and, most of all, personnel and political inputs for a variety of ultra-right causes and groups drawn together by transnational networks. It is essential to demobilize the national security establishment without distorting the play of social forces within society in such a way as to facilitate the rise of rightist politics and extra-legal manipulation of the policy process in constitutional democracies.

How can this transfer from the Cold War forms of security to the security arrangements appropriate to an era of geo-economic and eco-logical priorities be made without diluting the democratic ethos of the United States? Such a challenge is made even more difficult if the goal of promoting basic human needs of the poorer peoples of the world is also included as a high-priority responsibility of US foreign policy. It is un-fortunate that the United States appears to lack both an imaginative leader-ship and a bold and creative opposition at this time. The two political parties have not focused on this need for a post-Cold War vision of US foreign policy. The citizenry has seemed unduly complacent, approving of the greater moderateness of international life, but rather unconcerned about the ecological and economic shadows that fall across almost every careful account of the future. Perhaps, in the end, the Japanese challenge might prove beneficial, prodding post-Cold War diplomacy in a demilitar-izing direction and helping to wean the United States away from its sense of dependence on a war economy. At least, these facets of the Japanese example deserve far more attention than they have so far received.

A CONCLUDING WORLD ORDER NOTE

Internationalization cannot be accommodated within the framework of the state system as it has generally been understood. Many types of innovation will be needed, and are beginning to emerge: regionalization of economic life (Europe 1992); confederal breakdown of centralized multinational states (a future Soviet Union); major functional bargains (Law of the Seas Treaty, ozone depletion regime); procedures of accountability by governments and corporations for environmental negligence and criminality; experiments with a global concert of powers (i.e., a global version of the concert of Europe).

In this period of transition, two positive tendencies can ground our hopes for the future. The first tendency involves a restoration of some degree of governmental and public confidence that international institutions have an important role to play in providing stability and equity in this post-Cold War world. One can envisage the superpowers moving in a few years to establish peacekeeping forces at the disposal of the United Nations if, indeed, they renounce or confine their own interventionary options. International institutions can provide mechanisms for an unprecedented intensity of international co-operation, giving rise to higher levels of mutual understanding among states in international relations. The second tendency may be that the countries that have the greatest wealth and prosperity – the industrial countries of the world – will be induced to translate their present, rather nominal forms of co-operation into a much more co-ordinated strategy for addressing global environmental problems and the North–South disparity, grounding their real security in support for a strategy of sustainable eco-development (to borrow the rhetoric of the Bruntland Commission Report). These two levels of potentially enhanced international co-operation, if actualized, provide an enlarged period of time in which to solve the more structural crises of the state system: the crisis of the *porousness* of the state ('porous' in being unable to prevent the entry of undesirable elements – drugs, illegal immigrants, alien ideas, nuclear missiles, pollutants) and the crisis of *ecological decay* that can only be overcome if states co-operate in protecting the global interests and join together in seriously promoting the long-term interests of humanity.

A return to the themes of 'the Americanization of the world' and 'the Japanese challenge', given this new international situation and the policy consensus that has taken shape in the last five years, suggests an important zone of opportunity for both countries. The United States can explore paths that lead away from wasteful and dangerous reliance on a militarist foreign policy, while Japan can encourage this exploration by emphasizing the positive connection that exists between its economic achievements and its avoidance of commensurate militarization. The Americanization of the world, assuming it continues on the mass cultural level, can help persuade the United States that its influence in the world is not contingent upon its military prowess, but exists rather as a consequence of its high degree of success in achieving 'a good life' for the majority of its population. Similarly, Japan can overcome its reputation for passivity in global arenas by subsidizing the transition to a post-Cold War diplomacy based on high

ecological and equity priorities. Such positive prospects cannot be anticipated unless both governments are subject to pressures from below and
from without. A hopeful future, by this understanding, depends on the
rising vitality of transnational social movements and the gradual construction of a transnational democratic process that is dedicated to the establishment of a global polity committed to ecological viability, human rights and
a humane resource policy.

NOTES

1 *National Interest* (1989) 16:3–18; cp. Paul Kennedy, 'The (relative) decline of
   America' *The Atlantic Monthly* (1987) 29–37.
2 Compare, for example, a recent journalistic treatment of this theme: Randall
   Rothenberg, 'US ads increasingly attack Japanese and their culture' *New York
   Times*, 11 July 1990.
3 Speech at the European Nuclear Disarmament Convention, Helsinki, Finland, 4
   July 1990.
4 See R.B.J. Walker (1988), *One World/Many Worlds*, Boulder, Col.: Lynne
   Rienner.

Part II

Meanings and implications

Chapter 3

Interdependence and internationalization

Ogata Sadako

There is probably no other single topic that has been more often discussed in Japan in recent years than 'internationalization'. No clear agreement exists on the precise meaning of the term, but 'internationalization' is used to describe the current process of change taking place in Japan as well as the desired course of direction that Japan should follow. It is important to emphasize that 'internationalization' does not represent any sense of 'Japanization' or of influencing the outside world. No hegemonic sentiment is involved; rather, a commitment exists that Japan and Japanese society should adjust to an international environment that is becoming increasingly interdependent.

Often 'internationalization' is used interchangeably with 'interdependence'. For analytical purposes, however, these two concepts can be distinguished. It is true that both concepts relate to changes caused by rapid growth in international exchanges and contacts, but they represent different aspects of the same phenomenon. 'Interdependence' refers more directly to the development of interlocking relationships brought about by increased transactions involving money, goods, people or messages. 'Internationalization', on the other hand, is concerned with attitudinal changes in the face of growing interdependence. It may not be sufficiently realized that interdependence involves costs, especially at the social level. Faced with growing intrusion from the outside, a society may either choose to reject or contain the widespread effects emanating from interdependence, or it may decide to move in the direction of greater accommodation. The former may bring about a nationalistic backlash. The latter leads to internationalization. 'Internationalization', therefore, is a process that ensues when a given society pursues a course of adjusting to, and accepting changes brought about by, increasing interdependence.

What characterizes current developments in Japan is the acuteness with which the need for internationalization has been recognized by a wide range of business, political and opinion leaders. Until recently, however, Japanese society has remained relatively unaffected by outside change. Although international trade and foreign travel expanded, society maintained a high degree of exclusiveness. Not only the market, but also most social institutions – corporations, schools, professions – were understood to be for Japan and the Japanese only. A high degree of social mobility and open competition characterized Japanese society but opportunities were again mostly limited to Japanese. In the last decade, however, two factors have come to undermine the traditional exclusiveness of Japanese society. One is outside pressure in the form of a demand for market liberalization and social openness. The other is the impact of interdependence, which has necessitated changes in social attitudes and practices. Combined, these two factors have produced a strong awareness that internationalization may be the only course open to Japan to survive in today's world.

In fact, internationalization has been perceived by a wide range of Japanese leaders as the panacea for all kinds of imbalances to come to the fore in recent years. The most pronounced imbalance exists between an economy that has become global in its activities and impact, and a society that has remained largely traditional. Another imbalance can be found in the structure of the economy itself, between an ever more rational export-led sector of manufacturing and financing, and inefficient, heavily regulated and protected distribution and agriculture sectors. Significant imbalance can be observed in the movement of people, in which there is a clear excess of Japanese going abroad – whether students, scholars or businessmen – over foreigners coming to Japan for similar objectives.

How, then, is internationalization expected to lead to the correcting of these imbalances? It is a well-known fact that Japan's economy has developed steadily in the four decades since the war, and it now ranks second in terms of its GNP. Especially during the last decade, the surplus in Japan's balance of trade has increased markedly, and its net external assets had already reached more than US$240 billion by the end of 1987, making Japan the world's largest creditor nation. From the point of view of Japan's internationalization, however, it is important to note certain salient points that have conditioned the expansion of Japan's economy in the 1980s. The first and the most obvious point relates to the growth of the double deficits in the United States, which turned the US into the world's largest debtor nation. Related to this, and of equal importance, is the second point: the appreciation of the Japanese yen. This has triggered two developments. One is the acceleration in overseas investment on the part of Japan's manufacturers and financial institutions. The other is the growth of imports boosted by measures to stimulate domestic demand and liberalize markets.

Stepped-up economic activities following the appreciation of the yen have brought about social changes of great importance. On the one hand, there has been the 'push' effect of sending Japanese overseas to carry out business from foreign bases; on the other, the 'pull' effect of bringing into the country foreign businessmen and workers who try to profit from the high yen. In 1987, there were 270,000 Japanese living overseas for an extended period. These were mainly businessmen and their families engaged in trade, investment and manufacturing. This figure represents a 70 per cent increase over the last decade, and shows how Japanese economic activities have come to involve Japanese based abroad. Many of them are accompanied by their families. Some 40,000 Japanese children are estimated to be attending local or Japanese primary schools outside Japan. The increase in the number of Japanese schools, which are mostly concentrated in developing countries, has also been conspicuous. Children living in the industrially developed world, who attend local school during the week, are provided with supplementary Japanese language training outside normal school hours. In all, there are approximately 200 such facilities, which are managed jointly by the Japanese Ministry of Education and the Japanese business community.

The largest concentration of overseas Japanese is to be found in North America, followed by Western Europe and Asia. The number of Japanese in North America doubled from 50,688 in 1977 to 109,666 in 1987. A twofold increase is also found in the number of Japanese in Western Europe: from 35,452 in 1977 to 70,241 in 1987. However, although the number of Japanese living in Asian countries had been the largest, the increase has been more modest and has remained almost constant in the last five years at a little over 50,000. The relative decline of long-term Japanese residents in Asian countries reflects the fact that Japanese businesses set up in Asia are being increasingly managed by local employees, and that Japanese managers or technicians are overseeing the operations by making short visits.[1]

Apart from those engaged in business, a second major group of Japanese living abroad for an extended period comprises students and researchers. They numbered over 49,000 in 1987. An increasing number of students go abroad on short-term study programmes, mainly devoted to language training. The number of tourists is also on the rise. Nearly 8.5 million Japanese travelled abroad in 1988.

No conclusive generalization can be drawn at this time with regard to the social consequences of Japan's expanded economic activities overseas. Two areas would seem to require closer examination, however. One is the social and psychological impact of Japanese business operations abroad; the other is the impact of returnee long-term overseas residents on Japanese society. Both cases involve cross-cultural conflict and communication of a new and intense kind as their scale becomes unprecedented. They also call for additional changes and adjustments, not only on the part of the Japanese exposed to living and working in foreign environments, but also on the part of local employees of Japanese enterprises and business partners. Also, those Japanese who have no experience of living abroad will have to cope with fellow countrymen whose attitudes and values will have been altered by their experience abroad. The treatment of Japanese children who return after years of living overseas presents a poignant case.

Let us now examine the situation of foreign employees in Japanese enterprises. As of July 1988, there were 1,639,763 employees in Japanese businesses around the world. More than 1.1 million are engaged in manufacturing. The largest number, 787,450, is to be found in Asia. South Korea and Taiwan top the list, with Thailand coming third and Malaysia fourth. The second largest concentration, 373,249, is to be found in North America. In the United States alone, there are 331,737 employees in Japanese businesses. The third is in Western Europe, with a sizeable proportion of 118,374 employees in Japanese businesses. The greatest number, 34,280, is employed in the United Kingdom, followed by Germany with 24,016 and then Spain with 21,650. The characteristics of the employment pattern in Western Europe is that both in Great Britain and in Germany, employees of Japanese businesses are more or less evenly divided between the manufacturing sector and the trade and finance sector. In Spain they are almost exclusively engaged in manufacturing, a fact that reflects the expansion of Japanese automobiles, electronics and other manufacturing plants in that country.[2]

A number of surveys have been conducted on the effects of increased economic activity by Japanese corporations in the United States. The 1987 project on 'The Regional Underpinnings of the US–Japan Partnership', carried out by the Japan Center for International Exchange, provides interesting insights into the results of growing interaction between Japanese and Americans at the state level. Four states – Georgia, Tennessee, North Carolina and Indiana – were chosen for the 1987 survey, and an additional nine states were chosen for a 1989 survey. One of the most valuable contributions of the 1987 survey is to show how Japan's growing economic presence has stimulated local interest in Japanese culture, society and people. While there is an undercurrent of fear and resentment among Americans that Japan may not be playing fair, nor shouldering its share of global responsibility, there seems to be a growing curiosity in, and respect for, Japan. The study points to certain developments in these states resulting from Japan's increased economic presence: greater emphasis on education about Japan at the elementary and secondary school level; strengthening of Japanese or Asian related programmes of study at the university level; and establishment of Japan centres by the state authorities or business communities to provide information on Japan. These changes all show how Japan is inducing internationalization at the grass-roots level in the United States.[3]

By becoming directly linked with American workers, distributors and other business partners, Japanese business is also undergoing an intense learning process. While on the one hand some aspects of Japanese corporate culture, such as that emphasizing family-type unity and loyalty, seem to be gaining ground, on the other hand, American social values and practices seem to be making inroads. Questions concerning hiring and promotion, delegation of authority, discipline and work habits are all issues calling for understanding and adjustment. Japanese corporations are also learning to become more involved in the local communities. Participating in local philanthropic activities, for example, is a new experience for Japanese managers and their families. In the last few years, the Japan Federation of Economic Organizations has taken several initiatives to promote corporate philanthropy. It organized, for instance, the Council for Better Corporate Citizens to support community activities in foreign countries. It also created a 'One Per Cent Club' in order to encourage corporations to give at least 1 per cent of profits to philanthropic causes. Pursuing economic activities in an interdependent world is forcing business-men to turn into good citizens, not only in Japan, but also in their host countries. However, as the idea of good citizenship is culturally defined, the Japanese business community will have to continue to strengthen its learning capacity, as it expands its activities in Northern America, Western Europe, Asia and many other parts of the world.

Turning to the treatment of those who come back to Japan after extended stays overseas, the entry or re-entry of businessmen's children into the school system illustrates the problem in its most acute form. Most of the 40,000 schoolchildren who attend local or Japanese schools abroad will return to Japan at some point and face problems of adjustment. These range from the difficulty of catching up with the standardized curriculum of Japanese schools to the psychological struggle of behaving as a Japanese. While these are the types of difficulties children of any nationality face after spending years in a different cultural and national setting, the case of Japanese children tends to be more severe because of the highly standard-ized and competitive nature of Japanese society in general, and of the educational system in particular. Anyone who is not comfortable with the Japanese language, or does not know Japanese history or geography, is regarded with a certain disdain. In contrast, those fluent in foreign language are viewed with suspicion. In particular, those who are individual-istic or who take initiatives are considered uncooperative or even un-Japanese. In short, they are treated as if they were suffering from some defect. Most returnee children say that the schools and teachers spend most time in trying to correct their language, knowledge and even personality, rather than encouraging them to retain and develop what they have acquired abroad.

However, with the increase in the numbers of children returning from abroad, considerable improvement has been made in the situation during the last few years. The general commitment towards the 'internationaliz-ation' of Japan has contributed towards drawing national attention to the treatment of returnee children. Special classes have been set up in several national, local and private schools at the primary and secondary levels to deal with readjustment to Japanese society. A number of private schools now offer special quotas to facilitate returnee children's entry. At the university level, considerable improvement can also be noted. Over sixty universities have introduced a quota system for admitting these students on the basis of a different selection process. These universities include certain faculties at prestigious national universities, such as Tokyo and Kyoto. They base the entrance examination on a combination of internationally acknowledged qualifications, such as the scholastic aptitude tests and the international baccalaureate, together with short essays on various topics. The fact that corporations have begun to recruit Japanese university graduates with overseas experience, or even Japanese graduates of foreign universities, will help to alleviate the discriminatory practices that have prevailed in the past. In fact, the Provisional Commission on Educational Reform, which was set up to examine the status of Japanese education during the Nakasone era, stressed that the internationalization of Japanese education is the most important aspect of educational reform.

The question of the internationalization of Japanese education is not simply confined to the returnee children. Another category of growing concern is the foreign students from around the world who are attending Japanese universities. Japan still does not have a satisfactory programme for foreign students in terms of scale of intake, conditions, the number of scholarships, or the conferring of higher degrees. In 1988 the number of foreign students in Japan was 25,643. This reflects an average annual increase of nearly 20 per cent over the past five years. A sharp rise in numbers is expected and the government has set a target of 100,000 by the year 2000. The greatest number of students come from China, followed by Taiwan, Korea, Malaysia and the United States. Most foreign students pursue natural science and engineering courses, a pattern which reflects the growing need for scientists and technicians in Asian countries.[4]

Aside from the problems that arise from the inadequacies of the university system itself, the question of language has been considered a major obstacle to expanding foreign student programmes in Japan. This obstacle may be largely overcome as the teaching of Japanese spreads throughout the world, particularly in the Asia-Pacific region, and also as systematic improvements are made in the methods of Japanese language instruction. For a long time, Japanese people have tended to believe that their language is 'unique' and difficult for non-Japanese to master. With so many students presently studying Japanese in foreign countries, they are beginning to realize that their language, too, can be learned and used by others. Indeed, Japanese understanding of their own language has been gradually internationalized in recent years.

The issue of admitting foreign students, together with that of the influx of working students, trainees and foreign workers, has added new complications to the question of admitting foreigners into Japan. Working students are those who come to Japan not to attend universities, but to attend language or vocational schools. These students are permitted to work a maximum of twenty hours a week. The number of working students has increased rapidly, and reached 35,000 new arrivals in 1988. This represents a 2.5 increase over 1987.[5] The main objective of many of these working students increasingly seems to be to earn money rather than to learn a special skill or vocation. Similarly, trainees who come through private business arrangements also appear to be bent on acquiring income.

Indeed, the 'pull' factor of the appreciated yen has attracted new categories of foreigners to Japan. The most controversial of these is workers who enter Japan and work illegally. Japanese immigration law specifies certain categories of work in which the employment of foreigners is permitted. This excludes unskilled labour of any sort. Many of the illegal workers are deported: a sixfold increase between 1983 and 1988, when 14,314 were deported.[6] The composition of the illegal workforce can be projected on the basis of those who have been deported. Early on, the overwhelming majority of these were female entertainers from the Philippines, but recently the number of factory and construction workers has been on the upswing, particularly those from Bangladesh and Pakistan. The main motivation driving these Asian workers to Japan is the prospect of high income. Japanese wages are quite high by international standards, and the appreciated yen adds even more to the value of their earnings. In spite of the high cost of living, income is a strong temptation for workers from developing countries. On the Japanese side, there is shortage of manual and unskilled factory labour: the recent boom in the construction industry, in particular, has vividly illustrated the dearth of unskilled labour. There are now signs of a growing network of private employment agents, both in Japan and in the workers' countries of origin, that seeks ways of avoiding immigration control and of placing foreign workers in Japanese companies.

A wide debate is currently raging in Japan over how to deal with illegal foreign workers. Many studies have been conducted and proposals made by various advisory groups. The arguments range from those who insist upon the enforcement of strict measures to exclude foreign workers, to those who call for the opening up of the Japanese labour market. A report issued in April 1989 by a committee that examined the effects of international labour on the domestic labour market (set up by the Economic Planning Agency) stressed the importance of a system of accepting foreign workers under certain conditions, in order to eliminate illegal entries and to protect the human rights of foreign workers.[7] Japanese opinion polls reflect the existence of a divided view. In general, there appears to be public recognition of the economic needs existing on both sides; a majority supports a practical solution to allow a certain number of unskilled workers into Japan under certain conditions.[8]

The issue of illegal workers brings to the forefront the fundamental question of what kind of society Japan is to become in this increasingly interdependent world. A decade ago, when Japan's acceptance or rejection of Indo-Chinese refugees attracted considerable attention, the government took the initiative to admit them and set up the necessary legal framework prior to their arrival. In the case of the recent influx of illegal workers, however, economic realities have pre-empted the formulation of national policy. Their arrival has been accelerated not by war, as in the case of refugees, but by growing interdependence. This requires policy-making with long-term consequences in mind.

The growing number of Japanese returnees from abroad, the rapid increase in students from all over the world, the sudden influx of foreign workers – these are the phenomena forcing Japanese society to reappraise its traditional conservative attitudes and practices, and move in the direction of greater openness and tolerance. However, these societal changes should be applied not only to recent arrivals, but also to long-term residents who have suffered discrimination in the past. The question of the internationalization of Japanese society directly involves the status of the Korean, Chinese and other minority groups.

Indeed, the question of the Korean residents in Japan has become a serious issue of human rights and of humanitarian concern as well as of bilateral relations between Japan and Korea. There are over 670,000 Koreans living in Japan today. They were Japanese nationals until the end of the Second World War, but have remained in Japan as foreign nationals. Most, but by no means all, possess permanent rights of residence. However, since they are legally treated as foreigners in a country where they have lived all their lives and are likely to remain, Koreans have been subjected to various discriminatory practices. For example, they are required to be fingerprinted, and to carry alien registration cards. Moreover they are denied certain social security benefits and are discriminated against in the job market. Many adopt Japanese names in order to hide their ethnic origins.

Internationalization has affected Japanese concern over the status of the Koreans and other minority groups. When Japan became party to the Refugee Convention in 1981 in order to cope with the acceptance of Indo-Chinese refugees, Korean, Chinese and other long-term foreign residents also benefited from the expansion of social security and other measures. Enhanced awareness of human rights in recent years has also pushed the Korean issue to the fore. How Japanese society learns to deal with its minority groups will test its ability to live and work with peoples of other racial and national origins, whether abroad or within Japan. Advancing interdependence is accelerating the process of turning nations into pluralistic societies.

In the final analysis, political leadership will determine the pace and scope of Japan's internationalization. As already mentioned, Japan's internationalization has been triggered largely by economic developments, whether by way of expanding activities overseas or by drawing people into the country. Certain conditions must be met, however, if these developments are to lead towards further internationalization. The first is that the mobility of goods and people should continue to be improved. The second is that social systems and practices should be opened. The third is that pluralism should be encouraged and promoted in all spheres of national life. Political leaders can greatly influence these developments by taking decisions involving greater liberalization and deregulation, and by creating the environment necessary for such change. These measures bring high costs, both socially and politically.

Japanese political developments in recent years do not necessarily give cause for optimism. On the one hand, the Liberal Democratic Party faces political opposition that has grown in strength, and cannot easily compromise on the protection of traditional sectorial interests. On the other hand, the demands for market liberalization from abroad have intruded into areas requiring economic and social structural changes. The political costs of further internationalization will continue to be heavy. Strong voices must be raised by business and opinion leaders as well as by ordinary citizens and consumers to prod Japan's political leaders into following the path of internationalization. In these days of growing interdependence, internationalization is the only course left to all nations, and particularly to Japan.

NOTES

1 Statistics taken from Consular and Emigration Affairs Department, Ministry of Foreign Affairs, *Kaigai Zairyūhōjinsū Chōsa Tōkei* (Statistics on Overseas Japanese), 1988.
2 Statistics taken from *Tōyōkeizai, Shūkan Tōyōkeizai Rinjizōkan Kaigai Shinshutsu Kigyō Sōran 1989* (Special Issue of the Weekly Tōyōkeizai Surveying Japanese Business Abroad in 1989), pp. 150-3.
3 The Japan Center for International Exchange, *The Regional Underpinnings of the US–Japan Partnership*, 3, 1987.
4 Statistics taken from Science and International Affairs Bureau, Ministry of Education, *Wagakuni no Ryūgakusei Seido no Gaiyō* (Outline of Foreign Students in Japan), 1989.
5 Statistics taken from Ministry of Justice, *Shutsunyūkoku Kanri Tōkei Nenpō* (Annual Statistics of Entry and Exit of Aliens), 1989.
6 Statistics taken from Ministry of Justice, *Shōwa Rokujusannen ni Okeru Jōriku Kyōhisha oyobi Nyūkanhō Ihanjiken no Gaiyō ni tsuite* (Survey of Those Refused Entry and Those Violating the Entry and Exit Law in 1988), 1989.
7 *Rōdōryoku no Kokusaikan Idō no Kokunai Rōdō Shijō to ni Ataeru Eikyō ni kansuru Chōsa Hōkokushō* (Report on the Influence of International Labour Movement on the Domestic Labour Market), presented to the Planning Bureau, Economic Planning Agency, 1989.
8 See the chapter by Sugiyama Yasushi for further details.

Chapter 4

Internal and external aspects of internationalization

Sugiyama Yasushi

INTRODUCTION

The internationalization of Japanese society, along with the greying of the population and the impact of the scientific, technological and information revolutions, has been one of the most widely discussed social issues in Japan in recent years. Among the many factors contributing to this lively debate is the recognition by many Japanese that global interdependence is no longer an abstract concept but an inescapable reality that deeply affects their lives. This recognition has become more acute as Japan has become increasingly involved in the critical problems besetting the world, ranging from trade friction to environmental destruction. Second is the fact that Japan has become a major economic power, producing more than 10 per cent of the total gross national product of the capitalist world and main-taining the world's largest net assets overseas, with the resultant influence affecting the stability and prosperity of the entire globe. And third is the mounting criticism and pressure from overseas that Japan should open its doors to the outside world to a greater extent and should assume a more active role as a responsible member of the international community.

Despite the persistent interest in, and extensive discussions of, its im-plications for Japanese society, the term 'internationalization' itself has not been clearly defined; nor has a national consensus emerged regarding what is meant by being 'internationalized' or what this would require of the Japanese people. According to a study by the National Institute of Research Advancement, it is referred to as 'social phenomena which take place as a result of international exchange.'[1] A report by the Economic Planning Agency describes it as 'the expansion of the movement across national boundaries of goods, capital, information, people, and culture as the totality of all these.'[2] Yano Tōru of Kyoto University has characterized it as an effort to introduce international elements to a country or people with least friction with their identity.'[3] While Hatsuse Ryūhei of Kobe University has defined it as 'a process of opening Japan's heart to the outside world.'[4] This writer has explained it as 'a process of socio-cultural transformation of a society so as to adapt its nationalistic elements to a supra-nationalistic system by internalizing those norms, values, institutions and behaviour patterns which are known to have universal applications in the international community.'[5]

Internationalization in concrete terms is a process which proceeds at three different levels – that of nation, organization and individual. At the level of nation, it refers to, for example, the extent of co-operation with other nations, involving the movement of people, goods, capital and information across national boundaries; the standard of socio-political reforms; and the degree of political and economic interdependence with other nations. At the level of organization, it includes the extent of trans-national technological transfer; the establishment of multinational co-operation; and the exchange of students, scholars and other types of persons between educational and cultural organizations and civic groups. At the level of the individual, it entails the extent of knowledge of foreign languages and foreign countries; adaptability to life in foreign countries; and acquisition of the sensitivity, linguistic capabilities and other abilities necessary for international experiences.

Whereas the discussions of internationalization had in the past centred upon the quantitative aspects of international exchange in goods, people and information, those of more recent years have tended to stress the qualitative conditions or 'the state of mind' of the Japanese people in an international context. A typical expression of this view is found in the writings of Osaka University's Yamazaki Masakazu. In one of his essays, entitled 'An experiment in Japanese culture in world history – towards the second opening of the nation', Yamazaki asserts that the 'internationalization of Japan must be accompanied by drastic changes in Japanese society and its people, which may require "bloodletting" sacrifices on the part of Japan.' Calling on Japanese people to 'rediscover their identity', by re-examining their presumed cultural uniqueness, he argues that 'setting preconceived notions aside, we must polish our self-image in the tide of internationalization and temper it through cultural friction.' If the Japanese people succeed in doing this, he argues, Japan 'may be able to make an important contribution to the creation of a truly universal culture in the twenty-first century, thereby consummating a true internationalization.'[6]

With the upgrading of Japan's economic power and international role, the number of Japanese people travelling abroad has increased rapidly, rising from nearly 4 million in 1985 to close to 9 million in 1988. The number of Japanese residing abroad has also risen dramatically in recent years and stood at nearly half a million in 1988.[7]

Meanwhile, the number of foreigners visiting or staying in Japan has reached 2 million per year, while the scope of their activities has expanded. Japan's internationalization is now passing from the economic and techno-logical arena to that of interaction between people.[8] Travelling or living abroad, which may be viewed as one aspect of 'external internationalization', is no longer a matter of concern only to certain sectors of Japanese society, but to the Japanese public in general. At the same time, the problem of dealing with the increasing number of foreigners entering Japan, particularly those from Asian countries, who head to Japan's shores seeking employment, has become a key indicator of the degree of 'internal internationalization' in Japanese society. It has now become unavoidable for the Japanese government to pay due diplomatic attention to this matter as it is no longer a domestic issue, but one affecting Japan's relations with other Asian countries directly, thus affecting Japan's image abroad and the effectiveness of its conduct of international relations as a whole. It is in this context that the current debate on the internationalization of Japanese society has gained a new significance.

The purpose of this chapter is to examine the present state of, and the future prospects for, the internationalization of the Japanese people. It aims to shed light on the problem of Japan's internationalization in its two interrelated but separate dimensions: external and internal internationalization. The former refers to the process of deepening mutual understanding and appreciation between the Japanese and peoples abroad by means of various overseas public information and cultural exchange activities; the latter refers to the cultivation of internationally oriented attitudes, knowledge and skills among the Japanese people by means of formal and informal education at home. This chapter will examine first the present state of internationalization in Japan as reflected in the results of national public opinion surveys, and then explore the practical methods for promoting the internationalization of the Japanese people in both its external and internal realms.

JAPANESE PERCEPTION OF INTERNATIONALIZATION

What is the state of internationalization in Japan? How is the progress of internationalization viewed by the Japanese people? In this section, the Japanese people's perception of the internationalization of Japanese society will be examined on the basis of the results of national public opinion surveys. In a survey conducted by the Prime Minister's Office in October 1988 on Japanese foreign policy, including the prospects for Japan's internationalization, there was a noticeable increase in the number of those who were in favour of the increased internationalization of Japanese society. When asked to choose which view most closely represented their own with regard to Japan's internationalization, the percentage of those who thought 'Japan has an obligation to internationalize because of its status as a major power' increased from 40.8 per cent in a similar survey conducted in 1987 to 45.7 per cent in the 1988 survey. Respondents in this category outnumbered those who saw internationalization as 'an essential process in securing Japan's medium- and long-term prosperity', which also increased from 42 per cent to 44.9 per cent.[9]

As to the priority areas in which Japan's internationalization should be promoted, the percentage of those who favoured international co-operation, for example, contributions to international society in such fields as political and economic relations and technical assistance to developing countries, increased from 25.5 per cent to 27.3 per cent. This outranked the percentage who saw 'economic activities', such as the opening of the domestic market and changes in economic structure, as the main priority, which fell from 30.8 per cent to 25.7 per cent.[10]

As regards Japan's role in the international community, over half of the respondents (52.5 per cent) favoured 'contributing to the healthy development of the world economy'. 'Co-operating towards the advancement of

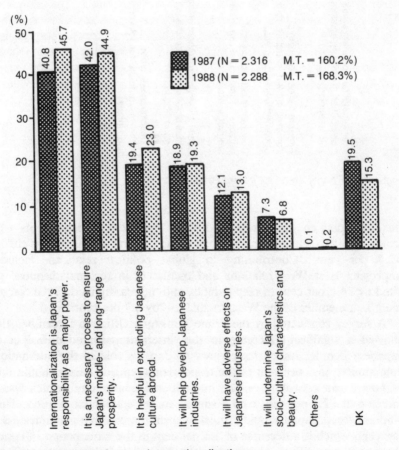

Figure 4.1 Japanese views on internationalization
Note: DK = don't knows

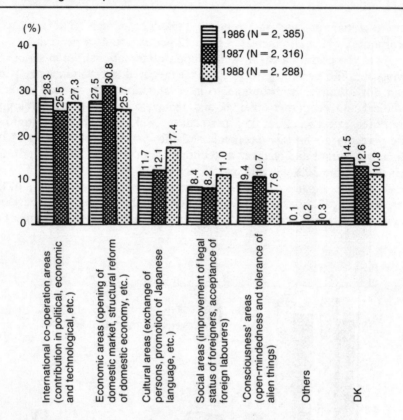

Figure 4.2 Priority areas for internationalization

the developing countries' was cited by 39.1 per cent of respondents, while 'contributing to scientific, technological and cultural exchange' was cited by 32.4 per cent. 'Contributing to global political relations, including improving East–West relations and mediating in regional disputes' was cited by 24.6 per cent of respondents, and 'increasing its defence commitment as a member of the Western alliance' by 8.7 per cent.[11]

A survey conducted by the Prime Minister's Office in December 1988 showed a significant increase in the 'international-mindedness' of the Japanese people. Asked their views on Japan's role in the international community, 45.6 per cent of the respondents replied, 'Japan should think of how it can contribute to the international community', which was an increase of 12.7 per cent over a similar survey conducted in 1985. Those who answered 'Japan should protect its own interests first', comprised 38.2 per cent, which is a decrease of 1.3 per cent in the same period.[12] Though there was some difference in percentage, both men and women were found to support the view that it would be important for Japan to think first of

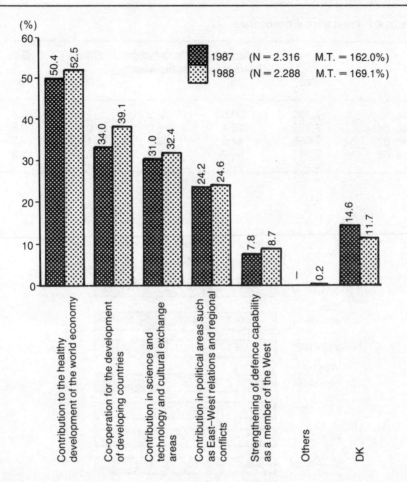

(%)

1987   (N = 2.316   M.T. = 162.0%)
1988   (N = 2.288   M.T. = 169.1%)

50.4 52.5

34.0 39.1

31.0 32.4

24.2 24.6

7.8 8.7

0.2

14.6 11.7

Contribution to the healthy development of the world economy

Co-operation for the development of developing countries

Contribution in science and technology and cultural exchange areas

Contribution in political areas such as East–West relations and regional conflicts

Strengthening of defence capability as a member of the West

Others

DK

Figure 4.3 Japan's role in the international community

contributing to the entire world. A large proportion of those who said Japan's interests should be protected first were found among over-50 age groups, and those who responded that Japan should place a higher priority on contribution to the world were found in the below-50 age groups, notably among those in their twenties. In previous surveys, the percentage of those who replied that Japan's interests should first be protected surpassed those who favoured a contribution to the world, but it is significant that in this survey the former responses exceeded the latter for the first time among both men and women.[13]

With regard to the increase in the number of foreigners working in Japan, 31.1 per cent of the respondents said it would be desirable to have more foreigners working in certain occupations, such as banking and

Table 4.1 International-mindedness

	No.	Japan's interest first %	Contribution to the world %	Others %	DK %
Dec. 85	7,780	39.5	32.9	1.2	26.4
Dec. 86	7,739	42.1	36.2	0.9	20.8
Dec. 87	7,655	42.5	38.2	1.4	17.9
Dec. 88	7,577	38.2	45.6	0.9	15.3

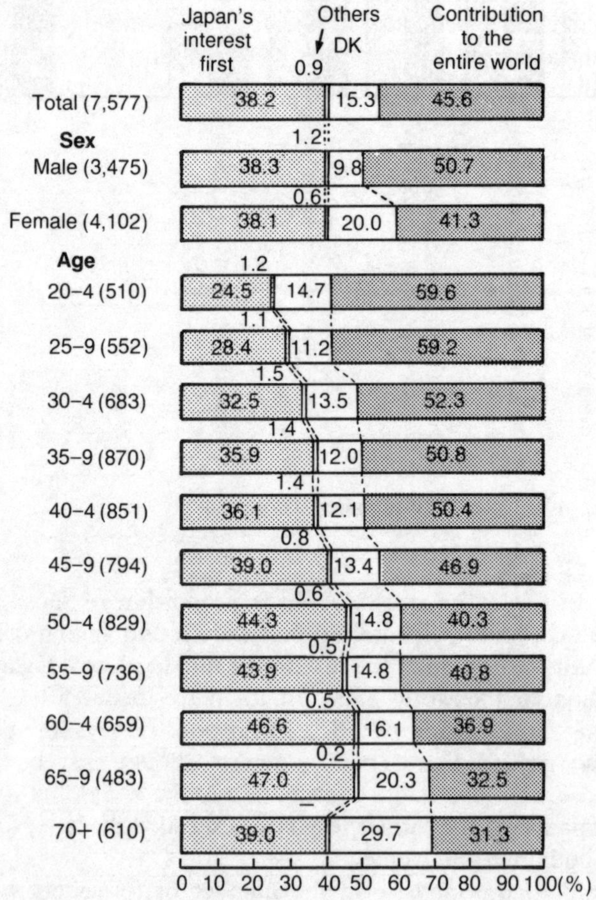

Figure 4.4 International-mindedness by gender

business, while 17.4 per cent opposed an increase. Less than a majority (44.6 per cent) said it would be preferable to keep the number at about the same level as at present. Those who supported having more foreigners were found to be more numerous among men aged 20–40 years, notably among those in their thirties.[14]

With respect to the future of Japanese culture and relations with foreign countries, 40.9 per cent of the respondents said 'Japan should attempt to learn first from foreign countries those things in which they excel', and 38.2 per cent replied 'Japan should develop its own things from now on.' By gender, about an equal proportion of men were in favour of Japan developing its own culture, science and technology (41.2 per cent) and of learning from other countries (42.6 per cent), but a slightly larger percentage of women preferred to learn from foreign countries (39.4 per cent) than those who were in favour of Japan developing its own culture, science and technology (35.7 per cent). As the age of respondents increased, those who were in favour of learning from foreign countries were slightly more numerous than those who preferred to develop Japan's indigenous culture and technology.[15]

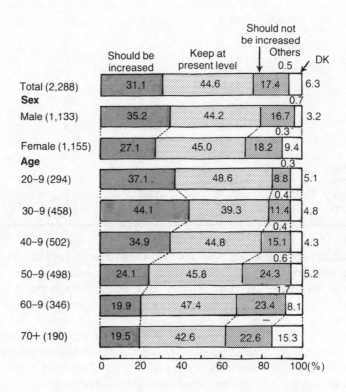

Figure 4.5 Foreign workers in Japan

Table 4.2 Japanese culture and foreign relations

	No.	Invent things Japanese %	Learn good things from abroad %	Undecided %	DK %
Dec. 85	7,780	36.1	35.4	14.5	13.9
Dec. 86	7,739	37.1	38.2	15.1	9.5
Dec. 87	7,655	36.7	39.8	15.5	8.0
Dec. 88	7,577	38.2	40.9	13.7	7.2

Table 4.3 The necessity of cultural exchange

		Should be promoted as top foreign policy priority %	To be pursued after economic and tech. co-operation %	Should keep it at the minimum %	Others %	DK %
Total	2,288	47.8	32.8	8.6	0.3	10.6
Sex						
Male	1,133	54.5	34.1	6.4	0.3	4.8
Female	1,155	41.1	31.5	10.8	0.3	16.3
Age						
20–9	294	53.7	34.4	4.8	–	7.1
30–9	458	52.0	32.5	7.4	0.2	7.9
40–9	502	51.2	31.9	8.4	0.6	8.0
50–9	498	44.8	34.5	11.4	0.2	9.0
60–9	346	43.1	33.5	9.5	0.3	13.6
70+	190	35.8	27.4	8.9	–	27.9
Education						
Elementary	655	30.4	35.1	14.4	0.2	20.0
Secondary	1,171	51.9	33.6	6.9	0.2	7.4
University	450	62.9	28.0	4.9	0.7	3.6

When asked to indicate whether cultural exchange between Japan and foreign countries was necessary, 47.8 per cent indicated that cultural exchange should be pursued actively as a major foreign policy priority, while 32.8 per cent thought that priority should be given to economic and technical co-operation, and that cultural exchange should be pursued subject to the availability of resources. Another 8.6 per cent indicated that 'cultural exchange should be limited to what is absolutely necessary for the maintenance of relations with other countries.'[16] The most popular category with regard to priority areas for cultural exchange was 'exchange programmes for youths', which accounted for 42.2 per cent of responses.

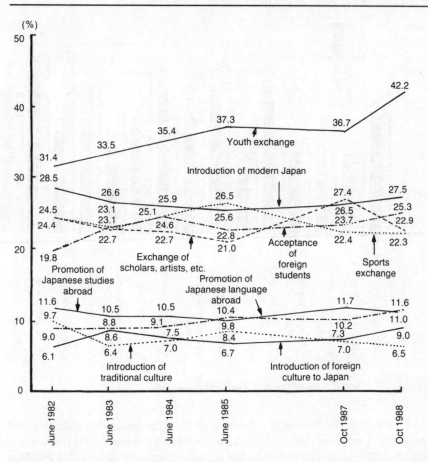

Figure 4.6 Priority areas for cultural exchange

This was followed by 'the provision of information about modern Japan' (27.5 per cent), 'the acceptance of foreign students' (25.3 per cent) 'exchange among scholars, artists and those involved in cultural activities' (22.9 per cent) and 'contact through sports' (22.3 per cent).[17]

In order to discover the state of internationalization in Japanese society, a survey was conducted by the Economic Planning Agency in October 1986. In this survey on national life, questions were asked on fourteen items to ascertain the people's awareness of the progress of internationalization over the decade 1976–86. The results of the survey indicate that, with regard to the area of information and goods, over 70 per cent of the respondents believed that internationalization had either 'progressed' or 'more or less progressed'. On the other hand, in the area of internationalization of people, such as 'foreign labourers', 'Japanese returnee children',

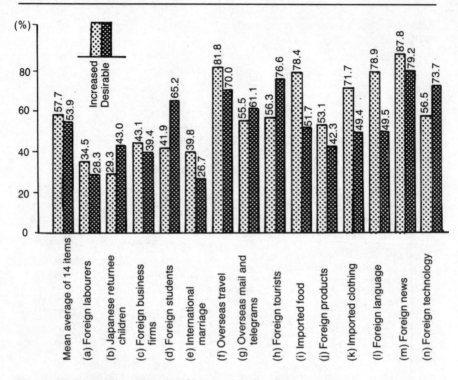

Figure 4.7 People's awareness of internationalization

and 'international marriage', those who thought internationalization had progressed were less than 40 per cent. The survey showed that there was a significant correlation between the actual progress of internationalization and the people's awareness of internationalization. That is to say, more people thought internationalization was progressing in those areas in which internationalization was actually taking place.[18]

The criteria for judging the progress of internationalization appear to vary according to the people's socio-economic status. The survey used an 'Internationalization Awareness Score' to find out the difference in the people's awareness of internationalization according to such socio-economic variables as sex, age, occupation, educational background, income and the size of community in which they lived. The Internationalization Awareness Score according to gender showed little difference between men and women, with the average score of 57.3 points for male and 58.1 points for female. However, there were considerable differences on certain items. Women scored high on such items as foreign clothing and other imported goods, and men on such items as foreign language and foreign news, which were related to their daily work. Both men and women showed declining Internationalization Awareness Scores in proportion to increasing age. The

Table 4.4 Internationalization Awareness Score (I)

Population	Total	Male	Female
Average	57.7	57.3	58.1
Age			
−19	64.9	64.5	65.4
20–9	64.7	62.9	66.3
30–9	59.8	58.5	60.9
40–9	56.7	57.9	55.5
50–9	52.5	50.0	55.5
60–74	49.2	53.0	44.8
Income			
−1,740,000	47.5	46.7	48.2
1,750,000–2,740,000	55.5	55.8	55.2
2,750,000–3,240,000	56.8	54.5	59.5
3,250,000–3,740,000	53.7	54.0	53.2
3,750,000–4,240,000	58.7	58.6	58.8
4,250,000–4,740,000	57.6	55.3	60.3
4,750,000–5,240,000	57.0	54.5	59.8
5,250,000–6,240,000	60.2	64.2	56.3
6,250,000–8,240,000	65.6	64.4	66.8
−8,250,000	64.6	62.5	67.4

Internationalization Awareness Score was notably low among men in their fifties. Women over 60 years of age, particularly those who were unemployed, registered low scores also, perhaps because their opportunities for activities outside the home decreased considerably. The Internationalization Awareness Score of people seemed to increase measurably as their income increased. This is reflected in the high score registered by those with extensive foreign travel experience compared to those without; and those with higher income tend to have more experience of foreign travel.

The Internationalization Awareness Score showed a direct correlation with the people's level of education, with 45.9 points for those with elementary school education and 70.4 points for those with university education. Between men and women, the difference due to educational background was smaller among men than women, with 48.2 points for men with elementary school education and 68.7 points for those with university education. This tendency was more apparent in respect of those items relating to economic activities such as acceptance of foreign workers, Japanese returnee children and foreign technology.

As regards occupation, professionals and college students generally scored higher, followed by white-collar workers, housewives, blue-collar workers, and agricultural and fishery workers. The fact that students scored highly may be attributed to the fact that they were young and were more interested in things international. The high scores registered by professional

Table 4.5 Internationalization Awareness Score (II)

	Total	Male	Female
Education			
Elementary school	45.9	48.2	43.1
Secondary school	52.3	50.8	53.6
High school	59.3	57.8	60.7
Junior college	65.8	65.6	65.9
University	70.4	68.7	78.6
Occupation			
Blue collar	55.0	55.2	54.3
White collar	58.3	56.8	60.1
Professional	63.8	63.7	64.3
Agriculture/fishery	45.7	48.6	39.9
Housewife	57.9	–	57.9
Student	64.0	63.0	65.3
Others	51.0	51.8	51.2
Community			
11 major cities	65.0	65.3	67.3
Over 300,000 pop.	59.5	58.9	60.2
Over 100,000 pop.	59.2	59.0	59.5
Below 100,000 pop.	55.4	55.8	55.1
Small towns	51.3	51.9	50.7

white-collar workers may be owing to their greater exposure to foreigners and things international, whereas the low scores for agricultural and fishery workers may be a result of their living in small communities with little contact with different social groups.

Those who lived in large urban communities tended to score higher on the Internationalization Awareness Scores, with 65.0 points for those who lived in eleven large cities, and 51.3 points for those who resided in small towns. The regional differences in the scores may be due to the fact that a majority of foreign residents live in eleven large cities located in nine prefectures and that foreign tourists tend to move around large cities; whereas both tourists and expensive imported goods are less likely to find their way into rural communities.[19]

Internationalization in Japanese society, according to these surveys, has thus been progressing rapidly. As to the Japanese people's awareness of this progress, the proportion of those feeling 'internationalization has increased' tends to be higher in respect to information and goods but lower in respect to people. As a majority of the people tends to think it is desirable to promote internationalization, the nation may be said to be generally in favour of even further internationalization. However, with regard to the internationalization of their own lives, such as making friends with foreigners or accepting foreign students in their homes, they seem to be less positive. This may suggest that, in spite of the considerable progress made towards the internationalization of their society, there still remain elements of closed-mindedness in the character and attitude of the Japanese people, and this appears to be one of the major obstacles to their internationalization. In the following pages, some of the practical measures to overcome these obstacles will be explored.[20]

EXTERNAL INTERNATIONALIZATION

As Japan's relations with the rest of the world have become both broader and deeper, friction between Japan and these countries has arisen in a number of areas. Although these differences are generally economic or political in nature, they are frequently grounded in a misunderstanding or inadequate understanding of each other's cultures and social practices. This is a clear indication of the increasing importance of ensuring that Japanese society is open to the rest of the world, not only materially and institutionally, but in the broadest sense of the term. It underlines the need to respond positively to the heightened interest in Japan and to work to ensure that present conditions in Japan are correctly understood by people overseas. Along with the effort to promote the internationalization of Japanese society, Japan must make further efforts to expand its internationalization activities externally through programmes of foreign cultural relations. The terms 'foreign cultural relations' used here refers to those activities and programmes carried out by both governmental and non-governmental organizations as part of the overall conduct of international relations for the purpose of promoting enhanced appreciation and understanding between the different cultures of the world. In Japan, it is generally perceived to entail two closely related but independent activities: overseas public information and cultural exchange. Overseas public information denotes those activities conducted by governmental organizations whereby information about government policies and the socio-economic background to these policies is communicated in order to create a favourable image and attitude among peoples in foreign countries. Cultural exchange refers to those activities that are conducted by both governmental and non-governmental organizations for the purpose of promoting increased understanding and appreciation of one's society and culture by broadening cultural, intellectual and artistic contacts and communication across national boundaries.[21] Japan's foreign cultural relations activities are carried out by a number of governmental, semi-governmental and private organizations and groups. The principal governmental organizations charged with the responsibility for the administration of Japan's foreign cultural policy are the Overseas Information Division and the Cultural Exchange Department of the Ministry of Foreign Affairs. The Ministry of Education, the Ministry of International Trade and Industry, the Prime Minister's Office and other agencies are also actively engaged in promoting overseas information and cultural programmes. Among semi-governmental organizations, the Japan Foundation, a public corporation under the supervision of the Foreign Ministry, is most actively involved in the administration of cultural exchange programmes. Although there has been a considerable expansion in recent years, Japan's foreign cultural relations activities fall clearly below those of the governments of the other major advanced industrial countries. A substantial increase in national effort is needed to implement effectively those activities which have become an important dimension in the conduct of Japanese foreign policy. These efforts must entail not only a quantitative increase in resources but also a more effective distribution of resources. The following are some suggestions which might help improve the effectiveness of Japan's foreign cultural activities.[22]

A consolidation of external cultural relations organizations

A basic requirement for the effective conduct of Japan's foreign cultural relations is to provide adequate facilities and qualified personnel for organizations involved in these activities. Major Western advanced industrial countries have active foreign cultural relations programmes, maintaining between 130 and 200 information and cultural centres around the world; Japan has only 28 information centres and ten Japan Foundation liaison offices. At the present time, one information centre is being opened each year. The establishment of Japan's overseas information and cultural centres needs to be greatly accelerated if its foreign cultural relations activities are to have any significant impact. Information and cultural centres abroad do not necessarily need to be administered by Japanese government organizations or Japanese citizens alone; these centres may be more effectively operated if they are administered as bi-national centres. Individuals of various professional backgrounds and nationalities may be hired to staff such centres.[23]

It will be necessary to improve the administrative functions of organizations engaged in overseas information and cultural exchange activities in Japan. Foreign cultural relations activities are presently being overseen by three types of institutes: governmental agencies, private organizations and business corporations. Although the activities of governmental organizations appear to be well co-ordinated (at least in avoiding overlapping responsibilities), overall and three-dimensional co-ordination is yet to be realized. Recognizing the importance of functionally organic foreign cultural relations activities, the establishment of a liaison/co-ordinating body for Japan's foreign cultural relations community should be considered. Because each of these three sectors recognizes the importance of international cultural relations, the volume of such activities will continue to expand. It will be desirable for governmental and non-governmental organizations engaged in overseas public information and cultural exchange activities to hold meetings periodically to exchange information and to co-ordinate their activities. Such meetings would enhance the effectiveness and efficiency of Japan's foreign cultural relations activities as a whole.[24]

Co-ordination of foreign cultural relations programmes

Exchange of persons is an effective means of deepening mutual understanding between peoples of different cultures, and, as such, it forms the basis of all international information and cultural exchange programmes. There is a variety of exchange programmes being conducted by different organizations in Japan, but with little mutual co-ordination or co-operation. For the purpose of introducing Japanese society and culture to people overseas, programmes which invite foreigners to Japan for short visits have been operated by various bodies. In order to carry out these activities more effectively, a comprehensive human exchange policy should be formulated. As the numbers of foreign invitees to Japan increase, it will become necessary to co-ordinate invitation programmes, taking into consideration such factors as the categories of persons to be invited, the objectives and duration of the visits, preparations by the host organizations, and the content of the programme. In order to evaluate the effectiveness of the programmes, it will be useful to conduct follow-up surveys of the invitees to find out whether these programmes are achieving their stated objectives. In identifying appropriate individuals to be invited, the co-operation of outside experts and area specialists should be actively solicited. As increasing numbers of Japanese scholars, artists, aid experts and other specialists are being sent abroad, it will be necessary to ascertain whether these persons are sent in line with the specific local needs and conditions. It will be desirable to build a national pool of candidates for various exchange of persons programmes so that the Japanese individuals most suited to the needs of the receiving countries may be sent.

In the field of overseas public information, it will be necessary to provide more effective assistance to foreign journalists gathering information in Japan. It is important to invite foreign opinion leaders to Japan, but it is even more important that Japan open its doors to foreign correspondents who are working in Japan. These foreign journalists and their news services are an important link in Japan's overseas public information and cultural relations activities. Regrettably, there has been considerable criticism by these correspondents, who feel that Japan is a country which keeps its doors closed to them by limiting their information-gathering activities. The aid they receive in fulfilling their task is passive, if given at all. Except for those who report on Foreign Ministry and Cabinet activities, foreign journalists are completely excluded from Japanese correspondent clubs and from all government agencies and offices. Such a situation is guaranteed to create a negative impression of Japan among these foreign reporters. Prompt steps need to be taken to extend as much assistance as is feasible to the foreign press in Japan.

In the area of education and academic exchange, it will be necessary to provide better services to foreign students and scholars studying and doing research in Japan. With the number of students from abroad increasing yearly, it is of critical importance for Japan to improve the educational and administrative facilities by which it receives and supports these students. At the same time, positive assistance and encouragement must be given to foreign scholars engaged in research and teaching in Japan. Students and scholars of Japanese affairs perform an important function as 'cultural mediators' by providing personalized interpretation and insight into things Japanese to the people of their own countries. Programmes of research assistance and financial aid should be extended, and assistance in other areas, such as orientation, counselling and housing, should be offered to facilitate their studies in Japan. Special consideration should be given to students and scholars from developing countries in view of the general scarcity of research funds available to them.[25]

The level of Japanese studies in a given country is closely related to the level of knowledge about Japan among the general public. The nature of Japanese studies varies from country to country, influenced by historical, cultural and other factors. Because of the importance of developing a core of Japan specialists in each country, programmes in support of Japanese studies abroad should be continued as a high priority.[26] In view of the trend in Japanese studies to lean towards the historical and humanistic aspects of traditional Japan, emphasis needs to be placed on modern studies of Japan in such disciplines as economics, sociology and political science. In response to the rising interest in the study of the Japanese language abroad, more systematic efforts are needed in the areas of training and exchange of Japanese language instructors, research and development of teaching materials, as well as 'indigenization' of Japanese language teaching abroad.

In the field of production and dissemination of printed materials, further efforts are needed to improve the quality of publications and the methods of distributing material to the appropriate institutions and individuals. Information material should be produced locally and distributed as frequently as possible. A mailing list of individuals should be kept and renewed periodically by information and cultural centres. In order to ascertain the reactions and interests of those receiving this material, readership surveys should be conducted periodically. Intellectual elites in each country, regardless of the country's state of development, hold roughly comparable higher educational qualifications. High-quality journals, introducing the different viewpoints of Japanese intellectuals, should be produced and distributed, preferably by private organizations rather than by governmentally administered information centres. More intensified efforts are needed to ensure that articles on Japan are published in the indigenous papers and journals of foreign countries. Only a fraction of the voluminous number of books published in Japan is translated for distribution overseas. More systematic efforts are needed to have Japanese books, particularly those in the social sciences, translated into English and other languages and distributed through commercial channels.[27]

Dissemination of information on Japan through the media can be an effective means of stimulating foreign interest in Japan. Given the high quality of audio-visual materials and telecommunications facilities available in Japan, more systematic attempts should be made to exploit these resources for overseas information and cultural activities. Co-operation needs to be extended to foreign producers of films and television programmes so that the potential for joint production and exchange of programmes will be increased. Technical problems inherent in exchange of audio-visual programmes, such as difference in audience taste, narration and superimposition, should be jointly studied, and the establishment of co-operative relationships between Japanese and foreign broadcasting stations, such as consultative joint committees and sister-station affiliation, should be actively promoted.[28]

Encouragement of private and corporate initiatives

One of the distinguishing features of contemporary international relations is the increasingly important role being played by private organizations, particularly in the field of cultural relations. Since cultural relations seek by their very nature to deepen mutual understanding and establish long-term friendly relations between peoples, it is desirable that activities in this field be based on broad popular support. The government should actively seek assistance and financial co-operation from corporations, organizations and individuals in the private sector in carrying out its international cultural relations activities. There has been an upsurge of interest in recent years among private organizations interested in promoting international cultural exchange. According to a survey conducted by the Japan Foundation, there were 560 private organizations and voluntary groups engaged in international exchange activities in Japan as of December 1985; this was an increase of nearly three times the number of private cultural exchange organizations that existed only five years earlier.[29] During the same period, there was also a marked increase in the number of private foundations that were established for the exclusive purpose of supporting activities in the field of international cultural exchange and co-operation. Every encouragement should be given to foster the development of these private organizations so that Japan's foreign cultural relations can be carried out with broad public support and co-operation.[30]

In order to improve the effectiveness of Japan's overseas information and cultural exchange activities, it is particularly important to solicit the co-operation of the Japanese business community. Japanese corporations should give international public relations a much higher priority than they have done in the past. A corporation should not consider overseas public information to be merely a technical matter, but should consider it a matter of top-management policy. Corporate management must become aware of the importance of international public information, particularly in light of recent criticism of Japan in the world press. At the same time, corporate activities should be made more consonant with the new age of internationalization by adopting a more sensitive personnel policy and by re-examining policies directed at overseas subsidiaries.

One of the major reasons for the growing criticism of Japan is the behaviour of Japanese corporations overseas. Top-level management must understand that its awareness of the changing international environment is inadequate, and it must reconsider the role of the Japanese economy within that environment. Management must reflect on its own inadequate control of Japanese corporate activity abroad. Japanese businessmen assigned to overseas posts tend to be preoccupied with the wishes of the home office and too anxious to contribute to a boost in sales and profit in the hope that they can soon return to Japan and improve their chances of promotion. This attitude prevents them from paying sufficient attention either to the feelings of the people in the host country or to the cultivation of friendly relations with the local community. Ministries and other government agencies as well as private corporations should offer carefully prepared pre-departure orientation and training programmes to their employees before sending them overseas, and give special consideration to their working conditions. The period of stay on overseas assignments should be lengthened to enable the representatives to devote themselves more fully to their work abroad, including the betterment of relations with the local community.[31]

Co-operating with developing countries

Co-operative cultural and educational programmes for developing countries seem especially significant in the sense that they promote mutual understanding and friendship and serve as a springboard for the self-development of such countries. There is a growing awareness in Japan that it should discharge its responsibilities to the international community by actively pursuing these programmes. In implementing foreign cultural relations programmes it is vital to carry them out systematically as long-term co-operative programmes, taking special care to assure their continuous operation. Special efforts must be made to understand the needs of the recipients of these programmes.

In administering co-operative programmes with developing countries, it is also important to carry out these programmes on their merits, either bilateral or multilateral, and these should not be regarded as mutually exclusive alternatives. Efforts should be made to institutionalize further a programme of sending teachers, researchers and administrators abroad and to provide effective orientation and facilities to such persons. Inasmuch as most of the developing countries are in the midst of nation building, training competent personnel is high on their agenda. Japan's programme of cultural and educational co-operation with developing countries should take cognizance of this fact and should take active steps to expand its programme of inviting students, teachers and other types of trainees from these countries. Consideration should also be paid to improving arrangements for hosting them, to include improving accommodation. Finally, it is important in undertaking these external internationalization programmes to encourage private corporations and organizations to initiate and conduct their own co-operation activities, including the hosting of students and trainees – for effective implementation of foreign cultural relations will depend upon the enthusiasm and commitment generated from the broadest possible segments of Japanese society.[32]

INTERNAL INTERNATIONALIZATION

In order to promote understanding and co-operation among peoples in the increasingly interdependent world of today, it is essential for the Japanese people to acquire a more internationally oriented outlook and attitude. In order for Japan to play a more effective role in the international community, it has become imperative for Japan to promote its 'internal' as well as its 'external' internationalization. Internal internationalization refers to the process of cultivating among the people those internationally oriented attitudes, knowledge and skills necessary for coping with the demands of an internationalizing society.

For the past one hundred years, the Japanese people have tried to transform their society into a modern nation through active importation and assimilation of Western culture. In their impulsiveness to acquire the piecemeal knowledge and techniques of the West, however, the Japanese have been remiss in their efforts to cultivate among themselves empathetic understanding and attitudes towards different peoples and cultures. The unique conditions attendant upon Japan's modernization, coupled with geographical barriers to daily intercourse with foreigners, have had the effect of inhibiting the sound growth of internationalism on the part of the Japanese and of fostering in them certain traits of ethnocentrism and insular patterns of behaviour.[33]

With the expansion of Japanese activities abroad, however, such an inward-looking orientation and the parochial attitudes which this has fostered have become a major obstacle in their relations with people overseas. Reflection upon the avenues to choose in Japan's search for internationalism, has shown that more concerted efforts are needed, through formal and informal educational processes, to inculcate among the Japanese people the importance of developing more internationally oriented attitudes and skills. It has become a basic requirement of Japan's educational system that each Japanese person be educated as an internationally minded individual, with abilities worthy of international trust and respect and with deep appreciation of the cultures and traditions of Japan as well as of other countries. Special consideration must be given to enrich the educational curricula for international understanding and, in particular, to encourage foreign language education so as to cultivate among Japanese students a sense of international-mindedness and a spirit of global co-operation. What follows is a list of some of the practical measures that need to be taken in order to promote the internationalization of the Japanese people.

Internationalization of education

If we define internationalization, as we do, as a process towards expanding interdependence and co-operation among nations and peoples, there is a necessity to make each nation's education more internationalizing in its aims, content and method. The fact that growing international interdependence brings problems and drawbacks in its wake provides all the greater inducement to internationalize the educational system of each country. Anyone who is going to be able to function as a citizen of a society that will be increasingly internationalized will have to be equipped with attitudes, knowledge and skills that relate not only to his own nation but also to the world at large. Education should aim to create an empathetic understanding of other peoples and cultures and a feeling of responsibility in the face of world problems. It should relate to the principles and methods of solving global problems, and provide tools with which to work in an increasingly interdependent world.[34]

Specifically, internationalized education should attempt to formulate the following:

1   open-mindedness, understanding and respect for all peoples, their cultures, values and life patterns;
2   insight into the relativity of one's own or national circumstances, values and life patterns; and
3   a positive attitude towards international co-operation and human solidarity, as well as the readiness and resolve to work for these goals.

Education should try to convey a knowledge of conditions in other countries – mainly through awareness of different political, economic, social, cultural, religious and economic structures and their interrelationships, and through an awareness of the different types of relations between countries and peoples. It should aim to develop the following:

1 ability to communicate, including competence in foreign languages and the ability to establish a rapport in a foreign milieu;
2 skill in retrieving information about other countries and international conditions; and
3 ability to make comparative observation and analyses from a global perspective.[35]

Expanding experiential education for international exchange

Current international education in Japan is, unfortunately, liable to go no further than instruction in conceptual knowledge. However, the content and method of education must also be improved so that each student is encouraged to gain first-hand experiences in international exchange in his or her educational process. We must draw up specific measures to promote educational activities for deepening international understanding and cultivating a spirit of international co-operation on the part of both youths and adults. Efforts must be made to expand existing programmes for sending people abroad, with the aim of cultivating an international outlook in primary and secondary school teachers; in leaders of youth and adult education; and in cultural and civic leaders. More imaginative and enlightened policies are needed with respect to the education of Japanese children abroad, especially in view of the need to cultivate people with more international attitudes and skills.[36]

Improving foreign language education

There is much room for improvement in current foreign language teaching, particularly English language education. First, it is necessary to specify the purposes of English language education at different school levels. Second, it is necessary to review the current teaching methods and their contents so that they can better serve people with different abilities and purposes. Entrance examinations involving English usage administered by colleges and universities should be improved so that applicants' English language abilities can be assessed accurately from a more diversified perspective. It may be worth considering using the results of such language proficiency tests as TOEFL (Test of English as a Foreign Language) to judge applicants' language skills.

A review of training programmes for foreign language teachers is called for. It is necessary to make the most of native speakers and of Japanese who studied at foreign colleges or universities. The current programme of employing foreigners as foreign language teachers in Japanese schools should be greatly expanded. With the co-operation of the Ministry of Foreign Affairs, the Ministry of Education and the Ministry of Home Affairs, some 2,000 young college graduates from the United States, Britain and other countries are now being invited to assist in the teaching of English in the lower and upper secondary schools throughout Japan under the Japan Exchange and Teaching (JET) Programme. Such programmes as this should be expanded so that at least one foreign teaching assistant is assigned to each secondary school in Japan, to teach not only English but other foreign languages and subjects, even including Japanese culture and history courses. Improved foreign language education, with expanded programmes for employing foreign teachers in Japanese schools, should contribute significantly towards the internationalization of the Japanese people.[37]

Internationalization of universities

Internationalism lies in the very idea of the university, which is to create and impart new knowledge detached from prevalent notions and national and other constraints. The internationalization of university education must enable the universities to realize this basic idea in the best possible manner and to develop it in deference to newly discovered problems for humanity and increasing global interdependence. The overarching goal for internationalizing university education should be to foster international understanding and co-operation, which also falls in line with the long-term interests of an interdependent world. In this way, education will create global openness, awareness and readiness to act as well as understand other peoples and cultures; it will give knowledge related to the world as a whole and promote the ability to communicate internationally; and it will prepare people for a career with international components and competence.[38]

Viewed from this perspective, it is imperative to make Japanese universities more internationalized so that more foreign students and faculty members can be invited and the number of internationally minded Japanese can be increased. It is necessary to extend the enrolment of foreign students and increase faculty members not only for the internationalization of Japanese universities but also for raising international levels of education and research and for better international co-operation and understanding. While students whose expenses are met by the Japanese government are given treatment which meets international standards, non-Japanese students who are self-supporting do not receive sufficient assistance. It is necessary to improve assistance for these self-supporting students through financial aid given by private scholarship organizations and corporations. It is also necessary for the government to work out measures to improve assistance given to these non-Japanese students who study at private schools.[39]

The internationalization of Japanese universities also necessitates increased flexibility in terms of the academic calendar and the transferability of credits. Further efforts are needed to introduce international elements into the curriculum and teaching methods of Japanese universities. Area studies, comparative cultural studies and other related programmes should be improved at the level of liberal arts education. It is important for Japanese universities to strengthen their curricula in the social sciences and humanities because studies in these disciplines provide a basis for an international frame of reference. Not only the literary works of European countries, for example, but also knowledge of Chinese and Indian classical literature is indispensable to the internationalization of university education.[40]

There is a need to consolidate educational research efforts in related academic fields so that the results of research may be more fully incorporated into the development of the international curricula of universities. Clearly, more encouragement and support must be given to all Japanese universities to expand their international exchange programmes, such as inviting larger numbers of foreign students and faculty members or sending more Japanese students and faculty members to universities abroad, particularly those in developing countries. Internationally speaking, it is extremely difficult for foreign students to obtain higher degrees from Japanese universities, especially in the social sciences and humanities. Such a state of affairs is not desirable from the viewpoint of the internationalization of Japanese universities and proper measures should be taken to rectify this situation.[41]

Improving the education of Japanese 'returnee' children

From the perspective of the internationalization of the Japanese people, children who have overseas experience should be viewed as a valuable resource. For the development of a global perspective among children, the experiences of these returnees should be shared with their classmates, rather than relegating the students concerned to special schools or classes. Further efforts must be made to ease the assimilation of returnee children into Japanese schools after returning home. It is also necessary to improve and expand measures aimed at promoting enrolment of the returnees at high schools, colleges and universities. The measures should include special quota systems or selection methods for the returnees.[42]

Promoting Japanese language education for foreigners

More systematic efforts should be made to promote the study of the Japanese language by foreigners as this will serve to create conditions for improved communication and understanding and further stimulate international exchange between foreigners and the Japanese people. Efforts must be made towards expediting the research and the development of the contents and the methods for teaching Japanese, providing programmes for education and training instructors of Japanese, and improving Japanese language education for foreign students who expect to be enrolled in Japanese universities. Japanese language education overseas should be facilitated in accordance with the promotion of Japanese language teaching in Japan. Japanese language skill tests for non-Japanese should be improved. Moreover a new qualification test to improve the quality of Japanese language teachers should be introduced.[43]

Improving arrangements for hosting foreign visitors

The Japanese mode of living is not always conducive to foreign visitors, and therefore special care should be taken hosting foreign students, trainees and other visitors. Housing accommodation, dormitories and other facilities are scarce and expensive, especially in large cities. In promoting future exchange activities, it will be necessary to increase the number of facilities for hosting foreign visitors. Further efforts should be made to improve the treatment of visitors in an unfamiliar environment, whether their stay in Japan is long or short, so that they can accomplish their objectives. Steps should be taken to establish reasonably priced accommodation in major cities to house foreign students and other visitors from abroad. Special attention should also be given to the qualitative improvement of facilities for foreign students, and the state should consider allowing a limited number of Japanese students to stay in this accommodation, since living together would be useful in enriching the experience of foreign students and improving the results of their study in Japan.[44]

Support for the internationalization of local communities

In recent years, developments in the internationalization of local communities have gained nationwide momentum, as indicated by the establishment in local government bodies of sections in charge of international exchange, an increase in sister-city affiliations and other international exchange activities at both the local government and the private sector levels.

In order to promote the internationalization of the Japanese people, it has become vital for the people who live in local communities to be exposed to things international, and to adjust their mode of thinking, that is, to accept foreign things and ideas with an open mind and to absorb what should be learnt. In recent years there have been a number of encouraging developments[45] in the internationalization of local communities and the government has given its full support to these developments. The Ministry of Foreign Affairs, for example, in 1986 established a Counselling Centre

for Internationalization in various local communities in order to answer
enquiries on international exchange and to facilitate the establishment of
sister-city affiliations and other activities, providing a useful contact point
for local governments and the private sector. The Foreign Ministry also
sends a Counselling Caravan for Internationalization, in which Ministry
officials visit local communities and answer enquiries on matters relating to
international exchange.[46]

Coping with the problems of foreign workers

The problems of foreign workers have attracted wide attention in recent
years in Japan and have become a symbolic issue in the internationalization
of Japanese society. Foreigners who enter Japan for the purpose of seeking
employment are currently dealt with in accordance with the Immigration
Control and Refugee Recognition Acts of 1951 and the subsequent policy
regarding the employment of unskilled workers approved by the Cabinet
on several occasions. Under current immigration law and government
policy, foreign workers, with the exception of businessmen, some university
teachers, and technical experts and skilled workers, are banned from
obtaining employment in Japan.[47]

Since about the end of 1975, there has been a sharp increase in the
number of foreigners, especially from South East and South Asian countries, who come to Japan for the ostensible purpose of sightseeing or
language study but choose to remain in Japan after the expiration of their
tourist visa to engage in unapproved activities or to be illegally employed.
Such illegal foreign workers have rapidly increased in number in the last
few years. It has been pointed out that studying at Japanese language
schools or training at companies serves to camouflage the activities of
illegal or unskilled labour.

The mass media have carried numerous accounts of the problems of
foreign workers in Japan, and various studies and proposals have been
submitted by the government, business, labour as well as academic groups
and individuals, as to how to resolve this vexing problem. As the results of
national public opinion surveys indicate, however, a national consensus on
this issue is yet to be formed. Every nation has its own system regulating
the entry and departure of foreign nationals. There are likely to be formidable obstacles to liberalizing the exchange of workers, particularly unskilled
workers from abroad. As part of the emerging global community of the
twenty-first century, however, it may become necessary for Japan to re-
examine the rationale and operation of its regulations concerning this type
of human transfer and to come up with a flexible response to the problem
in the spirit of international exchange and co-operation.[48]

CONCLUSION

The mass media in Japan these days are replete with such phrases as *kokusai kankaku* (international sense), *kokusai-sei* (international minded-ness), *kokusai-jin* (internationalized person), *kokusai kōryū* (international exchange), *kokusai kyōiku* (international education) and *kokusaika* (internationalization). Streams of books and articles are being published on the subject of internationalization, for example, on the 'internationalization of Japanese society', 'the conditions of internationalization', 'internationalization of the university', 'Japan's international responsibility', and so on. It appears as though 'internationalization' has become the 'buzz word' of the 1980s and is being used as a national goal almost in the way that economic growth was in the 1960s.

What is meant by 'internationalization' has not been made clear, and it seems to mean, if not all things to all men, at least many different things to many men. As currently used in the mass media, it generally refers to several different aspects of the interrelationship between Japan and the larger international community – the opening up of the Japanese economy; improving Japan's ability to participate in the world economic order; in general, becoming more like the rest of the advanced industrial societies. Much attention in the press is being directed at the question of how far along the road of internationalization Japan has come, what obstacles stand in its way, and how these obstacles can be overcome.

This chapter was an attempt to survey the present state of, and the prospects for, the internationalization of Japanese society with a particular focus on the internationalization of the people. We examined first the present state of internationalization in Japanese society as reflected in the results of national public opinion surveys and then explored the practical methods of promoting internationalization of the Japanese people. For the purpose of this chapter, the term 'internationalization' was conceptualized as a process of international exchange in goods, people and information within the international community; the notion of 'external' and 'internal' internationalization was used as an analytical tool with which to examine the problems of Japan's internationalization and to propose solutions to these problems.

Internationalization, conceived as a process of expanding international exchange and interdependence, affects many areas: international economics and politics; information and cultural communication; as well as global problems such as population growth, diminishing natural resources, environmental destruction, and so on. The process generates a need to make education more international. The fact that growing international interdependence brings problems and drawbacks in its train provides all the greater inducement to internationalize education. Anyone who is going to be able to function as a citizen of a society that will be increasingly internationalized will have to be equipped with attitudes, knowledge and skills that relate not only to his own nation or culture but also to the world at large.

This does not mean that education should try to eliminate affinity with one's environment or nation. Conflicts are bound to arise between short-term national interests, which are contrary to internationalistic endeavours, and long-term national interests which coincide with these. The concept of internationalized education must emphasize the longer-ranging but still relatively near-at-hand perspective on which national and international interests converge. The goal of international education to instill a sense of, and responsibility for, world citizenship does not mean that people can and should renounce their national origin or cultural identity. The national bonds of common purpose need to be replenished and enlarged, not eliminated. In short, internationalization of the people through enlightened education should be in the national interest.

With only a decade left before the dawn of the twenty-first century, Japan is caught up in a maelstrom of drastic social changes. In the short term, economic structural readjustment in many sectors will proceed. In the mid and long term, there are a number of problems with important implications for the future, such as the greying of the population; the scientific, technological and information revolutions; and the international-ization of society. There is an increasing realization that Japan's future security and prosperity can only be achieved by participation in interna-tionalization where it cannot survive in isolation from the rest of the world. There is a growing awareness that more concerted efforts must be made to improve and expand current activities and internationalization of the people on the external and internal dimensions.

It is expected that in the next century Japan will become more active in the global community, and the number of foreigners living in Japan will increase substantially. As the mobility of people increases around the globe, and particularly as Japan accepts a larger numbers of foreigners, opportunities for making contact with other cultures will expand. In asking others to understand Japanese lifestyles and values, the Japanese must also recognize those of others and strive continuously to ensure harmonious co-existence. Will the Japanese be able to display the level of tolerance that such a situation demands? Will they be able to adopt a more international outlook and orientation? Will they be able to overcome their traits of isolationism and ethnocentrism? Will the internationalization of the Japanese people be possible?

One optimistic view is that, since the Japanese have for hundreds of years been able to harmonize their own various beliefs and world views, they are clearly capable of such tolerance. The next generation will have had ample opportunity for contact with other cultures and worlds different from their own. If the new generation emerges with a different perspective from that of the older Japanese, there will naturally be more tolerance of other value systems. On the other hand, there is a more pessimistic view which holds that the development of a diverse system of values requires a clash of opposing absolutist values. Since Japan has never experienced serious internal religious or social conflict, this view maintains that it will be difficult to cultivate a real tolerance for a diversity of values. Whichever view is closer to reality, Japan can no longer avoid acting as part of the global community. No matter what the hurdles may be, the Japanese must learn tolerance for different value systems and co-existence with people of different cultural backgrounds.

As we stand on the threshold of the twenty-first century, the world in which we live is undergoing a rapid and far-reaching transformation. We are heading into an era in which global interdependence will be total. All nations, the large and the small, the rich and the poor, are already exposed to many forces and processes which are beyond their control, and all national boundaries have become permeable to the transnational impact of economic and political decisions made somewhere outside one's country. The fact of growing interdependence calls for new infrastructures and world views that will permit unprecedented levels of international co-operation far beyond any of the agreements that governments have been able to devise to date.

What is needed is no less than a change in our perception of the world around us. What is required is a new instrumentality for improving our capacity to listen to, and learn from, one another. These new modalities will have to be sensitive to the values and aspirations of all societies. It means delving deeply into the cultural and social roots of the Other, and evolving much more finely tuned perceptions of the world around us. It means increased insight, knowledge and ability to take part in and influence the interplay between conditions of local or national origins and factors of multinational or universal import. This speaks directly to the need to foster greater understanding and appreciation of the world's many cultures and peoples, and how they could interact and draw on one another so as to enable world civilizations to advance both in increasing unity and enriching diversity. In this process, internationalization of peoples plays an indispensable and a decisive role.

NOTES

1 Chūbū Shinkutankū Nettowaku, *Chiiki Shaika-no Kokusaika – Chūbu-ken no Genjō to Tenbō* (Internationalization of Local Communities – The Present State and Prospects for the Central Region), Tokyo: Sōgō Kenkyū Kaihatsu Kikō, 1982, p. 55.
2 Keizai Kikaku-chō Sōgō Keikaku-kyoku (ed.), *Sekai no Naka no Nihon – Sono Atarashii Yakuwari, Atarashii Katsuryoku – Waga Kuni Shakai Keizai no Kokusaika e no Kangaekata* (Japan in the World – Its New Role and New

Vitality – A Perspective for the Internationalization of Our Society and Economy), Tokyo: Ōkurashō – Insatsukyoku, 1984, p. 1. Keizai Kikaku-chō (ed.), *2000-nen no Nihon – Kokusaika, Kōreika, Seijuka-ka ni Sonaete* (Japan in the Year 2000 – Anticipating Internationalization, Greying of the Population, and Maturation of Society), Tokyo: Ōkurashō Insatsukyoku, 1982, pp. 85–99.

3　Yano Tōru, *Kokusaika no Imi-Ima Kokka o Koete* (The Meaning of Internationalization – Beyond the State Now), Tokyo: Nihon Hōsō Shuppan Kyōkai, 1986, p. 60.

4　Hatsuse Ryūhei, *Uchinaru Kokusaika* (Internal Internationalization), Tokyo: Sanrei Shobo, 1985, p. iii.

5　Sugiyama Yasushi, 'Nihonjin no Kokusaika – Naniga Mondai-ka' (Internationalization of the Japanese – What are the Issues?), *Kokusai Mondai* 321, December 1986, pp. 2–15. See also Glenn D. Hook, 'Internationalization of contemporary Japan', in *The Japan Foundation Newsletter*, xvii (1), August 1989, pp. 13–16; Herbert Passin, 'Overview – the internationalization of Japan,' in Hiroshi Mannari and Harumi Befu (eds), *The Challenge of Japan's Internationalization: Organization and Culture*, Tokyo: Kōdansha International, 1983, pp. 15–30.

6　Yamazaki Masakazu, 'Nihon Bunka no Sekai-shi-teki Jikken – Dai-ni no Kaikoku o Mezashite' (An Experiment in Japanese Culture in World History – Towards the Second Opening of the Nation), *Chūō Kōron*, June 1986, pp. 66–82; Kitamura Hiroshi, 'Inward internationalization: opening Japanese society to the world', *Speaking of Japan* 17 (71), November 1986, pp. 1–2.

7　*Asahi Shimbun*, 13 August 1989, p. 2.

8　*Yomiuri Shimbun*, 31 July 1989, p. 1.

9　Sōri-fu Kōhō-shitsu (ed.), *Gekkan Yoron Chōsa*, May 1989, p. 3.

10　Ibid., p. 5.

11　Ibid., p. 7.

12　Sōri-fu Kōhō-shitsu (ed.), *Gekkan Yoron Chōsa*, July 1989, pp. 37–9.

13　Ibid., p. 38.

14　Sōri-fū kōhō-shitsu (ed.), *Gekkan Yoron Chōsa*, May 1989, p. 6.

15　Ibid., p. 8.

16　Ibid., p. 8.

17　Ibid., p. 9.

18　Keizai Kikaku-chō (ed.), *Shōwa 61-nen Ban Kokumin Seikatsu Hakusho* (White Paper on National Life, Fiscal Year 1986), Tokyo: Ōkurashō Insatsu kyoku, 1986, p. 129.

19　Ibid., pp. 130–6.

20　Sofue Takao, *Nihon-jin no Kokusaisei-sono Kōzō Bunseki* (International-Mindedness of the Japanese – A Structural Analysis), Tokyo: Kimon Shuppan, 1989, pp. 14–29. See also, for somewhat critical analyses of the internationalization of the Japanese, Harumi Befu, 'Internationalization of Japan and Nihon Bunkaron', in Mannari and Befu (eds), op. cit., pp. 232–66; Ross E. Mouer and Yoshio Sugimoto, 'Internationalization as an ideology in Japanese society', in Mannari and Befu, op. cit., pp. 267–97, and Ronald Dore, 'The internationalization of Japan', *Pacific Affairs* 54 (4), Winter 1979, pp. 594–611.

21　Sugiyama Yasushi, 'Taigai bunka seisaku no genjō to kadai' (The Present State and Problems of Foreign Cultural Policy), *Kokusai Mondai* 338, May 1988, pp. 2–24; Kokusai Kōryū Kikin, *Kokusai Bunka Kōryū no Rinen to Seisaku* (Ideas and Policies in International Cultural Exchange) Tokyo: Kokusai Kōryū Kikin, 1984, pp. 273–83.

22 Sugiyama Yasushi, 'Japan's foreign cultural policy: an assessment', a paper presented at the 27th Annual Convention of the International Studies Association, Anaheim, California, 25–9 March 1986, pp. 37–62.
23 CDI, *Nihon no Kokusai Kōhō-Kōryū – Shogaikoku ni taisuru Bunka Jōhō no Teikyō no Jittai* (Japan's International Public Information Exchange: The State of Providing Cultural Information to Foreign Countries), Tokyo: Sōgō Kenkyū Kaihatsu Kikō, 1980, pp. 328–31.
24 Kaigai Kōhō Kyōkai, *Waga-Kuni Kaigai Kōhō Katsudō no Sōgō Senryaku Kenkyū* (A Study of the Overall Strategy for Japan's Overseas Public Information Activities), Tokyo: Kaigai Kōhō Kyōkai, 1986, pp. 339–41.
25 Saitō Makoto, Sugiyama Yasushi, *et al.*, *Kokusai Kankei ni okeru Bunka Kōryū* (Cultural Exchange in International Relations), Tokyo: Nihon Kokusai Mondai Kenkyūjo, 1983, pp. 25–60.
26 Shinbori Michiya, (ed.), *Chinichika no Tanjō* (The Birth of Japanologists), Tokyo: Yūshindo, 1986, pp. 151–231.
27 Matsuoka Norio, *Kaigai Kōhō no Jidai* (The Age of Overseas Public Information), Tokyo: Keizai Kōhō Senta, 1982, pp. 3–40.
28 Sugiyama Yasushi, 'Taigai Bunka Seisaku no Genjō to Kadai' (Situation and Tasks of External Cultural Policy), op cit., pp. 2–24; Kazuo Kawatake, *Nippon no Imeji-Masu Mejia no Kōka* (Japan's Image: Effects of the Mass Media), Tokyo: Nihon Hōsō Shuppan Kyōkai, 1988, pp. 177–210; and Takashi Tajima, 'Naze Kokusai Bunka Kōryū Nanoka' (Why International Cultural Exchange?), *Gaiko Foramu* 4, January 1989, pp. 29–34.
29 Kokusai Kōryū Kikin (ed.), *Waga Kuni no Kokusai Bunka Kōryū Dantai Ichiran* (Directory of International Cultural Exchange Organizations in Japan), Tokyo: Hara Shobo, 1985.
30 Nihon Kokusai Kōryū Senta, *Firansoropi no Yakuwari – Kokusai Shakai ni okeru Minkan Kikan no Yakuwari to Kinō* (The Role of Philanthropy: The Role and Functions of Non-Governmental Organizations in International Society), Tokyo: Sōgō Kenkyū Kaihatsu Kikō, 1988, pp. 61–8.
31 Iita Tsuneo and Kurisaka Yoshiro (eds), *Kaigai Kōhō Seifū to Kigyō no Kinkyū Kadai* (Overseas Public Information: An Urgent Task for the Government and Corporations), Tokyo: Yuhikaku, 1986, pp. 129–87; Igawa Toshio, *Kokusai-ka Jidai no Kaigai Chūzai in Ibunka e no Tekiō to Hito no Kokusaika* (Overseas Representatives in the Age of Internationalization: Cross-Cultural Adjustment and Internationalization of Peoples), Tokyo: Yuhikaku, 1987, pp. 1–12.
32 Okita Saburo, 'Keizai-Gijutsu Enjō Kara Chi-teki Enjō e' (From Economic and Technical Assistance to Intellectual Assistance), *Chūō Kōron*, August 1989, pp. 153–63.
33 Munakata Iwao, 'Henyō suru Kokusai Shakai to Kokusai-ka Kyōiku no Hōhō' (Changing International Society and Methods on Internationalization of Education), *Kokusai Mondai* 321, December 1986, pp. 16–30.
34 Kamijo Yasuko, *Kyōiku no Kokusaika ni kansuru Kenkyū* (A Study on Internationalization of Education), Tokyo: Taga Shuppan, 1989, pp. 133–48; Ishizuke Minoru, *Kokusaika e no Kyōiku* (Education for Internationalization), Kyoto: Mineruba Shobo, 1974, pp. 108–41; Monbushō, *Kyōiku, Gakujutsu, Bunka ni okeru Kokusai Kōryū* (International Exchange in Education, Science and Culture), Tokyo: Monbushō, 1975, pp. 19–50.
35 Iwabashi Fumikichi, *Kokusaika Jidai ni okeru Ningen Keisei* (Formation of Human Character in the Age of Internationalization), Tokyo: Gyōsei, 1982, pp. 189–210.
36 Edwin O. Reischauer, *The Japanese*, Boston: Belknap/Harvard University

Press, 1977, pp. 401–21; Edwin O. Reischauer, *The Meaning of Internationalization*, Tokyo: Tuttle, 1988, pp. 59–77.

37 *Asahi Shimbun*, 20 August 1989, p. 3.

38 Kobayashi Tetsuya, 'The internationalization of higher education in Japan', in Willian K. Cummings, Ikuo Amano and Kazuyuki Kitamura (eds), *Changes in the Japanese University: A Comparative Perspective*, NY: Praeger, 1979, pp. 166–84.

39 Kitamura Kazuyui, 'The internationalization of higher education in Japan', in *The Japan Foundation Newsletter* X (6), May 1983, pp. 1–9.

40 Jōchi Daigaku Kokusai Kankei Kenkyūjo, *Kokusai Kankei, Chiiki Kenkyū Kyōiku no Jittai Hōkoku* (Report on the Situation in International Relations and Area Study Education), Tokyo: Jōichi Daigaku Kokusai Kankei Kenkyūjo, 1984, pp. 171–9.

41 Sugiyama Yasushi, 'Internationalization of Japanese universities', a paper presented at the 28th Annual Meeting of the International Studies Association in Washington DC, 14–18 April 1987, pp. 68–76.

42 Kobayashi Tetsuya, *Kaigai Shijō Kyōiku-Kikoku Shijō Kyōiku* (Education of Japanese Children Abroad and Education of Returnee Children), Tokyo: Yuhikaku, 1981, pp. 324–9; Tokyo Gakugei Daigaku Kaigai Shijō Kyōiku Senta, *Kokusaika Jidai no Kyōiku – Kikoku Shijō Kyōiku no Kadai to Tenbō* (Education in the Age of Internationalization: The Tasks of and the Prospects for the Education of Returnee Children), Tokyo: Sōyū-sha, 1986, pp. 324–9.

43 CDI, *Nihongo Kyōiku oyobi Nihongo Fukyū Katsudō no Genjō to Kadai* (The Present State of and the Tasks for Japanese Language Education and Dissemination), Tokyo: Sōgō Kenkyū Kaihatsu Kikō, 1975, pp. 288–98.

44 Kanayama Nobuo, *Kokusai Kankaku to Nihonjin* (International-Mindedness and the Japanese), Tokyo: Nihon Hōsō Shuppan Kyōkai, 1989, pp. 193–202.

45 Kansai Jōhō Senta, *Chiiki kara no Kokusai Kōryū no Arikata no Kenkyū* (A Study of International Exchange on the Regional Level), Tokyo: Sōgō Kenkyū Kaihatsu Kikō, 1983, pp. 21–38; Yokohama-shi Kaigai Kōryū Kyōkai (ed.), *Tōshi to Kokusai-ka. Sono Riron to Jissen* (Cities and Internationalization: Theory and Practice), Tokyo: Kobuntō, 1983, pp. 17–67.

46 'Chihō no Jidai no Kokusai Bunka Kōryū Porishi' (International Cultural Exchange Policy in the Regional Era), *Warudo Puraza*, no. 3, March 1989, pp. 10–18. See also Nagasu Kazuji and Sakamoto Yoshikazu (eds), *Jichitai no Kokusai Kōryū* (International Exchange by Local Government), Tokyo: Gakuyō Shobo, 1983, pp. 3–40.

47 Hanami Tadashi and Kuwabara Yasuo (eds), *Asu no Gaikokujin Rōdō-sha* (Tomorrow's Foreign Workers), Tokyo: Tōyō Keizai Shinpō-sha, 1989; Ōnuma Yasuaki, 'Gaikokujin Rōdōsha – Dōnyū Giron no Kakerumon' (Foreign Workers: What's Missing in the Affirmative Argument?), *Chūō Kōron*, May 1988, pp. 96–117; Sakakibara Hidetsugu, 'Jinteki Sakoku Taisei Kono Nihon Shakai o Hōkai ni Michibiku' (The Isolationist System against People will Bring the Downfall of Japanese Society), *Chūō Kōron*, October 1987, pp. 96–117; and Nishiō Kanji, 'Rōdō Kaikokuka do Kentō shitemo Fukanō da' (The Opening of the Country to Foreign Workers is Impossible under any Circumstances), *Chūō Kōron*, September 1989, pp. 312–31.

48 Yamazaki Masakazu, 'Jinrui-shi-teki Kōken o mezashite' (Towards Contributing to the History of the Human Race), *Kokusai Kōryū* 44, October 1987, pp. 28–33; Yamazaki Masakazu, 'Kokusai Bunka Shakai o Mezashite', (Towards a Cultural International Society), International Symposium in Commemoration of the 15th Anniversary of the Founding of the Japan Foundation, December 1987, pp. 1–2.

Chapter 5

The internationalization of political thought
Liberal democracy in Japan

Tanaka Hiroshi

INTRODUCTION

Recently, the term 'internationalization' has gained wide currency in Japan. Bureaucrats, educators, businessmen, journalists and the public at large now use it to discuss the nation's domestic and international situation. Such usage seems necessary and important in view of the increased exchange of goods, information, capital, technology and people that takes place between Japan and the rest of the world.

Yet, if Japan's position in the world is on the ascendance, as the term 'internationalization' implies, the world clearly exhibits two contrastive attitudes in response. One is an appreciation of Japan's postwar economic success. Why was it that, despite its defeat in the Second World War and the enormous destruction caused by the Allied Powers, Japan recovered so quickly and went on to become one of the world's leading economic powers? Many answers have been given to that question, but no single, persuasive explanation is yet available. The other attitude towards Japan is one of suspicion and distrust. According to this view, Japan's economic success depends upon greed and unfettered global expansion, especially in Asia, North America and Western Europe. While Japanese success might be appreciated, its hyper-economic activity is thought to undermine each nation's economy and, eventually, the whole system. This suspicion extends to political and military issues, too. This is particularly true in South East Asia where, even today, the scars of war remain from Japan's aggression earlier in the twentieth century.

What should we do in these circumstances? Many Japanese citizens now enjoy their everyday life in a highly advanced consumer Japanese society, spend summer and winter holidays in Asia, North America or Europe, and buy expensive goods from around the world. In other words, the Japanese people now consume material wealth in abundance. This is not to say that people should not enjoy an affluent, internationalized lifestyle. But as a student of political theory, I must stress that Japan's internationalization has not been accompanied by the full acceptance of universal principles and values from the West. The internationalization of political ideas is critically lacking in Japan. This means, above all, that the idea of democracy and the diplomacy of peace are not institutionalized either in our lives or in our government. Without a proper global understanding and without a philosophical base, mere economic success cannot guarantee Japan's maturity as a leading nation in the world system.

Japan's modernization since 1868 has been a process of assimilation and rejection of Western political ideas. Was it possible to plant alien ideas and systems, such as constitutional monarchy and a parliamentary government, in a feudal nation? In this chapter I have chosen five important intellectuals and their contributions to political discourse in order to examine Japan's internationalization of ideas, and to grasp the degree of assimilation of Western political ideas in the process of Japan's political modernization since 1868. The approaches taken by these thinkers to the problems of democracy, modernization, power and international relations are the focus of my concern.

Japan has tried to introduce democratic values and institutions on at least four occasions in the past. The first occasion was the fifteen-year period from the Meiji Restoration and Meiji Enlightenment to the emergence of the People's Rights Movement (1860s to 1880s); the second was when Japan tried to modernize itself after promulgating a Prussian-style Constitution and establishing a national parliament based upon it (the 1890s); the third was the Taishō era of democracy (1910s to 1920s), when political, social and economic reforms appeared to have democratized Japan; and the fourth was the democratization of Japan by the Allied Powers after the Second World War. Japan's actual democratization took place only after 1945, but the idea of democratic government had been discussed by Japanese thinkers of liberal persuasion such as Katō Hiroyuki, Fukuzawa Yūkichi, Taguchi Ukichi, Kuga Katsunan and Hasegawa Nyozekan. As they highlight interesting and contrasting views on democracy, it is upon these thinkers that I wish to focus. The approaches taken by Fukuzawa and Katō to the formation of the Meiji state, attitudes towards China, and the nature of politics will be examined first. Then, the different views of three representative thinkers of Japanese liberalism – Taguchi, Kuga and Hasegawa – will be presented.

IMAGES OF THE NATION STATE BEFORE 1868

In the early 1860s, when the feudal regime was beginning to disintegrate and a new vision of the future was still on the horizon, both Fukuzawa and Katō tried to discern the essence of a nation state. Fukuzawa and Katō published their books in 1865 and 1860, respectively, in the hope of bolstering the decaying feudal regime. Obviously, under the chaotic situation which existed, they did not put forward prescriptions for a new society.

Rather, they intended to reorganize and repair the old system. For this reason, a blueprint for a modern Japan is difficult to find in their works. Moreover, they were not merely involved in scholarly investigation, for had Japan failed to modernize it might have suffered the colonial fate of other weak states. Hence a strong sense of nationalism, of defending the nation, informs their analyses.

Katō Hiroyuki's work, *Tonarigusa* (Our Neighbouring Nations), published in 1860, explored Western ideas and contemporary European political systems.[1] He was impressed by European ideas of equal citizenship and democratic rights. Also, since European parliamentary government worked efficiently, the dictatorship of a minority or the despotism of monarchies did not prevail to an overwhelming degree. The situation in the Orient was just the opposite of that in Europe. There, despotism or dictatorship was the rule in politics. How were the ideas of Western democracy introduced in Tokugawa Japan? First of all, it seemed unwise to criticize the Tokugawa regime directly, so Katō chose China as an example of a feudal, oriental nation. He entitled his book 'Our Neighbouring Nation' in reference to China. Thus an indirect attack on Japan was possible in his work.

There is a dialogue between two men who discussed the following three points in this book:

1 China's military defeat by the European powers starting with the Opium War (1840–2), and national disorder such as the Taiping Rebellion (1850–64) could be explained by three reasons. First, China did not learn Western technology thoroughly; consequently, its weaponry was outdated or obsolete. Second, China's political system was corrupt and inefficient. Third, China at the time lacked the national power required to repulse a Western invasion.
2 One way to modernize Chinese politics was by introducing a new system of government which would promise fairness and equality for all citizens. In this context, a Western-style parliamentary government appeared to be promising.
3 In case of emergency, lower-level governments should send a delegate to the capital in order to discuss critical national issues.

This was Katō's analysis of the Chinese situation. How was his prescription applicable to Japan? One answer to this question is as follows. A kind of nationwide assembly should immediately be formed to discuss urgent national issues. Since Katō seemed to imply that only samurai or clan elites from different regions should be chosen as delegates, it was not a democratic parliament as today. But when we consider the intellectual climate of Katō's era, his proposal should not be underrated. After all, he learned of these subjects only through reading foreign books.

On the other hand, Fukuzawa Yūkichi published his *Tōjin Ōrai*

(Transactions with the Chinese) in 1865.[2] It was based on his visits to the United States (1860) and England (1862), and his in-depth reading of foreign books. As a man of the Enlightenment, he warned the public that the opening of Japan to the world was Japan's only option. According to him, a sense of anti-Western antagonism and exclusionism, as expressed in the slogan 'Sonnō jōi' (Revere the Emperor and expel the Barbarians) was irrational and uncivilized, and had to be overcome. While Fukuzawa's book dealt mainly with China, it implied, like Katō's, transactions with both China and Europe. Let us briefly summarize Fukuzawa's work.

First, when European missions were sent to Japan, a majority of the Japanese people thought that foreign countries would take over Japan through advanced technology and military power. This type of emotional reaction to foreign visitors sometimes spurred terrorist acts against Europeans in Japan. Fukuzawa strongly opposed this reaction.

Second, he identified five regions of the world according to their level of civilization: America, Europe, Africa, Australia and Asia. Among the five, he placed both America and Europe in the advanced class whereas he classified Australia and Africa as less developed regions. Asia, which had once possessed an advanced civilization and had exerted great influence, was now unable to adapt to a new environment. The result, as seen in the case of China, was excessive national pride and ethnocentrism which prevented China from learning new ideas, science and technology from the West. In order to maintain its national independence and integrity, Japan should not follow the Chinese pattern.

Third, free trade was necessary for every nation so that goods could be exchanged. Here Fukuzawa seems to imply that peaceful and harmonious relations with the rest of the world, rather than military conquest, were important for the survival of Japan. Citing the example of Portugal, he observed that it was a relatively small nation yet maintained an influential position in the world. One reason for this was Portugal's wise domestic and foreign policies. Fukuzawa's voice, however, remained that of a minority. The majority insisted on militarization, especially the establishment of a powerful naval force in order to protect Japan from the colonial powers.

Both Katō and Fukuzawa examined the problems of the feudal regime (China) from the standpoint of the Western Enlightenment: Katō advocated parliamentary government while Fukuzawa called for opening of the nation to the West on the basis of free trade and peace. While neither thinker possessed a clear vision as to the precise nature of a future modern society, their theoretical understanding of the issue remains a focus of interest to political theorists. Clearly, both regarded China as an example of failed 'modernization' – a nation eroded by Western colonialism. Should Japan join in solidarity with China? To be a truly democratic nation, Japan should not colonize China as the European powers had done. In the event, however, Japan took the same path as the Western powers, and during the

Meiji, Taishō, and Shōwa eras became an expansionist, Western-type imperial power in Asia. Instead of fostering solidarity between the two nations, Japan exploited China. Democracy within a nation and solidarity among (weak) nations did not go hand in hand with Japan's political modernization.

IMAGES OF THE NATION STATE AFTER 1868

In 1868, Fukuzawa and Katō recognized that Japan was on the threshold of modernization, including political modernization. This change in the situation institutionalized their role as intellectuals. The changes brought about by the Meiji Restoration most importantly meant that the Tokugawa Shōgun, representing the samurai elite, was replaced by an Emperor, who during the 300 years of Tokugawa rule had held only nominal authority. Second, a majority of the ruling elite in the feudal period was replaced by a group of lower-status samurai, most of whom were ambitious young men from the domains of Satsuma (Kagoshima) and Chōshū (Yamaguchi). Although a radical transformation of Japan did not take place, the centre of political power shifted from the feudal authorities to a coalition of lower-status samurai leaders clustered around the Emperor. This change was not in itself revolutionary since it was unaccompanied by radical social and economic reforms.

What followed next was the difficult task of modernizing the country. From a political-science perspective, the formation of a nation state raises at least two questions. First, what type of dominant political ideology is to be chosen for that nation and what type of political institution is to be introduced? And second, what type of societal orientation and economic system is to be adopted? Fukuzawa and Katō provide interesting views on the Meiji government.

Katō's book, *Rikken Seitai Ryaku* (Constitutional Political Systems), published in 1868, is considered to be Japan's first major work on comparative politics.[3] In this work, the characteristics of different political systems are discussed generally, then specific systems are identified: monarchical dictatorship, non-despotic monarchical rule, aristocratic rule, constitutional monarchy and the republican system. According to Katō, Meiji Japan had just abandoned a dictatorship of the monarchical type and introduced a non-despotic monarchical rule. He did not venture to specify a suitable political system for Meiji Japan, but he seemed to support the idea of a constitutional monarchy. In 1869, he published another work on economy and trade entitled *Boeki Mondō* (Discourse on Trade).[4] In this work Katō identifies the advantages of free trade. Since many Japanese were influenced by traditional schools of thought, such as the *sakoku* policy (policy of isolation and exclusion) and anti-Western antagonism, his work represented a radical departure.

It was when Katō became more conservative, however, that his reputation was established. This is clearly illustrated in *Shinsei Taii* (The Real Meaning of Politics),[5] where his liberal political views are overshadowed by his opposition to democracy. Thus, although he called for the elimination of feudalism and rejected the idea that a citizen should sacrifice everything for his ruler, he favoured only a limited franchise with just a handful participating in politics. It was premature he argued, to grant political rights to uncivilized people and open a national Diet, as unlike people in the West, the Japanese people were lacking in education and culture.

As a champion of both nationalism and liberal enlightenment, Fuku-zawa Yūkichi tried to chart a course for Japanese politics and diplomacy through the murky waters of nineteenth-century realpolitik. His well-known three-volume work *Seiyō Jijō* (Conditions in the West) (1866–70),[6] *Gakumon no Susume* (The Encouragement of Learning) (1872–6)[7] and *Bunmeiron no Gairyaku* (An Outline of a Theory of Civilization) (1875)[8] contains insightful analyses of Japanese politics and civilization. The first volume, which actually consists of six separate books, discusses the advantages of free trade and constitutional government. In the second volume he argues that, by acquiring Western science and ideas, a liberal and egalitarian society could be established in Japan. Learning, he claims, makes people responsible and autonomous participants in society. From this he argues that once Japan has become a nation of independent citizens, then it can behave as a responsible country in world affairs. This was the essence of Fukuzawa's theory of development.

The publication in 1875 of *Bunmeiron no Gairyaku* (An Outline of a Theory of Civilization) marked Fukuzawa's zenith. The main theme of this book is how Japan can pursue national independence. He discusses diplomacy, political systems and overall societal transformation. Interestingly, Fukuzawa had by now abandoned his earlier optimism regarding international politics, believing instead that power politics is the rule of the game. Mere good faith could not assure a nation's independence. With regard to domestic politics, he warned both the government and its citizenry: the government should not employ coercive force against its people and the citizens should not use violence against their rulers. Only rationality could lead to peaceful national politics.

In summary, both Katō and Fukuzawa supported the idea of a Westernized form of government and civil society. Katō emphasized that modernization had to be initiated from above and regarded the German-type limited constitutional government as the most appropriate for Japan to adopt. Excessive democracy, as such, had to be firmly rejected. Fukuzawa, by comparison, argued that only civilized and well-informed citizens could establish a modern Japan.

THE PATH TO LIBERAL DEMOCRACY

In this section, the continuous development of liberalism will be discussed through an analysis of three liberal intellectuals – Taguchi Ukichi, Kuga Katsunan and Hasegawa Nyozekan. Taguchi and Kuga reflect the essence of Meiji liberalism and Hasegawa that of Taishō liberalism. Although all three supported the concept of liberalism, their approaches differed widely. We are therefore able to consider the development of liberalism through three different perspectives: Taguchi, a historian's perspective; Kuga, a nationalist's perspective; and Hasegawa, a social democrat's perspective.

Taguchi, 1855–1905: a historian's perspective

Taguchi Ukichi was born in 1855 at a time when Japan was forced to seriously consider abandoning its national isolation. On the one hand, foreign diplomatic missions were anxious to establish contact with Japan; on the other, the Tokugawa government unoffically allowed the study of Western culture and technology. Thus it was a period of uncertainty, but also a time of enlightenment for Japanese intellectuals.

Although Taguchi did not receive a formal academic education, he studied various subjects such as English, medicine, economics and history, and later became one of the leading intellectuals of Meiji Japan. During his career he was a translator, novelist, politician and businessman. He was not only a man of considerable intellectual talent and wide influence, he was also one of Japan's most renowned and respected historians. His numerous books include *Nihon Kaika Shōsi* (Japanese Civilization: a Concise Historical Overview) (1877–82),[9] *Jiyūbōeki Nihon Keizairon* (Free Trade and the Japanese Economy) (1878),[10] *Shina Kaika Shōshi* (A Concise History of Chinese Civilization) (1888)[11] and *Nihon Kaika no Seishitsu* (On the Nature of Japanese Civilization) (1885).[12]

While other Japanese scholars also wrote historical works, these were merely descriptive accounts of Western history and ideas lacking a global or comparative perspective, or else explanations of events and personalities in Japanese history. Often, books on Japanese history were written in isolation, without reference to the Western world at all, but not so Taguchi's. He was examining Japanese history within the framework of Western civilizations. On reading his work, especially *Japanese Civilization*, three distinctive rules of history can be discerned. One is the idea that enlightenment and progress are inevitable trends in society. Second is his belief that socio-political institutions, which are unable to adjust to new trends, are likely to be displaced by other innovative institutions. And third is that the Westernization and modernization initiated by the Meiji government is the only reliable means to establish a new nation state able to protect the citizen's life, freedom, rights and peace. Taguchi also believed that only the nation state could provide a framework for modern politics and society. Thus, to Taguchi, the state was not the reserve of the ruling elites or the rich; rather, its role was to protect the people's security.

What were the practical implications of his analysis? Two interesting points can be identified. First, Taguchi suggested that a new society should be free and open, providing equal rights for employers and employees, with the elimination of both the privileged and underprivileged. Hence his more provocative view on civilizations: Asian civilization was the preserve of an aristocratic minority, whereas European civilization was the product of an enlightened citizenry. Thus, the open and free society of the West offered a better opportunity for the development of civilization. The second was his proposal for the establishment of a free market economy. As outlined in his *Jiyūbōeki Nihon Keizairon* (Free Trade and the Japanese Economy), only free commercial interactions between nations could promise prosperity for all. He later elaborated on this theme by arguing that Japan should become 'a free republic' rather than a 'garrison state', since the path of military expansion would only bring national ruin.

Taguchi's historical view and his practical proposals are clear indicators of his liberalism. It was only his premature death in 1905 at the age of 50 that cut short his contribution to political thinking in Japan.

Kuga, 1857–1907: a nationalist's perspective

Taguchi's contemporary, Kuga Katsunan, was born into a samurai family in 1857 in Hirosaki (Aomori Prefecture), on the northern tip of Honshu. Like Taguchi, Kuga's career was short and multidimensional; he was a respected journalist, civil servant, translator and political activist.

He is best known as the founder of the newspaper, *Nihon*, which provided a liberal and democratic forum for political commentary after it was established in 1889, the year the Meiji Constitution was proclaimed.[13] Kuga's views were characterized by a mixture of liberalism and nationalism, two ideologies he found entirely complementary. Nationalism, according to Kuga, has two elements, 'the special improvement of national life' (*kokumin no tokuritsu*) with regard to Japan's external relations; and 'national unification' (*kokka tōitsu*) on the domestic stage. The first implied that relationships between nations should be equal and that no country should be permitted to colonize another. In other words, international relations should be democratic and peaceful. It is important to note that, for Kuga, the ordinary citizen's welfare and security, not the interests of big business or the ruling elites, were regarded as the decisive factors in world politics. While Japan was itself servilely negotiating an end to the unequal treaties imposed by the West during the 1860s, and behaving like another mini-European state, it was also becoming a military power at great cost to the Japanese people, not to mention the peoples of other Asian countries. Kuga's solution was the 'special improvement of national life'. It is clear that, for Kuga, the word 'national' referred not only to Japanese citizens but also to the other peoples of Asia. In short, even though the word 'nationalism' tends to evoke a sense of ethnocentrism and xenophobia, Kuga's nationalism was wider in its geographical scope than the boundaries of the Japanese nation. Here we can see his liberal understanding of Japan's role in Asia.

The second element was 'national unification' of Japan. Kuga was highly critical of both the Meiji government, which was split by regional factionalism (*hanbatsu seifu*), and the political parties which, in his view, were incapable of representing the real interests of the people. Thus neither the political elites nor the political parties were acting in order to unite Japan. A solution suggested by Kuga was to make the Emperor the centre of Japanese politics supported by the Meiji Constitution and a new national parliament (the Diet opened in 1890). He seemed to draw a parallel between Meiji Japan, and constitutional monarchy just after the Glorious Revolution of 1688. By establishing a British-type constitutional monarchy in Japan, Kuga hoped national unification could be fully achieved.

Kuga and his associates in the Society for Political Education (*Seikyōsha*) are usually regarded as anti-Western traditionalists. But Kuga was a nationalist of liberal persuasion and his understanding of world politics was logical and consistent. What was his attitude towards China? If he had indeed been a xenophobic nationalist, he would not have hesitated to recommend the military conquest of other Asian nations. But he consistently rejected that type of colonization. His view was that a militarized policy would be an obstruction to world peace: Japan should regard China as an equal partner and not as a colony to be exploited, and no Western policy to partition China should be tolerated. Again, in regard to Japan's colonial expansion, he criticized the government and argued that, 'war victories made our national interests far more fragile than before, and a strong army depends upon the impoverished mass of citizens.' In other words, a militaristic policy was being carried out at the cost of the masses. His comments on Japanese politics were atypical: the majority of 'nationalists' directly tied their 'nationalism' to military expansion outside Japan. Japanese victories in the Sino-Japanese War (1894–5) and the Russo-Japanese War (1904–5) promoted the type of nationalism Kuga rejected.

Kuga's liberalism is clear from the above. At the end of his life he suffered from illness and handed over his newspaper to a businessman in 1906. After his retirement in 1907 he died at the age of 50 in Kamakura.

Hasegawa, 1875–1969: a social democrat's perspective

Hasegawa Nyozekan was born in 1875 in Tokyo, and attended private academic institutions such as Meiji Law Institute (now Meiji University) and Tokyo Institute of Law (now Chūō University), where he studied law, politics and economics. His formal education was frequently interrupted owing to poor health and financial difficulties, so he never obtained a university qualification. Since it was the national universities, rather than the private institutes, that were expected to produce the future political, bureaucratic and economic elites of Japan, the course chartered by Hasegawa was atypical. But this in no way implies he was intellectually inferior to his peers at the more prestigious national universities. Indeed, he became one of the leading intellectuals of his day, despite not being a university professor and training his 'students' privately. Many of Japan's postwar political thinkers acknowledge their intellectual indebtedness to him.

Over his long career, which spanned from the Meiji period to the 1960s, Hasegawa had both a direct and indirect relationship with Taguchi and Kuga. After finishing his education, Hasegawa embarked on a career as a journalist by joining the staff of *Nihon*, the newspaper run by Kuga, who had influenced his thinking as a young man. Hasegawa highly valued 'Kuga liberalism', and considered it a privilege to be one of Kuga's associates. Hasegawa also benefited from the intellectual climate at the newspaper where many talented journalists of liberal persuasion worked. To a large extent, Japan's liberal tradition was founded and developed by Kuga and Hasegawa. On the other hand, while no personal connection existed between Hasegawa and Taguchi, Hasegawa highly respected the liberal historian. This is borne out by the fact that he later edited and published the collected works of Taguchi in 1928–9. Hasegawa here wished to treat Taguchi's analysis as a counterweight to authoritarianism and militarism. For Hasegawa, Taguchi's classical liberalism was not dated at all: Taguchi's ideas on free trade and the liberal state were useful concepts with which to attack Japan's non-democratic political institutions.

It is here important to recognize that, in the 1920s and 1930s, many communists and socialists were critical of liberalism. Although Hasegawa hoped for co-operation between the two groups in order to challenge the monolithic power of the Japanese state, no unified anti-governmental opposition was forthcoming. Despite this dashing of his personal hope, his role as an organizer and propagandist of the anti-fascist forces in Japan should be highly commended. His journal *Warera* (renamed *Hihan* from 1930) served as a forum for anti-statist discourse among liberals, social democrats, socialists and others of various ideological persuasion.[14]

Hasegawa's liberalism was different from that of Taguchi and Kuga. Hasegawa took note of the rising power of the working class and tried to incorporate this new trend into his liberalism. For him, it was not enough to discuss the political and economic structures of a liberal state; what was critically important was to pay more attention to the majority of the working class. Thus Hasegawa's liberalism was transformed from classical liberalism to that of a social democratic persuasion.

If we put these three Japanese liberals into a British context, interesting parallels can be drawn. Taguchi and Kuga can be compared to Jeremy Bentham as liberals who supported liberal democracy but did not positively incorporate the interest of the working class into their analysis. Hasegawa can be compared to John Stewart Mill as a liberal who could see the rise of the working class as a social force and revised liberalism. The main difference between the two groups may be summarized as follows: while Bentham understood the working class as a pivotal force in British society, he merely confirmed the essential rule of old liberalism – the one-man one-vote rule. Mill moved one step further by adding the collective right of the workers to his liberalism.

Here we have emphasized not only the continuity of liberalism in Japan, but also the changing nature of this concept as the socio-political environment of Japan changed from the Meiji to the Shōwa era.

JAPANESE POLITICS TODAY: A PHILOSOPHICAL EXAMINATION

As noted above, a powerful authoritarian state apparatus monopolized power in Japan until 1945, to the neglect of democratic rights and processes. Nevertheless, some intellectuals, a number of whom have been considered here, understood the reality of their times, and strove to democratize the nation's politics. Their prewar legacy of liberalism and the people's desire for peace provided fertile ground for the democratic reforms introduced during the American Occupation to take root. It is precisely because of the struggle for democracy by the Japanese themselves that the postwar 'gift' of democracy was not rejected. At the same time, however, the internationalization of Western political thought must be regarded as crucial to the modernization of Japanese politics, as we have seen. And, if we are to give meaning to the introduction of this thought, then two tasks must be urgently addressed.

One problem is the lack of a responsible opposition in Japanese politics. Although a majority of Japanese voters are committed to democracy, they tend to vote for the ruling Liberal Democratic Party (LDP) simply because the party promises economic well-being and the defence of vested interests. If a non-LDP party forms a new government, then the voters' status quo and vested rights could be undermined. As a result, the voters are likely to cast their ballots for the LDP. Under such conditions, a responsible opposition cannot emerge in Japanese politics. If democracy is a necessary condition for our life, then we need to encourage the development of a responsible opposition. As books written by James Harrington, John Locke, Baron de Montesquieu and other philosophers indicate, when one group monopolizes politics, only political decay and corruption result. The existence of a responsible opposition in Japan is thus essential.

Second, we can identify the lack of a global or universal perspective in Japan. Many people are unaware of what is happening outside Japan, and are unsure how to behave responsibly in the world. This applies to the individual traveller, corporations as well as to the government. We may be wealthy but we are not certain about how to use our wealth or resources. How do we deal with this issue? I believe that, if we understand correctly universal morals and principles, then we may be able to identify a reasonable and realistic position for Japan in the world. Thus, in conclusion, we may say that, in order to promote the internationalization of Japanese politics, we should improve our national politics and be aware of the universal principles of democracy.

NOTES

1   *Tonarigusa* (Our Neighbouring Nations), in *Meiji Bunka Zenshū* 7, Tokyo: Nihon Hyōronsha, 1929.
2   *Tōjin Ōrai* (Transaction with the Chinese), in *Meiji Bunka Zenshū*, vol. 1, Tokyo: Nihon Hyōronsha, 1929.
3   *Rikken Seitai Ryaku* (Constitutional Political Systems), in *Meiji Bunka ...*, vol. 7.
4   *Boeki Mondō*, (Discourse on Trade), in *Meiji Bunka Zenshū*, vol. 9.
5   *Shinsei Taii* (The Real Meaning of Politics), in *Meiji Bunka Zenshū*, vol. 5.
6   *Seiyō Jijō* (Conditions in the West), in *The Collected Works of Fukuzawa*, Tokyo: Iwanami Shoten, 1959, vol. 1.
7   *Gakumon no Susume* (The Encouragement of Learning), in *The Collected Works..*, vol. 3.
8   *Bunmeiron no Gairyaku* (An Outline of a Theory of Civilization), in *The Collected Works..*, vol. 4.
9   *Nihon Kaika Shōshi* (Japanese Civilization: A Concise Historical Overview) in *Teiken Taguchi Ukichi Zenshū* (The Collected Works of Taguchi Ukichi), Tokyo: The Association for the Publication of the Works of Taguchi Ukichi, 1928–9.
10 *Jiyūbōeki Nihon Keizairon* (Free Trade and the Japanese Economy), in *Teiken Taguchi ...*
11 *Shina Kaika Shōshi* (Chinese Civilization: A Concise History).
12 *Nihon Kaika no Seishiutsu* (On the Nature of Japanese Civilization), 1885.
13 *Nihon*, published from 1889 to 1905.
14 *Warera*, published 1919–30; *Hihan* published 1930–4.

REFERENCES

Bamba, N. and Howes, J.H. (eds) (1978), *Pacifism in Japan: The Christian and Socialist Tradition*, Kyoto: Minerva Press.

Blacker, C. (1964), *Japanese Enlightenment*, New York: Columbia University Press.

Dower, J.W. (ed.) (1975), *Origins of the Modern Japanese State*, New York: Pantheon.

Fukuzawa, Y. (1959) *The Collected Works of Fukuzawa*, Tokyo: Iwanami Shoten.

—— (1966), *Autobiography*, New York: Columbia University Press.

Hasegawa, N. (1984) *Aru Kokoro No Jijoden* (My Heartful Autobiography), Tokyo: Kodansha.

Ishida, T. (1952), *Meiji Seiji Shisoshi*, Tokyo: Miraisha.

Maruyama, M. (1963), *Thought and Behaviour in Modern Japanese Politics*, Oxford: OUP.

Matsuo, T. (1974), *Taisho Demokura shi* (Taisho Democracy), Tokyo: Iwanami Shoten.

Part III

Japan and the world economy

Chapter 6

Gearing economic policy to international harmony

Yamazawa Ippei

INTRODUCTION: HOW TO DEFINE THE INTERNATIONALIZATION OF ECONOMIC POLICY

The term 'internationalization' reflects a popular concern of the Japanese public. An agreed definition, however, is yet to emerge. Let me start, therefore, with an economist's perception of this term and proceed to a brief overview and evaluation of the recent performance of Japanese economic policy on the basis thereof.

As the chapters in this volume make clear, the definition of 'internationalization' differs between political scientists in Britain and America on the one hand, and those in Japan on the other. The former perceive internationalization as *doing to others*, while the latter perceive it as *adjusting to others*. A similar difference may be observed in the economist's definition as well, though it will be less obvious than in the case of the political scientist's.

The United Kingdom and the United States have maintained the world economic system for the past century. The United Kingdom acted as the centre of the gold standard before the First World War and the United States managed the de facto dollar standard after the Second World War. Their currencies, the pound and the dollar, were the international currencies. Recently, the Japanese yen has, to some extent, come to be regarded as an international currency, both in transactions and in foreign exchange reserves. This clearly reflects Japan's position as a strong creditor nation. Although the yen will not replace the dollar, it will take on a greater role in the multiple key currency system. Because Japanese monetary and fiscal policies will affect the stability of the international monetary system, it is essential that those in positions of authority are careful in their policy management. Playing an active role in this respect is a new aspect of Japanese economic policy. On the other hand, as Ogata Sadako correctly points out in an earlier chapter, there still remain many passive aspects of Japan's adjustment to the increasing interdependence of the world. In the economist's definition internationalization contains both passive and active aspects.

The internationalization of economic policy is not the same as the internationalization of the Japanese economy; that is, intensified out- and in-flows of commodities, labour and capital. Indeed Japan's economic policy is inevitably affected as foreign trade and factor movements are intensified relative to domestic economic activities. But a mere description of the restricted management of Japan's economic policy will not suffice. We have to analyse to what extent its external balance, or in looser terms 'international harmony', is taken into account in the Japanese management of economic policies.

It is commonly agreed that Japan should take a more active role in international affairs, commensurate with its economic capability and strengthened creditor position. How well is Japan prepared to meet these expectations? It seems there has emerged an increasing recognition within Japan of its greater international role; but how well has Japan's economic policy been geared to 'international harmony'?

IS INTERNATIONAL HARMONY A POLICY GOAL?

What does it mean to gear economic policy to international harmony? It does not imply a 'good neighbour' policy which benefits a nation's trading partners at the cost of its own economic well-being. It is simply not possible to favour all trading partners in a world of multilateral interdependence, where a favour to one partner may have an adverse affect on others. Such a policy would contradict the main aim of a government's economic policy, which is to maximize the welfare of its own people.

It is generally accepted that the primary objectives of economic policy are to provide full employment, price stability, economic equity and economic growth. External balance (defined as an overall balance of current and long-term capital accounts combined) is sometimes added to this list of policy aims; however, in principle, it is not so much a target as a constraint, since other policy objectives cannot be achieved without it. In a free market economy, an external imbalance tends to adjust automatically in the form of market discipline, either through exchange rate fluctuations or through changes in the quantity of money and the level of prices. There is therefore no need to produce economic policies geared to ensuring external balance. It is commonly argued that nations, like individuals, should by necessity survive on their own income. But this analogy no longer holds true on the international level. Nor, for the following reasons, does market force discipline automatically come into effect.

First, other objectives such as full employment and economic stability dominate the concerns of policymakers so that an external imbalance, if any, is not perceived as a strong constraint. Second, political interventions have occurred in market mechanisms to adjust or protect vested interests. Third, private firms have recently been so active in operating across borders that they can circumvent restrictions and regulations set by national governments more easily than before. Fourth, it has now become common for richer countries to assist in the economic development of poorer countries, regardless of historical or cultural ties. Fifth, it is no longer possible for an economy as large as Japan's to benefit from the world's free trade system without bearing some of the burden of maintaining it. The last two points, in particular, require Japan to pay additional consideration to 'international harmony'.

In the present context, external balance or international harmony cannot be left to the vagaries of market forces; it is a major policy concern of the Japanese government. Japan has been criticized recently by its trading partners for a lack of interest in maintaining 'international harmony'. It is important, however, to bear in mind that its external imbalance acts as a constraint on domestic economic growth and must therefore be resolved in a manner beneficial to Japan.

Conflicts with trading partners as well as criticism arising from a country's lack of attention to international harmony is not confined to Japan, but is common to all major trading countries. The United Kingdom also faces a conflict in its attitudes towards the creation of a Single European Market in 1992. While the EC Commission has been promoting a programme of economic integration, the UK government under Prime Minister Thatcher was reportedly less than enthusiastic over its implementation, and was reluctant to make a full commitment to European Monetary Union (EMU). At home, opposition parties and some members of the business community were highly critical of Prime Minister Thatcher's foot-dragging, and expressed concern that the United Kingdom may eventually become the odd one out in an integrated Single European Market. Abroad, other EC members complained that the attitude of the United Kingdom was detrimental to both European economic integration and the future existence of the EC as a whole.

Much of the criticism, however, has been misdirected, since Prime Minister Thatcher clearly seemed to appreciate the economic merits of the Single European Market and, in general, supported the 1992 integration programme. What concerned her government was how well European firms and industries were prepared for integration into the single market. If they are not, national regulations and restrictions will be reintroduced and the single market will not be realized.

HOW HAS THE ECONOMIC POLICY BEEN GEARED TO INTERNATIONAL HARMONY?

Let me briefly review Japan's economic policies in the 1980s and evaluate them on the basis of their contribution to 'international harmony'. Six policy measures will be reviewed: major economic policy, industrial policy, trade policy, foreign direct investment, development co-operation and institutional reform. They do not exhaust all relevant policies that could be reviewed, but represent the major areas of economic concern.

Macro-economic policy

In the past two decades the world economy has experienced enormous fluctuations in the price of petroleum and primary commodities. Major industrial economies have been affected by the sudden constraint on the availability of raw materials and energy input to their industries, and have tried to overcome these by implementing new policies and adjusting their industrial structures. Some countries have been more successful than others, and this has resulted in huge trade imbalances. Japan, with its high dependence on imported raw materials and energy, was affected most seriously by these fluctuations but has adjusted more effectively than its principal competitors, recovered more rapidly and, as a result, has increased its share of world production and trade.

On the other hand, Japan's superior performance has resulted in a persistent trade surplus with its major trading partners. Japan's trade surplus with the United States increased from US$12 billion in 1981 to US$51 billion in 1986. This bilateral trade imbalance also reflects the respective overall imbalances of the two countries. During the same period, Japan's overall trade surplus expanded from around US$20 billion to US$93 billion, whereas the overall trade deficit of the USA increased from US$28 billion to a staggering US$148 billion. Japan's prolonged trade surplus has aggravated trade conflicts with its major trading partners, especially with the United States, and both the restoration of external balance and the resolution of trade conflicts have become major policy concerns.

Japan's major economic policy has changed dramatically over the past two decades. At the time of the two major oil shocks of the 1970s, Japan, like other industrialized economies, altered its macro-economic policies in an attempt to overcome the adverse impact of higher oil prices. On each occasion Japan experienced minus economic growth, incurred a current account deficit, and suffered from the persistent threat of inflation. In response to these crises the government tightened the money supply and adopted an austere fiscal policy, especially after the second oil shock when the decline in economic growth was much less than in the first. Thereafter, the economy recovered quickly, mainly through export expansion, which added to the trade surplus.

After the G-5 agreement of September 1985, the government redirected its macro-economic policy mix towards a restoration of the external balance. The yen/dollar exchange rate shot up from 245 to almost 120 yen per dollar within three years. The Bank of Japan's rediscount rate was reduced to a historical low of 2.5 per cent in early 1987, and kept at that low level for a further two years. Government expenditure was expanded successively after 1986 and this was combined with a tax reduction. Both investment in plant by firms and household consumption were boosted, with the result that domestic demand has sustained the second longest boom since the Second World War.

Although a huge trade surplus is still with us (US$77 billion in 1989), this policy mix change provided a macro-economic framework within which the restructuring of the Japanese economy has begun to take place. First, slower growth itself forced firms and industries to undergo structural adjustment. Second, the rapid appreciation of the yen and improved terms of trade has on at least three occasions (in 1973 before the first oil crisis in 1978, and after 1985) severely hit export-oriented and import-competing industries and drastically undermined their competitive edge. Third, trade imbalance, trade conflicts, and the resulting series of market liberalization measures have encouraged imports and increased competition within the domestic market. Fourth, the stimulation of domestic demand has encouraged more firms to produce for the domestic market and to search for new products.

Industrial policy

Japan's industrial structure has undergone dramatic changes during the last two decades. The share in all industrial production of primary, consumer and basic material industries declined steadily throughout the 1980s (down to 26 per cent for the three industries combined in 1989), and this decline is expected to continue through the 1990s. On the other hand, this decrease was more than offset by sustained growth in the machinery and service industries. The machinery industry expanded rapidly during the past decade and is expected to continue to do so, but at a decelerated rate. The service industry has also expanded and will continue to do so at a faster rate hereafter. The increasing importance of the service industry reflects a move towards a more service-oriented economy. A careful examination of changes in the content, however, shows that much of this increase has occurred in intermediate input such as consulting, leasing and information services which support business activities, as well as parts and materials. These services were originally provided within individual machinery firms, but recently they have been hived off from their parent companies and now exist as independent firms in their own right. This will certainly have accounted for a large proportion of the statistical growth in the service sector.

The structural change referred to here is often described as a shift from 'Heavy, Thick, Long and Big' (H&B) to 'Light, Thin, Short, and Small' (L&S). Such H&B industries as basic materials (metals and chemicals) were the leading industries during the high growth period of the 1960s when they achieved economies of scale and cost reduction, thereby acquiring international competitiveness. However, increase in the price of petroleum and raw materials undermined their competitive edge, while slower growth after the oil shock resulted in under-utilization of existing capacities. Interest payment for underdepreciated capacities added a financial burden to the H&B industries. Retrenchment of existing capacities was the response favoured by many of these enterprises. On the other hand, the expansion of the machinery and service sectors has been a reflection of the shift to L&S industries. The greatest advantage which the machinery industry possesses compared to H&B industries is that it includes the production and assembly of a variety of parts. This not only makes it relatively free of energy and resource constraints, but allows for more rapid responses to the constant changes in technology and consumer taste.

Instead of mass production of a small variety of products, small-lot production of a large variety of products is required, and it has been achieved without increasing cost and with a shorter lead time. Fortunately, from a Japanese point of view, firms in the machinery sector possess the experience, organizational know-how and expertise to respond to this challenge, while a large domestic market with a high income level permits experimentations in new products. The shift from H&B to L&S has been apparent in all industries. Although there is no unambiguous definition for what constitutes either H&B or L&S, this transition is regarded as desirable in terms of industrial restructuring.

This structural change implies that Japan has outgrown its traditional catching-up industrialization (introducing new products and technology from the United States and Western Europe, mastering the technology and reducing production cost, thus achieving import substitution and then exporting abroad) and can itself explore new industrial frontiers. This will significantly affect the industrialization of Asian NIEs and countries whose industrial development has largely followed the Japanese pattern of moving from textiles to metals and then on to machinery.

The process has often been described as the 'flying geese' model of industrial development. Future restructuring of Japanese industries as well as increased direct foreign investment by Japanese firms will induce further industrial development in these countries. Ultimately, they too will lose the comparative advantages they now enjoy in certain industries as a result of ongoing global macro-economic adjustments.

These structural changes within Japan have also had a dramatic impact on areas of industrial specialization between Japan and her Asian neighbours. This has already been reflected in changes in Japan's export and import trade with these countries as well as in increasing direct investment by Japanese firms throughout the region. Imports of textiles and standardized electronics have increased from these Asian countries, while Japan's

export of parts and equipment has expanded, in line with the rapid industrialization of these countries. Thus Japan has enjoyed a healthy surplus
in the balance of trade with its neighbours, but this will decrease as import
substitution proceeds in these countries.

Structural change in the Japanese economy has also resulted from the
unfettered response by individual firms to changes in both the marketplace
and the supply of raw materials. But how has MITI's industrial policy
promoted this? MITI's industrial policy has so far been geared mainly to
the retrenchment of H&B industries as is evidenced by a series of
Depressed Industry Adjustment Laws enacted since 1978, although their
effectiveness remains the subject of considerable discussion. At the same
time, numerous MITI reports have also recommended a shift to L&S
industries as part of an overall strategy for restructuring the economy. The
Ministry no longer maintains the dominant role it adopted in the 1950s and
1960s in determining the direction of industrial development, selecting and
promoting the development of key industries. In most instances, MITI now
plays a subsidiary role in shaping state policy: that of providing moderate
financial assistance to small and medium firms and in general promoting
R&D activities.

Trade policy

Changes in the structure of exports and imports have corresponded to the
shift in the industrial structure from H&B to L&S. Metal exports have
declined rapidly while exports of light and high-tech machineries have
increased. In imports, raw materials and fuels have also declined, while
other manufactures, such as textile and steel, have increased. The share of
manufactured goods as a proportion of all imports expanded to 51 per cent
in 1989.

Japan's recent trade policies have been geared mainly to the resolution
of conflicts with its major trading partners. Various market liberalization
measures (reduction and removal of tariffs and non-tariff barriers;
improvement of standards and procedures for import; and deregulation of
such sectors of the economy as construction and finance) have been
implemented with the result that both competition and efficiency have
increased within the domestic market. On the other hand, voluntary export
restraints (VERs) have also been imposed on many machinery exports as a
result of bilateral negotiations with the United States and the European
Community. VERs may take the heat out of trade conflicts in the short
term, but they will cause serious distortions in the long term. Rigid market
share agreements among rival exporters tend to depress competition,
maintain higher prices and disadvantage both the consumer and user
industries.

A new aspect of Japan's trade policy is the increasing demand by

Japanese manufacturers for the imposition of import restrictions on goods from developing countries. In particular, imports of knitwear, steel-plate, and cement from Asian NIEs have increased so rapidly that domestic producers claim that this may undermine their efforts to reduce capacity at a time when domestic demand is stagnant. But bearing in mind Japan's enormous trade surplus with its partners, MITI has responded to their demands without resorting to the MFA restrictions, and has kept VERs at a minimum (knitwear and cotton yarns). At any rate, VERs will provide only a brief respite and import competition will eventually resume as the transfer of industry proceeds. The optimum policy is, of course, to encourage the domestic producers to adjust positively to industrial development and the changing pattern of trade based on vested interests at home. It will not be easy for domestic producers to make the painful decisions which will inevitably accompany these changes. The current Uruguay Round of the GATT negotiations provides a unique opportunity for Japan together with the United States and the EC to suppress the tendency towards managed trade.

Foreign direct investment

In the 1980s, changes in the macro-economic situation compelled Japanese firms to change their traditional strategy of producing at home and exporting abroad. One response was, of course, to shift further in the direction of L&S industries at home, while another was to increase foreign direct investment (FDI); that is, relocating Japanese production abroad and then selling the products there, exporting to third countries, or importing back to Japan.

Three regions – South East Asia, North America and Western Europe – have been the major recipients of direct investment, but investment patterns have differenced between the first and the last two. In South East Asia, Japanese firms have exported labour-intensive standardized types of production, in which their competitive edge had either been lost already or was under serious threat, while retaining more sophisticated parts of the production process which were capital and technology intensive.

Factories and plants relocated in this way remain reliant on parts and equipment which also have to be imported from Japan. On the other hand, FDIs in North America and Western Europe were initially stimulated by the threat of import restrictions and continuing trade conflicts between those countries and Japan. Once underway, however, they were quickly adapted as an integral part of a new global strategy for Japanese firms. Quite a few Japanese firms have implemented a corporate structure in which there are three headquarters – in Tokyo, the US and Europe – with each taking responsibility for its own part of the world, rather than the Tokyo office supervising global operations as in the past.

Development co-operation

As long as Japan's trade surplus continues, it will have to be recycled back to deficit countries. Active portfolio investment as well as active FDIs have contributed to the recycling of the Japanese surplus. Official Development Aid (ODA) plays a similar role in this respect. Indeed, a commitment to increase its ODA has, on numerous occasions, deflected criticism of Japan's trade policies, though this in no way detracts from some notable achievements in this area. Japan's ODA doubled between 1978 and 1980, doubled again between 1981 and 1985, and a third doubling, underway since 1986, is expected to be completed by 1992. In 1988, Japan's ODA amounted to US$9.1 billion, second only to the United States with US$9.8 billion. In addition to the more conventional types of co-operation, the Japanese government has recently introduced new forms of aid such as technical assistance to promote export industries in developing countries, preservation of tropical rain forests, and more efficient and pollution-free use of energy.

Japan is now also one of the largest contributors to multilateral aid programmes, and Japanese aid agencies (OECF, Ex-Im Bank and JAICA) co-operate closely with the World Bank, the IMF, and the Asian Development ment Bank. A Japanese 'Marshall Plan', tabled in 1987, proposed the transfer of a US$30 billion fund to developing nations over a three-year period, 1987–9. Over 90 per cent of this fund was committed for use in the first two years. In July 1989 the Japanese government proposed a two-year extension of this programme and an increase in the fund to US$650 billion. These transactions are completely untied to any commercial transaction. Japanese ODA has also encouraged private loans to developing countries, which amounted to US$26.8 billion in 1987 alone.

Despite its increasing economic influence, Japan does not seek to become a hegemon in international politics. The government is well aware that a strong foreign policy would be regarded with suspicion by Japan's neighbours, many of whom suffered from Japanese aggression in the past. Japan's increasing commitment to multilateral aid should therefore be interpreted as a conscious attempt on the part of the government to exercise economic influence while avoiding potentially awkward political involvements.

Institutional reform

There has been a growing awareness in Japan that adjustment in economic policy must be accompanied by institutional reform. In short, it is private firms and households who produce, consume and trade in the current institutional system, and their performance is largely determined by institutions as well as conventional policies. This has been recognized at the

OECD and at the Arche Summit Meeting in June 1989, which suggested specific institutional reforms to individual member countries.

Japan has been working on this issue since the early 1980s through two governmental advisory groups. The Maekawa Group (Study Group of Economic Structural Adjustment, 1985–6) focused on the external aspects of institutional reform and proposed improved access to the Japanese market, the promotion of manufactured imports, further promotion of structural adjustment in declining industries, and liberalization of the money and capital markets. The Administrative Reform Council (1981–3 and 1987) focused on governmental reorganization. Its first report (1983) resulted in the privatization of three state-owned enterprises (tobacco; telephone and telegram; and the national railroad). The second report (1989) proposed the deregulation of official administration in seven areas, including distribution systems, rice and other cereals. In addition, tax reform was promoted by the Ministry of Finance and a low consumer tax of 3 per cent was introduced over a wide range of commodities and services, thus reducing the government's reliance on direct taxation as a source of income. Furthermore, some form of land reform is unavoidable so as to rectify the abnormally high land prices in Japan.

FACTORS DETERRING INTERNATIONALIZATION

It has been shown thus far that Japan has pursued a policy of economic restructuring in response to external imbalances. Attempts have been made to reduce Japan's persistently high current account surplus and trade conflicts, particularly with the United States and the European Community, while at the same time taking on a greater role in the management of the world economy. These efforts should not, however, be regarded simply as an attempt to placate its major trading partners at the expense of internal balances. They have come about as a result of the government's recognition of the interrelationship between external imbalances (which, if left unchecked, could inhibit further economic expansion) and industrial restructuring and institutional reforms at home. Although the need for internationalization has largely been accepted, the government's efforts thus far have been widely misunderstood, both at home and abroad. This perception gap has on a number of occasions interfered with the process of restructuring. Let me briefly touch upon three specific instances when this has been the case.

First, industries and sectors directly affected by market liberalization suffer from adjustment difficulties and have therefore tended to resist policy changes. While the economy as a whole gains from liberalization, it is these industries and their employees who must endure plant closures and unemployment. The response has usually been to request adjustment assistance from the government, which, in effect, is no more than a form of compensation for lost earnings. Over time, these industries and sectors of the economy tend to act as special interest groups and resist further changes in policy. Labour-intensive industries and agriculture are typical examples of this sort of behaviour.

Second, although recent changes in Japan's policy management have clearly been intended to 'internationalize' the economy, it is difficult for the taxpayer to see how he or she will benefit from these changes. Similarly, Japan's trading partners remain sceptical of the government's commitment to liberalize both markets and institutions.

Third, the Japanese government has all too often given the impression that economic restructuring has come about only as a result of external pressures. This has been particularly evident in bilateral negotiations with the United States, when the government has employed the 'security card' to persuade industrial groups within Japan of the need to make trade concessions. Many voluntary export restraints as well as market liberalization measures have resulted from such manoeuvrings. External pressure has undoubtedly encouraged trade liberalization, but the frequent use of VERs and other managed trade practices will have adverse effects and result in serious distortions in the long run. Moreover, with the apparent ending of the Cold War, security concerns will increasingly give way to economic concerns as the determining factor in Japan–US relations. Resistance to external demands for institutional reform is likely to become more intense in the future, making it all the more important that the current restructuring not be misrepresented as simply a response to international criticism.

FUTURE PROSPECTS

What of the future prospects for Japan's efforts at gearing its economic policies to international harmony? Will they continue or not? Everything depends upon the capability of the Japanese government to co-ordinate its policies, both at home and abroad. The difficulties involved in this process should not be underestimated. In July 1989, the Liberal Democratic Party (LDP) lost its majority in the Upper House. The defeat was attributed both to the unpopularity of certain economic reforms undertaken by the government and to widespread anger at the involvement of prominent LDP politicians in the share-for-favour Recruit Scandal.

On the economic side, the introduction of a consumer tax and liberalization of farm imports were both economically justified. The tax reform was needed to prepare Japan for the demands of an ageing society, while the liberalization of farm trade was entirely in accordance with the recommendations of the GATT Uruguay Round negotiations. Both policies, however, became the focus of the Lower House election in February 1990, when the LDP was able to maintain its majority, thus ensuring continued political stability, but at the cost of reaffirming the influence of the agricultural lobby. What is more, by further strengthening controls on agricultural imports, the government has seriously undermined its own position within the framework of the current Uruguay Round negotiations, where Japan's ban on rice imports has become a major obstacle to progress. Some politicians have suggested a possible future change of policy, but there has been no official word on this at the time of writing.

Externally, economic conflict with the United States has continued to be Japan's major concern and the government has been serious in its attempt to conclude the US–Japan Consultation on Structural Issues (referred to as the Structural Impediments Initiative, or SII by the US). Senior government officials from both sides have met regularly with a view to removing or reducing structural impediments which have exacerbated the existing trade imbalance. Both sides have accepted that a satisfactory outcome will involve difficulties with domestic interest groups, such as the rice lobby in Japan, and will impose restraints on domestic policy management, particularly with regard to the mammoth US budget deficit. After a series of stiff negotiations stretching over ten months, the consultation was concluded in June 1990. Japan committed itself to a 60 per cent increase in public investment expenditure over the next decade and to the deregulation of the laws regarding the opening of large retail stores. On its own part, the United States agreed to a swift reduction of the budget deficit by curtailing government expenditure and increasing taxes. Nationalistic resentment was expressed by a vocal minority in Japan, but the majority of the population seems to have understood the necessity for this initiative and to have accepted the results of the consultation. Although bilateral negotiations of this type are by no means an ideal way of resolving trade disputes that affect the global economy, they do indicate that Japanese policy management has already been altered by the need for increased economic internationalization.

NOTE

For a detailed quantitative analysis of the restructuring of the Japanese economy, see Yamazawa Ippei (1990), *Economic Development and International Trade: A Japanese Mode*, Hawaii: University of Hawaii Press, ch. 9.

Chapter 7

The internationalization of Japanese capital

Sakamoto Katsuzō and Richard C. Conquest

INTRODUCTION

Since 1987, economic growth in Japan has been domestically generated and this growth is continuing steadily. This in itself marks an important change as in the previous forty years or so the economy was driven mainly by the export sector. During the 1980s Japan's current account surplus rose dramatically, as indicated in Table 7.1.

However, while the trade and current accounts have remained substantially in surplus, it can be seen that the long-term capital account has recorded deficits during this time. Furthermore, in most of these years the deficit on the capital account has actually been much larger than the surplus on the current account.

Consequently, Japan's economic and financial influence within the world economy has developed and grown so that it is now a major force in the global capital markets. This point may be emphasized by the fact that in 1985 Japan became the largest net creditor nation while, in the same year, the US ceased to be a creditor to the world and became its largest debtor. The Japanese surpluses arise from trade with the rest of the world but, even so, it is ironic that the process of internationalization is probably more difficult for Japan to achieve than almost any other country. There are clear cultural, geographical and historical reasons why foreign pressures and demands upon Japan to open its domestic economy and to liberalize its financial system are important. Some of these foreign demands have been welcomed by the Japanese authorities; others, in contrast, have been the subject of friction and tensions which have been resolved by negotiation.

THE INTERNATIONALIZATION OF JAPANESE CAPITAL

The Yen-Dollar Committee report of May 1984

This was an inter-governmental committee representing the US and Japan which first met in November 1983. This followed a visit to Japan by the then Secretary of the US Treasury, Donald T. Regan. The committee was

Table 7.1 Japan's balance of payments (US$: billion)

	Trade balance	Current account	Long-term capital
1980	2.1	−10.7	2.3
1981	19.9	4.7	−9.6
1982	18.0	6.8	−14.9
1983	31.4	20.7	−17.7
1984	44.2	35.0	−49.6
1985	55.9	49.1	−64.5
1986	92.8	85.8	−131.4
1987	96.3	87.0	−136.5
1988	95.0	79.6	−130.9

Source: Bank of Japan

mainly concerned with such issues as the liberalization of the Japanese money markets and interest rates, the Euro-yen market and foreign membership of the Tokyo Stock Exchange. The committee set out a strict schedule of reforms and in the event some of these were achieved within the stipulated time limit. Also, by February 1986, six foreign firms had for the first time gained membership of the Tokyo Stock Exchange.

The report of the Maekawa Committee of April 1986

The Maekawa Committee was appointed by the then Prime Minister, Nakasone Yasuhiro, shortly after the Group of Seven's 'Plaza Agreement' of September 1985. This agreement confirmed the depreciation of the US dollar, especially against the Japanese yen. The Maekawa Committee advised the Prime Minister to introduce policies which would bring about structural change in the Japanese economy and which would reduce Japan's dependence upon export-led growth. These policy initiatives were of such a radical nature that they could not be introduced through the usual political and administrative procedures.

The major recommendations of the committee were:

1 the expansion of domestic demand in order to stimulate domestically generated economic growth;
2 the transformation to an internationally harmonious industrial structure;
3 the further improvement of market access for imports and the encouragement of manufactured imports;
4 the stabilization of exchange rates and the liberalization and internationalization of financial and capital markets;
5 promotion of international co-operation and Japan's contribution to

the world economy, commensurate with its international status; and

6   the adoption of the appropriate fiscal and monetary policies for the realization of these objectives.

The most significant fact about the acceptance of the Maekawa Report was that the government's first concern was with international harmonization. This meant the reduction of both economic tensions and imbalances in trade and payments. The political realization was that, in the postwar period, the Japanese economy had become too large and too important to the world economy for the past patterns of behaviour to continue and that it had to become more compatible with the world economy.

The capital adequacy regulations of the Bank for International Settlements, December 1987

The BIS, whose members are the central banks of the major industrialized countries, decided to introduce common capital adequacy regulations which would apply to all banks transacting international business within the Group of Ten nations. According to the regulations, all qualified banks should achieve capital adequacy equal to 8 per cent of their total assets by 1992. The banks which were supposed to be most obviously and adversely affected by this were the Japanese banks, because their capital adequacy requirement was only about 3 per cent. The new regulations were intended to stabilize the management of international banking; for example, by adopting uniform criteria for the assessment of various forms of risk. However, this move was interpreted as an attempt to curb the expansion of the Japanese banks. In terms of the size of the total assets, no less than nine out of ten of the world's largest banks are Japanese. The actual result of the introduction of the new regulations was that the Japanese banks strengthened their capital base by issuing shares and convertible bonds; this has allowed them to continue the expansion of their international business.

The US Trade Act of 1988

In August 1988 the US Congress passed the Trade Act. This made free trade conditional by, for example, including retaliatory powers which the US authorities could use against trading partners which were deemed to employ practices harmful to American exports. Such retaliatory powers extend also to the trade in financial services. In August 1989 the issue of the primary dealership of the Japanese securities houses in the US Treasury Market was raised by the Federal Reserve Board because participation in the Japanese primary government bond market is more restricted. The FRB did, however, recognize that real efforts have been made and continue to be made to liberalize the Japanese government bond market. This is a good example of the way in which external pressures can be more persuasive than purely domestic pressures.

The House of Lords report on relations between the European Economic Community and Japan, June 1989

The House of Lords Select Committee on the European Community examined the intensity of competition in Japan and the high productivity of Japanese producers, comparing this with conditions in Europe. It concluded that the gap between the two would not narrow in the foreseeable future. The committee subsequently made numerous recommendations, among which was the suggestion that Japanese direct investment in the EEC should be welcomed. Such investment, it was argued, would strengthen manufacturing industry in the EEC and would lead to employment gains and the introduction of high-technology production techniques. However, the committee also cautioned that there should be a common EEC policy towards such direct investment from Japan.

The committee noted that, within the financial sector, Japanese participation was not regarded as a threat by European banks and securities houses. Rather, the participation of Japanese financial institutions was seen as enhancing the status of the City of London. On the other hand, the committee warned that the Tokyo financial market was likely to overshadow that of London by the mid-1990s, and was astonished that the City had not appeared to recognize this danger. Somewhat surprisingly, in view of this perception, no witness appearing before the committee expected the Japanese yen to displace the US dollar as the world's major currency.

The lessons of the Stock Market crash of October 1987

The real meaning and implications of the stock market crash of 19 October 1987 are still not fully understood. The Dow Jones 30 Index of the New York market plunged by 508 points or by 22.6 per cent: the most dramatic reversal since 1929. The recovery of the Tokyo market was extremely rapid, and by January 1988 it had overtaken New York in terms of the size of its market capitalization. These developments are suggestive of the significance of the shift of capital flows away from New York and towards Tokyo. These considerations are symptomatic of the kind of pressures and influences which have affected both the Japanese economy and its financial markets and which have contributed significantly to the efforts of the Japanese authorities and financial institutions to bring about reform and change.

STRUCTURAL CHANGE IN JAPAN'S FINANCIAL AND CAPITAL MARKETS

The accumulation of capital in Japan

The two decades following the Second World War saw a shortage of capital resources in Japan. This led to the regulation of the financial sector so that savings were encouraged while, at the same time, interest rates were maintained at levels below those which market forces would have determined. During the 1950s and 1960s a strong economic growth rate assisted Japan's accumulation of capital resources. Between 1960 and 1970 Japan's nominal GNP grew from ¥15 trillion to ¥73 trillion. At the same time, personal financial assets (excluding the financial assets of the corporate sector) increased from ¥13 trillion to ¥72 trillion. Thus, these two entities grew at virtually the same rate. During the 1970s, however, financial assets continued to expand more rapidly than GNP. This meant that financial assets as a ratio of GNP also rose, as shown in Table 7.2.

As recently as 1970, personal financial assets had the same value as nominal GNP, but by 1987 they had risen to 203 per cent of GNP, a twofold rise in less than twenty years. A major part of the growth in personal financial assets has been the steady rise of personal incomes together with the maintenance of a relatively high savings rate.

In the intermediate postwar period the entire financial system and particularly the structure of interest rates – including those of bonds – evolved within a regulatory framework. Towards the 1970s gradual change

Table 7.2 The growth of financial assets in Japan (yen: trillion)

	(A) Personal financial assets	% Change	(B) Nominal GNP	% Change	A/B
1960	13	–	15	–	87
1970	72	18.7*	73	17.2*	99
1980	347	17.0*	240	12.6*	145
1981	388	11.9	257	7.0	151
1982	429	10.6	270	5.0	159
1983	480	11.8	281	4.0	171
1984	528	10.1	298	6.4	177
1985	574	8.7	317	6.4	181
1986	643	12.0	331	4.4	194
1987	702	9.2	345	4.2	203
1988	792	12.8	366	6.1	216
1980–8	–	10.9*	–	5.4*	–

Note* Annual average 1960–70, 1970–80 and 1980–8
Source: Bank of Japan, Economic Planning Agency

and deregulation began. This has accelerated since 1975, when the government began to finance its substantial fiscal deficits with bond issues. This necessitated an improvement in the workings of the secondary bond market and therefore reforms were introduced. In the 1980s the Japanese economy finally reached the point at which, far from suffering from a deficiency of capital, it had accumulated financial resources which exceeded its own requirements. This is the obvious conclusion which is to be drawn from the rise in assets to GNP ratio shown in Table 7.2. As personal financial assets continued to accumulate, institutional investors such as the life insurance companies, banks and investment trusts, increased the scale of their operations. Table 7.3 illustrates this.

The figures indicate that the role of institutional investors is becoming increasingly important and that the share of assets under their management has more than doubled in the 1980s. The volume of transactions by institutional investors has greatly increased the activity of the financial markets. In these circumstances, and reflecting the needs of these institutions and other major corporations, the interest rate paid on big-lot deposits began to be liberalized. Over time the interest rate paid on smaller deposits has also been deregulated and in 1989 this process began to affect rates paid on small, personal deposits. A particularly important development took place in April 1988. The tax-free status of savings accounts (*Maruyū*) with the banks, the post office and other institutions, was abolished. Tax exemption had been used to encourage savings in the days of Japan's capital shortage. Its abolition marked the official recognition that the end of this period had finally been reached.

The impact of Japan's balance of payments

As was illustrated in Table 7.1, capital outflows from Japan have tended to surpass the size of the current account surplus. This draws attention to the structure of the capital account. The long-term capital account is made up of two key elements: assets and liabilities. Liabilities are made up of foreign investments in Japan and assets are Japan's overseas investments. During the 1970s, foreign portfolio investment in Japan was deregulated in order to stimulate capital inflows. In this period, foreign investment (so-called *gaijin toshi*) in Japan had a particularly important impact upon the Tokyo Stock Exchange. This was especially true in the years after 1969, when foreign investors introduced such criteria as Price Earnings Ratios in determining their investment decisions. However, during the 1980s, there was a substantial increase in Japanese investment in foreign countries. For example, overseas investment rose from US$10.8 billion in 1980 to US$149.8 billion in 1988. In the same period, foreign investment in Japan rose from US$13.1 billion to US$18.9 billion in 1988. In 1987 such investment actually declined.

Table 7.3 The assets of financial institutions (yen: trillion)

	1975	1980	1985	1986	1987	1988	1987/88
1 (All banks) Banking Accounts	105	175	270	295	332	366	+34
2 Life Insurance	12	25	51	62	74	91	+17
3 Non-Life Insurance	3	6	10	12	15	18	+3
4 Investment Trusts	4	7	20	31	45	52	+7
5 Total of 2+3+4	19	38	81	105	134	161	+27
Grand total	124	213	351	400	466	527	+61
Insurance and Investment Trusts (2+3+4) as percentage of grand total	15%	18%	23%	26%	29%	30%	44%

Source: Bank of Japan

As Table 7.4 makes clear, Japan's overseas investment was dominated by portfolio investment, while, for most of this period, direct investment was of much less significance. Furthermore, investment in securities has been mainly implemented by the financial institutions. This has increased from US$4 billion in 1980 to US$102 billion in 1986. It is equally clear from Table 7.4 that portfolio investment abroad has been overwhelmingly dominated by bonds, in particular US Treasury securities. This is because Japanese investors have sought a higher rate of interest than that available in the Japanese markets. In the primary US government bond market, Japanese investors have been conspicuously active and have typically taken up between 30 and 40 per cent of recent bond offers. As noted, personal financial assets have risen to more than twice the level of Japan's GNP. At the same time, foreign assets have been increasing, reflecting the long-term capital outflows described above. Japan's net overseas assets became the largest of any country in 1985, and in 1988 reached US$291 billion. Securities are by far the most important form of asset, while direct investment still accounts for a relatively small proportion of Japan's external worth. By 1988 investment in securities had reached US$427 billion – 51 per cent of all long-term assets. By comparison, direct investment totalled US$111 billion or 13 per cent of long-term assets, equivalent to about one-quarter of the value of portfolio investments.

This contrasts somewhat with the US position. America's holdings in overseas securities are only about one half as large as its holdings in direct investments. In these terms, Japan's asset profile is similar to that of the UK, where investors favour portfolio rather than direct investments. Japan's investment income reflects this enormous accumulation of foreign assets. The balance of investment income is set out in Table 7.5. If a comparison is made between the trade balance and the balance of investment earnings in the mid-1980s, it becomes clear that the latter was only about 10 per cent of the former. In 1988, however, this figure rose to the significantly higher level of 22 per cent. The implications of these trends for the structure of Japan's balance of payments may be summarized in the following way. First, Japanese investors are already in the process of diversifying the currency mix of their portfolio holdings. Of late, US dollar investment instruments have been the most important for these investors. However, the long period of dollar depreciation, which began in the first half of 1985, increased the need and incentive to reduce this exposure to one principal currency. Second, dollar investments were dominated by US Treasury bonds. The institutions are now seeking to diversify their portfolios with a greater emphasis upon equities. Third, the balance between indirect and direct overseas investment has already started to shift in favour of the latter. Thus, as recently as 1985, direct investment was equal to only about 10 per cent of indirect investment. By 1988 this figure had risen to about 40 per cent. Fourth, these trends will greatly assist the realization of

Table 7.4 Long-term capital balance (US$: billion)

	1979	1980	1981	1982	1983	1984	1985	1986	1987	1988
Balance	−13	2	−10	−15	−18	−50	−65	−131	−137	−131
Total assets	16	11	23	27	32	57	82	132	133	150
Direct Investment	3	2	5	5	4	6	6	14	20	34
Securities	6	4	9	10	16	31	60	102	88	87
Bonds	3	3	6	6	13	27	53	93	73	86
Total liabilities	3	13	13	12	14	7	17	1	−4	19

Source: Bank of Japan

Table 7.5 Japan's net assets and investment income (US$: billion)

	1980	1981	1982	1983	1984	1985	1986	1987	1988
Asset position									
Net assets	12	11	25	37	74	130	180	241	292
Total assets*	88	117	139	171	229	301	476	646	833
Direct investment	20	25	29	32	38	44	58	77	111
Securities	21	32	40	56	88	146	258	340	427
Income balance									
Credits	11	16	18	16	19	22	29	49	75
Net income	1	−1	2	3	4	7	9	17	21

Note * Long-term assets, excluding short-term assets
Source: Bank of Japan

the concept of international harmonization which was put forward by the Maekawa Report. Japan's direct investment flows are now massive by any calculation. This means that as Japanese corporations locate their production facilities outside Japan, they will be able to maintain their market share while reducing the need to export from Japan. These developments will also greatly assist in the process of reducing the Japanese current account surplus.

Further aspects of Japan's internationalization

In Japan, the liberalization of trade and exchange controls began in 1960, and between 1967 and 1973 the regulations relating to investment flows were eased in five major stages. In February 1973 the Japanese yen entered the floating exchange rate system which would soon include all the major currencies. In December 1980 new laws were introduced that related to exchange controls. Under the old law, every transaction involving foreign exchange had to be approved by the monetary authorities. Under the new system, all transactions are free of any requirement for official approval, although there are inevitably a few exceptions. Japan has therefore moved from a position of approval in principle to a position of freedom in principle.

In May of 1984 the report of the Yen-Dollar Committee was published. Its focus was the liberalization of Japan's financial markets and the internationalization of the Japanese yen. This pattern of bilateral discussions and negotiations soon extended beyond the bilateral US–Japan meetings. Soon Japan was involved in similar bilateral discussions with the UK, West Germany, France, Italy and Canada. This was a clear reflection not simply of the growing commercial and financial importance of Japan, but also of the growing friction which was affecting world trade.

Deregulation and liberalization have advanced in several areas of the capital and financial markets and some of these are outlined below:

Primary market deregulation

In the primary markets for the issuance of shares and corporate and government bonds, significant changes have occurred. For example, in the government bond market the issuing conditions have become more market determined. As noted above, this was necessitated by the substantial increase of issues after 1975 to finance Japan's fiscal deficits. The deregulation of the government bond market then triggered the growing use of other financial instruments such as Certificates of Deposits from 1979, and Money Market Certificates from 1985. These developments in turn brought about the liberalization of interest rates.

Asset management

The deregulation of asset management began in the 1980s, reflecting the accumulation of personal financial assets and the rapid growth of institutional investors such as pension and life insurance companies. The expansion of collective or institutionalized savings meant that the institutions themselves were exposed to a variety of market-related risks. Therefore, methods of hedging risks were developed. For example, a market in government bond futures was established in 1985. In 1988 the market stock index futures was created, and this was followed by the opening of the Tokyo stock and bond option market in 1989.

The easing of the regulation of capital outflows

In 1970 the first yen denomination foreign bond was issued by the Asian Development Bank and in the next year the World Bank also brought out an issue. This was the first time that the Tokyo market had been considered as a source of finance by foreigners. In December 1984 the Euro-yen bond market was liberalized. In 1970 investment trusts were awarded access to eight major foreign stock markets. In the following year this was extended to include insurance companies. In 1973 non-Japanese equities were quoted on the Tokyo Stock Exchange for the first time. Since then the number of foreign companies listed has risen from 6 to a total of 112 at the end of 1988. These measures have encouraged Japanese financial institutions to diversify their investments to include foreign securities. In the light of these developments, it is evident that the Japanese financial markets are being liberalized at a much faster pace than was envisaged by the Yen-Dollar Committee – which, of course, included US representatives. As a result of this, Japan's markets are becoming among the most free and deregulated of the major markets.

JAPAN AS A GLOBAL CREDITOR

As mentioned earlier, Japan has become the major creditor to the world economy, a position formerly held by the US and before that by the UK. This situation has resulted from a number of factors, such as the emergence of Japan's current account surplus, the high savings ratio, the lack of domestic investment opportunities, and the pressure of surplus liquidity in the domestic economy. Two aspects of this transformation are of particular importance: the trend of money flows in Japan, and Japan as the major exporter of capital.

The trend of money flows in Japan

Table 7.6 shows the financial balance of each sector. The Bank of Japan calculates this figure by taking the difference between the savings and investment of the sector. Therefore, positive figures indicate a surplus. For the rest of the world the negative sign means that Japan is exporting capital. The personal sector in Japan is always in surplus. This reflects the high savings rate which had been encouraged by the tax system until April 1988, when tax allowances on certain types of savings were abolished. During the 1980s the personal sector surplus remained at a high level but the decline in 1987 is accounted for by larger outlays on housing and increased consumer spending. The corporate business sector had the largest deficits until 1974: after this date the public sector incurred the biggest financial deficits. In 1988 the corporate sector once again incurred the largest financial deficit for the first time in fourteen years. This was due to heavy investment outlays on machinery, equipment and inventory. In contrast, the public sector deficit started to decline in 1987 and moved into surplus in 1988 for the first time since 1961. This change was brought about by the increasing profitability of the corporate sector which, in turn, generated large tax revenues.

In each of these sectors – personal, corporate and public – the changes in their financial positions were heavily influenced by government policy in 1987 and 1988. For example, the government wished to encourage greater expenditure upon consumer goods and this reduced the surplus of the

Table 7.6 Flow of funds in Japan (yen: trillion)

	Domestic sectors			
	Personal sector	Corporate sector	Public sector	Rest of world
1975	15.7	−5.1	−10.7	0.2
1976	18.9	−5.2	−12.5	−1.0
1977	20.5	−4.7	−13.4	−2.8
1978	22.5	−2.0	−18.5	−3.4
1979	20.1	−6.7	−17.4	1.9
1980	19.5	−8.3	−16.0	2.5
1981	28.1	−7.8	−18.7	−1.1
1982	29.0	−10.2	−18.6	−1.7
1983	29.0	−8.5	−19.0	−4.9
1984	29.3	−5.1	−17.2	−8.3
1985	31.0	−5.9	−13.1	−11.5
1986	33.7	−4.3	−13.7	−14.1
1987	27.3	−7.7	−4.8	−12.5
1988	27.7	−16.9	2.1	−10.1

Source: Bank of Japan

personal sector. One objective was to increase the demand for imported goods in order to reduce the trade surplus, in keeping with the recommendations of the Maekawa Report. The rest of the world's deficit – which means the yen denominated current account surplus – increased continuously until 1986 when it was the largest deficit sector. However, in 1987 the deficit started to decline, and the corporate sector then recorded the largest deficit.

As the rest of the world's deficit continued to increase, the overseas assets of Japan also rose consistently. On a money flow basis there is a necessity for the corporate sector's deficit to continue to widen. At present the public sector is in surplus and therefore the Japanese surplus with the rest of the world can decline only if the corporate sector's deficit increases. This is all the more true because the personal sector's surplus is not likely to decline sufficiently in the short term.

The major exporters of capital

The major exporter of capital during the 1960s was the United States. In terms of both portfolio and direct flows, Europe was the primary recipient. In common with Japan's present position, the US outflows at that time were greater than its current account surpluses. In keeping with the status of the dollar as the world's reserve currency, the US supplied liquidity to the world economy through direct and indirect investment. This resulted in the build-up of surplus liquidity in the world capital markets and particularly in the Euro-dollar market which increased the vulnerability and volatility of the exchange rate system.

By contrast, Japan's capital outflows in the 1980s have not resulted in such a build-up of international surplus liquidity. This is because the greater part of Japan's surplus liquidity has not been exported but has remained within the domestic economy. This is clearly reflected in the steep rise in the value of existing assets such as land, property and securities. In the mid-1970s the Organization of Petroleum Exporting Countries became the largest exporter of capital after the first 'oil shock' of 1973, which resulted in the huge increase of OPEC's current account surpluses. In fact, the largest surpluses were generated by the so-called 'low absorbers' – that is, countries whose small populations could not absorb substantially larger volumes of imported goods and therefore exported their surplus capital. The exported OPEC surpluses were recycled throughout the banking system of the US, Europe and Japan. This contributed to the massive and unsustainable accumulation of debt by the Latin American and other developing nations.

In these terms, it is necessary to consider Japan as a 'low absorber'. The Maekawa Committee was aware of the problem and for this reason advocated policies that would stimulate Japan's consumption of imports and, in particular, of manufactured goods. The continuing liberalization of the domestic market and its growing accessibility to foreign producers and exporters will continue. Again, in contrast to the utilization or recycling of the OPEC surpluses, Japan's capital exports will not result in financial instability of the kind seen in Latin America and Africa. The enormous growth of debt did nothing to stimulate the ability of the debtor countries to generate exports which were essential for debt servicing and repayment purposes. Japan's surplus liquidity is exported and invested by Japanese financial institutions such as banks, life insurance companies and corporations. The management of these funds is directly handled by Japanese companies. This is in marked contrast to the way in which the OPEC surpluses were recycled through financial intermediaries whose judgement, in terms of investment decisions, now appears to have been questionable.

In Japan's case, capital exports will not result in such chronic financial instability. By far the greatest part of these capital exports are directed at the industrialized or developed world. The capital is invested in the debt of states, for example the United States, and corporations which are easily able to service these debts. As has been seen, Japanese investors are also active purchasers of shares and this has no adverse financial implications for the issuers of these securities. The geographical distribution of Japan's long-term capital investment is set out in Table 7.7.

In the 1980s the US became the largest importer of Japanese capital and in 1988 it absorbed over US$61 billion out of Japan's total outflows of US$149 billion. However, in purely percentage terms, the US absorption of funds has peaked out and is now declining. Seen in global terms, in 1986 some 60 per cent of capital inflows were to the US and some 40 per cent of outflows were from Japan.

For the domestic and external reasons outlined in this chapter, it is certain that capital outflows from Japan will continue for the foreseeable

Table 7.7 The direction of Japanese capital outflows in 1988 (US$: million)

1988	Total	Securities	Direct
World	149,883	86,949	34,210
OECD	125,813	81,728	27,792
US	61,490	36,214	18,969
EEC	55,524	42,589	5,793
UK	16,322	10,699	2,908
West Germany	6,770	6,035	261
Australia	4,657	1,747	1,479
South East Asia	5,595	−453	2,688
Communist bloc	5,738	609	606
Others	7,416	−286	3,124

Source: Ministry of Finance; Bank of Japan

future. These outflows will, however, display two distinctive characteristics. First, Japanese institutional investors will continue to seek higher returns abroad than are available to them in the domestic markets – this is the process of diversification. However, it is probably true to say that portfolio investment flows peaked in 1986. Second, the Japanese corporate sector is under pressure to locate more of its production facilities abroad. This is particularly true of the exporting companies. Measures such as the US Trade Act and the creation of a Single European Market in 1992 have encouraged corporations to expand direct investment. In the past three years, for example, direct investment increased by more than 400 per cent to more than US$34 billion. This is obviously adding to the dynamism of the world economy.

IMPLICATIONS FOR THE FUTURE

The first and perhaps the most important implication of the developments which have been set out above is that there are definite limitations to Japan's international role and, in particular, to the role of the Japanese yen as a key currency in the world economy. There has, of course, been a major shift in the relative financial positions of the US and Japan. Until 1967, Japan was a net debtor to the world and in 1968 became a net creditor. For many years Japan's net position remained stable but in the past five years its creditor status has increased dramatically while at the same time the status of the US as a net debtor has increased in an equally dramatic way.

However, this does not mean that the Japanese yen could or should displace the US dollar as the world's key currency. In a number of respects, the Japanese yen still does not play its proper role in the world economy. There are three particular aspects of this. First, calculations carried out a few years ago indicated that the yen's use in the settlement of world trade was only about 2 per cent. Even in settlement of Japan's own trade, the yen's participation is disproportionately small. For example, in the early 1980s more than 60 per cent of Japan's exports and more than 90 per cent of its imports were denominated in US dollars. Second, as Table 7.8 indicates, the yen's status in the world's currency reserves does not reflect the fact that Japan is the world's second largest economy and has also been one of the most dynamic for several decades. Third, the under-utilization of the yen is the more surprising given the currency's strong performance in the foreign exchange market in the long term. However, this relative under-utilization is also seen clearly in the securities markets, which is the third aspect of this question. For example, the yen's use as a debt instrument is indicated by the currency structure of the international bond market, which is set out in Table 7.9.

The conclusion that arises from these observations is that the first task of the Japanese authorities is to bring about the necessary and complete

Table 7.8 Components of world currency reserves in 1988 (US$: billion)

	US$ equivalent	As % of total
US Dollar	379.0	62.8
Deutsche Mark	107.8	17.9
Yen	46.7	7.7
Sterling	19.5	3.2
French Franc	9.1	1.5
Swiss Franc	8.2	1.4

Source: Deutsche Bundesbank

Table 7.9 The currency structure of the bond market in 1988 (as % of total outstanding)

US Dollar	43.3
Swiss Franc	12.8
Yen	12.2
Deutsche Mark	9.6
Sterling	6.8
ECU	4.3

internationalization of the yen so that it plays a more substantive role in the world economy commensurate with Japan's economic and financial status. Similarly, Japan's capital markets must also play a full international role. These points also lead to another conclusion; namely, that it is still too early for the yen to be considered as a possible replacement for the US dollar as the world's reserve currency.

The second major point is that as well as considering the implications for the future, it is timely to consider also the lessons of the past. The era of the Pax Britannica – the years between 1815 and 1914 – were undoubtedly very successful in terms of the stability of the international economy. The UK emerged in the early years of the twentieth century as the largest creditor to the world economy. Britain also pursued a free trade policy more or less constantly from 1846 until 1932 and in fact incurred trade deficits for practically the whole of this period which were beneficial to her trading partners.

Britain's strong, invisible sector ensured that the country had a current account surplus – despite large trade deficits – and these surpluses were exported to build up overseas assets. Thus, in terms of both the visible and invisible sectors, the UK's influence upon the world economy was beneficial and world trade increased hugely from the 1840s. The working of the gold standard underpinned these events, with sterling being freely convertible. This enhanced London's position as the centre of the world economy and financial system.

This era of stability and progress was ended by the First World War, which eroded the UK's overseas assets and weakened its export economy fatally. The UK's economy could no longer carry the burden as the policeman of the world economy. This burden passed naturally to the US which was by far the leading economic power in the postwar period. However, the United States was unprepared to carry out this role. First, the US was a self-contained economy with a very low dependence upon overseas trade. Politically the US had been a reluctant participant in the First World War and soon returned to its isolationist tendencies. The Smoot Hawley Act of 1930 clearly indicated the trend of both economic and political thinking. The US was also underdeveloped in terms of its financial institutions; it was the weakness of this sector which precipitated the crash of 1929, an event which quickly produced a collapse of world liquidity and the disintegration of the world economy. One symptom of this disintegration was the spate of competitive devaluations which took place in the 1930s as each nation retreated from interdependence and attempted to export unemployment.

Second, the postwar era has been a more stable and constructive period in history. The US continued in its role as leader of the capitalist world, and this included its total commitment to economic reconstruction, as was illustrated by the extraordinary altruism of the Marshall Plan. In contrast to the interwar period, new institutions were created to avoid the mistakes of the past. The International Monetary Fund presided over the Bretton Woods fixed exchange rate system which, until 1971, provided a stable environment for reconstruction and avoided the reliance on competitive devaluations which had been so destructive in the 1930s. At the same time, the General Agreement on Tariffs and Trade sought to avoid the tariff wars and protectionist policies which had proved so self-defeating in the 1930s. Thus, the world economy has been sustained by the creation of new international institutions and by American leadership. However, the emergence of the twin fiscal and trade deficits has placed a question mark over the ability of the US effectively to continue its leadership role. The Trade Act of 1988 appears to have compromised its commitment to un-restricted free trade.

The third consideration focuses on the question: What should Japan's response to this situation be? There is only one possible reply: Japan should continue to support US leadership. This means Japan's continued move towards totally free trade and the higher volume of imports that this implies. In addition, Japan should continue to internationalize its capital resources and maintain the free movement of capital. The Japanese authorities should work to establish the yen's proper role in the world economy. In fact, the Japanese economy has been forced to adjust to the substantial appreciation of the yen in the 1980s. The appreciation should not be reversed; it should be sustained. The Japanese authorities at present support the strong yen policy. A depreciation would not be consistent with the status of a major or strong currency.

The problem of Japan's current account surpluses must be seen in relation to the changing nature of Japan's capital exports. As noted above, direct investment flows are increasing in proportion to indirect investment. This means that countries such as the UK will benefit from capital exports from Japan, which will in turn stimulate the growth of domestic production in the most dynamic sectors. The augmentation of the production capacity of the Japanese corporations abroad will reduce Japan's export earnings while fiscal and monetary policies in the domestic economy will stimulate imports – some of them produced by Japanese companies operating abroad. In this way, capital exports will increasingly contribute to the reduction of Japan's trade surplus – a major source of friction with the US and with the EEC.

In conclusion, the mistakes of the past are understood and should therefore be easily avoided in the future. In this there are perhaps four principal areas of concern. First, Japan's economic power has grown tremendously in the past few decades. However, the over-rapid transfer of politico-economic influence to Japan would be a serious mistake, in the same way that the transfer of power from the UK to the US in the 1920s contributed to economic turmoil. Second, the free trade system must be sustained and protectionism of the kind seen in the 1930s avoided. In doing so, the principle of interdependence must be upheld. Third, the free movement of capital should be sustained in the interests of both international investors and borrowers. This will also advance the internationalization of Japanese corporations – among others. And finally, the principle of stable currencies should be upheld in the way that Japan is supporting the strong yen.

Chapter 8

The internationalization of the Japanese automobile industry

Shimokawa Kōichi

INTRODUCTION

Recently, especially since the G-5 meeting of September 1985, the Japanese automobile industry has confronted difficult times owing to the appreciation of the yen. A number of export-oriented industries, including automobiles, electronics, machinery and steel, have been compelled to change their production strategies in view of the volatile international environment. In the case of the automobile industry, many Japanese automakers have established plants in North America, the biggest market in the world. At the same time, they have further strengthened their overseas production in Asia through both locally based KD ('knockdown') production, and by attempting to create an international division of labour within the region.

To date, Japanese automakers have established ten plants in North America, one plant in the UK (with a second currently under construction) and are promoting locally based production in developing areas, especially Asian NIEs. In 1988 Japanese firms produced about 1 million cars in the developed countries, and exported a similar number of KD sets, mainly to parts of Asia. In expanding their international business activities, Japanese automakers have been confronted with a wide range of difficulties, ranging from traditional labour–management problems and working practices to unwieldy and inefficient parts and components purchasing systems. These difficulties have occurred not only in developed countries like the United States, but in the developing countries as well. Here I will briefly describe the basic problems associated with transplant production in the developed countries and then discuss the situation in Asian NIEs in the light of the attempts by Japanese firms to expand overseas production.

JAPANESE CAR PRODUCTION IN NORTH AMERICA

As noted above, since the G-5 meeting of September 1985, the Japanese automobile industry has transformed the scope of its international

Figure 8.1 Overseas manufacturing operations by Japanese automakers in developed countries

Countries	United States of America						
Japanese makers	Honda	Nissan	Mazda	Mitsubishi	Toyota	Toyota	Fuji, Isuzu
Type of entry	Sole entry	Sole entry	Sole entry	Joint Venture with Chrysler	Joint Venture with GM	Sole entry	Joint Venture
Name of company	Honda of America Mfg., Inc.	Nissan Motor Manufacturing Corporation USA	Mazda Motor Manufacturing (USA) Corporation	Diamond-Star Motors Corporation	New United Motor Manufacturing Inc. (NUMMI)	Toyota Motor Manufacturing USA, Inc.	Subaru-Isuzu Automotive Inc.
Established / Paid-up capital	February 1978 $478 million	July 1980 $375 million	January 1985 $200 million	October 1985 $199.5 million	February 1984 $200 million	January 1986 $500 million	March 1987 $250 million
Share in equity	Honda of America 97.07% Honda 2.93%	Nissan (USA) 80% Nissan 20%	Mazda 100%	Mitsubishi 50% Chrysler 50%	Toyota 50% GM 50%	Toyota 20% Toyota (USA) 80%	Fuji 51% Isuzu 49%
Location	Marysville, Ohio	Smyrna, Tennessee	Flat Rock, Michigan	Bloomington-Normal, Illinois	Fremont, California	Georgetown, Kentucky	Lafayette, Indiana
Land area	First plant 870 acres; Second plant Undecided	783 acres; Engine plant 578 acres	395 acres	635 acres	210 acres	1,285 acres	870 acres
Vehicles/ parts produced	First plant Accord, Civic; Second plant	Nissan truck (1-ton pay load), Sentra, engines; Engines, steering components	MX-6 Probe	Mitsubishi Eclipse, Plymouth Laser	Prizm, Corolla	2-litre, 4-dr Camry sedan; Engines, axles, steering components	Leone-class passenger car (Fuji); small truck (Isuzu)
Production start-up month	Nov. 1982 for 1st assembly line; April 1986 for 2nd assembly line	June 1983 for Nissan truck; March 1985 for Sentra; summer 1989 for engines	September 1987	September 1988	December 1984	May 1988; Fall 1988 (axles); Fall 1989 (engines); 1990 (steering components)	September 1989
Annual production capacity	360,000 units	240,000 units (440,000 units in 1992)	240,000 units	240,000 units	250,000 units	200,000 units; To be determined	60,000 units each at start-up, 120,000 units each at full capacity
Employees	5,200	3,100 at the end of December 1988; 950	3,500	2,900	2,500	3,000; 500	1,700
Total investment	$250 million for 1st assembly line, $280 million for 2nd assembly line	$745 million; $600 million	$550 million	$600 million	$500 million	$800 million; $300 million	$500 million

Countries	Canada				United Kingdom				
Japanese makers	Honda	Toyota	Toyota	Suzuki	Nissan	Honda	Isuzu	Toyota	Toyota
Type of entry	Sole entry	Sole entry	Sole entry	Joint Venture with GM Canada	Sole entry	Sole entry	Joint Venture with GM	Sole entry	Sole entry
Name of company	Honda of Canada Mfg., Inc.	Toyota Motor Manufacturing Canada Inc.	Canadian Auto-parts Toyota Inc.	CAMI Automotive Inc.	Nissan Motor Manufacturing (UK) Limited	Honda of the UK Mfg., Ltd	IBC Vehicles Limited	To be determined	To be determined
Established	June 1984	January 1986	March 1983	December 1986	April 1984	February 1985	September 1987	To be determined	To be determined
Paid-up capital	C$200 million	C$250 million	C$7 million	C$202.5 million	£150 million	£50.935 million	£18 million	To be determined	To be determined
Share in equity	Honda of Canada 100%	Toyota 100%	Toyota 100%	Suzuki 50% GM Canada 50%	Nissan 100%	Honda 10.3% Honda of the UK 81.1% Other 8.6%	GM 60% Isuzu 40%	To be determined	To be determined
Location	Alliston, Ontario	Cambridge, Ontario	Delta, British Columbia	Ingersoll, Ontario	Tyne and Wear, England	Swindon, England	Luton, England	Burnaston, England	Shotton, Wales
Land area	450 acres	371 acres	14 acres	395 acres	801 acres	367 acres	59 acres	280 acres	130 acres
Vehicles/parts produced	Accord, Civic	1.6 litre Corolla sedan	Aluminium wheels	Cultus, Escudo	Bluebird, Micra-class passenger car, cylinder heads for engines	Mid-size car, engines	Fargo, Carry	1.8 litre Carina II	1.8 litre engines
Production start-up month	November 1986	November 1988	January 1985	April 1989	July 1986 for Bluebird; 1992 for Micra-class passenger car; early 1991 for cylinder heads	Mid 1989 for engines; late 1991 for mid-size car	September 1987	Late 1992	Late 1992
Annual production capacity	80,000 units at full capacity	50,000 units	240,000 wheels (40,000 wheels per month in 1989)	200,000 units	80,000 units for Bluebird (200,000 units for cars in 1992); 200,000 cylinder heads in 1993	100,000 units for mid-size car; 70,000 units for engines at full capacity	50,000 units	200,000 units (100,000 units in first stage)	200,000 units (100,000 units in first stage)
Employees	800	1,000	70 (135 in 1989)	2,500	2,000 at the end of December 1988	1,500 for cars and 150 for engines	2,000	3,000 (1,700 in first stage)	300 (200 in first stage)
Total investment	C$266 million	C$400 million	C$20 million (C$46 million in 1989)	C$615 million	£600 million	£300 million	£18 million	£700 million	£140 million

Note: Data included in the table above is based on individual manufacturers' official announcements as of July 1989.
Source: Japan Automobile Manufacturers Association, Inc. *The Motor Industry of Japan*, 1989

activities. Leading producers such as Toyota, Nissan, Honda, Mazda, Mitsubishi, Subaru, Isuzu and Suzuki have built ten automobile assembly plants, mainly in North America.

From the outset, Japanese automakers have been extremely cautious about setting up transplants, even in the United States. This is because of the large scale need for capital investment (almost US$1 billion), as well as differences in working practices and labour relations, different production systems and management styles, and parts procurement and material supply systems. The following were of particular concern to Japanese firms:

1 The unavailability of a highly educated and uniformly high-quality workforce comparable to that in Japan.
2 That the highly contractual nature of American business ethics would result in rigid working practices and overspecialization, which would hinder communication and co-ordination within the organization.
3 That Japanese-style management, with its emphasis on collective effort and reward, would be difficult to introduce.
4 That, as employees were less loyal to their companies, increased friction between labour and management would result.
5 That the existence of efficient and co-operative parts makers, so vital to the automobile industry, could not be relied upon.

Locally based production does, of course, bring certain advantages. These include:

1 the availability of raw materials at a lower cost due to the appreciation of the yen relative to the dollar;
2 reduced transportation costs;
3 avoidance of increased trade friction connected with restrictions on Japanese car imports;
4 heightened brand name and corporate image;
5 improved productivity and flexibility among workers in recent years, making it more likely that they would be receptive to Japanese-style management and the introduction of QC (Quality Control) circles.

The solution rested entirely with management's ability to minimize the disadvantages associated with locally based production, while making the best possible use of the indigenous workforce. From the producer's point of view, locally based production was feasible only if product quality could be maintained, and, in the case of the US, this meant combining innovative management techniques with the enthusiasm of the American workforce. Even before 1985, a number of automakers had experimented with transplant production in the United States. Honda led the way with the production of motorcycles in Ohio, and then ventured into full-scale mass production of automobiles. Honda was followed by Nissan, which began the production of small-size trucks before moving into small car production; and then Toyota, which employed UAW (United Auto Workers) members and entered into a joint production agreement with GM (General Motors) in Fremont, California. While all of these firms have displayed many of the managerial characteristics associated with Japanese corporations, important differences exist between the early initiatives taken by firms like Honda, Nissan and Toyota, on the one hand, and those of latecomers like Mitsubishi and Mazda, on the other, who only launched locally based production after 1985 when the yen had appreciated against the dollar. The first Japanese autoplants were located in rural parts of the southeast, far away from the baneful influence of both Detroit and the UAW, while late starters like Mitsubishi and Mazda, in partnership with Chrysler and Ford respectively, have endeavoured to conclude agreements with the UAW. This has been facilitated by shifts in union policy which now minimize job classification and accept multiskill workers rather than single-skill workers.

The single greatest problem facing Japanese managers in the US has been the procurement of reliable parts. Unlike in Japan, where each automaker relies on a supply of parts from suppliers with whom the company regularly does business and who takes full responsibility for any defective parts, US automakers had traditionally operated under a bidding system to acquire parts on a short-term basis. Since price was more important than quality, most parts were supplied by subcontractors who had neither the capital nor the incentive to invest in new technology. The result was a high proportion of defective parts and additional costs to the automakers. Japanese automakers dealt with this problem in two ways. Initially, locally based plants procured only about half of all their parts from local suppliers. In most cases, important parts like engines and steering equipment were supplied from Japan. At the same time, efforts were made to establish a more co-operative and co-ordinated relationship with the local suppliers. The attitude of Japanese automakers has been affected too by other considerations, like the appreciation of the yen against the dollar, which has increased the cost of parts imported from Japan; also by the 1988 Moss Agreement between MITI and the US Department of Commerce, which called for an increase in the local content ratio of cars produced in the US and for general improvement in the quality of locally manufactured parts. This is itself a reflection of the determination on the part of US automakers to catch up with their Japanese competitors.

Paralleling the expansion of locally based production by automakers, an increasing number of Japanese parts manufacturers have also set up overseas operations. In some cases this has gone hand in hand with a reduction in domestic output, while in others it has been in response to either the unavailability or unreliability of locally produced parts. There are now more than 180 such manufacturers. One result of this movement has been that the traditional affiliation between a parts manufacturer and a specific automaker has been loosened, thus stimulating the rapid diffusion of Japanese technology, the QC system, and production and management practices. Continued technology transfer of this type may well exert a decisive influence on the future of the automobile parts industry in Japan.

THE INTERNATIONALIZATION OF THE AUTOMOBILE INDUSTRY IN THE ASIAN NIEs

Among the most successful newcomers to the postwar automobile industry have been the Asian NIEs, particularly the Republic of Korea (ROK) and Taiwan. Korean automakers have been exporting finished products to parts of the developed world, notably North America, with considerable success since 1985, while Taiwan has specialized in the manufacture and export of automobile parts. The indications are that Taiwanese manufacturers intend to continue with this specialization with a view to becoming a centre for parts production in a future international division of labour within the automobile industry. Their successes have also stimulated the entry of other newly industrializing countries in Asia into automobile production, thus further encouraging the internationalization of the industry.

Historical experience makes it clear that the development of the automobile industry in newly industrializing nations inevitably creates a dilemma in industrial policy between the promotion of domestic production in response to domestic demand, on the one hand, and internationalization through the introduction of foreign capital and the acceptance of technology transfer, on the other. In the case of automobiles, which use a large number of parts and require a high standard of technology, increasing the local content ratio of parts to advance a policy of rapid domestic expansion will inevitably lead to higher costs along with quantitative restrictions in domestic market demand. This may also result in chronically poor product quality and low technological standards. If, on the other hand, internationalization is promoted through liberalization of the market, the advance of foreign capital and the import of parts may interfere with domestic production and inhibit the development of domestic parts producers.

With this dilemma in mind, the development of the automobile industry in newly industrializing countries requires the enhancement of the local content ratio and promotion of technological transfers through technical tie-ups and patent applications (despite cost penalties in the initial stages), expansion of the domestic market, and the strengthening of export competitiveness. Successful achievement of the first two conditions opens the automobile industry to further internationalization, thereby enhancing the third condition of building export competitiveness. The experiences of both the ROK and Taiwan reflect these conditions. The key to a view of the future is to ascertain how these and other Asian nations will construct a global strategic policy in the era of internationalization. In other words, the problem lies in how the automobile industries of this region will relate to their counterparts in the developed countries, and, in particular, how they will enhance their own technology and competitiveness through affiliation with the Japanese automobile industry.

THE INTERNATIONAL DIVISION OF LABOUR WITHIN THE AUTOMOBILE INDUSTRY: THE CASE OF TAIWAN AND THE ROK

A comparison of the characteristics of the automobile industries in the ROK and Taiwan produces some striking contrasts. Although both nations pursued a policy of encouraging domestic production and completely prohibited the import of Japanese-made cars, the ROK promoted the export of finished automobiles, while Taiwan exclusively exported parts. Contrasts are also apparent in the structure of their respective automobile industries: in the ROK, the state took the initiative by limiting the number of automakers to the three majors, and encouraging large-scale mass production. In Taiwan, however, where the government has neither limited the number of companies nor forced a reorganization of the industry, a total of seven medium- and small-scale automakers have been retained.

Korean automakers initially expanded production by combining low-wage costs and mass-production techniques to gain export competitiveness. Hyundai, for example, exported 120,000 of 240,000 cars produced in 1985, 300,000 of 320,000 in 1986; and 407,000 of 606,000 in 1987. Kia Motors, which had an extremely low export ratio until 1986, expanded rapidly thereafter, exporting 63,000 of 197,000 cars produced in 1987, with further increases planned for the future. Daewoo Motors, the third largest automaker, exported 71,000 of 162,000 cars produced in 1987, and is expected to double its exports in the very near future.

Unlike the way the ROK promoted its automobile industry, Taiwan employed a production policy geared to the needs of the domestic market which prevented large-scale mass producers like Hyundai Motors from coming into existence. Instead, there are several small-scale automakers, some capable of turning out 40,000–50,000 cars, and others 20,000–30,000 cars annually. Seven automakers competing with one another in 1987, for instance, produced a total of only slightly more than 220,000 cars. Because automobile production was designed exclusively for the domestic market, finished products were extremely expensive; even Japanese cars produced under licence were double the price of the equivalent model produced in Japan. Automobiles manufactured in Taiwan were suited exclusively to the domestic market, where the import of finished Japanese cars was prohibited, and were not competitive

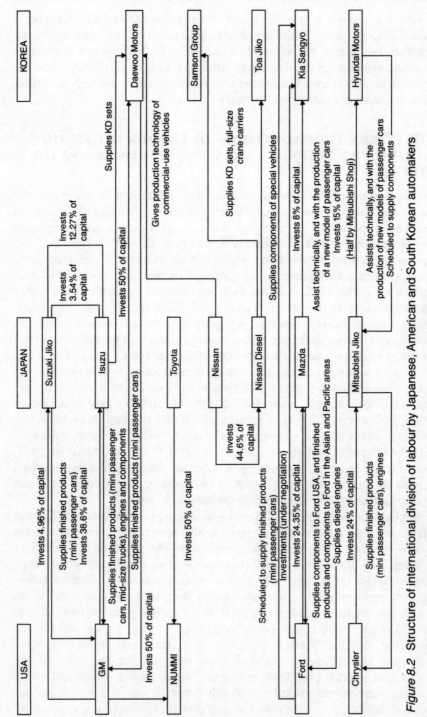

Figure 8.2 Structure of international division of labour by Japanese, American and South Korean automakers

Source: Japan Automobile Manufacturers Association Inc. *The Motor Industry of Japan*, May 1986.

Table 8.1 Korean automobile industry: change in output; registration of new cars; export/import; car ownership

	1960	1970	1980	1985	1986	1987
Output						
Passenger cars	–	14,487	57,225	264,458	457,383	793,125
Commercial-use vehicles	–	14,332	65,910	113,704	144,163	186,614
Registration of new cars						
(domestic products only)						
Passenger cars	–	–	45,972	136,159	156,464	249,448
Commercial-use vehicles	–	–	58,502	110,123	131,787	170,600
Export						
Passenger cars	–	–	14,655	119,210	298,878	535,231
Commercial-use vehicles	–	–	10,597	3,900	7,491	11,079
Import						
Passenger cars	141	14,087	1,027	643	2,124	n.a.
Commercial-use vehicles	168	8,235	2,675	3,865	2,341	n.a.
Ownership						
Both included	31,339	128,298	527,729	1,113,430	1,309,434	n.a.

Source: The Motor Industry Handbook (Nissan) 1988, p.40

internationally owing to both cost factors and low quality. On the other hand, the existence of a number of competing automakers encouraged the proliferation of parts makers, many of whom have become very active in the export of parts to the used-parts market in the United States. This area of export activity has expanded in recent years through joint ventures or technical tie-ups with manufacturers in developed countries, including Japan. Nevertheless, because of its policy of inhibiting the growth of high-risk, large-scale automobile production for export and, instead, concentrating on the domestic side, Taiwan has yet to find a solution to the problems of high costs and low standards. Hastily arranged joint ventures or industry-wide reorganization could create more problems than they solve, while the introduction of large-scale manufacturing would entail greater risks today than when the ROK first adopted this policy.

In response, the government appears gradually to be moving in the direction of decontrolling the market by lowering the local content ratio and accepting increased foreign capital investment. This will stimulate competition among Taiwanese automakers and allow them to participate in the international division of labour. To enhance its parts-manufacturing technology and development capability, Taiwan is also encouraging joint ventures with foreign firms, particularly Japanese, and the indications are that Taiwan intends to make itself a centre for parts production in the global division of labour.

Since the protection of the domestic automobile industry has been a major aspect of Taiwanese industrial policy for some years, any change in the regulations governing the local content ratio is bound to have a significant impact. In July 1978, for example, the government imposed a local content ratio of 70 per cent on automobiles with a gross weight of 3.5 tons or less, and in the following year introduced the Automobile Industry Development Promotion Act, which had the following objectives:

1 to increase the local content ratio,
2 to encourage the development of an export industry, and
3 to expand the capacity of parts manufacturing.

This regulation, too, was aimed exclusively at raising the self-supply rate for the domestic market. It in no way alleviated the problems of high cost and low quality, and therefore inhibited rather than stimulated exports. The government has recognized the limitation of fostering the automobile industry under such closed, isolated conditions, and has recently begun to stress the need for structural change within the industry in response to the international environment. The New Automobile Industry Development Bill, which was introduced in 1985, made provision for a staged reduction on the introduction of foreign capital, reduction of the local content ratio from the present 70 to 50 per cent after three years, and complete abolition of the local content ratio imposed on exported cars. To summarize, this

Table 8.2 China–Taiwan automobile industry: change in output; registration of new cars; import; car ownership

	1960	1970	1980	1985	1986	1987
Output						
Passenger cars	–	8,611	132,116	112,879	133,546	174,884
Commercial-use vehicles	–	279	464	38,801	39,732	49,300
Registration of new cars (domestic products only)						
Passenger cars	–	–	78,219	100,821	142,159	155,995
Commercial-use vehicles	–	–	52,231	52,592	53,648	73,837
Import						
Passenger cars	–	3,756	28,976	18,650	34,779	n.a.
Commercial-use vehicles	–	10,111	17,211	9,641	9,652	n.a.
Ownership						
Passenger cars	8,055	49,541	425,443	915,598	1,046,670	n.a.
Commercial-use vehicles	12,722	48,959	255,525	429,371	439,910	n.a.

Source: The Motor Industry Handbook (Nissan) 1988, p. 39.

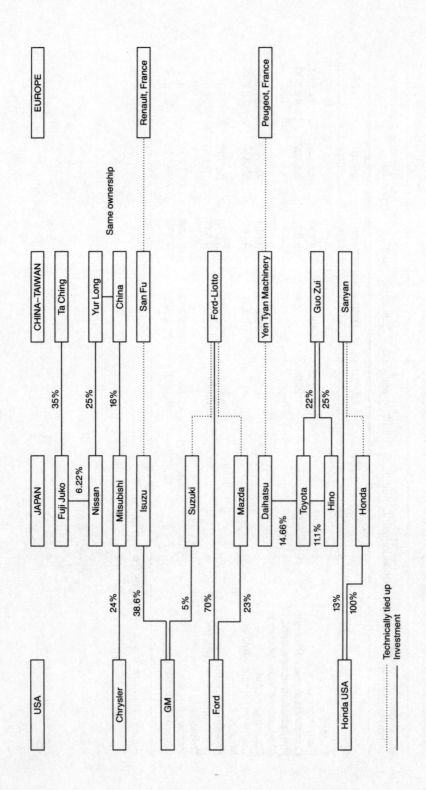

Figure 8.3 Structure of tie-ups by Chinese–Taiwanese automakers

Table 8.3 Key points of the New Automobile Industry Development Bill

Introduction of foreign capital and export ratio	1 For the manufacture of parts, joint ventures with manufacturers other than Chinese–Taiwanese ones should be encouraged as well, and the export ratio not fixed. 2 For the manufacture of finished products and complete export of all, joint ventures with manufacturers other than Chinese–Taiwanese ones should be encouraged as well. 3 For the manufacture and sales of finished products in China–Taiwan, joint ventures should be only with Chinese–Taiwanese manufacturers, and the export ratio and technological transfer plan must be approved by the administrative agency concerned.
Control on import of Japanese-made passenger cars	Restrictions on areas from which passenger cars are imported (imports should be exclusively from the US and the European countries) should be continued and reviewed after five years. If this control is abolished, it should be issued two years before the execution of the abolition.
Import duties	1 Passenger cars, and trucks with gross weight of 3.5 tons or less; to annually reduce from the present 60% to 30% in five years. 2 Parts: maintain the present 35% average for four years, and reduce to 25% in the sixth year. NOTE: The first year duties start to be reduced is not specifically dated.
Home parts production rate (home manufacture rate)	1 Passenger cars, and trucks with gross weight of 3.5 tons or less: maintain the present 70% for three years, and reduce to 50% three years after then. 2 Control on the home manufacture rate should not be applied to export cars. 3 Parts imported with foreign currencies obtained by exporting finished products and OEM parts can compensate for up to 20% of the home manufacture rate.
Tax reduction	Cars using the body, chassis and engine designed by Chinese–Taiwanese should be treated with a total reduction of 9% (3% each) in the commodity tax.

Source: The PR brochure issued by the Economic Dept as of 27 April, 1985

Table 8.4 Car part items with specified home manufacture rate and their rates for 1986

Full-size cars (includes chassis of large buses and trucks)	30% → 33%	Gross weight ranges from 3.5 to 7 tons. Plants which made an application must manufacture 3 of 15 items given at right in China–Taiwan.
	30% → 33%	Gross weight ranges from 7 to 15 tons. Plants which made an application must manufacture 2 of 15 items given at right in China–Taiwan.
	25% → 27%	Gross weight amounts to 15 tons or more. Plants which made an application must manufacture 2 of 15 items given at right in China–Taiwan.

①Piston ring and pin, ②Cam shaft (excludes semimanufactures), ③Inlet/outlet pipes, ④Clutch assembly, ⑤Flywheel and case, ⑥Brake and clutch master, ⑦Brake drum and operating cylinder, ⑧Rear wheel shaft and propeller shaft, ⑨Steering shaft, ⑩Steering assembly, ⑪Half steering gear housing, ⑫Chassis frame, ⑬Door (includes inner/outer plates), ⑭Front and rear panels, ⑮Frame.

Passenger cars (includes passenger cars, recreational vehicles and jeeps with gross weight of 3.5 tons or less)	70%	Plants which made at application must manufacture 3 of 15 items given at right in China–Taiwan, and 5 of 15 items there since 1986.

①Cylinder body, ②Cylinder head, ③Crank shaft (excludes semimanufactures), ④Cam shaft and gib assembly, ⑤Piston ring and pin, ⑥Clutch and flywheel (includes shift lever for automatic transmission), ⑦Transmission gear, ⑧Transmission case, ⑨Front/rear wheel shafts and propeller shaft, ⑩Steering assembly (includes steering wheel, general switch and connecting shaft), ⑪Steering gear housing, ⑫Brake assembly (includes disc type, drum type, vacuum power doubler, brake master), ⑬Door (includes inner/outer plates), ⑭Front, middle and rear frames, ⑮Engine head, front screw, rear door, trunk.

Small-size cars (includes 70% small trucks, passenger cars and combination passenger cars-and-trucks with gross weight of 3.5 tons or less)

Plants which made an application must manufacture 4 of 14 items given at right in China–Taiwan, and 6 of 15 items there since 1986.

① Cylinder body, ② Cylinder head, ③ Crank shaft (excludes semimanufactures), ④ Cam shaft and gib assembly, ⑤ Piston ring and pin, ⑥ Clutch and flywheel, ⑦ Transmission gear, ⑧ Transmission case, ⑨ Rear wheel shaft and propeller shaft, ⑩ Steering assembly (includes steering wheel, general switch and connecting shaft), ⑪ Steering gear housing, ⑫ Brake assembly (includes drum type, vacuum power doubler, brake master), ⑬ Door (high-mount car) and rear box (truck), ⑭ Front, middle and rear frames, ⑮ Front panel, rear door (high-mount car), or rear panel (small truck).

Source: The PR brochure issued by the Economic Dept, 3 December 1984

new government legislation encouraged the introduction of foreign capital and technology, with the objective of stimulating competition and encouraging the development of the automobile and parts industries and exporters well equipped to participate in the international division of labour.

In marked contrast to these changes in Taiwanese industrial policy, there are as yet no indications that the ROK is planning either a substantial reduction in the local content ratio of domestically produced cars, or a relaxation of the restrictions on the introduction of foreign capital. Under current regulations, the local ratio for cars produced for the domestic market is 98 per cent, and 95 per cent for the export market. If, however, the use of imported intermediate materials and certain special component parts is taken into account, the ratio drops to about 70 per cent. This is particularly true of cars produced for the export market, which require the importation of parts to meet various emission control and safety requirements. Such imported parts are normally assembled and installed in the ROK in order to satisfy the minimum local content ratio requirement. Although the ROK government has no intention of reducing the local content ratio, it has reduced or even exempted certain automobile parts from import duty provided they are destined for the export market. This may also account for the increasing presence of Japanese parts manufacturers in Korea. Nevertheless, some liberalization has taken place. For example, the limitation on the number of models which the three automakers could produce (imposed by the government in 1981) is being removed, and in future the introduction of foreign capital will be permitted if it encourages technology transfers. The free entry of foreign capital, which is increasingly common in other countries, however, is not expected to be authorized for the time being. It is also expected that import duties on finished passenger cars, excluding Japanese-made cars, will be reduced in stages.

The rapid growth of the Korean automobile industry and its success in exporting cars, particularly to North America, has attracted the attention of manufacturers around the world. The increase in the value of the market won since 1988, the saturation of the American small-car market, and renewed trade friction with the US have, however, made it clear that continued expansion will depend upon the development of new export markets, including Japan, and the introduction of new models for the luxury end of the North American market. To a great extent, success in these areas is dependent upon improved technology and quality control in the manufacture of parts. This in turn relies upon the willingness of the ROK to liberalize its industrial policies and encourage the participation of foreign manufacturers and parts makers in the domestic market.

The prescience of Japanese automakers in the ROK and Taiwan may be summarized in the following way. Korea's largest manufacturer, Hyundai

Motors, has technical and financial links with Mitsubishi Motors. In recent years Hyundai has grown increasingly independent of Mitsubishi in the development of new models, and this has resulted in a complementary division of labour between the two. The second largest Korean automaker, Kia, has a similar relationship with Mazda and produces the Mazda Festiva under licence. The third of the automakers, Daewoo, is in partnership with Isuzu and Suzuki as a result of its tie-up with General Motors. It also has an extremely limited relationship with Nissan involving the production of commercial vehicles. Aside from these, the major Japanese manufacturers, Toyota, Nissan and Honda, have no relationship with Korean automakers.

In Taiwan, the reverse is true and all domestic automakers have entered into technical or financial agreements with at least one of their Japanese counterparts. By and large these affiliations have resulted in the production of Japanese cars under licence for the domestic market, though Ford has begun to export Mazdas produced in Taiwan. Some Japanese automakers are also thought to be considering the possibility of creating a regional division of labour, with Taiwan as a centre for the production of car parts and components.

THE AUTOMOBILE INDUSTRY IN THAILAND AND ITS ROLE IN THE INTERNATIONAL DIVISION OF LABOUR

Thailand has thus far relied upon a policy of import substitution to promote domestic production. In doing so it has achieved a local content ratio of about 57 per cent, the highest among the ASEAN countries. This policy has done little to encourage the development of mass production (owing to the small size of the domestic market) and has inevitably resulted in high unit costs. A Japanese car produced in Thailand is double the cost of the same model produced in Japan. With a population of 48 million, car ownership in Thailand amounts to just over 1.4 million units, and annual sales of new cars average between 80,000 and 110,00 units. A striking feature of the industry in Thailand is that such a small number of cars is produced by no less than eight Japanese and three European automakers. There are a further 187 manufacturers of mechanical parts (including twenty-five major Japanese firms) and in cases where parts are unobtainable locally they must be manufactured by the automakers themselves. As a result of this and the small size of production lots, costs have remained high.

To compensate for the low scale of production and the lack of technology transfer in the parts industry, there are indications that parts production will have to be incorporated into an international division of labour. But to raise quality control standards to a level high enough to enable Thai producers to compete internationally will require considerably more expertise and capital than is currently available. And even if the

Table 8.5 Schedule for home car parts production in Thailand (announced in 1978)

	Target Score	Achieved Already	Scheduled to be Achieved					Achievement Rate (%)
			1st year	2nd year	3rd year	4th year	5th year	
1 Major engine parts	15.30						13.95	91.2
2 Other engine parts	7.00	1.65	0.15			1.39	0.17	48.0
3 Electric equipment parts	4.00	3.08	0.54					90.5
4 Wiring parts	2.00	1.50	0.15					82.5
5 Exhaust pipes	2.00	0.50		1.50				100.0
6 Fuel assembly	2.00		1.42			0.18		80.0
7 Wheels, tyres, etc.	10.00	10.00						100.0
8 Interior parts	4.25	1.41	2.18	0.15		0.15		91.5
9 Seats	5.00	4.65	0.35					100.0
10 Glass	2.50	0.75	1.75					100.0
11 Lamps	1.00					0.50		50.0
12 Suspension parts	3.50	1.43		1.47		0.12		86.3
13 Braking assembly	3.10		0.23			0.64		28.1
14 Clutch	1.90			0.54		0.15		36.3
15 Major body parts	23.00				6.50	0.78	1.37	37.6
16 Other body parts	1.45					1.11		76.6
17 Driving assembly	4.30							0
18 Steering assembly	2.95						0.89	30.2
19 Transmission assembly	3.75						1.79	47.7
20 Instrument panel parts	1.00							0
1–20 total	100.0	26.97*	6.77	3.66	6.50	5.02	18.17	
					Annual total			
21 Accessories	(7.70)	(2.00)	33.74	37.40	43.90	48.92	67.09	
					Grand total			

Note: The figures indicated by an asterisk include (2.00) of 21 accessories
Source: Thai no Kōgyōka: NAIC e no Chōsen (1987) (Thailand's Industrialization: A Challenge to NAIC), edited by Suematsu Akira and Yasuda Yasushi, Tokyo: Institute of Asian Economic Research.

Table 8.6 Thailand's automobile output

Automakers (Product brands)	1982	1983	1984	1985	1986
Bangchan General Assembly (Honda, Daihatsu, GM)	994	2,223	2,828	2,144	1,220
Isuzu Motor Thailand (Isuzu)	14,086	22,718	21,573	18,359	15,978
New Ara (Ford)[1]	–	–	–	–	1,584
Prince Motor Thailand (Nissan)[2]	2,214	2,620	2,522	1,061	67
Siam Automotive Industry (Nissan)	13,599[3]	17,125	17,855	12,149	10,573
Siam Motor & Nissan (Nissan)	4,139	6,886	5,435	2,526	2,207
Sukosol & Mazda Motor (Mazda)	4,790	6,796	6,338	5,402	5,791
Thai Hino Industry (Hino, Toyota)	3,524	4,732	4,502	2,379	2,115
Thai Swedish Assembly (Volvo)	437	539	774	654	643
T.A. Assembly Plant (Benz)	715	979	1,101	912	953
Toyota Motor Thailand (Toyota)	22,809	29,697	27,878	21,397	18,815
UDMI (Mitsubishi)	4,250	7,700	10,074	5,531	6,888
YMC Assembly (BMW, Peugeot, Citroen)	3,469	4,750	6,761	9,315	7,328
Total	77,270	109,261	111,037	82,106	74,162

(Unit: cars)

Source: Thailand Automobile Manufacturers Association, Inc.
Notes 1: Changed agency in 1985
2: Closed in February 1986
3: Stopped production of FIAT in 1986
4: On behalf of company reorganization, some company figures overlapped. Therefore some year totals differed with each company's total addition.

necessary machinery is provided, improved product quality will be dependent upon the morale of the workforce and the ability of local management to implement appropriate quality control procedures. Thus far the problem has been ensuring that the attitude of Japanese corporate management towards quality control is shared by locally recruited managers. The Thai government has adopted a policy of welcoming investment as a means of stimulating domestic production, promoting exports, encouraging technology transfers, and securing employment for indigenous workers. At the same time, however, the Board of Overseas Investment has instructed Japanese companies based in Thailand not to appoint Japanese employees as production line supervisors. This makes it particularly difficult to ensure that locally recruited Thai managers are as conscious of the need for strict quality control as their Japanese counterparts.

Despite a range of difficulties, including the recruitment of managerial staff, a general lack of industrial infrastructure and availability of raw and intermediate materials, Japanese automakers are attempting to incorporate Thailand within a regional division of labour. Some firms have begun to rely on Thai manufacturers for certain parts which do not require a high degree of precision tooling, while others have encouraged Japanese parts producers to set up in Thailand.

CONCLUSION

The appearance of a new age of industrialism, that of the Asia-Pacific, has caught the rest of the world unawares. 'Economic miracles' seem almost to be the order of the day in this region of the world. The automobile industry has played, and will continue to play, a significant role in the industrialization of these countries. The increasing domination of the global economy by multinationals, be they Japanese, American or European, has also made it clear that nations like the NIEs and Thailand will not be able to cling to isolated domestic production policies. The demand for technology transfer, and the contained development of an international division of labour, have necessitated the expansion and liberalization of domestic markets, and there are no signs of this trend abating. Throughout the region, Japanese car and parts manufacturers have taken on a dominant role in both technology transfer and the creation of a vertical division of labour. Initially, at least, the expansion of the Japanese automobile industry into Asia was stimulated by the unexpectedly rapid rise in the value of the yen against the dollar and the need to exploit new sources of low-wage labour. In the future, however, the international division of labour will be determined by factors other than relative labour costs, including increased technology transfer, the introduction and growth of mass production, and the liberalization of domestic markets throughout the region.

A precondition for the creation of a stable and lasting division of labour will be the diffusion of modern technology. This will enable the automotive parts and related industries to produce goods of a high enough standard to meet the requirements of markets in the developed countries. The most important of the related industries is the materials industry, which produces high-tech parts and components including brake systems, automatic transmission, emission control devices, electronic parts and so on. Because it would be virtually impossible to enhance technology in all of these fields simultaneously, a staged introduction or transfer of technology will be necessary. Paralleling this transfer, there is a need for an improvement in quality standards for all small parts, such as screws, nuts and bolts. Although an internationally acceptable definition of what constitutes quality standards may be impossible to achieve, a general co-ordination of quality standards within an acceptable range is not only possible, but absolutely essential. A comparison between the ROK, Taiwan and Thailand reveals significant differences in levels of industrialization, the positioning of the automobiles and parts industry, and industrial policy regarding automobile production. It seems that what is called for is the development of a more clearly defined industrial network within the international division of labour: the ROK concentrating on the mass production of automobiles by major firms; Taiwan as a centre for parts production; and Thailand engaging exclusively in small-lot production, importing raw and intermediate materials. In terms of practical application, Mitsubishi Motors is currently experimenting with such a system involving the ROK, Taiwan, Thailand, Malaysia and the Philippines. The results are likely to have an important impact on the industry as a whole.

Unlike the situation in the consumer electronics industry, where a horizontal division of labour has been in place for some time, this is not yet possible in the automobile industry, which requires a far greater number of parts and much higher quality standards. But, given the pace at which industrialization is proceeding, the increasingly close economic links which have already been formed, and the evolving division of labour between the NIEs and the ASEAN nations, the possibility of a horizontal division of labour emerging in the future cannot be ignored. For this to be achieved, it will first be necessary for Japanese, Korean and Taiwanese manufacturers to adjust and co-ordinate their corporate strategies. Whatever form it may take, it is clear that a new international division of labour within the automobile industry is beginning to emerge, and that the ROK, Taiwan, Thailand and the ASEAN countries will all play an important role in determining its future composition.

The internationalization of the Japanese automobile industry is only one aspect of the restructuring of the world economy. It does, however, indicate the range of difficulties which Japanese producers have encountered and will continue to encounter as they expand overseas. While each of the cases mentioned here has presented Japanese automakers and parts producers with a unique range of problems, there are, in fact, issues common to all. The single greatest challenge to Japanese industry is whether it can alter the traditional labour practices and production systems in the United States and the Asian NIEs. It will probably not be possible to impose a complete transformation, but resistance to change should diminish as the deficiencies of the present system become more apparent. Indeed, an awareness of just how badly the industry is functioning today – complicated job classifications, antagonistic labour–management relations and an obsolete parts procurement system – may provide the impetus for revolutionary changes in the future. It is also essential that locally recruited managers receive at least some of their training in Japan, since this will assist in the diffusion of Japanese methods of quality control, management and so on. The experience of Japanese firms in the United States, however, has made it clear that the imposition of rapid change from above is neither easy nor, in the long term, of benefit to management or to the workforce. Ways must be found of improving quality control, increasing productivity and encouraging initiatives from the shop floor, without alienating local management or unions. It will be through the gradual modification of existing practices and the careful introduction of Japanese technology and methods that a new industrial culture will emerge in an increasingly internationalized world.

Part IV

National and local politics

Chapter 9

Japan's political change towards internationalization
Grafted democracy and political recruitment

Yakushiji Taizō

FROM SECLUSION TO A WESTERN NATION STATE: A PRECONDITION

In the year 1588, while Elizabethan England was disposing of the Spanish Armada in a naval battle at Calais, Japan was approaching the end of an age of civil wars. In 1590, the civil wars ceased and the country was unified, first by Hideyoshi Toyotomi and later by his subordinate, Tokugawa Ieyasu. The year 1603 marked the establishment of the Tokugawa Shogunate, the same year in which Britain was unified under the House of Stuart. The Tokugawa regime lasted for nearly two and a half centuries without a single civil war or foreign invasion. Up until 1639, Japan was fully open to the external world, and many foreign missionaries and traders frequented Japan. They came to Japan to propagate the Christian faith and to export Japanese copper and silver for casting bronze. Competition over Japanese trade between the Dutch East Indian Company, stationed in Batavia (old name of Jakarta), and the English East Indian Company resulted in a victory for the Dutch, and the Netherlands was designated as Japan's sole trading partner during the isolationist period of the Tokugawa era.

Misunderstandings about the seclusive nature of the Tokugawa era are common. The European view is that Tokugawa Japan was completely isolated from the Western world. In fact, however, Japan remained open to Western influence. Seclusion merely implied a monopoly of foreign trade by the Tokugawa Shogunate. The Tokugawa government probably gathered news of European political affairs through the Dutch traders, including news concerning the European hegemonic war, better known as the Thirty Years' War. From 1618 to 1648, Europe was immersed in large-scale war against the Habsburg empire. In the aftermath of this war, the Westphalia Treaty defined the victors or victorious countries as nation states, countries of single national languages and independent governments. Tokugawa Japan was not, of course, a Western country, but it was functionally the same as a nation state, possessing national sovereignty and a single language. It had thus already met the requirements of a Western-style state long before the Meiji Restoration. In addition, the nation's domestic economy supported a stable population of 30 million. Edo (the old name of Tokyo) had a population of more than a million and had arrived at the stage of sophisticated capitalistic economy where modern commercial institutions were already operating.

The high-level development of the capitalistic economy and political stability during the Tokugawa period were the preconditions for the quick transformation of Japan into a Western-type modern '*Rechtsstaat*' following the Meiji Restoration. Political elites attempted to make Japan a hybrid of the British parliamentary monarchy and the Prussian constitutional empire by abolishing the hereditary clan class structure and creating a limited hereditary peerage and a vast number of social elites without patrimonial backgrounds. The creation of new elite classes resembled Prussia's dissolution of the Junker class. As in Prussia, new elites were recruited mainly through two routes: the military and the bureaucracy. The Japanese imperial university system was devised to attract, regardless of social background, the best and the brightest students from all over Japan. Politically, the House of Peers functioned as a political assembly. It was later complemented by the House of Representatives, whose members were elected through a limited electoral system. Only those who paid a considerable amount of national and local taxes were eligible to run for election. The country's policies were completely in the hands of the elite bureaucrats who served the country under the concept of *noblesse oblige*. Thus, up until the end of the Second World War, Japan had developed as the only Western-style nation state in Asia.

INTRODUCING GRAFTED DEMOCRACY

In pre-Second World War Japan, two major parties, the *Seiyūkai* and the *Minsei* parties, dominated Japanese parliamentary politics. In both parties, high-ranking government officials occupied the key posts. Many ex-bureaucrats from the Ministry of Home Affairs dominated the *Seiyūkai*, while those from the Ministry of Commerce and Industry (MITI's prewar name), and the Ministry of Foreign Affairs, controlled the *Minsei* Party. The Cabinets of both parties acted as a 'check and balance' on the House of Peers and the Privy Council under imperial sovereignty. In 1932, however, following the assassination of Prime Minister Inukai of the *Seiyūkai* in the 15 May *coup d'état*, Japan's prewar parliamentary political system came to an abrupt end. It was replaced by a militaristic government.

Japan's defeat in the Second World War heralded the introduction of a new political system. When the Allies met at Potsdam early in 1945 to settle Germany's future, they also discussed how the Japanese political system would be reformed in the postwar period. Churchill and Attlee insisted that Japan should return to a parliamentary monarchy with the Emperor retained as a figure-head. Truman and his American delegates, however, initially held the view that an American-style democracy should be introduced without an Emperor. Reflecting the fact that the Japanese Occupation was dominated by MacArthur's forces, the US finally introduced American-style democracy but preserved the imperial system. Subsequently, the Occupation forces abolished the powerful Ministry of Home Affairs and the Ministries of Navy and Army, purged prewar political elites and introduced American-style gubernatorial elections. In the prewar period, young officials of the Ministry of Home Affairs had been appointed as prefectural governors. In national politics, the long-suppressed Communist and Socialist parties were legalized, and Japan resumed a multiparty system. For a short period, in 1947, a socialist coalition government held power.

Despite a strong desire to democratize Japan, the American-led Occupation forces relaxed their military control with the advent of the Cold War. Fearing possible communist infiltration during the war, the Occupation authorities changed US policy after Truman concluded that Japan's economic recovery was imperative in order to make the nation both a political and economic fortress against communist influence. Social disorder caused by communist-dominated labour unions was another reason for this change in American policy. To facilitate economic reconstruction, political stability was necessary, and thus the purged prewar political elites were permitted to return to government and national politics. Then, in 1951, the peace treaty with Japan was signed in San Francisco, thereby hastening Japan's postwar return to the status of a sovereign state.

The political reshaping of Japan was then accelerated, and many prewar political and bureaucratic elites re-emerged. The first approach towards postwar political reshuffling was taken by the *Seiyūkai*'s former leader, Hatoyama Ichirō, who organized the new Liberal Party. In the first general election in 1946, the Liberal Party won, but before Hatoyama could form his Cabinet, the Occupation forces suddenly purged him. Subsequently, the ex-Ambassador to the UK, Yoshida Shigeru, assumed leadership of the Liberal Party and renamed it the Democratic Liberal Party. (The former name was again resumed in 1950 after the party absorbed some of Inukai's Democratic Party.) Following Hatoyama's purge in 1951, intra-party feuding within the Liberal Party intensified. Finally, Hatoyama split the party by creating the new Japan Democratic Party in 1954. While the two conservative parties competed with each other, the hitherto divided socialist parties merged in 1955 in order to fill the political vacuum. Fearing that there would be no chance of remaining in power as long as conservative in-fighting continued, the Liberal Party (Yoshida resigned in December 1954 and Ogata Taketora assumed the party presidency) and

Hatoyama's Democratic Party finally merged in 1955, thus creating the new Liberal Democratic Party (LDP). Since the year 1955 marked the beginning of new alignments, the postwar Japanese political system is often called the Year-55-Regime.

During the seven years of the Yoshida government, many ex-high-ranking government officials were recruited. For example, in the twenty-fourth general election for the House of Representatives in 1949, Yoshida recruited nearly fifty ex-high-ranking officials. They included the Ministry of Finance's ex-Vice-Minister Ikeda Hayato and the Ministry of Transportation's ex-Vice-Minister Satō Eisaku, both of whom later became Prime Ministers. These recruits became known as students of the 'Yoshida School'. Yoshida's motive for recruiting such high-ranking officials was to build a strong stand against the party politicians dominating Hatoyama's party. These ex-high-ranking officials led party politics in the newly created LDP as faction heads. By 1955, there were eight major LDP factions: the Satō faction, the Ikeda faction, the Ōno faction, the Ishii faction (originally, the Ogata faction), the Kishi faction, the Ishibashi faction (originally, the Hatoyama faction), the Kōno faction, and the Matsumura-Miki faction.

We have already noted that the Occupation forces attempted to destroy the prewar political system. Before long, however, the same system of elitist politics was resumed. What was the rationale for this? One possible answer may be that, due to the Cold War, the Occupation forces felt that the elite bureaucrats were indispensable as a vehicle to facilitate military control over economic reconstruction. The elite bureaucrats were those who already knew every facet of the social and economic affairs of Japan, since they had been transferred from one locality to another as either young tax office chiefs or as railroad station masters. Without them, military control was not possible. However, the admission of ex-government officials into postwar politics no doubt undermined earlier Occupation policy, which had been to introduce American-style democracy. It was here that American Occupation policies experienced a major setback.

Although the Occupation authorities could not help but allow the revival of the prewar political system in national politics, they did successfully democratize local politics, from which a new breed of politician was recruited. This was an obvious consequence of America's incomplete democratization of Japan, prior to the 1949 general election. A new class of politician was recruited for the 1947 election, which included Tanaka Kakuei, Nakasone Yasuhiro, and Suzuki Zenkō, all of whom later became Prime Minister. Special attention should be paid to Tanaka Kakuei. Although Tanaka had no connection with the government elite bureaucrats, his special skill in collecting political funds enabled him to climb the political ladder within the Yoshida School. After Satō resigned as Prime Minister, Tanaka took over his coalition and formed the new Tanaka faction. Tanaka's political success was, of course, partly due to his talents as a politician, but he was obviously a new type of politician who was more concerned with political transactions involving potential supporters and the distribution of pork-barrel benefits. In this sense, he was a typical grass-roots politician in the American mould.

In the prewar period, local politics had been dominated by wealthy landowners, while the political funding of the major parties came from both the rural gentry and the *zaibatsu*. The *Seiyūkai*, for example, was financially supported by the *Mitsui Zaibatsu*. Tanaka came from a poor social background, lacking both inherited wealth or links with *zaibatsu* money. How was he able to collect political funds, and from where? The answer lies in the fact that the Occupation authorities instituted both land reforms and ordered the dissolution of the *zaibatsu*. This meant that the sources of political funds would become far more diversified in the future, and that political talent would be needed to obtain alternative sources of financial support. Prewar politicians were impotent in this regard because they relied too heavily on organizationally collected money from the old landlord class or from the *zaibatsu*. In order to meet new challenges posed by postwar social and economic reform, political creativity was needed. Tanaka possessed just such creativity.

Tanaka's successful entry into the elitist Yoshida School resulted in the 'hybridization' of the mainstream of the LDP and intensified intra-party competition in exploring new political markets. At the national policy level, elite ex-bureaucrat politicians, in particular the *Kochikai* faction (another name of the Ikeda faction), formulated policy in close contact with the government, and at the local level, grass-roots politicians conducted pork-barrel political transactions. This two-tiered political system within the LDP was a consequence of the Occupation authority's incomplete implantation of American democracy. It was not full democracy, but half democracy which blended prewar Japanese elitist politics at the national level with American mass-democracy at the local level. Since American-style democracy was grafted upon prewar Japanese democracy (i.e., *noblesse oblige*), it is appropriate to refer to Japan's postwar political system as 'grafted democracy'. In short, the Year-55-Regime is the political realization of such grafted democracy.

FOCUS ON POLITICAL RECRUITS

For thirty-five years, since the start of the Year-55-Regime, the LDP has been continually in power. There are a multitude of reasons why the LDP has been able to maintain political power for such a long time. Among possible explanations, the catch-all party theorem seems most appropriate. As discussed above, the LDP started with eight major factions, and these groups fiercely competed with each other to expand their political market share, namely through garnering voter support. From the beginning, the

LDP has been an amalgamation of different political camps which are almost mini-parties in their own right. These mini-parties make every possible effort to gain party endorsements and campaign funds for their faction-based candidates. The Japanese electoral constituencies are such that two or more LDP candidates have to compete to fill a limited number of seats. Ideologically, the LDP's greatest source of support base has been among farmers and small shopkeepers, but intra-party competition between factions made it impossible for the LDP to rely entirely on such a narrow base of support. Therefore, the LDP has vigorously expanded its support base to include city dwellers and white-collar workers of large corporations, both of whom traditionally composed the support base for the opposition parties, in particular the Japan Socialist Party (JSP).

Japan's postwar economic development helped foster the gradual transformation of the LDP from a conservative ideological party to a catch-all party, as voters became increasingly conservative in defence of their economic well-being. The LDP appeared to many voters as a party which patronized their wealth. On the other hand, while the LDP has become ideologically free, the JSP has increasingly emphasized the importance of ideology, and has opposed policies proposed by the LDP government. Frustrated with the ideological stalemate within the JSP, a right-wing group left the JSP in 1960 to form the Democratic Socialist Party (DSP). In addition, a new Buddhist party, the Clean Government Party (CGP), with support among small shop and factory owners, came into existence in 1964. By the mid-1960s, Japan's multiparty politics was aligned with five major parties: the LDP, the JSP, the DSP, the CGP and the JCP (Japan Communist Party).

Party politics is a dynamic process with newly entering recruits as an input variable and old retiring politicians as an output variable. The party system then works with the remaining sums between election intervals. Thus, the degree to which a particular party is dynamically changing can be measured by how many and what type of new recruits have entered the political scene. If a party is dynamically predisposed to respond positively to dynamic changes in voters' demands, such a party might well supply a new type of politician. On the other hand, if a party is unable to respond to these changes, then its recruitment procedures are likely to reflect this: the result being that the same type of politician is continuously fed in.

Since the start of the Year-55-Regime, there have been twelve general elections, and in each election, new recruits entered national politics. Of course, not all of them lasted beyond the next election. Those who were re-elected, however, possessed the potential to climb up the political ladder and occupy key posts in the party. As far as the LDP is concerned, the excessive factional competition in elections created a simple promotion system, in which only those who could win six or seven consecutive elections became eligible for a Cabinet post or for the party's important committee chairmanships. Furthermore, when a new Cabinet is formed, ministerial posts are distributed on the basis of each faction's contribution to the LDP's victory in the election.

Figures 9.1 to 9.4 show the changing patterns of new recruits by their socio-political attributes. These figures are drawn in the following manner: first, the twenty-five new recruits are classified by their socio-political backgrounds, such as age, party affiliation, educational background, political background, etc.; and next, similarities of these socio-political attributes are extracted based on these individual groupings. As shown, the similarities in the socio-political attributes of new recruits in each election

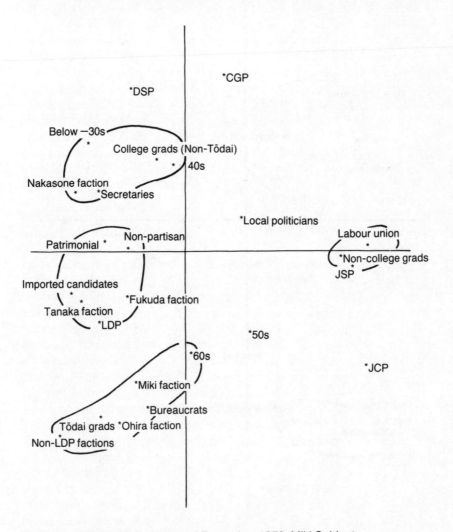

Figure 9.1 34th general election, 5 December 1976: Miki Cabinet

are plotted in a two-dimensional space: the horizontal co-ordinate represents political ideology such as progressive vs. conservative, and the vertical co-ordinate represents territorial jurisdiction or recruitment base, such as local vs. national.

Despite some minor anomalies, three clear patterns are thrown up by these figures. First, the JSP's recruitment pattern has remained relatively static. Its new recruits have largely emerged from the labour unions, and their educational backgrounds are not particularly high. However, as Figure 9.4 shows, the JSP has recently begun to recruit a new type of

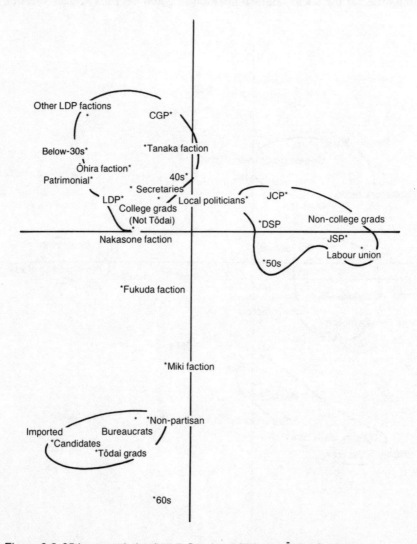

Figure 9.2 35th general election, 7 October 1979: 1st Ōhira Cabinet

politician from a wider base. Second, the LDP's recruitment patterns have shifted dramatically. There are basically three groups for the LDP: the centre of gravity group (primarily composed of the Prime Minister's faction along with its allied factions); the locally oriented (or grass-roots) group; and the nationally oriented (or bureaucratic) group. The composition of the first two groups has constantly been reshuffled, depending upon which LDP faction was in power or from which faction the Prime Minister came when the election took place. According to LDP rules, the party Secretary General is chosen from the Prime Minister's faction, and he is responsible

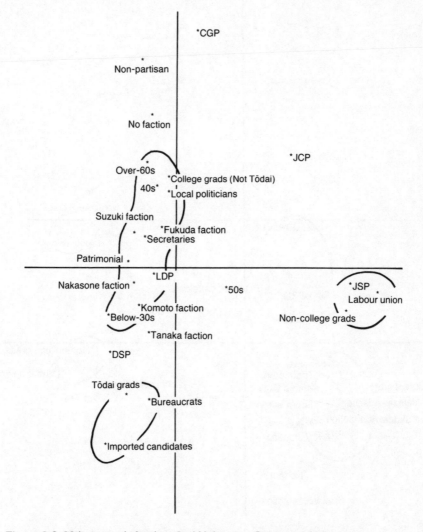

Figure 9.3 38th general election, 2nd Nakasone Cabinet, 1986

for co-ordinating the party's election strategy. That is why the LDP's centre of gravity has normally been occupied by the Prime Minister's faction. On the other hand, the characteristics of the nationally oriented group remained unchanged until the 1986 election. Their attributes indicate that the LDP's most prestigious faction, the *Kochikai*, has remained dependent upon ex-high-ranking government officials for recuitment. Third, the distance between the LDP and the JSP has widened, as the LDP's groups have gradually moved towards the vertical axis. This implies that, as far as political recruitment is concerned, the JSP has become more ideologically

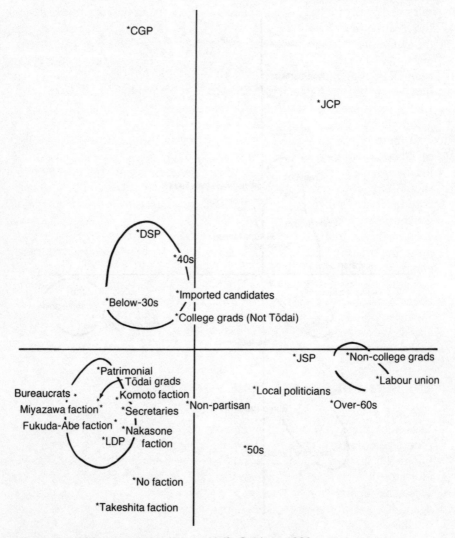

Figure 9.4 39th general election, 1st Kaifu Cabinet, 1990

oriented, and the LDP has, in contrast, become less ideologically dependent. Fourth, recently two opposition parties, the DSP and CGP, have
moved closer to the LDP pattern, and their new recruits are always locally
oriented. In the 1990 election, however, the CGP shifted from its previous
position.

Our analysis indicates that the secret of LDP rule throughout the entire
period of the Year-55-Regime lies in the scope of its sources of recruitment. In addition, the LDP's dynamically changing pattern of recruitment
implies severe competition amongst factions. Using an analogy from the
world of commerce, the LDP's factions resemble the mutually competitive
sales divisions of a large conglomerate, serving as an important vehicle for
the creation of new political customers. The so-called 'Recruit Scandal' and
the consequent landslide defeat of the LDP in the House of Councillors
election of July 1989 has generated much debate. In these discussions it has
often been suggested that the LDP has been immobilized by its inability to
dissolve the factions. The reality, however, is just the opposite. That is, the
LDP's factional system is an innovative device which enables the party to
avoid internal political paralysis.

If there is a vice associated with the factional system, it is that, because
of factional competition, the LDP increasingly draws new recruits from
locally oriented sources while isolating nationally oriented politicians. We
should also note that the new LDP started with the Yoshida School as a
core faction. Until the mid-1960s, LDP politicians of the Yoshida School
were primarily concerned with national and international issues such as
economic reconstruction, the opening of Japan's investment market and,
most importantly, the US–Japan security treaty. However, as factional
competition continued, the locally minded or pork-barrel type politician
has gradually come to dominate the LDP. Since this party has constantly
been in power, the LDP's shift to a locally minded party means that
Japanese politics has become more internalized and thus less internationalized. We will touch on this point from the viewpoint of voting behaviour
in the following discussion.

THE BIRTH OF JAPAN'S ISSUE VOTERS

The task assigned to the LDP in the 1960s was economic reconstruction.
Backed by the LDP's mission-oriented political alignment, the government
promulgated many laws which were designed to attain this objective.
Figure 9.5 shows a time series trend of law enactments. The declining curve
indicates a decrease in government law-making coinciding with the
successful completion of postwar socio-economic reconstruction. Here
again, it is worth noting that the laws were usually drafted by government
officials, not by the legislative staff of individual Diet members. The ratio
of laws prepared by the Diet members is less than 20 per cent.

According to the conventional theory of political economy, if the economy is in good shape, the party in power will steadily increase its voter support. This high correlation between economic performance and political support is observed in many Western countries such as the US and the UK. However, strangely enough, there is a reverse correlation in Japan. As is illustrated in Figure 9.6, although the Japanese economy grew throughout the 1960s and the first part of the 1970s, the LDP's rate of support steadily declined. This trend continued until about 1975, periodic fluctuations notwithstanding. From about 1977, the previous pattern reversed itself, and the LDP benefited from a sudden upsurge in its rate of support. During the mid-1970s, the Japanese economy entered a period of stagnation because of the two oil crises. Despite the economic difficulties that resulted, voters increasingly supported the party in power. It is not at all easy to account for this unusual state of affairs. What follows, is, therefore, an attempt to provide an interim analysis.

The first part of the support rate curve in Figure 9.6 illustrates the declining trend of law enactments in Figure 9.5. The coincidence may not be accidental, but may indicate that Japanese voters had positively acknowledged the role and contribution of government officials in the postwar socio-economic reconstruction of the nation. However, there was no way for them to express their appreciation. Since, during this period, the LDP was led by ex-high-ranking government officials, appreciation for government efforts was actually expressed by voting for the power-holding

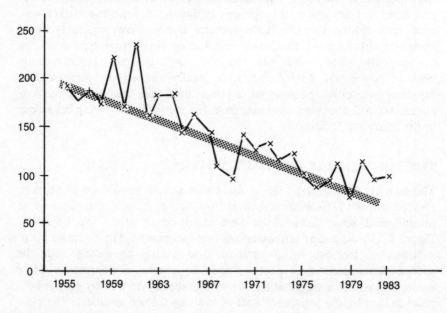

Figure 9.5 Total number of bills passed in Japan, 1955–83

LDP in elections. In other words, appreciation for the government was projected into support for the LDP. This so-called 'projection effect' implies that, as the government's role in socio-economic reconstruction approached an end, the LDP's support rate also declined.

Faced with external economic perturbations, such as the oil shocks caused by the wars in the Middle East, the Japanese economy entered a new stage of development. In short, the Japanese postwar economy was fully synchronized with the global economy during the period starting with the Nixon Shock in 1971 and the two oil crises in 1973 and 1979, respectively. Since Japanese voters were satisfied with the benefits of postwar prosperity, the new unsettled economic situation led them to fear for the future. Therefore, in expectation of the LDP's superior political management of the globally linked Japanese economy, they started to increase their support for that party. According to this so-called 'expectation' theory, voters' reactions are based not on a feedback process, but rather on a 'feed-forward' process. In feedback politics, voters respond to what the party in power did in the past; in feed-forward politics, voters react now by hoping that the party they support will solve future problems. The JSP's recruitment pattern until the 1986 election is a typical example of feedback politics, since new recruits had been chosen on the basis of their previous experience within the trade union movement. The LDP's recruitment pattern is feed-forward politics, since new recruits have been chosen from among a much wider variety of potential candidates.

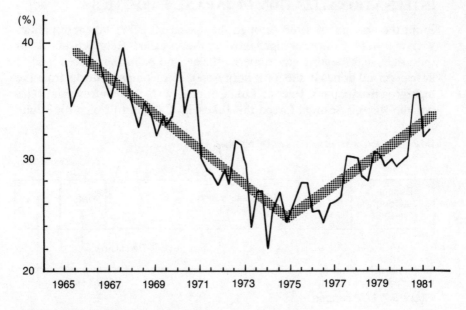

Figure 9.6 Polygonal-line phenomenon of LDP support rate

This shift in Japanese voter behaviour, based on the perceived ability of the political leadership to solve Japan's externally linked economic problems, indicates that Japanese voters are becoming what Nie refers to as 'issue voters'. The marked difference between partisan voters and issue voters is that the response of the latter is very quick and volatile depending on the issues they are most concerned with. In the 1986 general election, Nakasone Yasuhiro won a landslide victory, but shortly thereafter the voters were incensed by the introduction of a 3 per cent sales tax and elected an opposition party candidate in a by-election in Iwate Prefecture. In the aftermath of the LDP's overwhelming victory earlier in the year, Prime Minister Nakasone had argued that the victory was due to the party's success in attracting a new support cohort. His analysis, however, was flawed in that this new cohort could not be relied upon to give unquestioned support to the LDP on all issues.

In the event, Nakasone introduced a politically unpopular tax, relying on his landslide victory in 1986, but, as shown in Figure 9.7, the majority of voters who cast their vote for the LDP in 1986 were those who wished to preserve their conservative lifestyle, not the LDP's genuine partisan loyalists. This miscalculation of the LDP's support base may have caused the recent period of political turbulence. We will now consider this in greater detail.

CURRENT POLITICAL REALIGNMENTS AND THE INTERNATIONALIZATION OF JAPANESE POLITICS

From the autumn of 1988 through the spring of 1989, Japanese politics were in a state of disorder highlighted by the so-called 'Recruit Scandal'. In this affair, high-ranking government officials and politicians were found to have received bribes in the form of pre-marketed company stocks from the high-growth company Recruit Ltd. Coupled with the controversial sales tax, the Recruit Scandal forced the Takeshita Cabinet to resign on 3 June

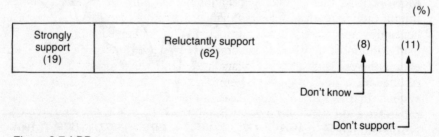

Do you support continuing with an LDP administration?

(%)

| Strongly support (19) | Reluctantly support (62) | (8) | (11) |

Don't know ⏌

Don't support ⏌

Figure 9.7 LDP support

Source: NHK Survey after the 1986 election

1989. Takeshita designated Foreign Minister Uno Sosuke as his successor. The Uno Cabinet, however, lasted for only two months and was forced to resign in the aftermath of a humiliating defeat in the House of Councillors election on 23 July. During the election campaign, the rate of support for the Uno Cabinet plummeted to 12 per cent, one of the lowest levels in the entire period of LDP's rule. This caused many people to forecast an LDP defeat in the forthcoming Lower House election. With respect to party support rates, the LDP's rates declined drastically from 50 to 26 per cent between March and July, while support for the JSP rose from 17 per cent to 28 per cent. Why did such a sharp decline in political support for the LDP occur in such a relatively short period of time? Is this a unique pheno- menon? The answer to the second question is 'no'; and we can find a parallel in the latter half of the Nixon Administration in the early 1970s.

In the 1968 presidential election, Nixon defeated Hubert Humphrey by a sizeable margin and became the thirty-seventh President of the United States. His phoenix-like revival was much appreciated by American voters who gave him a strong approval rating which reached 69 per cent according to a Gallop survey in February 1973. Nixon's popularity was based primarily on his role as a world statesman. With Henry Kissinger's aid, he opened diplomatic ties with China and terminated America's vexing war in Vietnam. The Watergate Scandal occurred suddenly at the height of Nixon's popularity, and even during the Watergate Hearings, there was only a moderate decline in support of his presidency. A sharp decline, however, began when he fired Special Prosecutor Cox on 20 October 1973, soon after the onset of an energy crisis brought on by war in the Middle East. When the Yom Kippur War broke out, Nixon immediately launched Project Independence, an energy conservation measure, and asked American citizens to lower their room temperatures by six degrees. Such a coercive measure so enraged the general public that voters who had hitherto supported Nixon began to question his leadership. A Gallop survey conducted in November 1973 showed that his popularity rate had declined drastically to a level of 20 per cent.

In the 1972 presidential election, the Democrats nominated George McGovern as their presidential candidate. During the Nixon Adminis- tration, the American economy had entered a new stage. American hegemony was under threat, particularly in global economics, and for many, the most humiliating economic measure introduced by Nixon was ending the exchangeability of dollars and gold. The so-called Nixon Shock resulted in a new monetary system, namely the floating exchange rate system. In the light of these developments, and armed with a liberal- progressive ideology, McGovern strongly criticized the performance of the Nixon Administration. A sharp cleavage of political ideology between McGovern and Nixon in the 1972 presidential campaign made a consider- able impact on the American public's voting behaviour.

Prior to this presidential election, American voters were generally partisan oriented. That is to say, they voted for either Republican or Democratic candidates according to traditional partisan affiliations which largely reflected their own socio-economic attributes, such as locality, income level, ethnic background and so on. For example, the Southern conservatives and the East-Coast minority workers would vote for a Democratic candidate, while Midwestern whites tended to vote Republican. Partisan voting of this type was possible as long as the two partisan candidates were ideologically close to each other. Since both candidates were equally conservative in issue areas, voters could not help but cast ballots based on partisan criteria.

According to Nie, McGovern's presidential nomination in 1972 completely undermined this traditional partisan voting pattern and gave birth to issue voting. Because Nixon and McGovern had completely different campaign platforms, American voters became more sensitive to various national as well as international issues. Nixon capitalized on this changing tide of voting behaviour, and hence won a landslide victory in the 1972 election. Throughout his remaining years in office, Nixon successfully retained popular support by satisfying the issue-oriented voter's expectations in the areas of foreign affairs and global economics. His overconfidence backed by high levels of popularity spilled over into arrogance, and he miscalculated that American voters would continue to provide him with partisan support. Consequently, he committed a fatal mistake by firing the Special Watergate Prosecutor and calling for the lowering of domicile temperatures. It was as a result of these miscalculations that Nixon was forced to resign the presidency in August 1974.

We can learn several lessons from the Nixon incident. First, a political scandal is not necessarily a primary cause for a sharp decline in popularity; rather, overconfidence and a miscalculation of the change in voting patterns are the main causes. A political scandal merely functions as a trigger mechanism. Applying this to Japanese politics, the decline of the Nakasone Cabinet's popularity was triggered by the Recruit Scandal, but primarily caused by Nakasone's overconfidence and miscalculation. Second, a landslide victory and a landslide defeat can occur in a relatively short time, since issue voters are quite volatile, depending on how they evaluate individual policies. Again, applying this to the Japanese case, Nakasone's landslide victory in 1986 was followed by an equally heavy defeat in the by-election in Iwate Prefecture in March 1987. Third, lagging behind by about fourteen years, the Americanization of voting patterns finally emerged in Japanese politics. This form of Americanization has also reflected the fact that Japan has become an international superstate, having synchronized its economy with the global economy. Thus, Japanese voters are increasingly concerned with international economic issues which are directly linked to their daily lives. However, because of the grafted nature of Japanese postwar politics, politicians have increasingly become local-issue oriented, thereby not meeting voters' demands.

The cleavage between deficiency on the supply side (i.e., the recruitment of new politicians and the government's policy-making) and growing concerns on the demand side (i.e., the issue oriented voting pattern) is a natural consequence of the Year-55-Regime. As we discussed earlier, the Year-55-Regime enabled Japan to become an economic superpower, and economic affluence caused Japanese voters to be issue oriented and conservative in lifestyle. In the meantime, under grafted democracy, (i.e., the political culture of the Year-55-Regime), politicians have become less international or national in their outlook. On the contrary, they have been increasingly local in their issue orientation. Therefore, as long as the Year-55-Regime continues, Japan's politics will remain chaotic. The current political turmoil in Japan would seem to indicate just such a system malfunction. In short, what is needed in Japanese politics is the internationalization of the supply side (i.e., the internationalization of politicians and parties as well as the electoral system). There are two different types of elections in the US, one for international and national issues (i.e., presidential election), and one for local issues (i.e., Congressional elections). Thus far, the Republican party has demonstrated strength in the former area, while the Democratic Party is predominant in the latter area. Under the current electoral system, Japanese voters are unable to differentiate between these two issue areas, and thus have become frustrated. To conclude, therefore, the internationalization of Japanese politics should centre on two reforms: the party system and the electoral system.

REFERENCES

Campbell, A., Converse, P.E., Miller, W.E., and Stokes, D.E. (1964) *The American Voter*, Cambridge, Mass: Harvard University Press.
Nie, N.H., Verba, S., and Petrocik, J.R. (1979) *The Changing American Voter*, Cambridge, Mass.: Harvard University Press.
Yakushiji Taizō (1967) *Seijika vs Kanryō*, (Politicians versus Bureaucrats) Tokyo: Tōyōkeisai.
—— (1990) *Political Constraints in Japanese Policy Making*, in Alan D. Romberg and Tadashi Yamamoto (eds), *Same Bed, Different Dreams: America and Japan - Societies in Transition*, New York: Council on Foreign Relations Press, pp. 118–28.

Chapter 10

The internationalization of Kanagawa Prefecture

Takahashi Susumu

THE CONCEPT OF INTERNATIONALIZATION

It has been argued recently both at home and abroad that policies promoting internationalization should be adopted by Japan. Although the term 'internationalization' now permeates the national agenda, its meaning remains ambiguous. The many research reports that have focused on Japan's policies of internationalization suggest that the term has been used in three different contexts, and agreement seems to exist among observers that policies directed at promoting internationalization have three distinct meanings.

1 'Internationalization', as an analytical concept, merely refers to the fact that, because of increased exchanges of people, communication and information across national boundaries, Japan has been closely inter-woven into global networks of interdependency. The term 'internationalization' in this sense has no positive or negative implications for government policy.

2 Internationalization has been proposed as one of the central policy goals of the national government, and may be defined in the following way: Japan must develop a new perspective on 'internationalization' in which emphasis is on the idea that Japan, as an active member of the world community, should contribute to the improvement of the living conditions of the peoples of other countries as well as its own. In the same context the following guiding principles have been put forward:

(a) Japan's economic and social institutions are to be internationally fair and managed by rules which are clear and understandable to all.

(b) Human resources are to be developed in Japan so as to enable its people to play a more active role in international society. Experiences that Japanese gain in foreign countries should be fully utilized upon their return to Japan.

(c) Japan's economic power is to be invested for the improvement of the welfare of the world, particularly in areas in which Japan has comparative advantage or expertise.

Although progressive in some respects, the above is typical of the reports submitted by government-sponsored policy councils or think-tanks, all of which have stressed the management of Japan's economic power.

3   The third way in which internationalization has been defined is for the purpose of promoting mutual understanding and co-operation at the grass-roots level. It is from this perspective that the 'People-to-People Diplomacy' of the Kanagawa Prefectural Government (hereafter, KPG) was initiated fifteen years ago. Since in this chapter the ideals and policies which constitute 'People-to-People Diplomacy', as pursued by the KPG, are addressed, it is worth noting that Kanagawa's policy of 'internationalization' has, from its inception, been distinguished by its emphasis on exchange.

PEOPLE-TO-PEOPLE DIPLOMACY: ORGANIZATION AND IDEALS

Organization

The KPG has promoted so-called 'People-to-People Diplomacy '(hereafter, PPD) since 1975, when Nagasu Kazuji, former Dean of the Department of Economics at the Yokohama National University, was elected to the governorship of Kanagawa Prefecture. The policy began with the reorganization of Kanagawa's Foreign Affairs Department, the main tasks of which were to manage passport offices and to handle the problems associated with US military bases in Kanagawa. In January 1976, an International Division was set up within the Foreign Affairs Department. The first mission of this new division was to establish links with similar organizations at the municipal level and to liaise with them. In 1977 the KPG established the Kanagawa International Association, and opened facilities in the centre of Yokohama in order to provide the 40,000 foreign residents of Kanagawa with opportunities for international exchange with each other and with Japanese citizens.

Fifteen years on, these initiatives no longer seem particularly significant, but it is worth noting that, at the local level in Japan, very few local governments maintain a special division on international affairs or support associations like the International Association. In most cases, local governments have tended to create small units within the General Administration Department, or else staff of the Secretariat Division have been assigned the task of promoting policies of internationalization. The strengths of the organizational structure of the PPD of the KPG are:

1   the size of the budget for internationalization,

2   the size of the full-time staff (at present the International Division has a staff of more than forty), and
3   the resulting improvement in the ability of staff to implement policies promoting internationalization.

In the past few years the KPG has taken further organizational steps to promote internationalization. In 1987, for instance, the KPG set up a Co-ordinating Committee on Internationalization Policy, composed of the heads of seven departments, including the Board of Education, Community Relations Department, Public Welfare Department, Labour Department, Commerce and Industry Department, and Foreign Affairs Department. By this action, the KPG has clearly demonstrated an under-standing that 'internationalization' is not confined to the arena of 'foreign' affairs.

Ideals

Governor Nagasu announced the basic ideals of PPD following a two-year study carried out under his direction. In September 1977, in a speech made at the Fourth Japanese–American Assembly (the so-called Shimoda Conference) before leading members of the Japanese business, political and academic worlds, he made the following three proposals:

The Japan that needs the world must become a Japan that the world needs

This goal stemmed from the recognition that Japan's export-driven eco-nomic development had resulted in enormous trade imbalances. Governor Nagasu proposed abandoning this one-sided relationship in the economic field, in favour of a basic transformation of Japan's role in the global community, from a 'Japan that needs the world' to a 'Japan that the world needs'. His proposal was addressed not only to national leaders, but also to local citizens, as he regards the support of the citizens as essential for achieving this goal. In his words 'foreign policies cannot be carried out unless they are supported by the people, for the network of world inter-dependence covers every part of our people's daily lives'.

To encourage popular support for this goal, Nagasu emphasized the importance of cultivating a sense of internationality among the people. 'Such a task,' he said, 'cannot possibly be adequately addressed by the diplomatic activities of the central government alone ... The promotion of closer personal communication through a variety of local government channels that represent regional communities, where people work, bring up children, laugh and cry, are extremely important and will produce good effects.'

Promoting cultural exchange at the local community level

Given Nagasu's emphasis upon local-level participation in the formulation and implementation of policy, it was inevitable that internationalization would go hand in hand with decentralization. The path towards decentralization that he chose was to create a viable and lively local community with a strong identity. If the regions and localities that form the basis of nations develop their own individual cultures and modes of living, strengthen region-to-region and locality-to-locality alliances, transcending the limits of national borders, they will make a very significant contribution towards the creation of an affluent world for all humanity.

Strengthening people-to-people relations between countries

To achieve the above-mentioned goals, Nagasu proposed the so-called *minsai-gaikō*, or 'People-to-People Diplomacy'. Although Nagasu recognized that diplomacy was monopolized by central government, he used the term *minsai-gaikō* as a means to emphasize the important role played by ordinary people in the creation of foreign policy. He summarized his attitude in the following way:

> The chances of success in diplomatic negotiations between national governments will be slim unless the people of the countries concerned agree to the matters in question and achieve a mutual understanding. The Japanese people have begun to realize that the maintenance of good international relations is directly connected with their daily lives and even with their very survival.

In this sense, PPD complements the diplomatic objectives of the central government. In other ways, however, Nagasu's policies represented a clean break with conventional forms of diplomacy. Two assumptions lie at the base of his PPD vision: first that the structure of international relations had been gradually changing from state-centric to transnational; and second, that central government diplomacy has been restricted by the development of transnational relations and interdependence. The aim of the PPD is to establish effective international networks that are capable of adapting themselves to the newly emerging international structures. Since PPD has its own objectives, logic and *modus operandi*, its initiatives will not necessarily be compatible with those of the state.

'PEOPLE-TO-PEOPLE DIPLOMACY': FOUR SPHERES OF ACTIVITY

Since its inception in 1975, PPD has gradually become central to prefectural life. At first the scope of PPD was very narrow, confining itself to identifying counterparts in other prefectures. As PPD has gradually gained in momentum, its scope of activities has widened. At present PPD consists of the following five main activities:

1 inter-prefectural relationships;
2 exchange programmes;
3 promoting peace programmes;
4 economic exchanges, co-operation, and assistance; and
5 People-to-People Diplomacy at home.

Inter-prefectural relationships

The KPG promotes two types of inter-prefectural relationship. First is sisterhood affiliation. This is based on sister-prefectural agreements with counterpart state governments. The KPG maintains relationships of this type with Maryland in the USA (since April 1981) and with Liaoning Province in China (since May 1983). The second involves relations without a formal sister-prefectural agreement. Such informal links are maintained with Goteborg och Bohus in Sweden (since September 1978), New South Wales in Australia (since 1979), Penang in Malaysia and Singapore (October 1980), Baden-Württemberg in Germany (since April 1984), and Odessa in the USSR (since April 1986). Although these relationships are mainly with the advanced nations of Europe and North America, as is the general trend in Japan, the KPG maintains more links of this kind than most other prefectural governments in Japan, where the average is three. Moreover, the KPG selects its partners on the basis of a carefully defined set of principles. The first is to promote *détente* between the two super-powers. Therefore, the KPG has established friendly relations with state governments in both the US and the USSR. The second is to create much closer contact with local governments among the middle-ranking powers like Sweden and Germany. The third is to create mutual under-standing and trust with other Asian countries. Governor Nagasu was well aware of the negative image of Japan held in Asian countries, and wanted the people of Asia to know that most Japanese people were determined to settle past grievances and promote future relationships based upon mutual trust. Above all, his concern focused on the establishment of normal relations with the people of China. When he signed the sisterhood affilia-tion agreement with the Liaoning Provincial government in 1984, Nagasu declared his opposition to all wars.

Exchange programmes

The KPG's exchange programmes, which are integral to inter-prefectural relationships, vary from country to country depending upon the counterpart local government. Generally speaking, however, these programmes normally include reciprocal good-will missions; exchanges of sports teams, cultural missions and language teachers; as well as the dispatch of economic missions. The most representative of these inter-prefectural programmes is the exchange programme with Liaoning. In this case, the KPG attempted to deepen contacts with the people of China by extending and intensifying cultural and personal exchange programmes under the slogan from 'people-to-people exchange to people-to-people co-operation'. Since 1984 the KPG has dispatched technical advisers to Liaoning and received their technical trainees. The most well-known and successful exchange to date involved the dispatch of technical advisers to a bicycle factory in Liaoning Province. One of the advisers analysed the physical characteristics of Chinese women and designed a woman's bicycle based on human engineering techniques. The new model 'Miss Bai-Shan' has become very popular, not only in Liaoning but throughout China. This is only one, albeit the most well-known, example of the KPG's success in providing technical assistance to an affiliated state government, and, based on this and other similar experiences, the KPG now has plans to send increased numbers of technical advisers to other developing countries.

Peace policy

Kanagawa prefectural declaration against nuclear weapons

In June 1984, the Kanagawa prefectural declaration against nuclear weapons was adopted after approval by both the prefectural government and the prefectural assembly. The declaration states that:

The abolition of nuclear weapons and the realization of everlasting peace is an earnest desire shared by all the people of Japan, the only country in the world to have suffered nuclear bombing. We, the citizens of Kanagawa Prefecture, wholeheartedly reaffirm the strong desire of the Japanese people.

Today, heightening international tensions caused by expanding nuclear armaments are threatening world peace and even the survival of the human race. We cannot help but appeal around the world for the abolition of nuclear weapons and for disarmament.

It is our responsibility to preserve this beautiful land of ours for our children and grandchildren and to see that they will be able to enjoy a life worth living.

We, the citizens of Kanagawa Prefecture, therefore declare that the three non-nuclear principles of 'not possessing, not manufacturing, and not permitting the entry into Japan of nuclear weapons' adopted by the

Japanese government as a fundamental national policy has this day become our prefectural policy too.

The early 1980s witnessed the emergence of the most extensive anti-nuclear armaments movement in Western Europe in the postwar period. During the same period, serious debates also arose in Japan over security issues, particularly the continued viability and observance of Japan's three non-nuclear principles. As deployment of the SS20 and Tomahawk missiles clearly illustrated, the nuclear arms race between the two super-powers had spread in the area around the Japanese archipelago, and in May 1981 former US Ambassador to Japan, Edwin Reischauer, revealed that nuclear weapons had, in fact, been brought into Japan. These developments provided the stimulus for the creation of a Prefectural Peace Policy since, with the exception of Okinawa, the highest concentration of US military bases in Japan is in Kanagawa. Of particular importance were Yokohama and Yokosuka, the home port for US aircraft carriers, cruisers and many SSBMs. In addition, considerable unease was expressed over the US Naval Air Facility in Atsugi City where, from 1982, a large number of aircraft from the carrier *Midway* had been conducting night landing exercises. The resulting noise and accidents had become a constant concern for Japanese communities located near the base. Finding itself at the forefront of superpower militarization, the KPG urged both the Japanese government and US authorities to consider a reduction in the number of US military facilities.

Further impetus for the creation of a peace policy was generated by the demands made by local activists and some municipalities for a nuclear-free declaration from the KPG. By 1984, more than half the municipalities in Kanagawa had issued nuclear-free declarations, about sixty citizen and labour organizations had submitted letters to the prefectural government or assembly requesting declarations against nuclear weapons, and more than 1.5 million citizens had signed a petition demanding the elimination of nuclear arms.

Indeed, Governor Nagasu himself had played an active role in the peace movement and the promotion of peace policies since 1981. In response to Reischauer's 1981 disclosure, for instance, Nagasu requested both the Japanese and American governments to adhere strictly to the three non-nuclear principles. In 1982, the KPG sponsored a 'Non-Nuclear Appeal for Children and Grandchildren' and dispatched five local representatives to the Second UN Special Session of the General Assembly devoted to disarmament. Early in 1983, Nagasu took the initiative in issuing a declaration against nuclear weapons by stating in the prefectural assembly that he wished to make a prefectural declaration against nuclear weapons reflecting the resolution of the prefectural assembly. This address to the prefectural assembly was the true starting point of a grass-roots movement incorporating appeals, requests, letters and petitions. The climax of this development was the adoption of a prefectural declaration against nuclear weapons. As this brief summary illustrates, Nagasu's positive support for the anti-nuclear weapons declaration was crucial to its adoption.

Implementing peace policy

In the 1980s many local governments (both prefectural and municipal) throughout Japan issued similar anti-nuclear declarations. As of 1986, the total figure stood at 946 out of a total of 3,302 municipalities nationally. Since adopting its declaration, the KPG has carried out a variety of peace policies, including:

1   The delivery of the prefectural declaration to all nuclear powers, various UN agencies, and sister states and prefectures abroad.
2   Publicizing the declaration through the prefectural public affairs magazine, posters, TV spots and so forth.
3   Publishing a series of booklets that covered wide-ranging nuclear problems including *Nuclear Weapons Notebook* (1986) and *Kanagawa Prefectural Declaration against Nuclear Weapons* (1987).
4   Forming networks of like-minded local governments at home and abroad. The KPG has played a very important role in the Authorities Liaison Council for Nuclear-Free Zones and Peace, the aim of which is to co-ordinate the peace policies of Japan's nuclear-free local governments. It has also participated in the International Conference of Nuclear-Free Zones Local Authorities (Cordoba, Spain in 1984 and Perugia, Italy in 1986).
5   Sponsoring many international academic conferences in Yokohama, the themes of which have been peace, disarmament, development, human rights and so on.
6   Finally, in 1988, the KPG began construction of a Kanagawa International Peace Museum as part of a joint project with the Kanagawa International Children's Museum. This International Peace Museum will provide for the study of war and peace in order to encourage the citizens of Kanagawa to be aware of the value of peace and the horrors of war.

Economic exchange programme

The original objective of PPD was to promote peace through mutual understanding at the individual citizen's level. Although the KPG has carried out wide-ranging activities aimed at both creating friendly inter-prefectural relationships and promoting peace policies, there has been a tendency to give low priority to international economic issues. In the early

stages of PPD, reciprocal exchange of economic missions between Kanagawa and Maryland was the only noteworthy economic activity. However,
encouraged by the need to revitalize its own regional economy in the early
1980s, the KPG has gradually developed systematic economic policies.

Kanagawa has historically been a centre for heavy industries such as
steel, electrical engineering and machines. But, with the current structural
shift of the Japanese economy away from the older heavy industries, the
KPG took the decision to embark upon a restructuring of the regional
economy. For example, the Second Kanagawa Plan announced by the
KPG provided a comprehensive programme for technological development
within the regional economy. A representative project is the Kanagawa
Science Park, which opened in Kawasaki City in 1989. Kanagawa Science
Park operates as an information centre focusing upon research and
development in the area of advanced technology as well as a facility for
joint experimental research and development directed at small or medium-
sized high-technology companies.

The KPG's international economic policy was linked with this far-
sighted plan for restructuring the regional economy. Governor Nagasu
began to emphasize the importance of economic co-operation with foreign
companies and local governments from the mid-1980s. At a symposium on
internationalization at the local level, held in 1985, he stated that PPD
would be more viable if international economic co-operation were
regarded as a crucial aspect of international co-operation. In response, the
KPG has aimed at becoming an international centre for economic co-
operation. The KPG's strategy has been to create multilateral economic
sister-city relationships with counterpart cities abroad. As of 1986, twelve
local municipalities in Kanagawa had established relationships with thirty-
one counterpart cities in twelve countries. However, in most cases these
relationships were bilateral, without an overall co-ordinating policy. The
KPG has attempted to change this by establishing a multilateral sister-city
network with the assistance of local municipalities throughout Kanagawa.

The KPG has concentrated its efforts in the economic sector and
consensus was quickly arrived at with the municipalities involved that
internationalization in the economic field was of decisive importance in the
development of the Kanagawa regional economy. The result of these
efforts was the Inter-Local Economic Exposition (ILEX) held 25 April–
1 May 1986. The main achievement of the ILEX was to open an Economic
Exchange Fair where more than thirty foreign cities that had ties with the
local municipalities in Kanagawa participated. The KPG has also pushed
forward joint projects for developing technology with counterpart cities
abroad. In the area of high technology, the KPG has maintained joint
projects with Baden-Württemberg in Germany, where many high-technology companies are located. Both the KPG and the state government of
Baden-Württemberg have invited high-technology industries from the

other side to their own high-technology industrial zones. As a result, some companies from Baden-Württemberg have begun operating in the Hakusan High-Tech Park in Yokohama. Japanese companies, however, have thus far had few incentives to expand their businesses into Germany.

The international economic policy of the KPG has not been restricted to the advanced countries. On the contrary, the KPG has oriented its policies towards the developing countries and top priority has been given to 'Minsai-kyōryoku', or economic assistance at the local level. the KPG has carried out its policy of economic assistance mainly in the following three fields.

The first phase of the KPG's economic assistance policy was to encourage the citizens of Kanagawa to gain a good understanding of North–South issues. For this purpose the KPG has published a series of booklets entitled Tami-chan. These were designed so that readers, especially children, could deepen their understanding of the present situation in the Third World by following Tami-chan's gradual appreciation of the gap between the North and South; global poverty; hunger and environmental damage; and also of the potential for economic assistance at the citizen's level. These booklets have been highly rated both by specialists in Third World Studies and by junior school teachers. The next phase in the programme was to promote technological assistance and transfer. Kanagawa has been very active in sending technical advisers to Third World Countries and in receiving trainees from them in return.

A further positive step taken by the KPG was to set up the Kanagawa Prefectural International Training Centre in 1987. This centre provides facilities for accommodation and training of representatives from Third World countries. The third initiative taken by the KPG has been to support the development of economic assistance programmes sponsored by various NGOs. This idea had its origins in the re-evaluation of the Central Government's Overseas Development Agency (ODA) budget. Although Japanese ODA had grown enormously in recent years, it has been criticized on the grounds that many projects are too strongly business orientated, and that economic assistance from the private sector is much smaller than that given in other advanced countries. The KPG has aimed at improving the quality of economic assistance by co-operating with grass-roots groups, such as the Japanese Volunteer Centre (JVC), and has engaged in private economic assistance. As a part of this policy, the KPG is now planning to start a local ODA programme with the support of grass-roots groups.

'People-to-People Diplomacy At Home'

In an English language pamphlet produced by the KPG, the basic objectives of 'PPD At Home' may be summarized as follows.

In the past, attention has not been paid to several tens of thousands of

Korean and Chinese living in Kanagawa Prefecture. In spite of the fact that
they should be regarded as 'equal residents', it is true to say that they still
suffer from deeply rooted prejudice and unreasonable discrimination.
Positive efforts are now being made to redress past and present injustices.
It is the ultimate goal to make Kanagawa an open community where people
of different nationalities and ethnic origins can enjoy harmonious lives.
Efforts to this end are termed 'People-to-People Diplomacy at Home', a
policy which Kanagawa Prefecture has spearheaded in Japan. 'PPD at
Home' – in other words, the internal internationalization of Kanagawa –
has become a top priority for the PPD in recent years. This was largely a
result of Governor Nagasu's conviction that unless discrimination against
foreign residents, particularly Korean and Chinese, was eliminated,
Kanagawa could not legitimize the basic idea of PPD, that of harmonious
'living together'. The generation of concrete policies aimed at ending
discrimination has also been stimulated by such issues as the arrival of
Indo-Chinese and other refugees, the growing number of overseas
students, and the recent influx of migrant workers from Asia.

The policy of 'PPD at Home' had two points of origin. First was the so-
called fingerprinting issue of the early 1980s. At the time, the Alien Registration Law of Japan, which has since been partially revised, required that
all aliens over the age of 16 who had resided in Japan for more than one
year renew their alien registration every five years. The law also obliged
foreigners to undergo fingerprinting, not only at the time of initial registration, but at each subsequent renewal of their alien registration. The entire
procedure had been delegated by the national government to local authorities throughout Japan. Early in the 1980s, a small number of Korean residents began to protest against these procedures, particularly fingerprinting,
claiming that these violated their human rights. When the Koreans were
prosecuted for infringement of the Alien Registration Law, some municipalities in Kanagawa came out in support of the protesters and made clear
their intention to sabotage the system. In the mid-1980s the fingerprinting
controversy became increasingly serious, both domestically and internationally, and has yet to be satisfactorily resolved.

The second point of origin was the suggestion by the International
Division of the KPG that the government should pay more attention to the
everyday lives of Korean and Chinese residents in Kanagawa. In response,
the KPG set up a study group on foreign residents in Kanagawa, and at the
same time publicized the problems faced by non-Japanese residents by
issuing several pamphlets. In 1985 the Kanagawa Prefecture Alien Residence Survey Committee published the results of a two-year study. This
survey covered only Korean and Chinese residents – since they accounted
for approximately three-quarters of all non-Japanese residents in
Kanagawa (Koreans numbered about 30,000, or 60 per cent of the total;
Chinese about 7,000, equivalent to 15 per cent), and had suffered a long

history of discrimination. This was the first such survey published by a local government in Japan since 1945. The results of this survey clearly revealed the circumstances of Korean and Chinese residents, and presented evidence that there remained considerable discrimination against them in such diverse areas as employment, welfare, education and so on. It also highlighted the fact that prejudice against them remains deeply rooted in Japanese society and that, for Korean and Chinese residents, the local community is a difficult place in which to live. Finally, the report suggested ways in which the prefectural government should respond in order to remodel Japanese society in such a way that non-Japanese residents could participate fully in the life of the community. In this way the local community could be a truly open society worthy of the title 'internationalized'. Based on the committee's proposals and in response to appeals from other concerned organizations, the KPG began to implement policies designed to improve the legal status and lives of non-Japanese residents, particularly Korean and Chinese. The following steps were among those taken.

1   The KPG decided to employ non-Japanese residents as technical staff within the medical service, engineering and education departments, excluding them only from the general administration staff. This exclusion is due to national legislation (Local Officials Act) which restricts the employment of non-Japanese by local governments.
2   The KPG has become increasingly active in dispelling prejudice against Korean and Chinese residents by encouraging the Japanese citizens of Kanagawa to become aware of the problems faced by their neighbours. In 1987, the KPG published a pamphlet for junior readers entitled *Living Together*, which included a short historical survey of the Korean community, a description of everyday life, and the history of discrimination against Korean residents in Kanagawa.
3   The KPG has made several efforts to formulate new fundamental policies that would complement internationalization at home, particularly in the field of human rights. In 1987, the KPG set up a study group on the promotion and protection of international human rights at the local level, and in 1988 cosponsored with the United Nations University the International Conference on Human Rights and the Citizen to commemorate the Fortieth Anniversary of the Universal Declaration of Human Rights.

CONCLUSION

The various programmes and projects which have been outlined here have not been without their critics, but, on the whole, Kanagawa's policy of PPD has been highly regarded not only by specialists in international relations and local administrators, but by citizens and grass-roots groups throughout Japan. Given Governor Nagasu's critical role in the formulation and implementation of strategies designed to encourage 'internationalization' throughout Kanagawa, it seems appropriate to conclude with an excerpt from one of his speeches. In it, he provides a broad outline for the future course of 'People-to-People Diplomacy':

> The people of the world are confronted with enormous changes. The various manifestations of the interdependence which has united the nations of the world more than ever before make us conscious that the global era is approaching. Perhaps the most encouraging development is that the concept of a common humanity has come to exert influence over central government activities in many countries. And where it has not, at least the dawning of it is discernible. At the same time, not only government-to-government relations, but also business-to-business relations, people-to-people relations and international relations between local communities have come to play a more important role in the thinking and activities of the people concerned. People now act and think on a worldwide scale.

NOTE

The material which forms the basis of this chapter is taken from unpublished documents of Kanagawa Prefecture.

Part V

Labour markets and migrant workers

Chapter 11

Migrant workers

The Japanese case in international perspective

Yoko Sellek and Michael A. Weiner

INTRODUCTION

In the coming decade Japan will face numerous challenges to its traditional identity as it seeks ways to address its new reponsibilities as an economic superpower. Among these will be the treatment of foreign workers, re- fugees and foreign students. Indeed, Japan's willingness to confront such issues will be viewed by many as a litmus test of its ability to assume the social and political roles of a major participant in world affairs. Over the past decade, the LDP government has attempted to deflect international pressure by, on the one hand, increasing its budget for overseas develop- ment assistance and expanding the number of places available at Japanese universities for foreign students, while, on the other hand, resisting demands to relax constraints on the entry of refugees and unskilled foreign workers. The issue of foreign workers, in particular, has been widely debated in the media. Proponents have argued that the employment of foreign labour would provide an opportunity to internationalize the domestic labour market at the same time as meeting labour shortages in particular industries. Others argue that migration to Japan is the inevitable result of the widening economic gap that exists between Japan and the developing nations of Asia; an outcome which cannot be 'legislated' away, and which could constitute part of Japan's economic assistance to these countries. Opponents, however, contend that the admission of migrant workers would have an adverse affect on general working conditions; would lead to the creation of an exploited underclass of poorly paid foreigners whose assimilation into a racially homogeneous society would prove impossible; and would give rise to a host of new social problems.

Given the tone of the debate as it has unfolded over the past few years, the migration of foreign workers to Japan may appear to be a recent phenomenon. Nothing, of course, could be further from the truth, as attested to by the presence of nearly 1 million people of Korean descent. It is equally important to recognize that, while the recent migration to Japan of workers from parts of South East Asia, Bangladesh, the Philippines and

South Korea exhibits certain specific characteristics, generally speaking there is nothing new about movements of this type. Capitalist development has always been dependent upon the migration of labour both within and across national boundaries, and the social history of Japanese industrialization is no exception to this rule. This latest phase in the internationalization of labour, involving the movement of workers from the peripheral and semi-peripheral dependencies of East Asia to the Japanese centre, should therefore be viewed not only as reflecting Japan's regional economic hegemony, but as a structural characteristic of the world capitalist economy.

Although Japan's present Immigration Law expressly prohibits the entry of unskilled workers, the government has considered this issue on at least three separate occasions during the past twenty years.[1] On each occasion, the state has rejected the option of permitting the recruitment of foreign workers, largely on the grounds that such an influx might endanger the seamless racial homogeneity of Japanese society. Such racial discourse is, of course, not unique to Japan, but has been used extensively with reference to certain types of immigration flows into Western Europe and the United States for more than a century. In the postwar period, however, unlike its Western counterparts, Japanese capital has, until recently, relied exclusively upon internal rural–urban migrations to meet its labour needs. In the past few years this situation has altered and large numbers of illegal foreign workers have entered the labour market to take on the jobs vacated by indigenous workers in certain sectors of the economy. Although the numbers have remained small, relative to the millions of temporary workers who entered Western Europe during the 1960s and the Gulf states during the 1970s, the intensity of the current debate reflects both the increasing flow of international migrants in response to the labour market needs of Japan, and the continued relevance of racial discourse within Japan.

Since the late 1970s, the international expansion of the Japanese economy has been very rapid. This period has been characterized principally by the strong yen and trade conflicts with the United States and Europe, but has also seen marked growth in the international exchange of 'goods', 'capital' and 'labour'. Certain aspects of 'labour' in particular, including technology, organizations and human capital, have moved beyond national boundaries and have become interdependent with the economies of other countries. Within this restructuring of the world economy, there has arisen a greater need for Japanese companies to employ highly skilled foreign workers.[2] The total number of foreign employees working within the scope of existing immigration law was estimated at about 36,000 at the end of 1987. This represents an 80 per cent increase over the corresponding figure for 1984.[3] The law states quite clearly that when a foreign national seeks employment, the 'authorities examine carefully the necessity of the proposed employment, considering factors such as the non-availability of, or possible substitution by, a Japanese national, the academic and/or professional career of the applicant, the conditions of employment, and the size and status of the potential employer'.[4] Foreign nationals qualifying for legal employment in Japan include entertainers, specialist business people, skilled labourers, academics, technicians and others who may benefit from special consideration. Table 11.1 indicates the status of residence under which engagement in professional or occupational activites is authorized by the government.

The employment of foreign nationals in categories other than those mentioned above is deemed to be illegal. Illegal employment also includes foreign employees who have engaged in activities other than those permitted under the status of residence, as well as individuals who have remained in Japan beyond the authorized period of residence. Such persons are usually referred to as 'illegal migrant workers'.[5] In 1986 there were an estimated 20,000 illegal migrant workers in Japan. By the end of 1987, this figure had more than doubled to approximately 50,000, with a further doubling occurring in 1988.[6] This increase is also reflected in the number of illegal workers apprehended by the police over the same period, with the number rising to over 14,000 in 1988, a sixfold increase over the corresponding figure for 1983. Despite the relatively small numbers

Table 11.1 The List of Status of Residence under which engagement in professional or occupational activities is authorized by the Japanese government

Status of Residence	Qualifying persons
4-1-5	Persons engaged in management of business, foreign trade or capital investment.
4-1-7	Lecturers and professors in full-time teaching at educational/research institutes.
4-1-9	Paid entertainers such as singers, actors, professional athletes, their managers and entourage.
4-1-12	Persons invited by public or private bodies in Japan for the purpose of furnishing high-level or specialized skills and know-how.
4-1-13	Persons engaging in skilled labour, e.g. cooks.
4-1-16-3	Persons who do not fall under any other status but are authorized to stay at the discretion of the Minister of Justice.

Note: The number in the three numerical series of status of residence designations indicate the article, paragraph and item or the Immigration-Control and Refugee-Recognition Act under which the status falls. Thus, 4-1-15 indicates Article 4, Paragraph 1, Item 5.
Source: The Immigration-Control and Refugee-Recognition Act.

involved, the government initiated a review of its policies concerning the entry of both skilled and unskilled foreign workers in 1987. The fundamental concern has been whether the government should ease restrictions on the entry and employment of foreign labour in the unskilled sector, further strengthen existing restrictions, or search for alternative solutions.[7] The recent revision of the Immigration Control Act (June 1990), while enlarging the scope of working activities for foreigners in certain skilled or professional categories, has further tightened the regulations concerning the recruitment and employment of unskilled foreign workers. In future, labour brokers and employers found guilty of hiring foreigners without proper visas will be subject either to fines up to maximum of ¥3,000,000, or up to three years' imprisonment.[8]

Lying behind these changes were the often expressed fears that a continued influx of unskilled migrant labour would generate social tensions identical to those experienced in a number of Western European nations. Anxieties were particularly strong over what may be termed cultural or ethnic contamination: the fear that temporary workers might over time be transformed into permanent settlers and marginalized into ethnic minorities. Such concerns are by no means unique to Japan and reflect a more generalized awareness that however much employers and governments may wish to regard migrant labour as a flexible and low-cost response to labour shortages, any short-term benefits may be outweighed by the long-term social and political costs.[9] That is to say, as workers they come to exert not only an influence on the balance of supply and demand in labour markets, but also on the economic and political environment in the countries from which they come and which receive them.

The remainder of this chapter will be given over to a discussion of the movement of foreign workers to Japan, set against the background of international labour migrations in the postwar period. After considering the various incentives underlying the international movement of labour, the Japanese case will be assessed in some detail. Particular emphasis will be placed on ascertaining why the issue of migrant workers, who constitute less than 0.3 per cent of the population, has generated such a furious debate in Japan.

Because Japanese terminology does not always provide a precise equivalent in English, the authors would like to make clear that the term 'unskilled labour' will be used in the context of labour requiring a low level of skill and providing very low levels of remuneration. Unskilled labourers (*tanjun rōdōsha*) are not necessarily 'unskilled' in terms of the quality of their labour, but are described as unskilled in terms of the type of work demanded of them.[10] Indeed, unskilled labourers may have been employed in areas requiring moderate or high levels of skill in the sending countries, but take on jobs requiring lower levels of skill in the receiving countries.

FOREIGN WORKERS IN THE CONTEXT OF THE GLOBAL MOVEMENT OF LABOUR

Studies of international migration have usually concentrated on three inter-related processes: the causes of migration; the focus of migration; and the consequences of migration. The causes and consequences of migration, in particular, have been the subject of numerous studies.[11] If this framework is applied to labour migration alone, the following issues need to be taken into account:

1 the incentives for migration, and
2 the influence of migration on the individual migrant worker and his/her family; on the receiving country or region; on the sending country or region; and on the relationship between the respective countries or regions.

In order to examine the second point, *viz.* the influence or consequences of migration, it is necessary to construct a framework of relevant factors and areas of influence. The Board of the Economic Planning Committee of MITI concluded that the factors which influence the receiving nations are:

1 the age, educational level and skills possessed by prospective migrant;
2 whether skilled labour is required and, if so, whether some form of technical training for migrants will be necessary;
3 how long migrants will be permitted to remain in employment, and the attitude of both sending and receiving countries towards the issue of family reunification; and
4 the legal status of migrant workers in the receiving country.

The same report identified the areas of influence as:

1 the migrant worker him/herself;
2 the economies, industries and labour markets (including the potential impact on unemployment and economic growth) in receiving nations or regions;
3 the societies, cultures and *national characteristics* of the receiving nations or regions, seen here in terms of acculturation or assimilation in the receiving nation; and
4 the international relations and domestic political environment of the receiving countries.

INCENTIVES TO PROMOTE THE MOVEMENT OF LABOUR

Why do people migrate? This is a question of enormous complexity, and one which does not lend itself to simple economistic answers. However, when discussing the incentives of individual migrant workers, there is a general consensus that, with the exception of political refugees and other types of involuntary migration such as the expulsion of Asians from Uganda in the 1970s, people crossing national boundaries in search of employment do so with the expectation that the benefit created by such migration will exceed any loss or cost associated with it. Migrants hope and/or judge that the market value of their labour will be greater in one location than in another – over and above transaction costs.

Most researchers into labour migration have approached the issue of incentives in one of two ways: by focusing on the objective/structural factors which influence individual workers; or by attempting to answer the question why, given a uniform set of objective/structural factors, some people choose to migrate while others do not. In other words, the emphasis is placed on the migrant's subjective account of incentives and his/her perception, evaluation and definition of his/her situation.

As Taylor has argued, however, there are particular problems associated with each approach. If we follow the first approach, that of assessing incentives purely on the basis of the influence exerted by objective-structural factors, then differential perception and evaluation tend to be ignored, whereas purposive-rational behaviour tends to be over-emphasized.[12] The traditional economistic 'push–pull' model is based on this approach, and suggests that migration is due to socio-economic imbalances between regions which result in certain factors 'pushing' persons away from an area of origin while others 'pull' them to an area of destination. Taylor concludes that this model 'subsumes all motives under the assumption of the maximization of want-satisfactions, so that the complex decision to migrate is reduced to a kind of mechanical balance of external and impersonal forces'.[13]

The second approach, based on the migrant's subjective account of incentives, is equally problematic given the enormous difficulties involved in assessing personal factors, such as intelligence, confidence and awareness of conditions which enter into the migrant's perception and evaluation of his or her own situation. As Jansen points out, without a reliable social survey, very little can be gleaned from the migrants themselves about their personal reasons for moving.[14] It is equally important to distinguish 'real' reasons from 'stated' reasons supplied by migrant workers.[15] Numerous attempts have been made by other commentators to develop alternatives to the 'push–pull' model by combining these two approaches.[16] Although research in this area is not yet well developed in Japan, some preliminary studies have been carried out.[17]

One such study on migration incentives was that undertaken by the Board of the Economic Planning Committee of Japan in 1989. The approach taken by the committee was largely limited to an investigation of the objective-structural factors influencing migration. It did, however, introduce 'evaluation' by individual migrant workers in order to 'screen' the objective-structural factors. A second modification of the conventional approach involved the application of a 'feedback' system which allowed for a degree of interlinking between objectively measured factors and individual incentives in the decision-making processes of migrant workers. It also introduced two distinct concepts, which are referred to as 'disparity' and 'network'.[18] In the present context, these two concepts, along with the historical 'factor' (the history of earlier migrations), have been employed to analyse the inducements of migrant workers in the case of Japan.

The decision-making process of individual migrant workers

The decision-making process of individual migrant workers as outlined by The Board of the Economic Planning Committee of Japan may be summarized in the following way.

In the first instance, migrant worker X evaluates his or her present conditions and the 'disparity' between 'expected benefit' and 'predicted loss' in terms of wages, job opportunities, lifestyle, and so on. The individual migrant also evaluates the system or 'network' which makes the movement possible and finds out how easy it is to move. As a result of these two evaluations, he/she may choose to move. Once the initial journey has been completed, the migrant will repeatedly re-evaluate the situation on the basis of post-migration experiences in the receiving nation. This may eventuate in the migrant seeking settler or permanent resident status.

This report regards the concepts of 'disparity' and 'network' to be of critical importance in the decision-making process. 'If the movement of labour is compared to a flow of water, disparity indicates water pressure. However, the flow of water will be reduced if the water channel is narrow. Network indicates a system or channel which allows the flow of water to run easily minimizing obstructions.'[19]

Disparity

Migration is governed by various incentives, but it should be noted that these incentives are subject to value judgement and evaluation by each individual migrant. Three principal incentives are likely to become subject to value judgement.

The first factor to be considered is, of course, the relative availability and demand for labour in the sending and receiving regions or nations. This is generally the case in internal rural–urban migrations where rural poverty precipitates movement off the land in search of employment in the cities. The greater the differentials between regions within a country, in terms of employment opportunities and wages, the more active migration will become. The principal destinations for such migrations have traditionally been the major commercial and industrial centres of the country concerned. As Todaro has noted, one of the most significant of postwar demographic phenomena, and the one that promises to loom even larger in the future, is the rapid growth of cities in developing nations.[20]

The geographic distribution of population in many developing nations is highly unbalanced in favour of the urban centres where most industrial production is concentrated. The supply of workers exceeds the demand for labour and this results in extremely high rates of unemployment or under-employment in urban areas. In many instances, internal rural–urban migration is considered as the most significant factor contributing to the size and rapid growth of urban populations and unemployment problems. The chance of obtaining a job in an urban area is closely related to the unemployment rate and this sort of self-limiting situation may drive the flow of labour abroad. According to Jansen,

> differential migration is the selectivity of certain persons or the tendency of certain groups (sex, age, class, and so on) to be more migratory than others ... to date the only differential which seems to have stood the test, in research undertaken in various countries and at various times, is that persons of young adult ages 20–34 are more prone to migrate than other groups.[21]

On the other hand, in the advanced countries the birth rate has been decreasing, more people are moving into the older age bracket and, in general, there is a shortage in the young workforce. As Castles points out, the expansion of mass production requires 'increasing division of labour, conveyor-line production, shift-work and piece work'. Castles further comments:

> This form of growth meant not only an increase in the number of workers needed, but also deskilling of large sections of the labour force. The new jobs were often dirty, monotonous, unhealthy and unpleasant. In a situation of expanding employment opportunities, some sections of the indigeneous workforce were able to refuse such jobs and move into skilled, supervisory and white-collar positions. Expansion could only be sustained by the large-scale import of workers compelled by their social, economic and legal position to take unpleasant jobs.[22]

Because of the increasing unavailability of indigenous workers and in an effort to obtain new sources of cheap labour, entrepreneurs will invest in automation at home while extracting both capital and production processes, particularly in low-technology and labour-intensive industries.[23] However, there are some industries which find it difficult or impossible to take such steps owing to their nature and the amount of the capital available. It is in these industries that the influx of migrant workers is generally most welcomed.

Economic incentive

The concept of disparity also includes economic inducement as an important factor in labour migration. This encompasses 'differences in working conditions and working hours, the stability of employment opportunities, the cost of movement, the cost of living, liability to taxation, social insurance benefits, and opportunities to acquire particular skills'.[24] The fundamental incentive here is the 'net income' for the individual migrant worker. In calculating this, the worker subtracts the actual costs of living in the receiving nation and the cost of travelling from the sending nation from the expected income and possible acquisition of skill through migration. Therefore, if large disparities exist in respective levels of economic development, especially in income levels between the sending and receiving countries, the movement of workers is driven by incentives of higher standards of living through working in a country of higher income and, in many cases, the possibility of being able to send money home.

Psychological incentive

Finally, there is the psychological incentive, which comprises such things as 'language, religion, distance between native country and receiving country, the acceptance of foreign workers by the nationals of the receiving country, the stability of the receiving society, possibilities for permanent residence'.[25] If the major international flows of labour today are considered, it is apparent that migrant workers do not necessarily move solely for reasons of economic inducement. For example, there is a tendency for workers to move between countries which share a common religious or cultural history, and also to move to neighbouring countries.[26] It has been suggested that 'one reason why there are many Pakistani and Bangladeshi workers in the Middle East is that they can continue with their own religion without hindrance or difficulty'.[27]

These are the three principal constituent incentives within the disparity concept. However, although marked differences may exist in the numbers of available workers, the supply and demand for labour, economic conditions, psychological elements, etc., in order to realize the movement of workers it is essential that there be a system, or 'network', to facilitate that movement. The existence of networks is thus another important determinant and in itself represents a concept governing labour migration.

Network

A network is a system which 'connects a sending country and a receiving country and which facilitates the movement of workers. It implies not only the support received when workers try to enter a country, but, more importantly, implies a system forming a "migration chain".'[28] This concept also takes into account the immigration control systems of both countries, labour agencies, transportation systems, and geographical conditions at the time when the migrants move. When the migrants start working, the concept comprises recruiters, information sources on employment, and the means to acquire practical know-how.

A further important component is communication with the migrants' countries of origin, which includes the means to receive and send information, the remittance system, and the ease or difficulty with which they can temporarily leave and re-enter the receiving country. The probability of obtaining work after returning home, and the possibility of settling down and becoming naturalized in the receiving country will also be components of any network.[29] All these factors contribute to the structure of the network and will play an important role in determining whether a mass movement of labour will occur.

It was suggested in the report of the Board of the Economic Planning Committee[30] that 'well-established networks can account for the movement of workers between particular pairs of countries' in addition to psychological incentives. They took as an example the present situation in Western European countries which are considered to constitute one of the major receiving areas in the world. When these countries opened their doors to large numbers of foreign workers in the late 1950s and 1960s, they formed a number of agreements for the recruitment of labour and thus established networks. In the case of West Germany, agreements were made with Italy, Greece, Spain, Turkey, Morocco, Portugal, Tunisia and Yugoslavia, and resulted in a threefold increase in the number of foreign labourers in that country between 1955 and 1960. In addition, certain Western European states have adopted policies such as offering migrant workers the same civil rights as other citizens and encouraging naturalization, which have further facilitated the expansion of networks.

Networks can be found in the movement of people between former colonies and the imperial power. In the case of Britain, for example, the major source of migrants after the Second World War and during the 1950s was the New Commonwealth (India, Pakistan and the West Indies).[31] By the mid-1950s, about 30,000 'black' workers were entering Britain every year without restriction and this flow continued until it was interrupted by declining economic demand. For Commonwealth citizens, special permission to enter Britain was not needed until 1962, and there were no legal obstacles to family migration until 1971.[32] In general, colonial migrants were afforded better legal rights than ordinary guest-worker type migrants, since the networks were originally established by the receiving nations (i.e., the metropolitan or colonial states).

Several examples of networks formed by governments have been cited, but networks can also appear in the private sector. In most cases the migrant worker's community is composed of his/her fellow migrants, all of whom transmit information about the situation in the receiving country to their friends and families at home. This in itself may give rise to a new influx of people who are connected in some way to the individual migrant such as his/her relatives, acquaintances or friends. Thus, by living in an environment which is not so very different from that of their native countries, the psychological pressure of living in a foreign country is somewhat reduced. At the same time, they create a block economic condition within the community and reduce their costs of living. In other words, they not only create a network, but further enhance labour flow by having a feedback effect through economic and other inducements.[33]

THE JAPANESE CASE

Disparity

Incentive caused by imbalances in the supply and demand for labour

The Japanese labour force has remained relatively stable thoughout much of the postwar period, with an annual rate of increase in the region of 1 per cent. However, following the anticipated labour peak in the mid-1990s, the number of school-leavers and other young people available for work is expected to decline and will not increase again for a least two decades.[34] Hayashi has predicted that 'if the labour force decreases gradually, the potential capability of economic supply in Japan will drop unless there is an influx of labour from outside or the productivity of labour increases by means of technological improvement'.[35] This process will be complemented by the depopulation of farming areas, which were the major sources of cheap, seasonal labour for Japanese industry in the 1960s and 1970s.

If this is the quantity side of demand, there is also a quality side which is associated with the unbalanced structure of the industrial market in Japan. Since the period of high economic growth in the 1970s, Japan has been trying to promote mechanization and robotization at home, while investing heavily in South East Asian countries where cheap and ready sources of labour exist. But the shortage of labour remains a very serious problem in industries demanding manual labour as well as in industries where labour cannot easily be exported, such as construction, demolition, small-sized manufacturing, and the service industry. The construction industry is a particularly good example, since it also typifies those areas in which there has been a consistent demand for foreign labour. Postwar reconstruction led to a boom in the construction industry which peaked in the mid-1960s and coincided with the Tokyo Olympics of 1964. During this lengthy period of expansion, the workforce also increased, absorbing both full-time and seasonal workers drawn principally from rural areas.

However, the 'administrative reforms' of the early 1980s which limited both public and private sector investment in new plants and equipment, led to a recession in the construction industry. Many workers were laid off or left their jobs and very few young people joined the industry's workforce during the next few years. Since 1986, however, the construction industry has steadily expanded. This has largely been a result of the government's implementation of certain recommendations contained in the Maekawa Report, the main purpose of which was to stimulate domestic demand. The sudden increase in the amount of capital available, which resulted from the easing of government regulations on both public and private sector investment, helped accelerate the redevelopment of cities and the construction of new buildings. The total amount of investment in the construction industry was around ¥50 billion between 1980 and 1985, but rose to ¥54 billion in 1986, ¥61 billion in 1987, ¥66 billion in 1988, and was expected to exceed ¥70 billion in 1989.[36]

In marked contrast to the situation in the 1950s and 1960s, however, the construction industry has been unable to draw on traditional sources of cheap labour, and this has resulted in a serious shortage of both skilled and unskilled workers. In addition to the difficulty in recruiting younger workers, it was estimated that about 40 per cent of the construction workers employed in 1988 were aged over 50. The main reason behind this trend is that labour conditions in the construction industry are far worse than in other industries. The expression '*Roku-K*' (six-K) in Japanese, which describes such industries as '*Kitanai*' (dirty), '*Kitsui*' (hard work), '*Kiken*' (dangerous), '*Kyūryō ga yasui*' (low wages), '*Kyūjitsu ga sukanai*' (few holidays) and '*Kakko ga warui*' (requiring little intelligence), graphically illustrates the unpopularity of the industry. Working outside, often in tall buildings and in inclement weather, involves taking serious risks, and the number of injuries and deaths in the industry is very high.[37] The average overtime per month is 120–150 hours and weekend holidays are rare. The average monthly income of unskilled workers in the industry is about 30 per cent less than that of unskilled workers in the manufacturing sector.[38]

Komai points out that 'the basis of these low wages and insecure working conditions was the existence of a stratified subcontract system'.[39] This stratified subcontract system is a hierarchical arrangement in which the prime subcontractor A subcontracts to B, who in turn subcontracts to C, and so on. This system has functioned as a safety valve for employers, allowing adjustment for economic and or seasonal fluctuations. It has also transferred the pressure on the prime subcontractor from the original contractor to the shoulders of the smaller subcontractors. At present there are about 5.5 million subcontractors working in the construction industry, and three-quarters of them work out of doors.[40] Among the 14,314 illegal migrant workers arrested in 1988, 26.8 per cent were working in the construction industry. Most of them were employed on light or unskilled jobs, such as fabricating scaffolding, demolishing buildings and other miscellaneous occupations. It has been reported that about half of the workers currently engaged in demolition work are migrant labourers.[41]

The situation among small to medium-sized manufacturing companies is very similar to that in the construction industry. To minimize labour costs, the larger manufacturing companies have increased their overseas investments while updating technology in Japanese factories and relying on the 'flexible production system' and 'computer-integrated manufacturing systems'. In practice, however, sufficient labour is not even available to produce the machines for these systems. This shortage of labour is even more acute among the smaller manufacturers who have played a major role in Japan's economic development during the postwar period. The hierarchically structured subcontracting system which characterizes the construction industry also exists in manufacturing, and two-thirds of all manufacturers are subcontractors.[42] There is a strong relationship between a given parent company and each subcontractor, with the latter subservient to the requirements of the former. Recently, parent companies have begun to exercise tighter controls over their subcontractors by, for example, demanding reductions in both the cost of goods and in delivery times. In these circumstances, working conditions in subcontracting companies have tended to deteriorate, making the recruitment and retention of labour even more difficult. Among illegal migrant workers arrested in 1988, 25.5 per cent were working for small and medium-sized manufacturers in, for example, the metal, food, printing, automobile or electronics industries.

Based on the mass production system, which has supported Japan's economic development since the Second World War, specialization in terms of function of labour in various industries has also expanded. Service industries not only operate across a variety of sectors, but new types of service industry have also emerged, such as the information industry, the manpower supply industry and the building maintenance industry. The development of these industries has produced an enormous number of job opportunities, and, in general, a shortage of labour can be found in those fields where working conditions are poor. In 1988, 12.9 per cent of illegal migrant workers arrested worked in service industries in positions such as building caretakers, window cleaners, messengers, security workers, refuse collectors, housekeepers, waitresses and waiters.[43]

The entertainment industry, particularly those areas referred to as the 'sex industry', relies almost exclusively on female 'labour'. In spite of the decreasing number of young Japanese women willing to work in this sector, the social demand has, if anything, increased. Between 1979 and 1987 most illegal migrant workers in Japan were young females working in this industry. Of 5,085 female illegal workers arrested in 1988, 87.3 per cent were hostesses, strippers or prostitutes. This number represents 32.9 per cent of the total number of illegal workers, both female and male, in the same year.[44] It has often been suggested that the so-called 'water trades' perform a vital function within Japanese society. According to this argument, Japanese businessmen are 'corporate soldiers', who are forced to work long and hard, whose lives are controlled by their companies and who often feel isolated. Such men partake of the favours provided by the sex industry as a way of relieving the pressures of the workplace. Within this closed system, it is further argued, both the businessmen and the women who provide them with comfort have significantly contributed to the development of the Japanese economy.[45]

The shortage of indigenous labour in the above-mentioned industries has been a major factor in the recent influx of migrant workers from other Asian countries. Before considering the imbalance in the supply and demand for labour in these countries, it may be useful to identify certain characteristics of the unskilled migrant workers coming to Japan. According to research carried out by the Immigration Bureau in Japan, a breakdown of the 14,314 illegal, unskilled migrant workers deported in 1988 may be summarized as follows:

1   By nationality: Filipinos, 37.6 per cent; Bangladeshis, 20.5 per cent; Pakistanis, 17.4 per cent; Thais, 9.6 per cent; Koreans, 7.2 per cent; Chinese (Taiwanese), 3.6 per cent; and others, 4.1 per cent.

2   By sex: males, 62.4 per cent; females, 37.6 per cent. Among Filipinos, 31.3 per cent were men, while among Thais the corresponding figure was 26.5 per cent. Filipinos and Thais formed 87.5 per cent of all female illegal immigrants. In comparison, of all male illegal immigrants, Bangladeshis, Pakistanis, Filipinos together constituted 79.7 per cent of the total. Table 11.2 shows the trend in illegal workers deported between 1982 and 1988 according to sex and major nationality.

3   By age: those between the ages of 20 and 40 constituted 89 per cent of the total number deported (1987 figures). Of females, 83 per cent were in their twenties (most in their early twenties).

4   By length of employment: approximately 80 per cent had worked for less than one year (1986 figure).

5   By level of earnings: 40.6 per cent of male and 30.9 per cent of female illegal migrant workers deported in 1986 claimed they had earned between ¥100,000 and ¥500,000 per month (equivalent to approximately £400–£2,000). It should be noted, however, that as these figures are based on personal claims by the deportees, they may contain significant inaccuracies.[46]

In addition to the number of illegal workers deported each year, numerous would-be workers using forged passports or visas, or in some other way

Table 11.2 The number of foreigners refused entry 1983–8

	1983	1984	1985	1986	1987	1988
Pakistani	7	79	153	596	1,355	4,288
Bangladeshi	0	24	18	146	707	3,233
Korean	197	68	53	80	133	1,070
Thai	191	184	343	457	389	996
Malaysian	2	18	7	2	40	394
Filipino	588	633	417	929	1,034	365
Chinese (Taiwanese)	277	203	224	402	293	253
Others	115	105	125	139	200	508

Source: The Statistics of the Immigration Bureau of the Ministry of Justice, as cited in Board of the Economic Planning Committee (1989: 155).

attempting to conceal the purpose of their visit to Japan, are turned away by immigration officials at the time of their arrival. Table 11.2 illustrates the recent trend in the numbers of workers refused entry according to nationality.

Most commentators are agreed that the outflow of migrant workers from Asian countries has passed through three stages since the Second World War.[47] According to Komai, for example, the first stage involved the outflow from former colonies to the metropolitan or colonizing states. This would include the movement of workers, and in some cases their families, from India and Pakistan to Britain, from the Philippines to the United States, and from Korea to Japan. The second stage was the outflow of Asian workers to various destinations in the Middle East and, in particular, the Gulf states during the construction boom which followed the oil shock of 1973. The third stage, which has been with us since 1985, has been characterized by a decrease in the demand for migrant workers in the Middle East owing to the decline in the number of new construction projects throughout the region. It has been predicted that many Asian countries will begin the search for new areas where they can export surplus labour.

Todaro classifies the common characteristics of developing countries into six broad categories:

> low levels of living, low levels of productivity, high rates of population growth and dependency burdens, high and rising levels of unemployment and under-employment, significant dependence on agricultural production and primary-product exports, and dominance, dependence, and vulnerability in international relations. Birth rates in less developed Asian countries are generally at very high levels.[48]

He also notes that:

> current rates of open unemployment in the developing countries average between 10 and 15 per cent of the urban labour force ... unemployment among young people aged 15 to 24, many of whom have received a formal education, is typically almost twice as high as the overall national average.[49]

A number of Asian governments have promoted labour exportation policies for several years in an attempt to reduce the number of under-employed and unemployed. Such policies have also been partly founded on the expectation that migrant worker remittances would provide an important new source of foreign exchange for the labour-exporting country.[50] The Philippines, China and Korea have all asked the Japanese government to accept more of their workers, while the most recent five-year economic plan adopted by the government of the Philippines for the years 1987–92 calls for the encouragement of labour exports.[51]

Economic incentive

This is by far the strongest inducement for workers coming to Japan. Japan's dominant economic position in relation to its Asian neighbours has been reinforced by the massive revaluations of the yen in 1983 and 1986. Japanese income levels are now among the highest in the world; as is clearly illustrated in Table 11.3, enormous disparities in per capita GNP between Japan and other Asian countries exist.

There is more than a fivefold difference in per capita GNP between Japan and its closest competitor the Republic of Korea, while in comparison with Burma or Bangladesh the difference is even more marked. The high cost of living and the double structure of income between large and small companies and between full and part-time employment represent negative economic inducements, but in countries with much lower income levels, the streets of Japan appear to be paved with gold.

Network

The establishment of networks has to a large extent been inhibited by the strict application of Japan's immigration laws. The present Immigration Control Act, which prohibits the entry of unskilled migrant workers, was passed in 1952. From then until the mid-1970s, when the number of seasonal workers available for industrial labour fell off sharply owing to very high growth in the economy, there were discussions as to whether the country should use foreign labourers in unskilled industrial fields. However, on three separate occasions (in 1967, 1973 and 1976) the Cabinet decided not to accept such workers. As a result, the wages of

Table 11.3 GNP for Asian countries, 1987

	Per capita GNP (US$)	Comparative Index
Japan	15,770	100
Korea	2,690	17.1
Malaysia	1,800	11.4
Thailand	840	5.3
Philippines	590	3.7
Indonesia	450	2.9
Pakistan	350	2.2
China	300	1.9
Bangladesh	160	1.0

Source: World Bank Atlas, 1988

indigenous workers increased at an annual rate of more than 10 per cent; the retirement age was extended to 60, and women were encouraged to return to work after marriage; annual working hours decreased from 2,660 hours in the mid-1960s to 2,100 hours in 1970; and the wage differential between large and small firms was reduced. At the same time, emphasis was placed on mechanization and automation and per capita production suddenly increased. Therefore, in spite of large increases in wages, consumption prices increased only slightly, wholesale prices remained stable, and the Japanese economy managed to become a high-wage economy within a relatively short period.[52]

The basis for a private network, however, first appeared in the 1970s. The combined effect of the phenomenal growth in the Japanese economy and the increasing value of the yen has provided increased opportunities for many Japanese to go abroad, both as tourists and on business. This, in turn, has facilitated the transmission of information about Japan throughout the developing countries of Asia. Japan's dominant position in both regional trade and investment has also enhanced its image as an affluent land of opportunity and potential destination for migrant workers.[53]

The rapid increase in the number of illegal workers entering Japan in recent years has been accompanied by a similar rise in the numbers of private agents and labour brokers operating in both the sending countries and in Japan.[54] The system of recruitment by private agents is one which has a long history in the sending countries of Asia and has developed in parallel with the process of emigration.[55] In Japan, cases involving private domestic and foreign agents recruiting illegal migrant workers and furnishing them to potential employers have been increasing rapidly since late 1985. Of 8,131 illegal workers deported in 1986, 87 per cent had some contact with private agents in finding employment.[56] Although it is unknown whether the 'private agents' include the workers' acquaintances, relatives or friends, intervention by private agents is regarded as an integral part of the migration process. It is estimated that in 1987 about 31 per cent of private agents were Japanese and 69 per cent were of the same nationality as the arrested illegal workers.[57]

The ways in which these private agents form networks tend to vary both between and within individual industries. In the case of female workers, for example, where most 'illegals' are employed as nightclub hostesses, nude dancers and prostitutes,[58] private networks were first established in response to international condemnation of Asian 'sex' tours for Japanese businessmen. Until recently it had been common practice in Japan to reward company employees with expenses-paid weekends in Manila, Bangkok or Seoul. At the start of the 1980s, however, a campaign was mounted by Japanese and Asian feminists against this type of Japanese sex tourism. In Manila, Filipino women took to the streets during a state visit by Prime Minister Suzuki in 1981, causing the latter considerable embarrassment. In response to the drying-up of this lucrative source of income, the same agents who had been responsible for organizing sex tours of Asian capitals began flying Asian women to Japan for the same purpose. The vulnerability of these illegal workers to exploitation by unscrupulous employers and labour brokers has been exacerbated by the unregulated nature of the entertainment industry and the increasing involvement of criminal gangs in the employment network. Numerous incidents involving forced labour without pay and forced prostitution have been reported, but the victims, fearful of deportation, have been understandably reluctant to approach the police.

Private networks have also been organized in the residential areas, where there is a high concentration of migrant workers. This is particularly evident in the case of illegal Korean workers, whose presence is actively supported by the long-established Korean community. It has been estimated that nearly 40 per cent of all illegal Korean migrant workers live in the Osaka area, which also contains the largest and most important Korean community in Japan.[59] Illegal workers of other nationalities have also grouped in certain geographical locations and in Tokyo, for example, one particular area is now referred to as the 'ethnic triangle' because of the presence of large numbers of migrant workers.[60] Further networks have been created by other organizations whose motives are purely economic. Japanese companies, for example, have learned to circumvent immigration regulations by employing migrant workers under the category of 'trainees'. By law, 'trainee' status is defined as a person taken on by a public or private organization in Japan to acquire an industrial technique or skills (status of residence 4-1-6-2). However, there have been many cases where vocational facilities have been minimal or entirely lacking, and the trainees themselves have been exploited as cheap labour.[61]

Historical factor

Although the government has been at pains to disassociate the current migration of Asian workers from the migration of hundreds of thousands of impoverished Koreans to Japan between 1910 and 1945, there is little doubt that present-day attitudes and policies have been largely shaped by the presence of nearly 1 million Korean residents who also constitute approximately 80 per cent of the total resident foreign population. The treatment and legal status of Korean residents should therefore be regarded not only as producing a historical precedent, but as a matter closely related to the civil liberties of Asian workers in general. While it would not be appropriate to discuss here the history of the Korean residents in any great detail, its relevance to the current debate cannot be underestimated.[62]

Throughout the period when Korea was governed by Japan (1910–45), Koreans were permitted to live and work anywhere within the empire. Although Korean residents, as citizens of the empire, possessed Japanese nationality, they did not enjoy the same rights of citizenship as accorded to 'pure' Japanese. Moreover, as members of a subordinate race, they were expected to take their proper place at the base of the social and economic hierarchy. Discrimination and oppression were a daily feature in the lives of these colonial guest workers, particularly between 1939 and 1945 when hundreds of thousands of Koreans were conscripted as replacement labour in the mines and factories of Japan. The liberation of Korea from Japanese colonial rule in 1945 did not in itself result in a marked improvement in the status of Korean residents. On the contrary, the few rights which they had possessed prior to 1945 were lost in 1952, when the Japanese government withdrew Japanese nationality from all Korean (and Taiwanese) residents. Since that time, the status of Korean residents has been regulated by a host of laws, ordinances and international agreements between Japan and the Republic of Korea. To a great extent, these have only served to isolate Koreans from mainstream society further and to institutionalize discrimination in employment, education, housing and access to social welfare. Some of the more overt forms of institutionalized discrimination have recently disappeared with the removal of the so-called Nationality Clause, which excluded foreign nationals from employment in the public sector and from most forms of social welfare.

An important catalyst in the government's decision to rescind the Nationality Clause was the strength of the Korean residents' movement, but other external factors also played a role. Pressure on the government began to build following the arrival of refugees from Indo-China in 1975. In the same year, Japan participated in an international summit for advanced countries and began, perhaps for the first time, to feel pressure from the West to adopt a more liberal stance towards foreign residents. Initially the government was only prepared to allow the boat people to stay temporarily until they could be moved to third countries, but eventually decided to allow them to reside in Japan. This was followed in 1979 by Japan's belated ratification of the Universal Declaration of Human Rights. In 1981 Japan ratified the International Covenant Relating to the Status of Refugees, and this resulted in the modification of laws governing the status of foreign residents and the removal of the Nationality Clause. But, while the willingness of the government to meet its obligations under international law deserves recognition, there is ample evidence of the persistence of discrimination against Korean and other long-term Asian residents.

CONCLUSION

In this chapter we have attempted a preliminary assessment of the influx of foreign workers into Japan as a part of the international movement of labour. Owing to limitations of space, certain important aspects of the issue have not been considered and we would like to touch upon them here as subjects for future analysis.

One important factor influencing labour migration is the social and economic condition of specific groups of the population within the sending countries. The individuals who actually migrate are not the people at the bottom of the social structure. There is usually a particular group or class within a society for whom the macro-inducements of foreign work are greatest, and for whom the possibility of migration is a viable alternative to remaining at home. In Japan, 'illegal' migrant workers are mainly aged between 20 and 40 and, being in general younger than Japanese workers in the same industrial field, often provide a higher quality of labour. This is the principal reason why the government is concerned that these workers may generate unemployment among native Japanese workers. Further analysis of those groups with high potential to move to Japan in the future is now necessary. Second, the level of what may be called the 'maturity' o particular sources of foreign labour should be analysed. This implies the need to set in an appropriate historical context the inflows of specific sectors of the foreign labour market through categorization of workers in terms of, for example, pioneer workers, 'second-wave' migrants, those stimulated into movement by specific events in their native countries and so forth. Finally, we should amend our approach to the topic of migrant labour to distinguish labour, which is measured principally in economic terms, from the workers themselves, who should be considered in social terms as well. It is extremely difficult to discuss labour in its broadest sense, since it has so many different attributes which themselves can be further subdivided, but we should at least attempt to analyse in some detail the changes in the characteristics of migrant labour which have been brought about by the restructuring of the world economy.

NOTES

1 The entry into and conditions of residence in Japan of all foreigners, including those who are to be employed, are regulated by The Immigration-Control and Refugee-Recognition Act (Cabinet Order no. 319 of 1951, referred to as the Immigration Control Act). The concrete procedural matters, etc. are stipulated by Immigration-Control and Refugee-Recognition Act Enforcement Regulations (Ministry of Justice ordinance no. 54 of 1981, referred to as the Immigration Regulation). For further explanation, see Immigration Bureau in Japan 1988, p. 3.
2 Tezuka (1989a, 1989b) describes this period in the history of Japanese economy in detail.
3 Unless it is specifically mentioned, all statistical data are cited from *Zairyū Gaikokujin Tōkei*, Ministry of Justice (1988).
4 Immigration Bureau (1988), p. 11.
5 For further explanations, see Immigration Bureau in Japan (1989) p. 59, in particular, the section entitled 'On violations'.
6 Komai (1989a), p. 29.
7 Komai (1989a) and the Planning Committee of the House of Councillors (1989) categorized the various opinions and divided them into 'the closed-door policy', 'the open-door policy', and others.
8 The revision of the Immigration Control Act was not finalized in the 1989 spring session of the Diet.
9 Mori (1984), p. 259.
10 The Japanese, '*tanjun rōdōsha*' is not a suitable word to describe 'unskilled workers' because the word '*tanjun*' can also mean 'simple' or 'not clever', and can be used as a derogatory term.
11 This section has benefited greatly from the work of Yorimitsu (1988) p. 8.
12 Taylor (1969), p. 99.
13 Ibid.
14 Jansen (1970), p. 20.
15 Taylor (1969), p. 100.
16 The study of the incentives of migration has received considerable scholarly attention in Western countries. For example, see Lee (1969) as an example of the alternative approaches. Alternatively, see Kosinski and Prothero (1975) who summarize various approaches.
17 The study of the incentives with specific reference to Japan is still limited compared to the volume of study on other countries. However, see Morita (1987), Yorimitsu (1988) and Kuwahara (1988).
18 The Board of the Economic Planning Committee of Japan (1989), p. 36.
19 Ibid.
20 Todaro (1977), p. 264.
21 Jansen (1970), p. 14.
22 Castles et al. (1984), p. 2.
23 Ibid., p. 3.
24 The Board of the Economic Planning Committee of Japan (1989), p. 38.
25 Ibid.
26 For example, Central and South America (particularly Mexico) to the United States, Southern Europe and North Africa to advanced European countries, and Asia to the Middle East.
27 The Board of the Economic Planning Committee of Japan (1989), p. 38.
28 Ibid.
29 Further explanation of the components is provided by the Board of the Economic Planning Committee (1989) p. 38.
30 Ibid., p. 40.
31 According to Castles (1984) p. 232, 'The New Commonwealth comprises those countries of the British Commonwealth in 1973.'
32 In 1971 the British government further restricted Commonwealth emigration by placing limitations on the entry of dependants.

33 This explanation is based on work by the Board of the Economic Planning Bureau of Japan (1989) p. 40.
34 This analysis of the projected workforce in Japan is based on the statistical figures presented by the Board of Economic Planning Committee of Japan.
35 Hayashi (1990), p. 13.
36 Asano (1990), p. 128.
37 Komai (1989f), p. 92.
38 For further explanation about working conditions in the construction industry, see Asano (1990) p. 131.
39 Komai (1989f), p. 92.
40 This figure is from Komai (1989f) p. 92.
41 This case was reported in the Tokyo area.
42 Komai (1989h), p. 8.
43 Komai (1989i), pp. 78–80.
44 Komai (1989e), p. 23.
45 Tanaka and Miyoshi (1988), p. 29.
46 Immigration Bureau (1988), pp. 80–8; see also Komai (1989b), p. 75.
47 Komai (1989j), p. 29.
48 Todaro (1977), p. 27.
49 Ibid., p. 38.
50 It should be noted that Singapore is 27.
49 Ibid., p. 38.
50 It should be noted that Singapore is excluded from the list of sending countries.
51 In the case of the Philippines it is an obligation of the migrant workers to remit more than 50 per cent of their income earned abroad to the Philippines, and in addition, they must pay between 1 and 3 per cent of their overseas income to the Filipino government in tax.
52 Takanashi (1990), pp. 21–2.
53 For example, see Gonoi (1989); *Karabaw-no-kai* (1988); Matsuda (1988); Matsui (1988); and Tanaka (1988).
54 Komai (1989c), pp. 27–8.
55 This is particularly true in Bangkok where there are more than 500 private recruitment agencies for Thai migrant workers.
56 Komai (1989c), p. 27.
57 Ibid.
58 Although the persons identified as prostitutes are relatively small in number, some of those classified as hostesses are considered to be engaged in prostitution (Komai 1989e).
59 Komai (1989g), p. 79.
60 Komai (1990), p. 89. Here the word 'ethnic' implies East Asian countries.
61 Since they are treated as 'trainees', large deductions are made from their wages to cover subsistence. For further discussion on this topic see Komai (1989d) pp. 26–31.
62 See Weiner (1989).

REFERENCES

Asano, M. (1990) 'Kensetsu Rasshu no Seika, Ote ga Hitorijime' (The Result of the Boom in the Construction Industry – Most of the Benefit Taken by Large Companies), *Rōdō Undō*, No. 291, pp. 128–31.
Board of the Economic Planning Committee, Ministry of International Trade and Industry in Japan (eds.), (1989) *Gaikokujin Rōdōsha to Keizaishakai no Shinro* (Migrant Workers and Their Impact on the Economy), Tokyo: Ōkurashō Insatsukyoku.
Castles, S. (ed.) (1984) *Here for Good – Western Europe's New Ethnic Minorities*, London: Pluto Press.
Gonoi, H. (1989) *Dekasegi Gaijin Zankoku Monogatari* (An Account of the Brutal Treatment of Foreign Migrant Workers), Tokyo: Eru Shuppan.
Hayashi, T. (1990) 'Aete Nihon Keizai no Shikaku o Tou' (What is the Blind Spot in the Japanese Economy?), *Japanese Economist*, Vol. 68, No. 2, pp. 10–15.
Immigration Bureau, Ministry of Justice in Japan (ed.) (1988) *Employment of Foreign Nationals: Questions and Answers*, Tokyo: Nihon Kajo Shuppan.

Jansen, C.J. (1970) 'Migration: a sociological problem', *Readings in the Sociology of Migration*, London: Pergamon Press.

Karabau-no-kai (eds.) (1988) *Gaikokujin Rōdōsha no Gōhōka ni Mukete* (Aiming at the Legalization of Migrant Workers), Tokyo: Shinchiheisha.

Komai, H. (1989a) 'Gaikokujin Rōdōsha Hitsuzenron, Sakokuron, Kaikokuron o Koete' (Why it is Essential to Accept Migrant Workers – Beyond the Closed-Door Policy and the Open-Door Policy), *Japanese Economist*, Vol. 67, No. 34, pp. 28–33.

—— (1989b) 'Fuhōshūrōsha to iu Rakuin' (The Tag of Illegal Migrant Worker), *Japanese Economist*, Vol. 67, No. 36, pp. 72–7.

—— (1989c) 'Anyaku Suru Assen Brōkā' (Behind-the-Scene Labour Brokers), *Japanese Economist*, Vol. 67, No. 37, pp. 26–31.

—— (1989d) 'Teichingin Rōdōsha toshite no Gijutsu Kenshūsei' (Trainees as Labour with Low Wages), *Japanese Economist*, Vol. 67, No. 38, pp. 62–7.

—— (1989e) 'Sore wa Josei kara Hajimatta' (It Started with Women), *Japanese Economist*, Vol. 67, No. 41, pp. 22–7.

—— (1989f) 'Kaikokuron o Shuchō Shihajimeta Kensetsugyōkai' (The Construction Industry Begins to Consider an Open-Door Policy), *Japanese Economist*, Vol. 67, No. 42, pp. 90–5.

—— (1989g) 'Kensetsu Gemba no Gaikokujin Rōdōsha (Migrant Workers on Construction Sites), *Japanese Economist*, Vol. 67, No. 45, pp. 76–81.

—— (1989h) 'Rōdōryoku Busoku ni Naku Chūshō Shitauke Seizōgyō' (Medium and Small Sized Manufacturing Subcontractors Suffer from a Shortage of Labour), *Japanese Economist*, Vol. 67, No. 46, pp. 78–83.

—— (1989i) 'Sābisu Sangyō e no Tairyō Shinshutsu' (Large Numbers of Migrant Workers Make Inroads into Service Industries), *Japanese Economist*, Vol. 67, No. 48, pp. 78–83.

—— (1989j) 'Rōdōryoku Yushutsu ga Kōzōka Sareta Ajia' (Asian Countries which have Structured the Export of Labour), *Japanese Economist*, Vol. 67, No. 51, pp. 28–33.

—— (1990) 'Hinjaku na Kyojū Kankyō ni Kurushimu Gaikokujin Rōdōsha' (Migrant Workers Suffer from a Poor Residential Environment), *Japanese Economist*, Vol. 68, No. 2, pp. 88–95.

Kosinski, L.A. and Prothero, R.M. (1975) 'Introduction: the study of migration' in L.A. Kosinski and R.M. Prothero (eds) *People on the Move, Studies on Internal Migration*, London: Methuen.

Kuwahara, Y. (1988) 'Sekiyu Kikigo no Kokusai Rōdōryoku no Dōtai' (International Labour Fluctuations After the Oil Shock), *Nihon Rōdōkyōkai Zasshi*, No. 348, pp. 34–47.

Lee, E.S. (1969) 'A theory of migration' in J.A. Jackson (ed.) *Migration*, Cambridge: Cambridge University Press.

Matsuda, M. (1988) 'Baikai Sareru Ajia no Onnatachi' (Asian Women Treated like Slaves), *Hōgaku Seminā Zōkan, Gaikokujin Rōdōsha to Jinken* (Hōgaku Seminar Special Issue – Migrant Workers and Their Human Rights), Vol. 42, pp. 30–41.

Matsui, Y. (1988) 'Jinken Shingai ni Naku' (Weep Over the Violation of Human Rights) in A. Utsumi and Y. Matsui (eds) *Ajia kara Kita Dekasegi Rōdōshatachi* (Migrant Workers from Asia), Tokyo: Akashi Shoten.

Ministry of Justice in Japan (ed.) (1988) *Zairyū Gaikokujin Tōkei* (Statistics Foreign Residents in Japan), Tokyo: Okurasho Insatsu Kyoku.

Mori, H. (1984) 'Yōroppa Ijū Rōdōsha Mondai to Kokusai Rōdō Undō – Nishi Doitsu o Chūshin Toshite' (The Issue of Migrant Workers in Europe and International Migration – a Case Study of West Germany), in Shakai Seisaku Gyōshō Iinkai (ed.) *Kokusaika Suru Rōdō Mondai to Shakai Seisaku* (Internationalized Labour Issues and Social Policy), Tokyo: Keibunsha.

Morita, Y. (ed.) (1987) *Kokusai Rōdōryoku Idō* (International Movement of Labour), Tokyo: Tokyo Daigaku Shuppankai.

Planning Committee of the House of Councillors in Japan (ed.) (1989) 'Gaikokujin Rōdōsha o Meguru Rongi to Shiten' (Discussions and Viewpoints on Migrant Workers), *Rippō to Chōsa, Bessatsu*, Tokyo: Chūo Insatsu.

Takanashi, A. (1990) 'Fusoku to Kajo no Konzai o Dō Kaiketsu Suru' (How Should We Solve the Problem of Shortage and Excess), *Japanese Economist*, Vol. 68, No. 11, pp. 18–27.

Tanaka, H. (1988) 'Ajiajin Rōdōsha to Gaikokujin Sabetsu no Rekishi' (Asian Workers and the History of Discrimination Against Foreigners), in *Hōgaku Seminā Zōkan, Gaikokujin*

Rōdōsha to Jinken (Hōgaku Seminar Special Issue – Migrant Workers and Their Human Rights), Vol. 42, pp. 88–95.

Tanaka, H. and Miyoshi, A. (eds) (1988) 'Zadankai, Gaikokujin Rōdōsha o Meguru Mondaiten – Sono Jittai to Kore kara no Taiō' (Problems of Migrant Workers – the Present Situation and Counter-Measures for the Future), *Gendai no Esupri*, No. 249, pp. 9–40.

Taylor, R.C. (1969) 'Migration and motivation: a study of determinants and types', in J.A. Jackson (ed.), *Sociological Studies 2: Migration*, Cambridge: Cambridge University Press.

Tezuka, K. (1989a) *Gaikokujin Rōdōsha* (Foreign Migrant Workers), Tokyo: Nihon Keizai Shinbunsha.

—— (1989b) 'Rōshi Kankei no Kokusaika to Rōdōhō no Aratana Tenkai' (The Internationalization of Labour Relations and New Developments in Labour Law), *Kikan Rōdōhō*, No. 150, pp. 42–60.

Todaro, M.P. (1977) *Economic Development in the Third World*, 4th edition, 1989, New York: Longman Inc.

Weiner, M. (1989) *The Origins of the Korean Community in Japan 1910–1923*, Manchester: Manchester University Press.

Yorimitsu, M. (1988) 'Gaikokujin Rōdōsha Ukeire Mondai e no Ichi Shiten' (One View on the Acceptance of Migrant Workers), *Nihon Rōdōkyōkai Zasshi* (Magazine of the Association of Labour in Japan), No. 348, pp. 3–13.

Chapter 12

Reciprocity and migrant workers

Hatsuse Ryūhei

INTRODUCTION

Japan became an economic superpower in the 1980s. With the strengthening of the yen, foreign goods became widely available within Japan, and such imported goods as Scotch whisky and American cigarettes are now no longer regarded as luxury items for the wealthy. In 1988 more than 7 million Japanese travelled abroad. In terms of consumption and sight-seeing, economic internationalization has bestowed enormous benefits upon the Japanese people.

Economic internationalization has involved not only the freer movement of goods, capital and services, but of people as well. An unanticipated and what many regard as an unwelcome result of Japan's emergence as a regional hegemon has been the recent influx of large numbers of unskilled workers from the peripheral and semi-peripheral states of Asia. For Japan this movement of people has become a problem demanding urgent social and institutional solutions.

Government policy throughout the post-1945 period has been to prohibit the entry of unskilled foreign workers. Two types of illegal foreign worker can be identified: first, those who are engaged in activities, usually but not exclusively economic, outside those permitted under their visa status; and second, foreigners who remain in Japan after their visa has expired. In reality, of course, a considerable overlap exists between these two categories, and a sizeable proportion of the illegal workers presently in Japan entered the country on short-stay tourist visas. Such individuals are not regarded as criminals in a strictly legal sense, though they are subject to deportation under existing immigration law.

The unanticipated introduction of large numbers of migrant workers from Asia has presented Japan with an apparently insoluble dilemma. On the one hand, a clear need exists for labour of this type in certain sectors of the economy that are currently suffering from severe shortages of labour. On the other hand, there is widespread concern that the presence of foreign workers could have a negative social impact on Japan. There are an estimated 120,000–150,000 illegal migrant workers (1988), mainly young unaccompanied men and women from the Philippines, Bangladesh, Pakistan, Thailand, Korea and China, currently employed throughout Japan. As in other similar situations, the conditions under which they live and work are inferior to those which all but the most destitute Japanese workers would tolerate.

This unexpected development has generated considerable debate among journalists, bureaucrats, academics, trade-unionists and within the business community as a whole. There is, as one might expect, a wide divergence of opinion, ranging from demands for tighter border controls, the need for a flexible source of labour in certain sectors of the economy, questions of human rights and labour protection for illegal as well as approved foreign workers, racial discrimination, and the necessity for Japan to meet its obligations as a major economic power. While persuasive arguments have been mounted, both for and against the admission of migrant workers, a consensus has yet to emerge which would satisfy all the criteria outlined above. Added to this is the fact that, despite the formation of a range of Japanese support groups, none of the major political parties has adopted a clear position on the issue. This 'decision of indecision' has resulted in a tacit acceptance of the status quo and the continued exploitation of migrant workers by unscrupulous employers and labour brokers.

In the view of this writer it is essential that the issue of migrant workers in Japan be considered in the broader context of North–South relations in Asia. Second, it should be the responsibility of the Japanese people to ensure that the social costs of immigration and repatriation are not borne solely by the immigrants themselves. Third, it must be acknowledged that some temporary workers may become permanent resident aliens and, in some instances, even naturalize. Consequently, foreign workers must not be evaluated only in terms of their labour power. Fourth, efforts must be made to ensure that the protection guaranteed to Japanese workers under existing labour legislation is extended to all foreign workers as well. This is extremely important since migrant workers, working on the fringes of the Japanese economy, are particularly vulnerable to exploitation and discriminatory treatment in terms of living and working conditions. Fifth, it should not be overlooked that, in regard to international migration, many nations recognize as legitimate the reunion of a family divided by migration. Regulations governing family reunification must therefore be incorporated in any future legislation. Sixth, and finally, as Zolberg has remarked:

> It is probably the case that truly free international migrations would on balance affect a radical redistribution of resources and opportunities to the benefit of the peoples originally located in the semi-periphery and the periphery. This might in the long run benefit humanity as a whole, but it would undoubtedly impose in the short run drastic costs on the population of the affluent countries.[1]

In an ideal world, of course, the solution would be to allow the unrestricted entry of foreign workers. But every nation, without exception, imposes some limits on who, and how many, aliens it will admit. In the present situation it would simply not be feasible for Japan to permit the un-regulated entry of migrant labour. Unlike the EEC, where rough equival-ence in levels of employment and income among the member states allows for unrestricted movement across national boundaries, the free movement of people in Asia would, as in the case of internal rural–urban migration in the developing countries, be largely a movement in one direction, with a massive flow of migrant workers to Japan. However appealing it may at first appear, the unlimited entry of large numbers of mostly unskilled foreign workers is not an appropriate response to the current situation.

In the circumstances, the only workable solution will be for the Japanese people and government to bear the social costs of migration itself while imposing an enforceable ceiling on the number of migrant workers permitted to enter the country. Although by no means unproblematic, an interim solution might be to accept an agreed number of workers from those countries which have accepted both Japanese investment and the basing of Japanese-managed factories within their borders. At the same time, Japan would bear certain of the social costs of immigration. This would, at least to some extent, be a response to the fact that positions of authority in Japanese corporate offices in Asia are monopolized by Japan-ese executives and that the social costs of the Japanese presence is borne solely by the host nations in Asia.

TRENDS IN ILLEGAL IMMIGRATION TO JAPAN

Historically speaking, migration to Japan is not a new phenomenon. The present-day Korean community is a legacy of the massive migration of Koreans to Japan between 1910 and 1945. At times the population flow from Korea was voluntary, responding to labour market needs in Japan, but between 1939 and 1945 nearly 1 million Koreans and a further 40,000 Chinese were conscripted for work as replacement labour in the mines and construction sites throughout wartime Japan. At the end of the war there were an estimated 2 million Koreans resident in Japan. The present-day community, numbering approximately 700,000, is the largest ethnic minority in Japan. Its members continue to suffer from discrimination in employment (in both the public and private sectors), housing, education and in the provision of a wide range of social services.

Labour shortages have been a recurrent problem since the 1960s, when the possibility of importing labour was first considered. At that time, however, shortages were overcome through reliance on seasonal migrations from rural areas within Japan, increased automation, or through direct investment in South East and East Asia. Similarly, the labour shortages of the 1970s and 1980s were surmounted by increased reliance on part-time and temporary workers – most often students and housewives. In the past few years, however, acute labour shortages have developed in immovable industries (the construction industry and the rapidly expanding service sector), as well as in sm.ll subcontracting firms which lack the capital to either rationalize production or invest overseas. Wages and working conditions in these areas are poor by comparison with other sectors of the economy. As in other similar situations, illegal migrant workers, who are willing to accept inferior living and working conditions, have provided employers with a new source of cheap, flexible labour.

At this juncture it may be beneficial to highlight the situation of these illegal workers by comparing their number with those of other types of working foreign residents. There are three categories of foreigners that need to be considered in this respect: permanent residents, foreign residents with work permits, and illegal migrant workers. Estimates of the total number of illegal workers in Japan vary considerably, but, according to figures provided by the Immigration Bureau of the Ministry of Justice, a total of 70,000 foreigners overstayed their visas in June 1988: most of these were suspected to be working illegally. If we add to this figure the more than 20,000 foreign workers (mainly Chinese) who entered the country as language students but who are obliged to work far more than the twenty hours a week permitted under their status (in order to pay school fees, housing and other ancillary costs), a few thousand factory trainees who are forced to work illegally, and those who are working illegally but have not been apprehended, the total for 1988 was in the region of 120,000–150,000. While this figure represents only 0.25 per cent of the total working population, it corresponds to approximately one-third of the total number of permanent foreign residents employed in Japan, and exceeds the number of those foreigners working legally (see Table 12.1).

Most male migrants find employment on the margins of industry; in small factories; in day or week labouring in the construction industry; or in

Table 12.1 Legally employed foreigners (at the end of each year)

Visa status	Enter-tainer	Business man	Special permission for language	Special permission for other jobs	Skilled labour	Professors	Technical advisers	Total
1984	7,346	5,943	1,799	3,004	1,366	1,007	13	20,478
1986	10,357	7,148	4,264	6,242	1,502	1,120	12	30,645
1987	12,880	7,216	5,553	7,956	1,510	1,184	15	36,314

Source: The Immigration Office of the Ministry of Justice (ed.) Statistics of Foreigners in Japan (in Japanese)

the service sector. In general, they take on the jobs either which have been vacated by indigenous workers, or in areas where the recruitment and retention of labour presents particular difficulties. In the case of male workers, the bulk have been drawn from China, Korea and the Philippines, though there has been a recent upsurge in migration from Bangladesh and Pakistan (see Tables 12.2 & 12.3). As in Western Europe, migrants in Japan do the low-paid, dirty, physically taxing and dangerous work which is avoided by indigenous workers.

This is borne out by the results of a survey of foreign workers in Tokyo and two adjacent industrial cities (Kawasaki and Kawaguchi). Here it was found that foreign workers were employed by 26.8 per cent of the metal-working, welding and plating firms, ironworks and foundries surveyed; 20.7 per cent of the bookbinding firms surveyed; and 15.8 per cent of the general and electrical machinery firms surveyed. A total of 11.3 per cent of the firms surveyed had at some time in the past employed foreign workers,

Table 12.2 Apprehended illegal workers, 1983–8

	1983	1984	1985	1986	1987	1988
Total	2,339	4,783	5,629	8,131	11,307	14,314
m	200	350	687	2,186	4,289	8,929
f	2,139	4,433	4,942	5,945	7,018	5,385
Filipino	1,041	2,983	3,927	6,297	8,027	5,386
m	29	96	349	1,500	2,253	1,688
f	1,012	2,887	3,578	4,797	5,774	3,698
Bangladeshi	0	0	1	58	438	2,942
m	0	0	1	58	437	2,939
f	0	0	0	0	1	3
Pakistani	7	3	36	196	905	2,497
m	7	3	36	196	905	2,495
f	0	0	0	0	0	2
Thai	557	1,132	1,073	990	1,067	1,388
m	39	54	120	164	290	369
f	518	1,078	953	826	777	1,019
Korean	114	61	76	119	208	1,033
m	24	34	35	69	109	769
f	90	27	41	50	99	264
Chinese*	528	466	427	356	494	502
m	85	136	126	161	210	230
f	443	330	301	195	284	272

Source: Statistics of the Immigration Bureau of the Ministry of Justice
Notes: m: male
    f: female
   *almost all Taiwanese

Table 12.3 Apprehended illegal workers, January–December 1988

	Total	Construction	Small factory	Auxiliary	Hostess	Nude dancer	Prostitute	Shop assistant	Waiter/waitress
Total									
m	8,929	3,807	3,486	765	–	4	–	283	170
f	5,385	31	165	120	4,359	205	140	105	63
Filipino									
m	1,688	984	294	129	–	0	–	50	132
f	3,698	2	39	46	3,169	143	101	43	39
Bangladeshi									
m	2,939	927	1,555	278	–	0	–	115	11
f	3	0	2	0	0	0	0	0	0
Pakistani									
m	2,495	920	1,277	154	–	0	–	35	12
f	2	1	1	0	0	0	0	0	0
Thai									
m	369	100	129	77	–	0	0	33	5
f	1,019	0	13	7	936	1	32	12	8
Korean									
m	769	599	112	13	–	0	–	6	0
f	264	28	93	32	53	0	0	11	4
Taiwanese									
m	223	22	19	71	–	1	–	40	7
f	269	0	10	29	163	1	3	38	9
Malaysian									
m	265	221	21	18	–	0	–	0	0
f	14	0	5	4	3	0	0	1	0
%	100	26.8	25.5	6.2	30.5	1.5	0.9	2.7	1.6

Source: Statistics of the Immigration Bureau of the Ministry of Justice

and over 12 per cent were currently employing foreign workers.[2] According to a further survey of part-time jobs held by students of Japanese language schools, it was found that 51.1 per cent were employed in the service sector as, for example, waiters or waitresses, a further 26.5 per cent in construction or factory work, and 10.7 per cent in some type of clerical work.[3] In addition to the categories listed above, migrant workers have also found employment in a wide range of areas including laundries, food processing, car washes, noodle shops, public baths, wholesale markets, farming, and as delivery boys and office cleaners. As illegal workers, they are barred from taking up work in transportation, hotels, catering, the health service, or as regular workers in large factories. This represents a significant departure from the situation in postwar Western Europe.

Although labour migration is usually regarded primarily as a young male phenomenon, this is not the case in Asia. A specific characteristic of the Japanese case is the large number of young female workers, particularly from Thailand and the Philippines. Relatively few of these women find employment outside the service sector, and most work as hostesses in small nightclubs or bars.

In general, wages for migrant workers are between 20 and 50 per cent lower than those paid to their Japanese counterparts. For the period 1988–9, the daily wage rate ranged from ¥4,000–10,000 with an average of about ¥7,000. Rates of pay are determined not only by market demand, but in some instances are affected by the nationality of individual workers. Although wage levels satisfy the legal requirements set down by the Minimum Wage Law, migrant incomes do not allow for much more than a subsistence level existence in Japan, where living expenses are extremely high. However, if they send as little as 20 per cent of their monthly income to their families back home, it is not difficult to imagine how much better off these families are through these remittances.

FACTORS AFFECTING IMMIGRATION

In general, all the sending countries have a relative surplus of population or a high unemployment rate. In addition, the governments of the Philippines, Pakistan, Bangladesh and China all have policies which promote labour migration. The governments of China (1988), the Philippines (1987) and Korea (1988) have all been successful in their attempts to persuade the Japanese government to facilitate the employment of migrant labour. In the case of Korean migrants, however, restrictions on the entry of unskilled workers appear to have been consistently circumvented. Owing to the existence of extensive family networks, particularly in the Osaka area (where the bulk of the Korean community is located), hundreds of Koreans are reported to have found employment in small family-operated concerns after having entered Japan on a visa to visit relatives. A similar situation has arisen within the resident Chinese community, which has well-established links with other Chinese communities throughout the region. It is no coincidence that half of the thousands of boat people who arrived in Japan in the summer of 1989 were, in fact, Chinese from Fukien Province, a region with particularly strong social and economic ties with overseas Chinese communities throughout South East and East Asia. Although these individuals were later repatriated to China, there is another network linking certain language schools in Japan with labour brokers in Shanghai.

The strongest inducement for migration, however, is the enormous wage gap that exists between the sending countries and Japan (see Table 12.4). According to statistics provided by the widely respected *Tōyō Keizai Shimpō*, a comparison of the average wage for factory workers in manufacturing reveals the following differentials. Taking Japan as 100, Korea = 18, Thailand = 5.5, the Philippines = 5.3, and China = 1.5 (1986). Figures for the same year provided by Jetro (Japanese External Trade Organization) and the Ministry of Labour paint a very similar picture. Thus, one hour of wage labour in Japan is equivalent to twenty hours in the Philippines and sixty hours in China. In other words, a Chinese worker who had saved the equivalent of one year's income after a two-year sojourn in Japan would be able to maintain him/herself in China for a further sixty-six years at present levels. Similarly, a Filipino worker who had managed to save the equivalent of two years' income after a stay of three years in Japan, would be able to live on his or her savings for the next forty years in the home country. Although a number of variables have not been factored into these estimates, they do highlight current income differentials. The

Table 12.4 Economic gap in Asia, 1986

	Pop. (million)	GNP/ capita (US$)	Exports (million (US$)	Imports (million (US$)	Remittances (million US$)	Wage (Japan = 100)
Japan	121.5	12,840	210,757	127,553		100.0
Korea	41.5	2,370	34,715	31,584	—	18.0
China	1,054.0	300	31,148	43,172	208	1.5
Philippines	57.3	560	4,771	5,394	163	5.3
Thailand	42.6	810	8,794	9,178	—	5.5
Malaysia	16.1	1,830	13,874	10,829	—	7.9
Bangladesh	103.2	160	880	2,701	586	
India	781.4	290	11,741	16,269	2,000	
Pakistan	99.2	350	3,384	5,377	2,632	
Sri Lanka	16.1	400	1,215	1,958	324	

Sources: The World Bank, *World Development Report 1988*; ILO, *Yearbook of Labour Statistics 1987*

role of economic factors is given added significance when one considers that Japanese society is relatively closed to foreigners, and that immigrants have experienced great difficulty in settling there in the past. For example, the total number of Vietnamese refugees who have settled in Japan is less than 10,000. This pales by comparison with the number for the United States (720,000), Canada and Australia (120,000 each), and France (110,000).[4]

THE CURRENT DEBATE IN JAPAN

Concern over the potential consequences of accepting migrant labour from Asian countries has revealed a wide range of opinions even within the state bureaucracy. The Ministry of Justice, which has responsibility for administering immigration and nationality laws, has consistently opposed any relaxation of the current regulations and, instead, has called for tighter controls. The Ministry of Labour has also reacted negatively, although this appears to have been motivated by its concern over poor working conditions. The Board of Economic Planning has recently taken a more liberal position on this issue, while the Foreign Ministry, reflecting its concern with improving relations with the rest of Asia, has favoured the limited employment of foreign workers. The Ministry of International Trade and Industry, on the other hand, has adopted what amounts to a wait-and-see policy. Most trade unions have consistently opposed the use of foreign workers on the grounds that it could result in a deterioration of wages and working conditions for Japanese workers.

While some commentators argue that the employment of unskilled foreigners would be of practical economic benefit to both the sending and receiving countries, others point out that the real solution to the north–south divide in Asia lies in creating jobs in the sending countries through increased direct investment and expanded development assistance. Proponents also argue that legalization would mean immediate protection for workers who are presently exploited and discriminated against, while opponents stress that discrimination against foreign workers cannot simply be legislated away. Similar divisions are apparent between those who favour employment as a means of responding to the demands of the labour market, and those who are fearful that a future contraction of the market would lead to the creation of a large unassimilated pool of foreign workers. Anxieties such as these are dismissed by proponents who are convinced that migrants would voluntarily repatriate, since Japan would not be a hospitable environment for unemployed foreigners. Proponents argue that a better-quality labour force can be obtained from immigrants, while opponents stress that labour shortages should be overcome through the rationalization of the labour process, and that continued dependence on human resources will hinder this. However, proponents can argue in response that some jobs will never be mechanized and automated.

Still others claim that the employment of foreign workers would provide an ideal opportunity to internationalize Japan. Opponents remain extremely sceptical and argue that the continued existence of combined occupational and racial discrimination in Japan would result in increased social tensions. Proponents also point out that immigrants will not stop coming to Japan even if they remain illegal, while opponents argue that such workers will flood into Japan once restrictions are eased, and hence they should not be given legal standing. This lack of consensus has been reflected in a number of surveys. In response to a survey carried out by the Immigration Bureau in October 1987, for instance, nearly 65 per cent responded that the presence of illegal foreign workers was 'undesirable', while 26 per cent believed that they were 'permissible to some extent'. In a second poll carried out in February 1988, however, more than 45 per cent of the respondents replied that the employment of illegal workers was 'not recommended but inevitable', while 39 per cent felt this to be unacceptable. Some 52 per cent of those polled approved of the limited introduction of unskilled labour from Asia, and 24 per cent of the respondents supported the existing policy of excluding such workers (survey carried out by the Prime Minister's Office at the request of the Immigration Bureau). There are those, of course, who argue that the employment of foreign workers is inevitable, and this would appear to be borne out by the fact that a quarter of all small and medium-sized manufacturing firms in and around Tokyo have employed foreign workers. When asked whether they would do so again in the future if restrictions were removed, 54 per cent replied in the affirmative, while 27 per cent, expressing anxieties over differences in language and culture, indicated that they would not do so.[5] Thus public opinion has begun to move gradually towards the acceptance of foreign workers.

At least a partial response to the current situation can be found in the decision to revise the Immigration and Refugee Recognition Law (from 1 June 1990). The principal aims of this revision are threefold. First, to relax the regulations governing the activities of certain categories of skilled foreign workers, e.g. lawyers, doctors, dentists, accountants, teachers of English, designers and company transferees. Second, to tighten existing controls on the recruitment and employment of illegal foreign workers (primarily unskilled labour). Third, after the June 1990 deadline, any employer or labour broker found guilty of making use of unauthorized foreign workers (who entered Japan after the deadline) will be liable to a fine of up to a maximum of ¥2 million or imprisonment for up to three years. It is difficult to determine at this stage the impact of this legislation, since the status of illegal migrants who entered Japan before 1 June has in fact been left ambiguous. We may regard this as giving *de facto* legal status to those migrants already in Japan, though the government is unlikely to share this interpretation. It is also clear that, although the revision will curtail the flow of migrant labour, it will not be possible to cut it off entirely. At the same time, by making the employment of migrant workers a criminal offence, the government will have simply forced the employment issue underground. It is probable that, as a result, the status of such workers will become increasingly tenuous and that working conditions will deteriorate further.

MIGRATION AND DISCRIMINATION IN JAPAN

The history of Western industrialization has been accompanied by the colonization of other areas of the world. Japan's development as a modern state also followed this pattern, which resulted in the annexation of Taiwan in 1895, part of China (Kwantung Lease Land) in 1905, Korea as a protectorate in 1905 and as a colony in 1910, and finally Manchuria in 1931. In the ideology of the state, imperial expansion was justified not only in economic or political terms, but as a natural expression of Japanese superiority. The people of Asia, by comparison, were found to be sadly lacking in the very qualities which had allowed Japan to avoid foreign domination. As a result, the peoples of China and Korea were regarded as inferior races whose fate it was to serve the needs of imperial Japan. Many thousands of Koreans migrated to Japan where they were exploited as cheap colonial labour, and held in contempt as the bearers of an alien and inferior culture. Although many of the more overt forms of discrimination have since disappeared, Chinese, Korean and other Asian residents in Japan still suffer from the effects of prejudice at both the institutional and personal level.

The total number of foreign residents in Japan at the end of 1988 was 868,000. This included 677,000 Koreans, 129,000 Chinese, 33,000 Americans (excluding military personnel and their dependants) and 32,000 Filipinos. As a group, foreign residents make up less than 1 per cent of a total population in excess of 120 million. Until quite recently, however, the application of various nationality restrictions limited their access to better employment, better business opportunities, higher education and a range of social welfare benefits. National health insurance programmes, pensions, public housing and student scholarships were all closed to them until the early 1980s. Most of these barriers have been lifted both as a result of the efforts of Korean and other foreign resident associations, and as a consequence of Japan's ratification of the International Refugee Convention in 1981. Professorships at national universities were opened to foreigners in 1982, although such appointments are normally made for only three years. Some municipal governments employ foreign nationals as civil servants or teachers. Nevertheless, discrimination against foreign residents at the institutional level remains widespread. Foreigners are, in principle, prohibited from taking up positions within the national civil service, or as teachers at most primary and secondary schools within the state sector, and only rarely are they employed above the clerical level by municipal governments. Foreigners are still required to undergo the humiliation of fingerprinting, and Asians in particular continue to face discrimination in employment and in access to financial services and housing.

In his analysis of racism in contemporary Britain, John Solomos makes the following observation:

> In practice the most resonant themes in contemporary racial discourses are not concerned with absolute notions of racial superiority, but with the threats which black communities are seen to represent to the cultural, political and religious homogeneity of white British society.[6]

So close are the parallels between Britain and Japan that one is tempted to replace the word 'black' with 'Asian' and 'white British' with 'Japanese'. In both cases, discrimination against foreigners is deeply rooted in a belief in the cultural and ethnic homogeneity of the nation. Such racial ideologies as these also find expression in the fear of cultural pollution, as exemplified by former Prime Minister Nakasone's ill-judged reference in 1986 to ethnic diversity as a cause of educational under achievement in the United States. In defending his remarks, Nakasone suggested that his intention had not been to criticize the United States, but to stress the fact that Japan's higher standard of educational achievement was due to an absence of ethnic conflict.[7] In both Britain and Japan, nativist concerns with ethnic homogeneity are embedded in all institutions. There are, however, differences between the two which should not be ignored. In Japan, notions of mono-ethnicity and racial exclusivity have an almost tribal character which rejects not only non-Japanese within Japan, but Japanese who have been contaminated by extensive contact with the outside. The children of businessmen who are posted abroad risk bullying when they re-enter the Japanese school system, while the hundreds of Japanese war orphans who had been abandoned in China at the end of the Second World War and came to Japan during the 1980s were at first welcomed and then segregated from the rest of society. Thus the Japanese even discriminate against other types of Japanese.

Of course, migrant workers are doubly disadvantaged since their illegal status prevents them from protesting against discriminatory employment and social practices (housing, health, religion, entertainment and social life). Although the Ministry of Labour has indicated that protective labour legislation covers all workers, regardless of nationality or legal status, illegal migrants have little choice but to accept inferior wages and working conditions. To do otherwise would be tantamount to inviting deportation, since they would have no choice but to make themselves known to the authorities in any labour dispute. In fact, there is very little likelihood that protective legislation will be applied so long as their labour itself is illegal. As a result, the migrant worker lives in near complete isolation from the majority community, which benefits from his or her labour. Thus the migrant workers in Japan share many of the disadvantages and characteristics of their European counterparts, whom Cohen describes in the following way:

> Rather they are sad, fearful, pathetic individuals desperate to escape intolerable conditions at the periphery of the regional political economy, thrown about by forces they at first only dimly comprehend, and forced to accept conditions of housing, employment and health care that permits a maximum level of exploitation. Such individuals, like many other migrant workers, are ideologically habituated into tolerating.[8]

Thanks to their presence, the Japanese can be free from unpleasant, dirty or dangerous work. Thanks to their illegality, the Japanese can also escape the burden of further social costs and the fear of ghettos being built around them. This is an unjustifiable situation which demands immediate action. Some have suggested that the answer lies in accepting a limited number of foreign workers. But, unless immigration controls were rigorously enforced, this would actually result in a continuance of, or increase in, illegal migration to Japan. The reasons for this are as follows. First, an estimated 20–30 per cent would, for various reasons, refuse to return home after the expiry of their visas. Second, the status of even legal workers would become tenuous if there were a sudden downturn in the economy. Even if their work permits were revoked, it is unlikely that all would voluntarily repatriate. On the other hand, Japan would risk international censure if it attempted to repatriate them forcibly. Third, illegal workers would retain their principal attraction to employers, that of providing the cheapest, most flexible source of labour. Fourth, since the demand for cheap unskilled labour would be likely to exceed the supply of approved workers, the migration of illegal workers would continue. This had certainly been the case in Western Europe. As Castles has remarked:

> Small, marginal businesses were in favour of continued entry of workers, but wanted their rights to be kept as limited as possible, in order to prevent job-changing or demands for better pay. The best possible worker for many marginal businesses was the illegal immigrant without a work permit, completely lacking in rights and hence an easy target for exploitation.[9]

Personnel managers in small companies in Tokyo point to the following advantages in employing illegal foreign workers:

1   work in earnest at simple and dirty jobs that Japanese would not do;
2   no troublesome procedures in employing then;

3   no need to consider social security benefits; and
4   lower wages.[10]

It is high time to try to rectify the injustice of inflicting suffering on migrant workers only. In international relations, the ideal treatment of different peoples is to provide complete equality. The second best is to provide reciprocally identical treatment by both nations concerned. Reciprocity is inferior to complete equality, but superior to ethnocentric or racist treatment, and far better than waging war.

AN INTERIM SOLUTION

The free movement of people across national borders, while attractive from a humanitarian point of view, is simply not possible where enormous disparities in levels of income exist between the nations concerned. In effect this would mean the lifting of borders, accompanied by enormous population flows which, in turn, would lead to the creation of migrant worker ghettos in the industrialized states. Here I would like to introduce the idea of reciprocity as a means to change Japan's policy of refusing entry to unskilled foreign workers. In essence, this means that nations would send and receive an equivalent number of people to work, regardless of any qualitative differences in the types of employment. Japanese are posted to Asian countries as managers, supervisors or trainees within subsidiary companies. Asians come from overseas to work in Japan as unskilled workers or hostesses. The two are equivalent in the sense that they both work. However, a complete matching of work content between the sending and receiving nation is not feasible in the Asian north–south context; it would amount to barter trade, leading to little human exchange.

The Foreign Ministry has reported that there were 42,305 Japanese employees and their families residing in Asian countries in 1987. The greatest number (8,999) were living in Hong Kong; followed by Singapore, 7,798; Indonesia, 5,341; Thailand, 4,715; Taiwan, 4,100; China, 2,784; Malaysia, 2,776; Korea, 1,967; the Philippines, 1,405; India, 928; Sri Lanka, 372; Bangladesh, 307; and Pakistan, 277. Under the sort of system proposed here, Japan would be obliged to accept an equivalent number of workers from the countries listed above. Bearing in mind, however, that Singapore itself suffers from labour shortages and that Hong Kong has not sent any workers to Japan, their quotas could be reassigned to other participating countries. The resulting figures would be: China, 6,000; Thailand and Indonesia, 5,000 each; the Philippines, Bangladesh and Pakistan, 4,500; Malaysia and Korea, 3,000 each; India and Sri Lanka, 1,000. If we also accept that Japan, as an economic superpower, should bear an unequal burden under any such arrangement, the above quotas could be multiplied by three which would produce a total of 128,000.

Multiplying these quotas by five would produce a total of 210,000, a figure slightly larger than the number of Japanese company employees and their families residing abroad in 1987.

The figures presented above are no more than a rough approximation of how arrangements of this sort could operate. Under the idea of reciprocity as outlined here, Japan would also undertake to bear the full social costs of providing language tuition, further education opportunities, as well as vocational training and rehabilitation for foreign workers. The people and the government would further guarantee that foreign workers would be entitled to equal pay and conditions of service, equal access to housing and the full range of social security benefits. On the other hand, immediate steps must be taken to end the activities of employers and brokers involved in the illegal recruitment and employment of foreign workers. In addition to imposing heavy fines on those agencies found to be trafficking in illegal labour, the government should also seek ways of establishing a network of Japanese language schools in Japan and other Asian countries. By doing so, the government would effectively put an end to the many private employment agencies which currently masquerade as language schools. Finally, an immediate amnesty should be offered to all illegally employed workers presently in Japan.

Some might argue that this programme of work exchange amounts to little more than a reshaping of border controls, an experiment which, on past experience in other countries, is unlikely to prove successful in Japan. Nevertheless, I believe that it may work if the following conditions are all satisfied:

1   the rigorous enforcement of stringent border controls (not a difficult task given that Japan has no continguous land frontier);
2   public support for a complete clamp down on illegal workers;
3   the introduction of stiff penalties for employers and brokers who break the law;
4   police enforcement of the law against the employment of illegal workers; and
5   a state-sponsored programme of labour recruitment.[11]

If the government has the political will to disregard the enormous profits which are generated by the use of illegal workers and if it can satisfy the above criteria, this programme would have the effect of immediately relieving the suffering of the illegal workers presently exploited. Even in this case, however, the number of illegal migrant workers might not be greatly reduced, as mentioned earlier.

CONCLUSION

The acceptance of migrant workers on a reciprocal basis should not be regarded as anything more than an interim response to the current injustices that they suffer. It does not, for example, address what many consider to be the fundamental factor in international labour migration, namely unequal economic development. By implication this means that Japan must also take a more prominent role in the economic and social development of the region as a whole, through increased direct investment, an expansion of its overseas aid programmes, the encouragement of NGO activities, and by increasing its imports from Asia. The issue of labour migration to Japan is one aspect of the north–south problem and must be resolved within that context. Any moves in this direction must also be accompanied by an amelioration of the status of Korean, Chinese and other long-term foreign residents.

NOTES

1 A.R. Zolberg (1978) 'International migration policies in a changing world system', in W.H. McNeilland and R.S. Adam (eds), *Human Migration*, London: Indiana University Press, p. 280.
2 T. Iyotani and T. Naito (1989) 'Tokyo no Kokusaika de Tenkan Serareru Chūsho Kighō' (Small/medium enterprises at the crossroads of internationalization) *Ekonomisuto*, 5 September, pp. 44–9.
3 Cited in H. Komai (1989) 'Gaikokujin Rōdōsha Hitsuzenron, Sakokron Kaikokuron wo Koete' (Why it is Essential to Accept Foreign Workers, Beyond the Closed-Door Policy and the Open-Door Policy) Part 1, *Ekonomisuto*, 15 August, pp. 28–33.
4 Figures given are of 1988. Cited in ibid.
5 T. Iyotani and T. Naito (1989) 'Tokyo no Kokusaika de Tenkan Serareru Chusho Kighō' (Small/medium enterprises at the crossroads of internationalization).
6 J. Solomos (1989) *Race and Racism in Contemporary Britain*, London: Macmillan, p. 127.
7 Ashai Shimbun, 24 September 1985, cited in P. Tasker (1987) *Inside Japan*, London: Penguin, pp. 15–16.
8 R. Cohen (1987) *The New Helots*, Hants: Gower, p. 178.
9 S. Castles, H. Booth and T. Wallace (1984) *Here for Good – Western Europe's New Ethnic Minorities*, London: Pluto, p. 31.
10 Cited in H. Komai (1989) 'Gaikokujin Rōdōsha Hitsuzenron, Sakokron Kaikokuron wo Koete' (Why it is Essential to Accept Foreign Workers, Beyond the Closed-Door Policy and the Open-Door Policy).
11 R. Cohen (1987) *The New Helots*.

REFERENCES

In this chapter Japanese language material, except for statistics and surveys, has not been included. Interested readers should refer to Hatsuse, R., 'Gaikokujin Rōdō' (Foreign Labour), *Kobe Hōgaku Zasshi*, 39 (2) (September 1989): 299–335.

Ajiaijin Rōdōsha Mondai (ed.) (1988) *The Asian Worker's Handbook*, Tokyo: Akashi Shoten.
Anderson, B. (1983) *Imagined Communities*, London: Verso.
Beer, L.W. (1981) 'Group rights and individual rights in Japan', *Asian Survey*, 21 (4): 438–53.
Castles, S., Booth, H. and Wallace, T. (1984) *Here for Good – Western Europe's New Ethnic Minorities*, London: Pluto.
Cohen, R. (1987) *The New Helots*, Hants: Gower.
Fujibayashi, H. (interviewer and ed.) (1990) 'Gaikokujin Rōdōsha Ukeire Mondai wa doko ni' (Whether To Accept Foreign Workers), *Sekai*, January: 52–67.
Iyotani, T. and Naito, T. (1989) 'Tokyo no Kokusaika de Tenkan Serareru Chūsho Kigyō' (Small/medium enterprises at the crossroads of internationalization) *Ekonomisuto*, 5 September 1989: 44–9.
Japan Immigration Association (ed.) (1987) *A Guide to Residence and Registration Procedures in Japan for Foreign Nationals (New Edition)*, Tokyo: Nippon Kajo Shuppan.
Komai, H. (1989) 'Gaikokujin Rōdōsha Hitsuzenron, Sakokuron Kaikokuron wo Koete (Why it is Essential to Accept Foreign Workers, Beyond the Closed-Door Policy and the Open-Door Policy), Part 1, *Ekonomisuto*, 15 August, pp. 28–33.
—— (1990) 'Gaikokujin Rōdōsha Hitsuzenron, Sakokuron Kaikokuron wo Koete (Why it is Essential to Accept Foreign Workers, Beyond the Closed-Door Policy and the Open-Door Policy; Proposing a Policy for Foreign Workers), Part 2, *Ekonomisuto*, 20 March, pp. 84–8.
Miles, R. (1989) *Racism*, London: Routledge.
Popham, P. (1990) 'Working for the Yen', *The Independent Magazine*, 13 January: 22–7.
Solomos, J. (1989) *Race and Racism in Contemporary Britain*, London: Macmillan.
Study Group, Immigration Bureau, Ministry of Justice (1988) *Employment of Foreign Nationals: Questions and Answers*, Tokyo: Nippon Kajo Shuppan.
Tasker, P. (1987) *Inside Japan*, London: Penguin.
Zolberg, A.R. (1978) 'International migration policies in a changing world system', in W.H. McNeilland and R.S. Adam (eds), *Human Migration*, London: Indiana University Press.

Chapter 13

The trade union response to migrant workers

Nimura Kazuo

INTRODUCTION

The issue of foreign workers has recently become the focus of concern for a number of individual researchers and other institutions (government, trade unions and academics).[1] Until 1987 this issue was taken up in one or two articles per month in the Monthly Bibliography of Labour Publications, compiled by the Ōhara Institute for Social Research of Hosei University, and published in the *Monthly Journal of the Japan Institute of Labour*. Since 1988 this figure has gradually risen to more than ten articles per month.

The migration of foreign workers to Japan has its origins in the rapid appreciation of the yen following the G-5 meeting of 1985. Of particular concern has been the increase in the number of so-called *Fuhō Shūrō Gaikokujin* (illegally employed foreign workers). According to figures published by the Immigration Bureau of the Ministry of Justice, in 1988 a total of 14,314 persons were arrested for violations of the Immigration Control Law. This represents a 26.6 per cent increase over the figure for 1982, and a sixfold increase over 1977.[2] This increase has also been characterized by a significant rise in the number of males among those classified as illegal workers.

Viewed purely in numerical terms, however, the issue of foreign workers has not yet become a serious social problem. At the end of 1988, the number of foreigners resident in Japan amounted to 941,005, only 0.8 per cent of the total population. Of these, 648,012 (mainly Koreans and Chinese whose families had been living in Japan since before the war) held rights of permanent residence.[3] Excluding permanent residents, there were approximately 30,000 further foreign residents who had been issued with work permits. Aside from these, the number of illegal foreign workers who had continued to reside and work in Japan after the expiration of their visa was estimated at around 130,000.[4] We can conclude from these estimates that the current number of foreign workers in Japan, excluding holders of permanent resident rights, is between 150,000–200,000. This represents no more than 0.3 per cent of a total working population of more than 61 million.

Why then has the issue of foreign workers begun to generate so much debate? One reason is that, by comparison with other countries, most Japanese regard their country as racially, culturally and linguistically homogeneous, and are therefore extremely concerned that an influx of foreign workers will lead to a multitude of social problems. A further reason is that jurisdictional disputes within the government have intensified concern over this issue. In the light of this, and with a view to regulating the increase in illegal foreign workers, the Ministry of Justice initiated a review of the Bill Concerning Enterprises Employing Foreign Workers in December 1986, and in the following year approved the proposals put forward by an internal working party. In response to this, The Ministry of Labour set up the Association for Research on the Problem of Foreign Workers in December 1987, and, at the end of March 1988, published its reply in the form of a report entitled 'The Way Forward for the Acceptance of Foreign Workers'. The Economic Planning Agency also established its own research association and approved its proposals. In addition, the Prime Minister's Office, the Foreign Ministry and MITI all carried out surveys on this issue, or continued with reviews of existing government policies. The various research bodies created within the government included not only academics, but representatives from various employers' organizations and the trade unions. This ensured that a wide range of opinion would be incorporated in the final reports.

Since people are naturally concerned about problems which may develop in the near future and how to deal with them, this issue is increasingly being taken up by central and regional government as a legal and administrative problem. As a consequence, the issue of foreign workers has become the focus of considerable attention and debate. There has, however, been surprisingly little discussion concerning the relationship between foreign workers and the Japanese trade union movement, though as we will see, both *Rengō* (All Japan Confederation of Private Sector Trade Unions) and *Sōhyō* (General Council of Trade Unions in Japan) have made clear their respective policies concerning foreign workers. Unions in the construction industry, as well as a number of unions across particular industries, have also begun to discuss the problems involved. Their policies, however, have amounted to little more than calling for government studies of the current situation, and demanding that appropriate action be taken. Hardly any effort has been made by the movement itself to consider what the unions themselves should be doing to address this issue.

In common with other countries where the issue of foreign workers has arisen, the position of Japanese trade unions is largely a passive one. It is management which has the ability to determine whether or not the company will employ foreign workers, and, if so, how many. Moreover, it is central government policy which controls the entry of foreign workers as a whole, and which also determines the right of entry as well as the length and conditions of stay for individual workers. The trade unions have no rights in these areas. It may be that the passive position adopted by the trade unions is also accounted for by the fact that most Japanese workers do not yet regard foreign workers as a threat. Seen in this light, the union stance is perhaps not so surprising.[5] But it is the ordinary Japanese worker who is in daily contact with foreign workers, and it is also the Japanese worker whose employment opportunities stand to be restricted by increases in the number of foreign workers, thus exposing him or her to the threat of unemployment. The future relationship between Japanese and foreign workers will thus depend on how the Japanese trade unions respond to these issues. In the long term, increases in the number of foreign workers will probably be unavoidable. The question of whether they are to work in harmony or in conflict with Japanese workers is not only central to the current debate over foreign labour, but also to the future of the Japanese trade union movement.

Moreover, the trade unions do play a clearly defined role in the determination of government policy. Both employers' groups and the unions send representatives to various government select committees of inquiry within the Ministry of Labour and elsewhere. *Rengō*, now the central national trade union organization, has issued policy statements on education and economics as well as on labour matters in an attempt to widen its influence. Trade unions will have to become involved in the process of formulating new directions in policy with regard to the issue of foreign workers. It will therefore be necessary to know what Japanese trade union leaders are thinking about the whole question. Furthermore, since the majority of Japanese trade unions are enterprise unions, it is also possible that they will influence individual company policies on the question of foreign workers.[6]

The presence of foreign workers was first considered as a problem of employment, but it is now widely recognized to have implications beyond purely economic concerns. Given the experiences of other industrial democracies, the importation of foreign labour is likely to exert a profound influence on wider social issues such as education, the urban environment and housing. Consequently, there are calls from some quarters for a complete ban on the employment of foreign workers. Nevertheless, the views of those who regard this issue as an opportunity for Japan's relatively closed society to become more open are gradually gaining ground. The latter view is shared by this author.

At present, one of the central areas of debate over official policy is how to find ways of preventing the 'issue' from becoming a 'problem'. Until now, government policy has in principle prohibited the entry of all unskilled workers, though this has clearly not been a foolproof deterrent. Another possible solution would be to regulate the flow of foreign workers by creating a ceiling on the number permitted to enter the country. This author is also of the opinion that such a course of action is worthy of serious consideration. It takes time before people of very different cultures, with different backgrounds and customs, are able to understand one another. There can be no doubt that gradually increasing the number of foreign workers over time would be preferable to allowing them to flood in *en masse*. What is more, there is also the possibility that political crises could erupt in neighbouring countries with the result that the number of exiles entering Japan might rapidly increase.

One important element has tended to be overlooked in the current debate on the issue of foreign workers, namely, the vital need for foreign workers to create their own movement and their own organizations in order to safeguard their human rights. However much careful consideration is given to this aspect politically, it will be impossible to prevent completely the emergence of prejudice against foreign workers. The matter clearly requires careful political and administrative consideration, but the government continues to affirm the view that 'Japan is a racially homogeneous nation state'. As is shown by the fact that many people still believe this 'myth' to be true, the sense of racial, linguistic and cultural solidarity within Japanese society is clearly strong. It has been suggested that in both Britain and Japan there exists a sense of insularity as island nations. Unlike Japan, however, Britain contains within its borders four separate countries, and regards itself as a multi-racial society, having for centuries absorbed people of many races from Europe and the Commonwealth. Social groups in Japan, in contrast, clearly discriminate on the basis of who is inside and who is outside the group (*uchi to soto*), and the tradition of doing so has very deep roots. Futhermore, there is a marked tendency within Japanese social groups, including companies, to discriminate against and to exclude, either consciously or unconsciously, minorities that do not conform to the values of the group. In a society with such characteristics, there is strong psychological resistance to accepting into one's group people who appear, even superficially, to be different from oneself.

In the short term, there is no problem provided they are taken in as guests. Initially, at least, the attitude may well be 'by all means, let's be hospitable', but how long would such an attitude survive among Japanese workers when they realize that those foreigners, who were supposed to be their workmates, hold a different set of cultural values? Is it not more likely that, especially in the case of non-white foreign workers, the effort to understand those different values and customs will give way to an insistence on conformity, summed up in the maxim 'when in Japan, do as the Japanese do'? In the transition to a more 'open society', capable of accepting people of different races and nationalities, it will be very difficult to avoid friction and confrontation. One can easily imagine that such friction and conflict will take the form of emotionally based prejudice and discrimination on the grounds of race and nationality. In fact, one does not need to imagine this sort of scenario, since Japanese society has already experienced such behaviour.

There is, for example, the oft-cited example of the more than 2 million Koreans who were brought to Japan, either forcibly or under duress, and were put to work in the mines and on construction sites during the Second World War. In theory, Koreans were at that time considered to be not foreigners, but Japanese nationals. They received a special education, the objective of which was to transform them into loyal subjects of the Emperor. The cost of this transformation was the eradication of Korean culture. There are still those who would argue that such things occurred because of the unusual circumstances during the war and that the situation is different now. However, Koreans have lived in Japan as foreigners since the war, and have been subject to various forms of discrimination at the hands of the Japanese – and such discrimination persists today. Koreans encounter discrimination in employment, particularly within the civil service, in courtship and marriage, and in terms of access to social welfare provision. Only very recently has the situation undergone a slight improvement with the removal of the so-called Nationality Clause, which had limited the right to a state pension, child benefit and access to public housing to Japanese nationals. Nevertheless, there still remains the nagging problem of alien registration with its compulsory fingerprinting, not to mention the fact that although Koreans are obliged to pay the same taxes as Japanese citizens, they posses neither the right to vote, nor the right to stand for public office.

In recent years the position of Koreans in Japanese society has improved somewhat. Since 1977 it has been possible for foreigners to take the entrance examination for the judiciary, and the restriction which limited candidacy for the Nippon Telegraph and Telephone Public Corporation's entrance examination to Japanese citizens has also been lifted. In 1984, the nationality clause relating to postmen was removed, and in 1986 non-Japanese became eligible for employment as nurses in hospitals operated by local authorities. There is no doubt that the organized movement of Korean people living in Japan has been one of the leading forces which has worked to bring about these changes.[7]

It is essential, therefore, that the issue of foreign workers is not considered solely on the basis of what will be in the best interests of Japan. It is imperative that they be perceived as human beings with the same human rights as Japanese, and not simply as commodities to be traded in the marketplace. This might seem obvious, but those who consider themselves to be 'realists' dismiss such considerations as mere sentimentality. The result is that the weak legal, social and economic position of foreign workers is taken advantage of, their human rights are abused, and instances of exploitation are either ignored or not taken seriously. The so-called 'illegal immigrants' are the most vulnerable group of all. In the view of this author, the creation of an environment in which foreign workers will be able to demand their own rights is an absolute necessity. Legislation alone will not guarantee their basic human rights, nor will it necessarily end discrimination and prejudice. This has already been proven in Japan and other countries. The deciding factor in any defence of human rights is organized action taken by the aggrieved individuals themselves, in this case, foreign workers. To resolve the problem of foreign workers in Japan, it is therefore absolutely necessary to create the conditions in which such action can develop. Certainly, both central and local government have an important role to play in this, but an even more important role can be taken on by the trade unions. The following discussion will therefore consider the policy objectives which Japanese trade unions currently pursue with regard to foreign workers; the actions which the unions are actually taking; and the type of role the unions can or cannot play in the future.

JAPANESE TRADE UNION OBJECTIVES

National organizations

Rengō: All-Japan Confederation of Private Sector Trade Unions

Formed in November 1987 around a nucleus of large corporate enterprise unions, *Rengō*, with a current membership in excess of 5.5 million, is today the largest national trade union organization, far outstripping *Sōhyō*. In November 1989, *Sōhyō* formally disbanded and merged with *Rengō*, leaving the latter as the national trade union organization in Japan. In March 1988, *Rengō* published the following policy objectives with regard to the issue of foreign workers.[8]

Basic principles

1 Opposition to the free and unconditional entry of foreign workers.
2 Where foreign workers are employed, their employment must be in balance with that of Japanese workers. Before criteria for employment are clarified, the conditions of the environment in which foreign workers are to live and work must be determined and a national consensus among the Japanese people obtained.
3 Conditions for determining specific criteria for acceptance:

   (a) That there should be no adverse effects on national employment practices and conditions of labour.

(b) That employers' responsibilities should be clear.
(c) That the employment engaged in by foreign workers should have some social value.
(d) That the burden of responsibility to pay should be made clear if social costs are incurred by the foreign workers.
(e) That the views of Japanese workers be sufficiently taken into account.

4   That the participation of trade unions in the determination and application of such criteria should be guaranteed.
5   That fair and just labour standards be established to guarantee equal rights with Japanese workers.
6   That illegal practices be eradicated.
7   That employment opportunities in foreign workers' countries of origin be expanded by increasing Japanese overseas aid and by accepting more foreign trainees.

Demands submitted to government

1   The situation of foreign workers in Japan should be investigated and clarified.
2   A 'Foreign Workers' Policy Review Body', consisting of representatives from government, trade unions, management and the academic world, should be set up to generate a national consensus on the question.
3   Disciplinary measures against employers who employ foreign workers illegally should be tightened and the workers involved deported. They should, however, receive protection from the state until the time of their deportation.
4   Study in Japan for overseas trainees and postgraduate students should be actively promoted.
5   Trade unions should be involved in the expansion of overseas aid programmes and in ODA planning discussions.
6   A rational policy of economic growth should be maintained and an overall employment policy be promoted in order to achieve an optimum employment environment.
7   Policies to tackle areas of instability in the labour market (part-time work, day labourers, etc.) should be more actively pursued.
8   Minimum labour standards should be raised.

Sōhyō: General Council of Trade Unions in Japan

Sōhyō, which has played a major role in a variety of social movements since the American Occupation, including the trade union and peace movements, disbanded in November 1989 in order to merge with *Rengō*.

However, on the issue of foreign workers, the policies of the two organizations revealed considerable differences in outlook. Since a new unified
policy has yet to emerge, it may be useful to refer briefly to *Sōhyō*'s policy
statement for 1988 which contained the following:[9]

Basic principles

1   The issue of foreign workers is not simply a question of labour supply.
    It needs to be carefully studied from a broad overall perspective.
2   The terms of the Universal Declaration on Human Rights of 1948, and
    ILO Convention 97 (Convention concerning Migration for Employ-
    ment (revised 1949)) must be respected.
3   The present system of controls (in accordance with the Immigration
    Control Law) should be revised with a view to advancing international-
    ization and preventing illegal employment.
4   Anti-discrimination measures are needed to guarantee and safeguard
    foreign workers' human rights. Technical education and training
    policies as well as Japanese language training facilities are essential
    prerequisites for the employment of foreign workers.
5   There is an urgent need for strict penalties for those employing workers
    illegally and for special measures to deal with the workers so
    employed.
6   The viability of an overall quota system to control the number of
    foreign workers ought to be investigated. Official overseas aid
    programmes which are directly connected with the creation and expan-
    sion of employment opportunities must contribute towards employ-
    ment programmes in foreign workers' countries of origin.

Urgent demands

1   Policies must be based upon respect for human rights.
2   Serious problems can be expected from any rush to employ foreign
    workers in the present worsening climate for employment.
3   The current situation with regard to foreign workers needs to be
    urgently reviewed. The extent to which the Labour Standards Law is
    being adhered to (non-payment of wages, lack of respect for human
    rights, etc.) needs to be investigated and special measures enacted to
    protect workers' rights.

AREAS OF DIFFERENCE BETWEEN *RENGŌ* AND *SŌHYŌ*

In terms of their concrete policies, there was considerable common ground
between these two organizations. Both were, for example, opposed to the
entry of unskilled labourers, and united in: first, the demand for overseas

aid to stimulate employment in the sending countries; second, the need for more punitive measures to be taken against companies and individuals who employed illegal workers; and third, the need for Japanese language provision and technical training with a view to creating a hospitable environment for foreign workers.

In the basic principles which underlay these proposals, however, the two organizations differed widely. Whereas *Rengō* laid emphasis on security of employment for Japanese workers and preventing a decline in working conditions, *Sōhyō* had as its main priorities the human rights of foreign workers and the abolition of discrimination against them. This difference in 'basic principles' was also reflected in the attitude of the two organizations towards the policies of the Ministry of Labour. The final report of the ministry's Study Group on the Issue of Foreign Workers was published in December 1988. *Rengō* welcomed the report and called for 'the full co-operation of all concerned government departments in the urgent implementation of the many recommendations contained in the report'. *Sōhyō*, on the other hand, criticized the report, claiming that it 'did not make provision for the kind of thorough conditions of entry seen in Europe and the USA', and that it merely proposed 'an extension of the present restrictions on entry as a means of confirming the present situation', a course of action which would not lead to the resolution of the problem.

Superficially it would appear that *Sōhyō* was firmly opposed to increasing the number of foreign workers permitted to enter the country. In fact, however, *Sōhyō* was more positively disposed towards the entry of foreign workers than was *Rengō*. There were, for example, voices within *Sōhyō* that favoured the introduction of a 'labour permit system', under which the number of foreign workers permitted to enter the country would equal the number of Japanese working abroad. There had also been criticism from within *Sōhyō* of an earlier proposal put forward by the Ministry of Labour for the creation of an 'employment permission system', under which work permits for foreign workers would be issued to the companies employing them rather than to the individual workers themselves. *Sōhyō* had itself been pressing for a system which would entail the issuing of permits to individual workers. A number of citizens' groups have also urged that human rights for foreign workers be given legal backing. *Rengō*, however, not only opposed any such legislation, but insisted that illegal foreign workers be deported. In a general sense, the problem was that both *Rengō* and *Sōhyō* had largely limited their activities to pressing the government to act on their respective proposals, but had given little consideration to what the trade unions themselves could do. It could even be said that *Rengō* had done little more than demand official recognition of the need for trade union representation in the debate on the issue of foreign workers.

INDUSTRIAL FEDERATIONS OF TRADE UNION ORGANIZATIONS

Zenkensōren: National Federation of Construction Workers' Unions

The first union organizations to address the issue of foreign workers were sectoral union organizations in the construction industry in which large numbers of foreigners were already employed. Among these, one of the first to examine the problem and to take action was *Zenkensōren* which represents 385,000 construction workers, such as carpenters and plasterers. In October 1986 and again in May 1987, *Zenkensōren* called on major construction companies and housing companies, 'not to make use of foreign labour as illegal workers'. This led to the first case of conflict between workers over the issue when in June 1987, an organization calling itself the *Karabaw* Group, which supports Filipino workers in Japan, complained that *Zenkensōren's* campaign 'infringed the human rights of foreign workers'.

The first paragraph of the section relating to foreign workers in the policy statement passed by the October 1988 *Zenkensōren* Conference deals with the matter in detail.[10] It states that there are an estimated 100,000 foreigners working in Japan who entered the country illegally and declares the union's 'opposition to illegal employment', giving as the main reason the fact that 'at a time when even Japanese workers are not guaranteed fair wages and decent working conditions, there is the danger that such practices will drive wages and working conditions down even further'. The same policy statement claims that a major reason for the issue of foreign workers becoming a problem, especially in the construction industry, lies in the rising value of the yen. It also notes that an even more significant factor is that shortages of skilled workers have developed owing to increases in the numbers of workers changing jobs, which in turn is caused by the construction industry's practice of laying off workers once jobs are completed. Whenever times have been difficult, the statement continues, big companies have immediately reduced the value of contracts for their subcontractors, have laid off workers and cut their wages. Consequently, even if large general contractors were to give assurances that they would not hire foreign workers who had entered the country illegally, their subcontractors would still continue to do so, because, if they did not, jobs would not be completed. Furthermore, if a slump were to hit the industry again in the future, the first to suffer would be the foreign workers, who are particularly vulnerable to lay-offs. In the event of this taking place, there is no doubt that serious social problems would ensue.

In an attempt to strengthen its argument against the use of foreign labour, the statement goes on to cite the experience of various European countries where migrant foreign workers have been employed. The introduction of foreign workers, it claims, has led to numerous problems in the areas of social welfare, education and in the maintenance of public order. Two-tier labour markets have developed as European workers have refrained from taking low-paid jobs with poor working conditions, leaving employers in such businesses entirely dependent on foreign labour. The result has been human rights' problems fed by racial discrimination. Most countries now encourage their foreign workers to return home, but the numbers have not dropped.

As for the use of unskilled foreign labour, currently the main focus of debate, the statement notes that even the majority of construction companies oppose it, despite the fact that they are keen to cut their labour costs. The document also points out that a special characteristic of the Japanese construction industry is that there are no firm job demarcations between skilled and unskilled work. A new worker doing unskilled work gradually acquires skills on the job and eventually becomes recognized as a skilled worker. On the other hand, skilled workers continue to do unskilled work. Since it is therefore difficult to distinguish between skilled and unskilled work, the statement concludes that *Zenkensōren* 'is opposed, in principle, to the employment of any foreign workers in the construction industry, whether skilled or unskilled'.

On the question of labour shortages in the construction industry, the policy statement emphasizes the need to recruit labour from other industries currently in structural difficulties and to make the construction industry a more attractive industry in which to work, principally by raising wage levels and the standard of working conditions throughout the industry as a whole. The statement also calls on the Japanese government to implement positive and effective programmes of overseas aid which will lead to increased employment opportunities in the sending countries, thus rendering it unnecessary for them to have to travel abroad to find employment.

In conclusion, the statement deals with American and Korean demands for the liberalization of the construction industry in Japan, and calls for assurances from the Japanese government that, if foreign companies are allowed access to major Japanese domestic construction projects, no adverse effects on Japanese workers will result from the employment of foreign workers. According to certain newspaper reports, the situation within unions of this type contradicts the image they would like to present to the public. This is illustrated by the fact that there is concern among self-employed foremen, who make up about 10 per cent of the membership of *Zenkensōren*, over the lack of new apprentices. Many of these foremen have expressed a desire to bring in foreign workers as auxiliaries to bridge the gap.[11]

Zōsenjūki-Rōren: Confederation of Shipbuilding and Engineering Workers' Unions

With the slump in the shipbuilding industry which began in the 1970s, the membership of *Zōsenjūki-rōren* fell from 233,000 in 1976 to 166,000 in 1986 and to 127,000 in 1988. In its policy statement for 1988 the confederation included the following declaration of its opposition to the employment of unskilled foreign workers:[12]

> Given the rapid changes now affecting the structure of Japanese industry, with the consequent loss of many jobs for manual workers, it is clear that the introduction of unskilled foreign labour will lead to large-scale unemployment among Japanese workers. At the same time, in view of the friction which has developed between foreign workers and local people in the developed countries of America and Europe, and the social tensions resulting from such friction, it cannot be accepted that Japan should open its doors to allow in unskilled foreign labour. Japanese companies should not forget that they exist to provide employment first and foremost for Japanese people and also to ensure a livelihood which, as Japanese, the people will not feel ashamed of. This Confederation calls on the government to recognize that international co-operation means striving to the utmost to help developing countries raise their standards of living by promoting free trade, increasing ODA levels and assisting in the creation of jobs in those countries that need them.

Unions in support of foreign workers

From the kind of statements quoted above, it would appear that Japanese unions are united in their opposition to the employment of unskilled foreign workers, but there are a few unions which have come out in support of foreign workers:

Sōhyō Osaka Higashi District Amalgamated Union – Union Higōrō[13]

Formed in 1983 in the east district of the city of Osaka by the (*Sōhyō*) Osaka Higashi District Council of Trade Unions, Union *Higōrō* (the name is an abbreviation: *Higashi* (east); *Gōdō* (amalgamated); *Rōsō* (union)), is a small union, with several hundred members drawn from various industries including beauticians, cooks, drivers and so forth. The focus of the union's activities is mutual aid, towards which the members pay ¥600 (just over £2.00 at current exchange rates) per month as a part of their union dues and which includes a telephone consultation network. The union's motto is 'Workers support each other and fight all forms of discrimination.' As part of its struggle against all forms of discrimination, the union began to concern itself with the problems of Asian migrant workers and has produced the following English leaflet for those workers:

> To Asian Friends,
>
> We inform you of the following facts concerning your rights in Japan.
>
> Your mimimum conditions such as working hours and wages are guaranteed in Japan by the Labour Standards Law and the Minimum Wages Law whatever your jobs are. The above-mentioned rights are under protection while you work in this country no matter what types of visa you have. However, Japanese managers and company owners do not always observe these laws.
>
> We, UNION *HIGORO*, protect your rights from unfair practices of managers. Please feel free to come and talk over your troubles with us. For information and assistance, call 941-1169.

Edogawa Union[14]

This union was formed in 1984 by the Edogawa District Council of Trade Unions in the east district of Tokyo. More than half of its 300 members are part-time workers. It is a union of individual members, that is, of the self-employed, of people who work at home and also of unemployed people. The union has been conducting a campaign in support of foreign workers since 1986, when it was consulted on the question of the parentage of a child born to a Filipino woman and a Japanese man. It has been involved in solving problems of non-payment of wages and is currently investigating the situation of foreign workers in its area.

(Sōhyō) Zenkokuippan Tokyo Nanbu – *South Tokyo local branch of the National Union of General Workers*[15]

(Sōhyō) Zenkokuippan draws its members from shops and small businesses, and the South Tokyo branch is based in the downtown area of the city. It is an unusual union in Japan in that 10 per cent of its members (260 out of a total of 2,600) are foreigners, all of whom are English language teachers, and this has enabled the union to offer an English language labour consultation service.

Another feature of the union is its support of the Bangladesh Buddhist Association of Japan. This is an organization of Bangladeshi Buddhists resident in Japan, and whose religion is a minority faith in their own country. Its aim is not only to provide a mutual aid framework for Bangladeshis, but also to introduce Japanese and Bangladeshis to each other's cultures. The Association finances itself from money earned from teaching Japanese and from contributions from the low wages of its members, and arranges for promising young people from Bangladesh to come over to Japan. To defend their rights, it is essential that foreign workers should form their own organizations, and, from this point of view, the existence of a body such as this association is very significant.

Kotobuki – *solidarity with foreign migrant workers*[16]

This group, founded in May 1987, is more commonly known as the *Karabaw* Group; the word means 'water buffalo' in Tagalog, the language of most of the Filipino day labourers who gather at specified recruiting areas in Yokohama to obtain a day's work from construction companies and other employers. The group is not a trade union as such, but rather a social pressure group which takes as its aim the legalization of all forms of work undertaken by foreigners, including unskilled workers.

The founding nucleus of the group was, however, the day labourers' union in Kotobuki-cho, an area of Yokohama. The group is campaigning for legalization of entry for all categories of foreign worker. This is largely due to the fact that while illegal foreign workers are guaranteed accident insurance and welfare benefits by law, relatively few 'illegals' actually exercise these rights in cases of non-payment of wages or non-payment of accident compensation. This, in turn, is because they are afraid of arrest and deportation by the immigration authorities. The root cause of such problems lies in the strict limits on the entry of foreign workers set by the government. Consequently, whereas assistance or support from other unions usually takes the form of telephone advice services and help with problems of non-payment of wages, for example, the Kotobuki group's campaign is directed at gaining official recognition of the residence rights of those foreign workers currently in Japan, and also at legalization of entry for all foreign workers, including unskilled workers. The group has published a booklet, *Towards Legalization For Foreign Workers* and puts out a newsheet in Japanese and English aimed at increasing support for its campaign. It also campaigns against *Zenkensōren's* efforts to persuade construction companies to refuse employment to illegal workers.

The *Karabaw* Group is also pressing for the implementation of four other demands:

1   the establishment of state-run employment agencies for foreign workers which will uphold the principle of the individual's free choice in selecting employment;
2   the establishment of advice centres for foreign workers where they can receive advice on medical matters, employment concerns and social problems in general;
3   the provision of free language training for foreign workers which would provide them with the necessary linguistic skills for daily life in Japan; and

4   the safeguarding of foreign workers' rights through the application of
     all Japanese law to foreign workers, beginning with the principle of
     equal pay for equal work.

All the unions supporting foreign workers then are small-scale organizations with only a few hundred members each, most of whom are day
labourers, part-timers and employees of small businesses. They are 'general
unions' based on their geographical area of activity and not on the workplace itself, and are thus outside the mainstream of Japanese unionism
which is overwhelmingly made up of enterprise unions. Most are also
independent of any larger organization, though some have received assistance from local branches of *Sōhyō*. Their activities in support of foreign
workers are, for the most part, concerned with non-payment of wages and
solving problems associated with industrial accidents. Membership is open
to foreign workers, but the number of actual foreign participants is low.

PROBLEMS AND PROSPECTS

The issue of foreign workers poses awkward questions for Japanese trade
unions, which are caught between their principles and their actual policies.
Traditionally, the trade union movement has based its policies on the
principles of internationalism and international worker solidarity. Japanese
trade unions have been no exception. The organization from which
Japanese trade unions can be said to originate, the Friends of Labour, was
founded in San Francisco in 1891 by migrant workers from Japan who,
despite the discrimination they suffered at the hands of American workers,
realized that ordinary American people owed their high standard of living
to the trade union movement, and worked to transplant trade unionism to
Japan. One of the leading figures of the Friends of Labour, Takano
Fusataro, became acquainted with Samuel Gompers and was chosen to be
the AFL organizer for Japan. On his return, he set out to promote the
spread of trade unionism.[17] Since then, Japanese trade unions have
benefited greatly from their contacts with foreign trade unions, not least
from the existence of the ILO. Against such a background, if Japanese
trade unions proclaim their loyalty to principles of international solidarity
and then proceed to demand the exclusion of foreign workers, they will be
criticized by those foreign workers for compromising their own principles.

Nevertheless, trade unions exist primarily to improve working conditions
for their members and to safeguard the jobs of their members. From that
point of view, it is only natural that trade unions in any country would
oppose the employment of foreign workers, because a sudden influx of
large numbers of foreign workers accustomed to working for low wages in
their own country would obviously be to the advantage of management and
to the considerable disadvantage of the indigenous workforce. It is there-

fore only natural that employers should be positively in favour of employing foreign workers while the attitude of trade unions is negative. Since the construction industry is notoriously vulnerable to fluctuations in the economy and is already absorbing 'illegal' foreign migrant workers, the unions in that industry in particular cannot be criticized for warning against any increases in the number of foreign workers, or for opposing the entry of such workers.

What concerns this writer, however, is the fact that most Japanese trade unions are dealing with the issue of foreign workers solely from the point of view of defending the working conditions and the jobs of Japanese workers; they are not conscious of the need to solve the dilemma that their actions place them in – in which their own traditions risk being compromised.

Most observers agree that, in the long term, Japan will be unable to avoid increases in the number of foreign workers. If that view proves to be correct, then the day will eventually come when Japanese trade unions will be forced to consider seriously the prospect of accepting foreign workers as members. Many unions in the West are currently making energetic efforts to attract such workers. They may not have been in favour of this course of action when foreign workers first entered their countries, but these unions have realized that if they are to maintain their own strength, then they have no other choice but to do so. This realization has yet to dawn on trade unions in Japan.

One reason why they do not feel the need to recruit foreign workers no doubt lies in the fact that the number of such workers in Japan is still very small. What is more, foreign workers themselves also show little interest in joining trade unions. Most of them, after all, are temporary migrant workers, who simply wish to make as much money as they can in a short period of time and then return to their own countries. They do not see the merit of becoming a member of a trade union, in paying union dues and becoming involved in union actions that do not quickly result in more money. Furthermore, many of the illegal immigrants are employed in small businesses which are not unionized; they live in constant fear of detection and arrest by the immigration authorities. Understandably, they would not feel enthusiastic about becoming involved in union activity. Even if some do join a union when faced with a problem at work, they tend to leave again when the problem has been resolved.

Trade union leaders need to consider the fact that the policies their unions formulate now will have a considerable bearing on the way that relations with foreign workers develop in the future. If they begin by adopting a hostile stance towards foreign workers, they will lose their trust, and it will be difficult to regain. One cannot help feeling concern therefore at the kind of policy statements put out by *Rengō* and *Zenkensōren*, which call on the government to deport 'illegal workers'.

CONCLUSION

Since the end of the war, Japanese trade unions, in particular *Sōhyō*, have provided great human and financial support for a variety of social movements and campaigns. In order to link up with *Rengō*, *Sōhyō* dissolved itself in November 1989. What policies will *Rengō* then pursue with regard to the employment of foreign migrant workers? It will not be sufficient to limit its activities to the periodic submission of requests to the government for appropriate action, although such government action will always be necessary. The trade unions need to take a long-term view and find their own solutions to the problem. For example, they ought to apply themselves more to the task of raising the level of the working conditions of foreign workers to those of Japanese workers, irrespective of questions of 'legality'. Another particularly important task for the unions is to protect those workers who suffer exploitation and human rights abuses because their 'illegal' employment puts them in a weak legal position. Rather than the government, it should be the trade unions which provide centres where foreign workers can go for help in confidence, without having to fear deportation as 'illegal workers'. Such actions would serve to raise the Japanese trade union movement in the estimation of foreign workers and would prepare the way for unionization of foreign workers in the years to come.

However, at the moment, Japanese trade unions do not seem predisposed to accept such advice. On the contrary, it is more likely to be rejected out of hand with unrealistic emotional arguments. Given their present attitude, it is unlikely that Japanese trade unions will make the kind of effort to recruit foreign workers that unions in Europe and America are now making. This is because most Japanese trade unions are 'enterprise unions' whose members are all full-time regular workers. However, there exists throughout Japanese industry today a great number of 'false part-timers' (*giji paato*) who are part-time workers in name only and who, in fact, work virtually the same hours as full-time regular workers. Whereas full-time employees are guaranteed jobs for life under the so-called 'life-time employment' system, the short-term contracts of the part-time workers are subject to periodic renewal. Companies use this pool of part-time labour as a 'buffer' against changes in an economic climate which requires flexibility in employment policy, and the full-time unionized employees understand only too well that this means a stable employment situation for themselves. Many union members even consider it appropriate that their own relatively high wages are guaranteed by the existence of the lower-paid, part-time employees.

From the end of the war until the 1950s 'company democracy' was one of the unions' main slogans, and, to a certain extent they succeeded in removing the distinctions between white-collar workers. They were also successful in having many temporary workers upgraded to full-time status. With the high economic growth of the 1960s and 1970s, however, Japanese union members became the members of a 'new labour aristocracy', which accepted the need for 'false part-time workers' to guarantee its own stability of employment. This has been the main reason why the unionization of part-time workers has not made much progress. Of course, there has also been a reluctance on the part of part-time workers themselves to join unions, but more important has been the negative attitude of the full-time employees who have not wanted their part-time colleagues to join them. One can therefore understand why there has been no interest at all among the enterprise unions in recruiting foreign workers who are hired on the same short-term basis as part-time Japanese employees. Neither can any such interest be expected to develop in the foreseeable future. Nevertheless, some Japanese unions are open to accepting foreign workers as members. These are the new-style 'community unions' which began to appear within the trade union movement in 1983 and have since spread rapidly across the country. At the end of 1987 they numbered more than thirty.[18] Their organizing strength is still slight and, as in the case of the Edogawa Union and Union *Higōrō*, membership is measured in the hundreds rather than thousands.

The number of part-time workers has risen sharply and has been one important factor which has caused a drop in union membership relative to potential membership year by year. Both *Sōhyō* and *Rengō* had therefore begun to emphasize the importance of more active recruiting campaigns. If, on the other hand, the community union movement continues to grow, then the character of the trade union movement as a whole will change and may very well become more amenable to accepting foreign workers. This is not, however, a development which can be expected in the near future.

AUTHOR'S NOTE

This chapter is a revised version of a paper presented at a conference held in September 1989 and does not therefore refer to a significant development which has since taken place. This is the re-organization of the Japanese labour union movement. On 21 and 22 September 1989 – precisely the time when the Sheffield Conference was being held – *Sōhyō* held its final annual conference. A resolution to dissolve the organization was formally passed at that time, and came into effect two months later, on 21 November 1989. On the same day, *Rengō* accepted into membership its first public sector unions, and changed its name to The Japanese Trade Union Confederation ('new' *Rengō*) with a membership of 8 million.

Also on 21 November 1989 the communist trade unions, which had either refused to join the new organization or had their applications for membership rejected, formed *Zenrōren* (The National Confederation of

Trade Unions), with 1.4 million members. A further national confederation also founded at this time was *Zenrōkyō* (The National Trade Union Council), made up of unions associated with the left wing of the Japan Socialist Party which had not joined the new *Rengō*. The effect of these changes is that two of the organizations referred to in this paper, *Sōhyō* and (old) *Rengō* – now no longer exist.

Nevertheless, the new *Rengō* has inherited the basic policy position of its defunct namesake, and is not expected to alter its policies on the foreign worker issue in the near future. And although the two national federations (*Sōhyō* and (old) *Rengō*) have disappeared, their constituent unions such as the National Construction Workers' Union (*Zenkenkyō*) continue to exist. To this extent, therefore, the outline of union policy contained in this chapter is still a reflection of the current situation, and has not become a mere historical record. Nor have these organizational changes altered the main thrust of the author's argument.

It is appropriate to refer briefly to other changes that have taken place since the paper was presented. The first of these was the revision of the Immigration Control and Refugee Recognition Law enacted on 8 December 1989. The revised law came into effect in July 1990, and imposed penalties on the recruiters and employers of illegal immigrants, whose activities had gone unchecked until that time. It is as yet unclear what the effects of this revision will be.

The continuing buoyancy of the economy has created an even greater labour shortage, resulting in a significant change in employer attitudes. In particular, there has been a rise in the number of employers in the restaurant and food preparation sector and in the construction sector who are actively seeking foreign workers, including unskilled labour. The government too is considering whether to accept unskilled workers under the title of 'trainees'. It is therefore quite likely that the situation will change dramatically in the near future.

NOTES

1 Publications in Japanese include: Saeki 1989; Hanami and Kuwahara 1989; Ōhara Shakai Mondai Kenkyūjo (Ōhara Institute for Social Research 1989); and Kantō Bengoshi Kai Rengōkai (Kantō Federation of Lawyers' Associations) 1990. A specialist journal on the topic is *Kokusai Jinryu*, published by the Immigration Association. The Immigration Bureau co-operates in editing this journal, which contains up-to-date immigration statistics and other pertinent materials. In English, see: Kuwahara 1988; Foreign Workers' Affairs Office 1989; Mori 1990; and Study Group, Immigration Bureau 1988. This last publication outlines in Japanese and English the policies of the Immigration Bureau. *Ajiajin Rōdōsha Mondai Kondankai* 1988, a private support organization for Asian workers, sets out in English and Japanese the legal rights of foreign workers.
2 Immigration Bureau 1978; 1983; 1989.

3 Yamagami (1990).
4 Mori (1990).
5 An exception is the All Japan Seamen's Union. In the shipping industry, members of the union had for some time seen their jobs going to foreigners under the flag of convenience system. On 25 October 1989, the All Japan Seamen's Union reached an agreement with the employers to allow Japanese and foreign seamen to serve together on the so-called 'Maru-ships' – Japanese flag carriers on loan. See *Asahi Shimbun*, 26 October 1989; *Kai-iin*, January 1990; and *Nihon Rōdō Nenkan*, vol. 60, 1990: 272.
6 Enterprise unions account for 90 per cent of all unions and 80 per cent of all unionized workers (Shirai 1979: 18).
7 For a more detailed discussion of the movement for the abolition of such discrimination see *Pak-kun wo Kakomu Kai* 1974; *Zainichi Kankoku/ Chōsenjin no Kokumin Nenkin wo Motomeru Kai* 1984; Nagai 1989; and Oka and Mizuno 1989. There are many local authorities that continue to apply a nationality clause in relation to the employment of public servants. Very few actually employ non-Japanese nationals. According to figures published by the Ministry of Home Affairs, 1 April 1989, a total of 1,616 foreign nationals were employed by local authorities, and of these 539 were full-time employees.
8 *Rengō Seisaku Shiryō*, no 47, and *Ōhara Shakai Mondai Kenkyū Zasshi*, 6 July 1990.
9 *Sōhyō Seisaku Shū* 1988; *Ōhara Shakai Mondai Kenkyū Zasshi*, 6 July 1990.
10 *Platform of the Thirtieth Conference of Zenkensōren*; *Background Materials of the Thirtieth Conference of Zenkensōren*; and *Ōhara Shakai Mondai Kenkyū Zasshi*, 6 July 1990.
11 Asahi Shimbun, 1 August 1988.
12 Record of measures proposed at the Nineteenth Conference of *Zōsenjūki-rōren* 24–26 August 1988.
13 *Community Union Kenkyū-kai* 1988: 44–51.
14 *Gekkan Sōhyō*, May 1989 and *Community Union Kenkyū-kai*.
15 Interview with Watanabe Ben, Vice Chairman of the National Union of General Workers, Tokyo Chapter, South District, 30 November 1988.
16 *Karabaw no Kai*, September 1987; 1988.
17 *Karabaw no Kai*, September 1987; 1988.
18 Nimura (1979).

REFERENCES

Ajiajin Rōdōsha Mondai Kondankai (ed.) (1988) *Ajiajin Deskasegi Rōdōsha Techō* (The Asian Worker's Handbook), Tokyo: Akashi Shoten.
Foreign Workers' Affairs Office, Ministry of Labour (ed.) (1989) 'Response to foreign worker issue', *Japan Labour Bulletin*, October.
Gekkan Sōhyō, May 1989.
Hanami, T. and Kuwahara, Y. (ed.) (1989) *Ashita no Tonaribito Gaikokujin Rōdōsha* (Tomorrows Neighbours, Foreign Workers), Tokyo: Tōyō Keizai Shimpōsha.
Immigration Bureau, Ministry of Justice (1978, 1983, 1989) *Shutsunyū Koku Kanri Tōkei Nenpō* (Annual Report on Immigration Statistics), Tokyo.
—— (1988) *Employment of Foreign Nationals: Questions and Answers* Tokyo: Nihon Kajo Shuppan.
Kai-in, January 1990.
Kantō Bengōshi kai Rengōkai (ed.) (1990) *Gaikokujin Rōdōsha no Shūrō to Jinken*

(The Employment and Human Rights of Foreign Workers), Tokyo: Akashi Shoten.
Karabaw no Kai (ed.) (1987) 'Firipinjin Dekasegi Rōdōsha to no Rentai wo Motemete' (A Call for Solidarity with Filipino Migrant Workers), *Shinchi-hei*, September.
—— (1988) *Gaikokujin Rōdōsha no Gōhōka ni Mukete*, (Towards the Legalization of Foreign Workers), Tokyo: Shinchi-Heisha.
Kenkyū-kai Community Union (ed.) (1988) *Community Union Sengen* (Declaration of the Community Union), Tokyo: Dai-ichi Shorin.
Kuwahara, Y. (1988) 'Towards re-establishing a foreign workers' policy', *Japan Labour Bulletin*, November.
Mori, H. (1990) 'An estimate of the influx of illegal workers into Japan (1975–1988)', *Journal of International Studies*, March.
Nagai, K. (1989) *Eijyū Gaikokujin to Kōmu Shūnin-ken – Nanaju Man-nin wo Shimedasu Ronri*, (The Right of Permanant Resident Foreigners to Employment as Public Officials: The Exclusion of 700,000 People) Tokyo: Tsuge Shobo.
Nimura, K. (1979) 'Shokkō Giyūkai to Kashū Nihonjin Kutsukō Dōmeikai' (The Union of Japanese Shoemakers in Canada and the Society of Labour Volunteers), *Reimeikai Nihon Rōdō Undō no Saikentō* (A Reassessment of the Earliest Period of the Japanese Labour Movement), Tokyo: Junposha.
Ōhara Shakai Mondai Kenkyūjo (ed.) (1989, 1990) 'Nihon ni okeru Gaikokujin Rōdōsha' (The Problem of Foreign Workers in Japan), *Nihon Rōdō Nenkan*, nos 59, 60, Tokyo: Ōhara Shakai Mondai Kenkyūjo.
—— (1990) *Ōhara Shakai Mondai Kenkyūjo Zasshi* June–July.
Oka, M. and Mizuno, S. (1989) *Gaikokujin ga Kōmuin ni natte ii jya nai ka to iu Hon* (Why Shouldn't Foreigners Become Public Officials), Tokyo: Komichi Shobo.
Pak-kun wo Kakomu Kai (1974) *Minzoku Sabetsu; Hitachi Shūshoku Sabetsu Kyūdan* (Racial Discrimination: The Struggle Against Employment Practices at Hitachi), Tokyo: Aki Shobo.
Rengō (1989) Showa 63–64 'Nendo Seisaku Seido Yōkyū-Ketsuron to Dōkō' (Policy Demands for 1988–89 – Conclusions and Trends), *Rengō Seisaku Shiryō* (Rengō Policy Documents), Tokyo.
Saeki, T. (1989) *'Nihon ni okeru Gaikokujin Rōdōsha Mondai ni Kansuru Bunken Mokuroku'* (A Catalogue of Materials Concerning the Issue of Foreign Workers in Japan) *Ōhara Shakai Mondai Kenkyūjo* Zasshi, nos 368–73, July–December.
Shirai, T. (1984) *Kigyō Betsu Kumiai* (Enterprise Unions), Tokyo: Chuo Koronsha.
Yamagami, S. (1990) 'Kakō no Zairyū Gaikokujin Tōkei ni mita Zairyū Gaikokujin no Sui-i' (A Statistical Survey of the Changes in the Composition of the Resident Foreign Community), *Kokusai Jinryū*, February.
Zainichi Kankoku/Chōsenjin no Kokumin Nenkin wo Motomeru Kai (ed.) (1984) *Kokuseki Sabetsu to no Tatakai* (The Battle Against Nationality Discrimination), Tokyo: Gaifusha.
Zenkensōren (1989) 'Zenkensōren Dai-30 Kai Teiki Taikai Undō Hōshin' (Campaign Platform for the All-Japan General Confederation of Construction Workers' Unions) *Dō Taikai Shiryō* (Documents of the 30th Annual Conference).
Zensōsenjūkikai Rōdō Kumiai Rengōkai (1988) *Dai-19 Kai Teiki Taikai Giansho* (Motions at the Nineteenth Annual Conference of the All-Japan Confederation of Shipbuilding and Heavy Engineering Workers' Unions).

Part VI

Education and the individual

Chapter 14

The internationalization of education

Ehara Takekazu

GROWING CONCERN OVER THE INTERNATIONALIZATION OF EDUCATION

The internationalization of education is one of the major issues in the field of contemporary Japanese education. In the reports published by the National Council of Educational Reform (*Rinkyōshin*), for example, measures to cope with the internationalization of society are listed as one of the top eight major issues. The council recommendations appearing in the fourth and final report include

1 educational measures for Japanese children living abroad;
2 improving the procedures for accepting foreign students;
3 reviewing foreign language education;
4 improving Japanese language teaching facilities for foreign students;
5 restructuring the Japanese higher education system from an international perspective; and
6 establishing a clear identity as a Japanese and regarding oneself in relative terms.[1]

The latest *White Paper on Japanese Education*, published by the Ministry of Education in 1988, proposed five measures for encouraging the internationalization of Japanese society:

1 enabling the younger generation to make a contribution to an internationalized society;
2 international exchange and co-operation in education, culture and sports;
3 promotion of student exchange programmes;
4 improvement of the teaching of the Japanese language to foreigners; and
5 enhancement of the education of Japanese children living abroad, as well as those who have returned from a long stay abroad.[2]

The internationalization of education has, in fact, been of concern since modernization was adopted as a political goal by the Meiji state more than 100 years ago. During the last two decades, and especially in the 1980s, however, it has become of even greater concern. There are three reasons for this. First, with Japan's rapid economic growth since 1955, human and material exchange between Japan and other nations has increased dramatically. The widespread structural changes in Japanese society and in its international relations, which this has resulted in, have been discussed in various publications.[3] Table 14.1 shows how increased internationalization has affected Japanese society in terms of a number of key indicators.[4] For instance, the number of foreign visitors to Japan increased 2.7 times between 1970 and 1985, although the number of registered aliens increased only 1.2 times during the same period. Per capita import of consumer goods grew 3.7 times during this same fifteen-year period. On the other hand, the number of Japanese going abroad grew 7.5 times, while the number of children returning from abroad in 1985 showed a more than sixfold increase over that in 1971.

Second, there has been a growing demand for students with the experience and training necessary to develop knowledge and skills for life in an internationalized society. In other words, the importance of internationalizing individuals through education has been increasingly recognized by government, the business community and the public at large.[5]

Third, it must also be acknowledged that demands from outside Japan for the internationalization of education have increased since the 1970s. UNESCO, for example, issued 'The Recommendation Concerning Education for International Understanding, Co-operation and Peace and Education relating to Human Rights and Fundamental Freedoms' in 1974. In addition, the OECD published a series of reviews of national education policies in member countries in the 1970s, including one that examined educational policy and planning in Japan. In the last chapter of this report, entitled 'Education for world participation', the OECD examiners recommended the internationalization of Japanese education, adding that:

> Today there is a *need for new attitudes.* The world can no longer be seen simply as a market in which skills and raw materials can be acquired and products sold. Internationalism has acquired a new meaning. A hundred years ago, after the Meiji Restoration, Japan entered the international stage sending Japanese abroad to learn and work on behalf of their country. Today, the demands made on Japan, as on the other member countries, are for international participation on *behalf of the world.*[6]

From this perspective, the authors reviewed some aspects of Japanese education, including foreign language teaching, study abroad, the opening-up of Japanese educational institutions to foreigners, and training for world roles. Since that time, there has been consistent criticism from within Japan of the closed system of Japanese education, particularly higher education.[7]

Table 14.1 The effects of increased internationalization on Japanese society

Indicators	1970	1975	1980	1985
a) Alien residents and foreign visitors				
Number of registered aliens (10,000 persons)	70.8	75.2	78.3	85.1
Foreign visitors to Japan	85.4	81.2	131.7	232.7
b) Japanese living abroad (1,000 persons)	63.4	137.5	193.8	237.5
Number of employees of private companies and their families living abroad	40.0	90.8	131.5	159.2
Number of students, researchers, teachers, and their families living abroad	8.9	19.8	31.8	40.6
Others	14.5	26.9	30.5	37.7
c) Number of Japanese going abroad (10,000 persons)	66.3	246.6	390.9	494.8
Number of Japanese tourists going abroad	31.9	202.7	326.9	402.4
d) Number of children returning from abroad	1,543	4,598	7,504	10,196
e) International marriages	5,546	6,045	7,261	12,181
f) Number of drug smugglers reported to the Prosecutor's Office	88	139	233	354
g) Per capita import of consumer goods (yen per Japanese)	12,506	31,774	41,313	46,395
h) Rate of dependence on imported edible agricultural products (%)	22	26	28	29
i) Number of overseas telephone calls (units)	218	857	2,343	9,563

Source: Social Policy Bureau, Economic Planning Agency 1987: 102-5

This has also been paralleled by international criticism, principally from China and Korea, of the content of history textbooks currently approved for use in Japanese state sector schools.

A TENTATIVE DEFINITION OF 'INTERNATIONALIZATION OF EDUCATION'

What does the term 'internationalization of education' mean? The lack of an agreed definition has permitted considerable ambiguity and uncritical usage among educators and other commentators. By way of introduction, therefore, it might be useful to provide a tentative definition of 'internationalization of education', which follows on from the work of Ebuchi Kazuhiro.[8]

In November 1988, an OECD International Seminar on Higher Education and the Flow of Foreign Students was held in Hiroshima. In his keynote address, Ebuchi claimed that there was significant difference in meaning between the word 'internationalization' in English and its Japanese counterpart '*kokusaika*'. According to the 1961 edition of *The Oxford English Dictionary*, for example, the definition given for the word 'internationalize' is 'to render international in character or use; especially, in modern politics, to bring (a country, territory and so on) under the combined government or protection of two or more different nations.' Likewise, the 1973 edition of *The Random House Dictionary of the English Language* defines the word 'internationalize' as 'to make international; to bring under international control'. In both dictionaries the word 'internationalize' is identified as a transitive verb. The implication is that the English-speaking peoples of the West tend to see themselves as active subjects and other people outside of their countries more as objects.

In contrast, the Japanese equivalent, that is, '*kokusaika suru*', is an intransitive verb, which designates 'being in a process of becoming' international. According to the first edition of *Shogakukan Kokugo Daijiten*, published in 1981, the noun form of the word '*kokusaika*', is defined as '*sekai ni tsuyō suru yōni naru koto*', which literally means 'the process of becoming accepted by the rest of the world'. Similar explanations and attitudes towards *kokusaika* can be found not only in other Japanese dictionaries, but also in many articles and books published in Japanese. It seems that the Japanese generally consider internationalization to involve the process of becoming international.

In view of these differences between English and Japanese usage, and current Japanese attitudes towards *kokusaika*, a tentative definition of 'internationalization of education' would be as follows (this definition is a slightly modified version of that given by Ebuchi):

> Internationalization of education is a process by which educational provision of the education system becomes more sophisticated, enriched and broadly applicable to the younger generation from all backgrounds and countries, emphasizing especially the possible development of programmes which are internationally and cross-culturally compatible, with a view towards providing all of the younger generation with the experiences and training necessary to develop knowledge and skills for life in a world characterized by increasing international exchange.

Three further points arise in relation to this definition. First of all, in this definition the verb 'become' is used, because the Japanese translation of 'internationalization', that is, '*kokusaika*' is recognized by most Japanese, including educational researchers, as 'a process of becoming accepted by the rest of the world'. The semantic difference between the English and Japanese terminology may well derive from the particular historical experience and ways in which each nation has participated in the world community. The Japanese concept of 'internationalization of education' may therefore be more accessible to people who live in less politically dominant countries, such as Belgium and the Netherlands within the European Community.

Second, the Japanese tend to conceive of 'internationalization' as not only a process of 'becoming' or a state of 'being' international, but also a definite goal to be attained. In this sense, it seems that the term 'internationalization of education' has a positive value for the Japanese.

Third, the question must be asked: What kind of knowledge and skills should the younger generation develop for their life in an internationalized society? But, rather than offering a list of the particular skills and gobbets of knowledge, which would arguably be prerequisites, a more generalized response seems appropriate. An interesting example is to be found in Kurimoto's statement that: 'To live in an internationalized society is to live in plural cultures and to have a good command of plural social systems'.[9] It seems that the first thing the younger generation should do is to acquire knowledge and skills which enable them to regard themselves and their daily lives in relative terms.

THE MAIN REQUIREMENTS FOR EDUCATION AIMED AT FOSTERING AN INTERNATIONALIZED SOCIETY

The main requirements for education aimed at fostering an internationalized society are summarized in Table 14.2. It should be noted, however, that the categories listed here are neither discrete nor exhaustive, but represent areas where educational management can, and should, be adapted to the needs of an internationalizing society. For reasons of space, the current situation in Japan and problems related to each item in Table 14.2 are discussed only briefly in the following sections.

Education for internationalization

International education includes all educative efforts which aim at fostering an international orientation in knowledge and attitudes. The aim of international education is to give the younger generation opportunities to obtain knowledge and insight into foreign culture, the history and geography of other countries, and to acquire certain attitudes which constitute international solidarity, rejection of racial prejudice, understanding of other cultures and social systems, and so on.[10] Under the present *Courses of*

Table 14.2 Main requirements for education aimed at fostering an internationalized society

---

I **Education for internationalization**
  1 Education in international understanding, or international education
  2 Foreign language education:
    (a) education in English as an international language of communication
    (b) regional foreign language education
  3 Japanese language education
II **Internationalizing the education system**
  1 Universalizing school structures
  2 Special institutional arrangements:
    (a) programmes for Japanese children living abroad and those who have returned from a long stay overseas
    (b) programmes for foreigners living in Japan
    (c) international schools

Study for Elementary and Secondary Schools, international education is not regarded as an independent area of the curriculum, but is taught as a part of subjects such as moral education and social studies. According to the new *Course of Study for Upper Secondary Schools,* which was issued by the Ministry of Education in 1989, world history is expected to be a required subject for all students from 1994. At the higher education level, there is now a boom in establishing new departments, which have names with the prefix 'international', such as International Relations, International Politics and International Culture. There were thirty-eight such departments in 1988, an approximate threefold increase over 1978.[11] Nevertheless, there still remains considerable scope for improvement, in terms of both the number of courses and departments in existence and the quality of the materials in use. The way in which foreign countries and cultures are treated in school textbooks, for example, is in need of drastic improvement.

Education for internationalization should also include increased emphasis on foreign language provision. Though some might disagree, English is the principal language used in international communication, and is likely to remain so for the foreseeable future. In response to this, today's Japanese students are provided with many more opportunities to hear and speak English than were former generations. English instruction at Japanese secondary schools has been improved substantially over the past thirty years. Even so, further effort is required in response to the rising number of Japanese who study and work abroad. At the same time, more opportunities to learn the languages of neighbouring countries, including China, Korea, Thailand and Indonesia, should also be provided.

Figure 14.1 shows the number of foreigners learning Japanese both in

Japan and in other countries. Figure 14.2 gives the number of Japanese language teachers and of institutions offering Japanese language courses in Japan. Despite, or perhaps due to, the remarkable upsurge in interest which has occurred in the past few years, there is an urgent need for expansion of and improvement in initial and in-service training programmes for Japanese language teachers. The development of appropriate teaching methods and materials is also needed.

Internationalizing the education system

Universalizing school structures requires, among other things, standardizing diplomas and degrees, admission and graduation requirements, and transfer procedures for students at different institutions on a transnational basis. It also requires a review of the school calendar, curricula, educational facilities and equipment, and staff exchange programmes. Table 14.3 reveals that over 57,000 Japanese students went abroad to study in 1987, and that most of them went to North America. Figure 14.3 gives the number of foreign students in Japan: as indicated in Table 14.4, most of them are from Asian countries. The government plans to increase the number of foreign students studying in Japan to 100,000 by the beginning of the twenty-first century. In order to achieve this goal, a wide range of measures, including the expansion of Japanese government scholarships and the improvement of living accommodation for students, must be implemented.[12]

It is only within the last decade that the Ministry of Education has permitted the employment of foreign teachers within the state sector. In 1986, the Ministry of Education extended invitations to 2,400 foreign teachers and scholars, and in 1988, a total of 839 foreigners were employed at national institutions of higher education as either full-time or part-time teachers. Most of them were teaching foreign languages.[13] Table 14.5 shows that in 1988, almost 1,400 foreign young people were employed as teaching assistants in Japanese schools under the JET (Japan Exchange and Teaching) Programme, which had been introduced in the previous year.

The number of Japanese teachers sent abroad by the Ministry of Education in 1987 is given in Table 14.6. The first programme was designated as a short-term, in-service training scheme for elementary and secondary school teachers, which would enable them to broaden their horizons and international perspectives. Under the second programme, foreign language teachers at universities are sent to countries where the language of their speciality is spoken. In addition to the programmes provided by the Ministry of Education, there are other mechanisms for sending university teachers and researchers abroad, including scholarships provided by the Japan Society for the Promotion of Science. In 1987, a total of 3,973

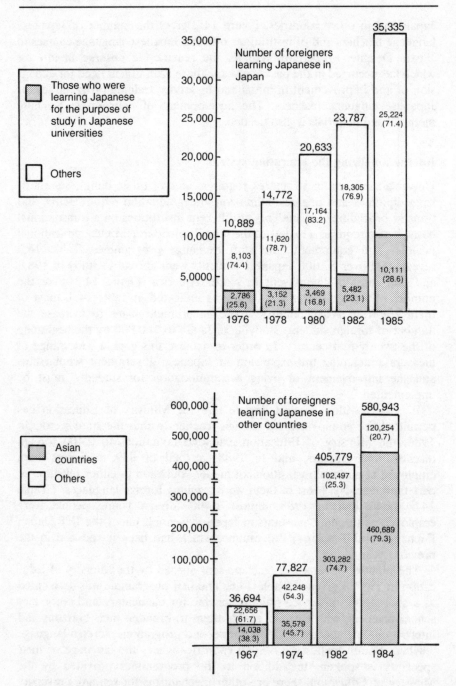

Figure 14.1 Trends in the number of foreigners learning Japanese

Source: Ministry of Education, Science and Culture, Japan 1986: 66

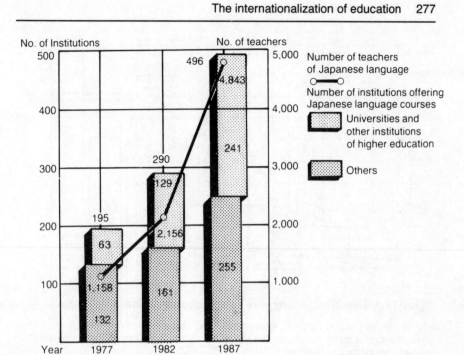

Figure 14.2 Trends in the number of Japanese language teachers and institutions offering Japanese language courses

Source: Ministry of Education, Science and Culture, 1989a: 53

Table 14.3 Number of Japanese students going abroad for study, by region, 1987

Region	No. of students	% Distribution
Asia	10,039	17.5
Middle and Near East	77	0.1
Africa	212	0.4
Pacific	2,267	3.9
North America	30,908	53.8
Latin America	297	0.5
Europe	13,684	23.8
Total	57,484	100.0

Source: Ministry of Education, Science and Culture, Japan 1989b: 69

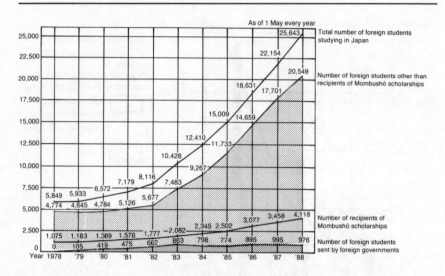

Figure 14.3 Trends in the number of foreign students in Japan, 1978–88

Source: Ministry of Education, Science and Culture, 1989a: 52
Note: 'Foreign students sent by foreign governments' are those sent by the governments of China, Indonesia and Malaysia.

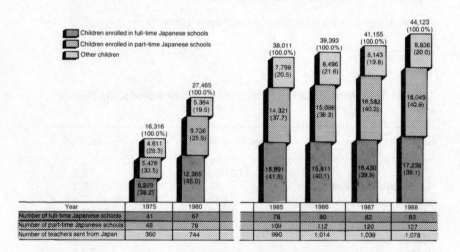

Figure 14.4 Trends in the number of Japanese children living overseas, 1975–88

Source: Ministry of Education, Science and Culture, 1989a: 54
Note: The number of 'Japanese children living overseas' signifies children aged 6–15 as of May each year. 'Other children' are those not enrolled in Japanese schools, either full time or part time.

Table 14.4 Foreign students in Japan, 1987

Region	No. of students	% Distribution
Asia	19,569	88.4
Middle and Near East	139	0.6
Africa	222	1.0
Pacific	158	0.7
North America	1,003	4.5
Latin America	491	2.2
Europe	572	2.6
Total	22,154	100.0

Source: Ministry of Education, Science and Culture, Japan 1989b: 68

Table 14.5 Number of foreign teaching assistants invited under the JET programme, 1988

Country of origin	English fellows	Co-ordinators for international exchange
US	837	39
UK	250	1
Australia	128	13
New Zealand	33	1
Canada	116	6
Ireland	20	–
Total	1,384	60

Source: Ministry of Education, Science and Culture, 1989b: 71

Table 14.6 Number of teachers sent abroad during the school year, 1987

Categories of programme	No. of teachers
1 Programme for sending elementary and secondary school teachers abroad	3,027
2 Programme for sending foreign language teachers abroad	244
3 Programme for sending university teachers abroad	702

Source: Ministry of Education, Science and Culture, 1989b: 71

university lecturers, teachers and researchers were sent to foreign countries under these three programmes.

As shown in Figure 14.4, more than 44,000 Japanese children were living overseas in 1988. Their distribution by region is shown in Figure 14.5. In 1987, a total of 11,000 Japanese children had returned from a long stay overseas. These returnee children, as they are known, face enormous difficulties in readjusting to life in Japan.[14] One of the problems to be solved is how to ensure that a positive value is attached to these foreign experiences in later life. Because excessive competition in entrance examinations is a predominant feature of Japanese education, children who have lived overseas also experience immense difficulties in adapting to the rigid Japanese system after they have returned home.

Another area of educational priority which has recently become the focus of considerable attention is the type and quality of education available to Korean residents in Japan. According to *The Immigration Control Statistics* published by the Ministry of Justice, there were 686,000 Korean nationals living in Japan in 1984, and they constituted approximately three-quarters of the entire foreign resident population. Most of them are Koreans who migrated, often involuntarily, to Japan as labourers before and during the Second World War, and their descendants. The number of Korean children attending schools in Japan is estimated at about 130,000. A quarter of them attend one of the 163 Korean schools in operation in Japan, and the remainder attend Japanese-maintained or private schools.[15]

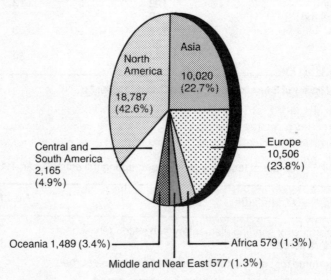

Figure 14.5 Distribution of children living abroad, by region, 1988

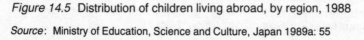

Source: Ministry of Education, Science and Culture, Japan 1989a: 55

There are two problems related to the schooling of these children in terms of the internationalization of Japanese education.[16] The first problem concerns the legal position of Korean schools. Most of them have been established without any formal approval from the government or have been approved by prefectural government as miscellaneous schools. As a result, graduates from these schools are at a disadvantage in terms of both admission to university and future employment. The second relates to the question of *Minzoku Kyōiku*, or ethnic education for Korean children attending Japanese schools. Stated briefly, the problem is how, on the one hand, to provide an equivalent education for both Korean and Japanese children while, at the same time, encouraging the preservation of a Korean cultural and social heritage.

A further test of Japan's commitment to internationalize its education system has been provided by the recent migration of a large number of workers from South East Asia, the Philippines, Korea and China, who have entered Japan in response to both the demand for manual labour in certain industries and the increased reluctance of young Japanese to take up employment in these areas. If Japan accepts more foreign workers in the future, education for them and for their children will have to be given careful consideration. It is hoped that in this respect Japan will be able to draw on the postwar experiences of many Western European states in drawing up education programmes for foreign residents.[17] The National Council of Educational Reform has recommended the establishment of new international schools, where foreign children and Japanese children who have returned from overseas can study together with other Japanese students. This programme is, however, still in the planning stage.

CONCLUSION

In some respects the internationalization of education in Japan appears to be quite advanced, at least in comparison with other industrialized states. Although the term itself has become something of a 'buzz word', 'internationalization' is clearly a part of the national agenda in Japan. Much, however, remains to be done. Returnee children continue to suffer from both overt and covert forms of discrimination; education remains dominated by an examination system in which the accumulation of facts takes precedence over the ability to analyse and question; and universities are ill-equipped to provide an adequate education for foreign students.

As self-appointed curator of Japanese culture, the Ministry of Education continues to obstruct the employment of Korean or Chinese residents within the state sector, while refusing to acknowledge the relevance of ethnic education for national minorities. If, as Ogata suggests in Chapter 3, internationalization must take place at the level of values and attitudes, then the establishment of departments of international relations within universities will not necessarily lead to the creation of an 'internationally oriented' environment. Nor, for that matter, will this be achieved through the employment of foreign language (English) assistants, or an increase in the number of student exchange programmes. For internationalization to succeed, education, at both the formal and informal levels, must inculcate the values and skills commensurate with citizenship in a global society. The challenge for Japan today is no less than it was 120 years ago when the leaders of the new Meiji state sought to create an educational system which would lay the foundations of empire.

NOTES

1   National Council on Educational Reform (1988) *Reports on Educational Reform*, Tokyo: National Council on Educational Reform, pp. 513–18.
2   Mombushō (1988) (ed.) *Kyōiku Hakusho: Wagakuni no Bunkyo Seisaku* (White Paper on Education 1988: Educational Policy in Japan), Tokyo: Ōkurashō Insatsukyoku, pp. 400–1.
3   E. Hamaguchi (1989) (ed.) *Kokusaika to Jōhōka* (Internationalization and the Information Society), Tokyo: Nippon Hōsō Shuppan Kyōkai (NHK), pp. 193–9; A. Sawada and K. Kadowaki (1990) *Nihonjin no Kokusaika* (The Internationalization of Japanese People), Tokyo: Nihon Keizai Shimbunsha, pp. 28–47.
4   Social Policy Bureau, Economic Planning Agency (1987) *1987 New Social Indicators: Result of 1987 Calculations Based on NSI*, Tokyo: Ōkurashō Insatsukyoku, pp. 102–7.
5   K. Kurimoto (1985) *Kokusaika Jidai to Nihonjin* (The Age of Internationalization and the Japanese), Tokyo: Nippon Hōsō Shuppan Kyōkai, pp. 190–2.
6   OECD (1971) *Review of National Policies for Education: JAPAN*, Paris: OECD, p. 112.
7   T. Kobayshi (1986) 'The internationalization of Japanese education', *Comparative Education*, 22(1), p. 66; T. Kobayshi (1979) 'The internationalization of Japanese higher education), in W.K. Cummings, I. Amano, and K. Kitamura (eds) *Changes in the Japanese University*, New York: Praeger. K. Kitamura (1984) *Daigaku Kyōiku no Kokusaika* (The Internationalization of University Education), Tokyo: Tamagawa Daigaku Shuppanbu, pp. 163–74.
8   K. Ebuchi (1988) 'Foreign students and internationalization of the university from the Japanese perspective', keynote address given at the International Seminar on the Higher Education and the Flow of Foreign Students, Hiroshima University, November; K. Ebuchi (1989) 'Kokusaika no bunseki shiten to daigaku shihyō settei no kokoromi', (The concept of internationalization: a semantic analysis with special reference to the internationalization of higher education), *Research in Higher Education – Daigaku Ronshū*, 18: 29–52.
9   K. Kurimoto (1985) *Kokusaika Jidai to Nihonjin* (The Age of Internationalization and the Japanese), p. 43.
10   T. Husen (1985) 'International education', in T. Husen and T.N. Postlethwaite (eds) *The International Encyclopedia of Education: Research and Studies*, Oxford: Pergamon, p. 2662; K. Sanuki (1984) 'Kokusaika Shakai ni okeru Kyōkai Kandai no Shiten to Tenbō', (Basic Viewpoints and Perspectives on Education in an Internationalized Society), *Kyōikugaku Kenkyū*, 51 (3), p. 2.
11   Mombusho (1988) (ed.) *Kyōiku Hakusho: Wagakuni no Bunkyo Seisaku*

(White Paper on Education 1988: Educational Policy in Japan), pp. 402–4.

12 Ministry of Education, Science and Culture, Japan (1989a) *MONBUSHŌ 1989*, Tokyo: Ministry of Science, Education and Culture, Japan, p. 52.

13 Ministry of Education, Science and Culture, Japan (1989b) *Development of Education in Japan 1986–1988: Report for Submission to the 41st Session of the International Conference on Education*, Tokyo: Ministry of Science, Education and Culture, Japan, p. 72.

14 T. Kobayshi (1989) 'Educational problems of "returning children"', in J.H. Shields, Jr (ed.) *Japanese Schooling: Patterns of Socialization, Equality, and Political Control*, University Park: Pennsylvania State University Press, pp. 187–8.

15 M. Ishizuki and M. Suzuki (1988) (ed.) *Gendai Nihon no Kyōiku to Kokusaika* (Contemporary Japanese Education and Internationalization), Tokyo: Fukumura Shuppan, p. 76; T. Kobayshi (1986) 'The internationalization of Japanese education', *Comparative Education*, 22 (1), p. 69.

16 T. Kobayshi (1981) 'Nihon no kyōiku no kokusaika' (The Internationalization of University Education), in M. Shinbori (ed.) *Nihon no Kyōiku* (Education in Japan), Tokyo: Yushindo, p. 92.

17 Centre for Education Research and Innovation (CERI) (1987a) *Multicultural Education*, Paris: OECD; Centre for Education Research and Innovation (CERI) (1987b) *Immigrants' Children at School*, Paris: OECD.

Chapter 15

Data protection and the individual

Horibe Masao

INDIVIDUALISM AND PRIVACY

Many of the concepts widely used in political and legal discourse in Japan today find their roots in the influences arising from internationalization since the modernization of the state in the Meiji era. For instance, *kojin* (individual) and or *kojinshugi* (individualism) are concepts invented in that era. Surprisingly, however, the word *puraibashii* (privacy) did not enter widespread usage in the academic world until the latter half of the 1950s and among the public until 1961, when a lawsuit was filed against a famous novelist and his publisher for the invasion of privacy. The plaintiff used the word *puraibashii* in his suit. Legal scholars, who have conducted research into the development of the right to privacy in Anglo-American law, have tried to translate the term into Japanese, but as yet, no commonly accepted translation exists. In other words, we have been unable to invent a new Japanese word acceptable to the public.

As privacy is closely connected with individualism, this chapter will examine 'the individual' or 'individualism' as embodied in the concept of 'privacy' or 'the right to privacy' and the related concept '*kojin jōhō*' (individual/personal information or individual/personal data) in the context of the internationalization as well as the 'informationization' of Japanese society. The term 'internationalization', as used in Japan in the field of law, has two meanings: first, to Westernize or Americanize the Japanese legal system. Second, to raise the standard of the Japanese legal system to the international level. The term will be used here in this latter sense. *Jōhōka shakai* (information society), a term originally invented in Japan, is here divided into three categories: the mass media information society of the 1960s; the computer information society of the 1970s; and the network information society of the 1980s. This division, which is based on the characteristic features of information society in Japan in each period, will be outlined later in connection with the development of the notion of privacy or personal data.

PRESENT STATE OF PRIVACY PROTECTION

In Japan the Act for the Protection of Computer-Processed Personal Data Held by Administrative Organs (hereafter referred to as the Personal Data Protection Act) was enacted in December 1988. This Act, which came into force on 1 October 1989 is, with a number of exceptions, intended to apply to national government organs and to personal data processed by computer systems. Prior to this, several hundred by-laws relating to personal data protection were introduced by municipal governments, the earliest one dating back to 1975. According to a Ministry of Home Affairs survey, as of 1 January 1990, 630 by-laws have been enacted by Japanese prefectures and municipalities. As there are 3,315 prefectures and municipalities (forty-seven prefectures and 3,268 municipalities) in Japan, the figure of 630 amounts to approximately 19 per cent of the total. The situation is bound to change in the near future, because prefectural or metropolitan governments such as Nagano, Kanagawa, Tokyo and Fukuoka are investigating this type of legislation. In fact, in March 1990 the Kanagawa Prefectural Government became the first prefectural government in Japan to enact a personal data protection by-law.

During the legislative process leading up to the drafting of the 1988 Personal Data Protection Act, the opinion had been expressed in some quarters that national law should also apply to prefectural and municipal governments. However, due among other things to Article 92 of the Japanese Constitution, which guarantees the principle of local autonomy, the view that prefectural and municipal bodies should each devise their own measures concerning personal data protection was upheld. Section 26 of the Personal Data Protection Act stipulates that 'where a local government conducts computer processing, etc. of personal data, they shall, taking into account national measures under the provision of this Act, strive to take steps to secure proper handling of personal data and to implement them.' Local governments will be greatly influenced by this provision.

The situation in the private sector can be contrasted with that in the public sector. At the national level, a Cabinet decision has been taken concerning personal data protection for the private sector in line with measures for the public sector. In essence, this decision states that 'the respective ministries and agencies concerned shall continue to advance their deliberations into personal data protection while striving for the necessary consultations and co-ordination, and shall take proper measure as occasions arises.' This is the content of the Cabinet decision of 24 January 1989, with the phrase 'shall take proper measures as occasion arises' representing a new addition to past decisions. In the public sector, the implementation of this decision was first undertaken by the Ministry of International Trade and Industry (MITI) on 18 April 1989. In some areas of the private sector, moreover, guidelines have already been adopted independently, such as The Centre for Financial Industry Information Systems' (FIISC) 'Guidelines on the Protection of Personal Data for Financial Institutions', adopted in March 1987, and the 'Guidelines on the Protection of Personal Data in the Private Sector' of the Japan Information Processing Development Centre (JIPDEC), agreed upon in March 1988. The MITI and private sector developments will be discussed later.

In addition, a number of by-laws enacted by local governments apply to the private sector as well as to the public sector. The 1990 Kanagawa Prefecture Personal Data Protection By-law is a representative example. Furthermore, we must mention the existence of laws at the national level which, in certain specific fields, make provisions for the partial protection of personal data in the private sector, such as Instalment Sales Act and the Act on the Regulation of Money Lending. Finally, the Telecommunications Business Act provides that 'the secrecy of communication being handled by a telecommunication carrier shall not be violated'.

INFORMATION SOCIETY AND THE EMERGENCE OF PRIVACY ISSUES

Classifying information society

The terms 'privacy' and 'personal data' are known to almost everyone in Japan today. They are widely employed to denote a direct connection with the personal interests of the individual. The current debate in Japan concerning these issues may be viewed as the result of:

1   the development of an information society;
2   international influences; and
3   heightened public awareness.

The first is considered pivotal for the discussion. The term 'information society' conjures up different images for different people. Here it is used to mean:

1   a society in which mass media have developed and the volume of information has rapidly increased ('mass media information society');
2   a society in which computers have come to be used to process large quantities of information ('computer information society'); and
3   a society in which data networking has evolved due to the rapid developments in, and combinations of, both computer and communications technology, and in which – together with the great increase in the volume of information – the flow of information has greatly expanded, not only within national borders, but also internationally ('network information society').

The issues of privacy and the right to privacy can be examined in accordance with these three types of information societies. That is, privacy can be classified as first, mass media privacy; second, computer privacy; and third, network privacy, Likewise, if we address the question of the right to privacy, then we are concerned with the rights to mass media privacy, computer privacy and network privacy. These expressions have been coined from the viewpoint of the symbolic content of the words 'mass media', 'computer', and 'networks'. In Japan these three types of society and privacy have arisen in a phased manner, with the mass media information society (mass media privacy) appearing in the 1960s, the computer information society (computer privacy) in the 1970s, and the network information society (network privacy) in the 1980s. Viewed within this typological framework, we can say that it was the mass media information society which brought forth the concept 'information society', and which, in turn, gave rise to the 'privacy' problem in Japan. In other words, today's privacy debate has its origins in this kind of society.

The *After the Banquet* case and court decision

A much-discussed topic in the first period was a lawsuit seeking compensation and a public apology for an alleged invasion of privacy caused by *After the Banquet,* a novel by Mishima Yukio. The plaintiff, an unsuccessful socialist candidate for the 1959 Tokyo gubernatorial election and one-time Foreign Minister, alleged in March 1961 that the defendant had, without his consent, written a *roman à clef* based on him and his former wife. This was a symbolic event in terms of the mass media information society. Since the plaintiff used the word 'privacy' in his 1961 suit, 'privacy' came into general use after this. It could well be said that the benefits of concepts such as 'private life', 'personal affairs', and 'personal secrets' – which until then had been understood only vaguely – became crystallized in the term 'privacy', thereby bringing the problem to a head. The case promoted scholarly research into the approach to the right to privacy in the United States and Europe.

On 28 September 1964, the Tokyo District Court awarded the plaintiff most of the ¥800,000 (approximately £800 at the time) damages requested. This was then the largest damages awarded in a privacy or defamation case. In establishing this new right, the District Court declared that respect for, and protection of, an individual's dignity in a mass communication society was no longer merely a matter of ethics; rather, this personal interest was elevated to a legal right, to be protected against unlawful infringement. The court defined the right to privacy as 'the legal guarantee or right of not having one's private life unreasonably disclosed to the public'. Moreover, it found that the right was recognized in statutory provision covering certain aspects of privacy and was guaranteed under the

Constitutional requirement that 'all of the people shall be respected as individuals'. Although welcomed by lawyers, the judgment was criticized by the literary community, who feared the curtailment of freedom of expression. While this decision concerned only one of the many aspects of the right to privacy, it set the direction for future developments.

THE COMPUTER INFORMATION SOCIETY AND THE SEARCH FOR PRIVACY PROTECTION

The 1960s, when the right to mass media privacy was first acknowledged, may also be characterized as a period of extremely rapid advancement in the use of computers. However, compared to the US and Western Europe, the debate on privacy in relation to computers emerged somewhat later in Japan. For it was only at the end of the 1960s that the question of an information society characterized by computers, and of computers themselves and their relation to privacy, came to be discussed in public documents. Subsequently, in the 1970s, public interest in the issue of privacy increased dramatically. During this period, the plan for a Unified Individual Code System (People Coding System), and the opposition movement against it, drew the nation's attention to the issue of privacy, especially in relation to computers. The opposition movement, led by *Zendentsu* (National Union of Telecommunications Workers), warned of the dangers to democratic control under this proposed coding system, and at the 44th General Meeting of *Sōhyō* (General Council of Trade Unions of Japan) in August 1972, *Zendentsu*, together with *Jichirō* (All Japan Prefectural and Municipal Workers' Union) put forward a resolution for the protection of privacy in relation to computers, emphasizing its importance. Furthermore, in co-operation with the *Denkirōren* (Japanese Federation of Electrical Machine Workers' Union) and *Jichirō, Zendentsu* issued a call for a nationwide campaign. This bore fruit on 15 November of the same year when, with the participation of scholars and other members of the intelligentsia, the Central Committee for the Protection of Privacy and for Opposition to a Comprehensive Numbering System for the People, was formed.

In the midst of this heightened awareness of 'privacy', as evidenced by the opposition movement, the incumbent Director of the Administrative Management Agency was finally prompted on 7 April 1973 to state in the Diet that a final decision on the introduction of unified individual codes should be taken after a careful study of world developments and in the context of a national consensus. Against the backdrop of these events in the early 1970s, concern over the issue of privacy intensified later in the decade. In particular, 1975 can be singled out as a peak year in the debate on privacy. Some examples of important events early in that year include the following.

February A report to restrict disclosure of information from a person's family register was presented by the Council on Administration of Civil Matters, a consultative body of the Ministry of Justice.

March The Administrative Management Agency, Prime Minister's Office, published the results of a public opinion poll concerning privacy. Kunitachi City, Tokyo, enacted a privacy protection by-law. The Socialist Party put a personal data protection bill before the Diet.

April The Administrative Management and Inspection Commission, a consultative body of the Administrative Management Agency, submitted an interim report concerning the protection of privacy in the use of computers.

Furthermore, the relationship between privacy and numerous different fields was discussed during this period. These included medical care, education, libraries, data communications, taxpayer number codes, administrative investigations, disclosure of tax data, the obligation to guard professional secrets, the secrecy of communications, detailed statements of telephone bills, the flow of international information, personal credit information, investigations of victims of the atomic bombs, investigation of the handicapped, the right to investigate state affairs, the obligation to bear witness, the real estate registration system, national census, private detective agencies, police investigations and so on.

As is clear from the above, the 1970s witnessed a great diversification in concern about privacy. However, in contrast to developments in the US and Western Europe, the national government did not propose legislation to protect privacy at this time. The situation at the municipal level was different. Spurred on in part by the precedent set by Kunitachi City's by-law, several municipal governments enacted similar legislation. As of 1 April 1979, twenty-eight municipalities had passed such by-laws. These can basically be understood as efforts to answer the question of how to protect computer privacy in a computer information society. Also, during this period, the right to privacy increasingly came to be regarded as 'an individual's right to control the circulation of information relating to him or herself'.

NETWORK INFORMATION SOCIETY AND PERSONAL DATA PROTECTION

The OECD guidelines and The Committee on the Protection of Privacy

During the 1970s, laws to protect personal data were passed in the United States and Western Europe. The Organization for Economic Co-operation and Development (OECD), moreover, adopted the *Recommendation of the Council Concerning Guidelines Governing the Protection of Privacy and Transborder Flows of Personal Data* on 23 September 1980. Australia, Canada, Ireland, Turkey and the United Kingdom abstained, but Japan did not. Thus, at the beginning of the 1980s, in the midst of this international activity, the need for legislation on personal data protection was finally accepted at the national level in Japan. The recommendations of this international body exerted a major influence on the Japanese Government in this respect. In January 1981, the Administrative Management Agency (now the Management and Co-ordination Agency) set up a Committee on the Protection of Privacy in order to study the issue, both domestically and overseas. The committee presented a report entitled the 'Protection of Privacy in the Processing of Personal Data' to the Director of the Administrative Management Agency in July 1982. The main feature of this report was to acknowledge the necessity of enacting a new law based on the following five fundamental principles for the protection of privacy.

1 Collection restriction

The purposes of collecting personal data should be clearly specified and the data to be collected should be restricted to that which is necessary to achieve these purposes. In addition, data collection should be carried out by legitimate and fair means (this corresponds to the Collection Limitation Principle and the Purpose Specification Principle of the OECD guidelines).

2 Use restriction

The use of personal data should, in principle, be restricted to the purposes for which it was collected (this corresponds to the Use Limitation Principle of the OECD guidelines).

3 Individual participation

Appropriate means should be available for individuals to know of the existence and details of data held on them, and to request correction thereof as necessary (this corresponds to the Openness Principle and the Individual Participation Principle of the OECD guidelines).

4 Proper management

Personal data collected and stored should be accurate and kept up to date, and reasonable safeguards against risk of loss, destruction, falsification and improper transfer should be taken (this corresponds to the Data Quality Principle and the Security Safeguards Principle of the OECD guidelines).

5 *Accountability*

The responsibility assigned to a data controller for the protection of privacy should be clearly defined (this corresponds to the Accountability Principle of the OECD guidelines). An additional feature of this report was its attempt to address the issues of privacy in relation to information society, in particular network information society, as follows:

> The privacy of an individual has become increasingly threatened as radical technological innovations in information processing and communication have made possible the rapid and massive processing of data and various kinds of data concerning individuals have come to be collected, stored and used much more widely.

Unfortunately, the report was not tied directly to any legislation at the national level.

The Provisional Commission on Administrative Reform and Cabinet decisions

Subsequent to the initiatives outlined above, issues relating to privacy were examined by the Provisional Commission on Administrative Reform, an advisory body to the Prime Minister. The commission's final report, published on 14 March 1983, declared:

> a positive approach to setting up the necessary system for the protection of personal data, including legal measures, should be taken considering developments in the administrative information system and trends in public opinion, as well as developments in other countries with respect to the operation of the system. In establishing means of protection, close consultation and co-ordination among the ministries and agencies concerned will be necessary.

Following submission of the report, the Cabinet decided consecutively in May 1983, January 1984, December 1984 and December 1985 that the government should scrutinize and develop the necessary system, including legal measures, designed to facilitate the protection of personal data held by government agencies. The relevant part of the Cabinet decision made in December 1985 reads: 'Regarding the protection of personal data held by government agencies, the government shall continuously scrutinize and develop the necessary systems, including appropriate legal measures, and shall endeavour to formulate its policy as soon as possible.' Under Cabinet mandate, the Government examined concrete measures to protect personal data held by government organs, through the Inter-Ministerial Meeting for Administrative Information Systems, which consisted of personal data protection staff at each ministry and agency.

Personal Data in Administrative Organs and the Personal Data Protection Act

In addition to the inter-ministerial meeting, the government also set up a Study Group on the Protection of Personal Data in Administrative Organs inside the Management and Co-ordination Agency. This study group held meetings from July 1985 to December 1986 and carried out research on personal data protection, listening to the opinions of ministries and agencies. Its report, recommending that a law on the protection of personal data be introduced, was issued in December 1986. All the national dailies gave space to the report and took it up in their editorials. Finally, we should take note of the Ministry of Home Affairs committee on personal data protection. In October 1987, after meeting for two and a half years, this committee issued its report, 'Protection of Personal Data in Local Governments'.

In the wake of these investigations, a 'Bill to Protect Computer-Processed Personal Data Held by Administrative Organs', which finally saw the light of day in the form of a Cabinet decision on 28 April 1988, was presented to the Diet. Deliberations took place in the Extraordinary Session of the Diet and four expert witnesses (including the author) appeared before the Cabinet Committee of the House of Representatives in October. The Bill was approved by a majority of the House of Representatives on 18 November and by the House of Councillors on 9 December. It was promulgated on 16 December 1988 and came into force on 1 October 1989 as provided for by Cabinet Order. In the case of the provisions on the disclosure and correction of personal data, however, these are to be enforced as from a day fixed by Cabinet Order within not more than two years, beginning with the day of promulgation. The Act will be summarized later.

The private sector

The term 'private sector' covers a wide range of entities, from firms specializing in direct marketing to financial organizations and the press. During Diet deliberation on the above Bill, the problem of the private sector was raised, and in the supplementary resolution of the Lower and Upper House Committees, the following item was included: 'Considering the fact that the need for measures on personal data protection applies not only to national government organs of the public sector, but likewise to the private sector, the government is to advance promptly its investigations'. Thereupon, as stated above, a Cabinet decision was made instructing the ministries and agencies concerned to move ahead with their investigations and devise measures as necessary. The systematization of personal data protection has been underway in certain areas of the private sector and well-known examples will be mentioned later.

Local government by-laws on personal data protection

As stated above, as of 1 January 1990, 630 local public bodies had passed by-laws on personal data protection, and the Kanagawa Prefectural Government enacted the Personal Data Protection By-Law in March 1990. The by-laws contain both common features and differences: the most important differences being whether or not the legislation is intended to cover the private sector and the manual processing of personal data. The recent tendency has been to pass by-laws applicable to the private sector as well as to manually processed data. Among such by-laws the above-mentioned Kanagawa Prefecture Personal Data Protection By-Law of 1990 is noteworthy as a positive and comprehensive example of this kind of legislation. Before the enactment of this by-law, the Study Group on the Promotion of Personal Data Protection, consisting of twenty-five members appointed by the Governor of Kanagawa Prefecture, investigated, from November 1988 to August 1989, how to formulate a system of personal data protection in Kanagawa. Its report, 'A Proposal for a System of Personal Data Protection in Kanagawa Prefecture', was submitted to the Governor on 7 September 1989. An important aspect of this proposal is a section on a 'system for the protection of personal data held by the private sector', including 'clarifying the obligations of entrepreneurs', 'guidance and encouragement of self-regulation', 'relief measures relating to individual cases', and 'heightening awareness among prefectural citizens'. The by-law drafted based on this proposal was passed unanimously in the Prefectural Assembly on 26 March 1990. Most provisions will come into force on 1 October, but some provisions on 1 April 1990.

At the local government level, the network information society has fostered a sense of anxiety among citizens regarding their privacy. This calls for urgent, positive and comprehensive measures for the protection of privacy.

THE PERSONAL DATA PROTECTION ACT 1988

Purpose and scope of the Act

The purpose of the Act is 'in view of the development of computer processing of personal data in administrative organs, to protect the rights and interests of individuals while ensuring the proper and smooth operation of public administration, by stipulating basic matters concerning the handling of computer-processed personal data held by administrative organs' (section 1). The primary aim of the Act is the protection of 'the rights and interests of individuals' and the secondary goal is to ensure 'the proper and smooth operation of public administration'.

The Act covers 'computer-processed personal data' and 'administrative organs'. These terms are defined in the Act (section 2). 'Computer processing' means 'input, storage, editing, working, modifying, updating, retrieval, erasure, output or any other processing similar to them which is conducted by using computers'. In the future, the protection of manually processed personal data is also to be considered. 'Personal data' are 'data which relate to a living individual who can be identified from names, date of birth or other descriptions contained in the data or from a number, symbol or other mark assigned to the individual.' This definition resembles the definition of personal data provided for in section 1 of the United Kingdom Data Protection Act 1984.

'Administrative organs' are mainly national administrative organs. As mentioned earlier, during the legislative process the opinion was expressed in some quarters that a national law should apply to prefectural and municipal governments. One of the reasons for this is the desirability of securing conformity in measures between national and local governments. However, in addition to the principle of local autonomy guaranteed by the Constitution, differences in organizational structures and services between the national government and various local governments contributed to sectorial legislation.

Personal data processing regulations

Chapter 2 of the Act is concerned chiefly with regulations pertaining to personal data processing such as:

1 Limitations on holding personal data

Administration organs shall, in holding personal data files, confine their actions to cases necessary to perform the competent functions provided for by law and specify their purposes as much as possible (section 4).

2 Security and accuracy of personal data

Heads of administrative organs shall strive to take measures necessary to prevent leakage, loss, or destruction of personal data and for other proper management, and to ensure that the processed data is accurate within the extent necessary for file-holding purposes (section 5).

3 Prior notification in holding personal data files

Heads of administrative organs shall notify in advance the Director-General of the Management and Co-ordination Agency of the names of the personal data files; the name of the holding organs and the organization in charge of functions for which the files are used; the purpose of holding the files; the files record items and their extent; the method of collecting the processed data; and the name and location of the organization which accepts individuals' requests to access their personal data, etc., (section 6). There are, it should be noted, some exceptions to the rule.

4 Compilation and inspection of personal data files directory

Heads of administrative organs shall compile a directory stating the matters noted and make it available for public inspection (section 7).

5 Public notice of personal data files

The Director-General of the Management and Co-ordination Agency shall make public in the offical gazette at least annually the notified matters (section 8).

6 Limitation on the use and finishing of personal data

The processed data shall not be used or furnished for purposes other than the purpose for which the files are held, except when they shall be used within the holding organs or furnished to persons other than the holding organs in accordance with the provisions of the law (section 9).

Right of individuals

Chapter 3 of the Act stipulates disclosure and correction of personal data. Disclosure is recognized as a legal right. The main content of this chapter is as follows.

Any person may request in writing of the heads of holding organs the disclosure of the processed data of which that person is the data subject. However, this shall not apply to the personal data files recording matters concerning school records or entrance examinations in schools; diagnosis and treatment in hospitals, clinics or maternity clinics; criminal cases or disposals by public prosecutors, public prosecuting officers or judicial police officers, or execution of sentences (section 13).

With regard to the correction of personal data, the Study Group on the Protection of Personal Data Administrative Organs set up in July 1985, touched on earlier, had two alternative ideas, one giving the legal right to request correction and the other treating it as proposal. The Act adopted the latter (section 17). In any case, the Act should be re-examined as a whole in the light of the development of information society and the conditions under which it is implemented.

MEASURES FOR PERSONAL DATA PROTECTION IN THE PRIVATE SECTOR

Following Cabinet recommendations, the Ministry of International Trade and Industry (MITI) investigated measures for protection in the private sector, issuing a document on 18 April 1989 entitled, 'Concerning the Protection of Computer Personal Data in the Private Sector'. The document states:

> MITI has up until now taken such measures as giving guidance by issuing a circular notice to business associations, principally with regard to the handling of consumer credit data. Regarding the protection of computer-processed personal data in the private sector, the Sub-Committee on the Protection of Personal Data, Horibe Masao of the Informationization Committee, an advisory group of the Director-General of the Machinery and Information Industries Bureau, has carried out investigations at the same time as listening to the views of various consumer-related organizations since May 1988, based upon the study pursued by the Japan Information Processing Development Centre (JIPDEC).

The document then goes on: 'On 18 April 1988, the report of the said sub-committee was published under the title "Concerning the Protection of Computer-Processed Personal Data in the Private Sector (Guidelines)".' Based upon this, it adds that:

> MITI decided to adopt the following policies as a set of immediate measures, based upon the report, with the object of urging entrepreneurs and business associations to further their measures and to forge steadily ahead with consumer protection in this matter.

The following three points are then touched upon:

1   Business associations are directed to foster thorough knowledge of the sub-committee's report among entrepreneurs and to carry out investigations necessary for the enactment of concrete guidelines based upon the report in accordance with the characteristics of their business activities.
2   In order to actively promote systematic measures by business associations in this matter, the said associations are directed to take measures such as establishing organizations to deal with this matter, and to set up organizations able to respond suitably to outside enquiries concerning this subject.
3   Together with the further promotion of measures, mainly by business associations, to contribute to the protection of consumers, a 'Registry System for Measures on Personal Data Protection' (tentative name) is to be established and published. This will list the systematic measures

taken by each business association and outside enquiry references, and is to be properly updated in accordance with future developments. The report consists of (1) Background and Basic Points of View; and (2) Guidelines and Matters for Consideration, and the JIPDEC Guidelines set out in the annexe.

At JIPDEC, the committee on Privacy of Protection in the Private Sector began investigations in January 1986. Guidelines were enacted in March 1988 based on the OECD guidelines. In the case of the Special Committee on Personal Data Protection of the Centre for Financial Industry Information Systems (FISC), where investigations had begun at about the same time as at JIPDEC, their Guidelines on the Protection of Personal Data for Financial Institutions were adopted in March of the previous year. These guidelines are based on the OECD guidelines; and 'financial institutions' covers insurance companies, as well as financial institutions in the strict sense. The Directors of the Banking Bureau and of the Securities Bureau of the Ministry of Finance expressed the following views in respect of the guidelines:

It is thought that, along with the rapid development in recent years of information processing using computers, it has become necessary to take proper action concerning the protection of privacy under these circumstances. The recent independent enactment by the Centre for Financial Industry Information Systems, along with the agreement of finance-related businesses in relation to the 'Guidelines on the Protection of Personal Data for Financial Institutions' was quite timely. Hereafter, it is thought that each financial organization will be taking proper actions based on the guidelines, and it is the intention of this bureau to take a keen interest in observing developments.

The guidelines drew considerable attention as an example of comprehensive independent rules covering a specific field of the private sector. Furthermore, it was referred to in a report of a Commission of Inquiry set up by the Ministry of Finance. That is, the 19 May 1987 Report of the Commission of Inquiry on the Insurance Industry points out that, in the indemnity insurance industry, it is necessary to handle personal data properly and to compile detailed rules relating to the concrete application of such data in accordance with the guidelines.

The MITI policy, as mentioned above, will play a very important role in this matter, because MITI implemented the Report of the Personal Data Protection Sub-Committee by issuing circular notices to the business associations concerned on 28 June and promulgated the Rule on the Register concerning the Measures for the Protection of Computer-Processed Personal Data in the official gazette on 7 July 1989.

CONCLUSION

Legislation to protect the right to privacy in Japan has advanced considerably over the last decade, on the local and national levels as well as in the private sector. As we have seen, the development of a more complex information society – from 'mass media information society', through 'computer information society', to 'network information society' – has led to an increasing awareness of the need for legislation to protect the individual's right to privacy in Japan. Local governments, under pressure from their citizens, were quick to take up the challenges posed by burgeoning 'informationization', and to legislate to protect privacy. Progress has also been made in the private sector. Moreover, with the passage of the 1988 Personal Data Protection Act, the central government has accepted the implications of the 'network information society', and has legislated to protect the individual's privacy. With the passage of this legislation, Japanese law on the 'right to privacy' has become internationalized. Here, the role of the OECD in placing the issue on the international agenda should be positively evaluated. It is to be hoped that, in the implementation of this and other laws to protect an individual's right to privacy, Japan will maintain an international standard.

REFERENCES

Horibe, M. *Gendai no Puraibashii* (Contemporary Privacy), Tokyo: Iwanami Shoten.
—— (1988) *Puraibashii to Kōdō Jōhōka Shakai* (Privacy and the Advanced Information Society), Tokyo: Iwanami Shoten.
—— (1989) 'Privacy in Japan: the development of policy on personal data protection', in *Japan Computer Quarterly*: 78: 3–11.
—— 'A tentative English translation of the Japanese Personal Data Protection Act 1988', unpublished.

Part VII

The future

Chapter 16

Towards a new departure
Alternatives for Japan

Nagai Michio

RESPONSIBILITIES AS AN ECONOMIC POWER

Japan and its people are now standing at an important turning point in history. Indeed, the history of Japan and the history of the world are now intertwined as never before. It is in this context that the problems accompanying Japan's development as an economic power need to be addressed.

After Japan's defeat in 1945, the continued political and economic existence of the country was in doubt, and many people were on the verge of starvation. Though increased industrial activity during the Korean War period triggered the recovery of its economy, Japan had only a 3 per cent share of the world GNP in 1955. Not at that time a member of the OECD, the organization of advanced industrial countries, Japan was regarded by commentators in the West as a developing country, or what was then called an 'underdeveloped' country. The United States, in particular, acted as Japan's protector during and after the Occupation period and most Americans, Japanese and other people, regarded the relationship between the two as one between protector and protected. It was as a part of this 'special relationship' that the government and people of Japan were able to establish economic, political, social and educational systems to promote the national interest.

Under these circumstances, from the beginning of the 1950s, the Japanese economy took its first step towards recovery and eventually entered a period of remarkable development lasting some thirty years. In the 1960s the world as a whole enjoyed prosperity, but Japan recorded real economic growth rates of over 10 per cent annually. Ikeda Hayato, who took office as Prime Minister in July 1960, introduced the political slogan 'income doubling', but actually an unprecedented tripling of the average income was achieved by the end of the decade. However, what especially attracted the attention of the US and other advanced industrial countries was the amazing performance and adaptability demonstrated by Japan during the oil crises that rocked the global economy twice in the

1970s. At this juncture Japan's GNP exceeded 10 per cent of the world total, or about one half of the 20 per cent share of the United States.

In the 1980s, Japan developed further as an economic power, strengthened domestic production capacity, and took its position as the third major power in the international market, together with the US and Europe. The Japan of the immediate postwar era and the Japan of the 1980s are so different it is sometimes difficult to accept that they are one and the same country. Similarly, the relationship between the US and Japan has changed from one of protector and protected to one of competitors.

As a result of such changes, Japan now shoulders new responsibilities. First, it has to assume its share of responsibility as an equal partner in the world economy and promote free trade. Efforts are continuing, therefore, through GATT negotiations, to open the Japanese market to the free flow of agricultural products. Second, the current reality in Japan is far from the government's official position on market liberalization, which was set forth in the Maekawa Report.[1] The US government then pointed out that Japan, a special case by the standards of the West, could not be a satisfactory partner in the free market economy unless changes took place in its distribution system, enterprise affiliation patterns, and customary business practices. European countries and the NIEs (Newly Industrialized Economies) were also demanding that Japan open its markets. It was finally agreed, based on a proposal by the US government, to hold discussions from September 1989 onward on economic structures relevant to the relationship between the two countries. Third, in contrast to the position of Japan, the US (the leader of the world economy) is now suffering unprecedented deficits in both the federal budget and the trade balance. Other countries, including Japan, are therefore faced with the problem of co-operating to revitalize the US economy in order to maintain stability and growth in the world economy. Under such continually changing circumstances, what role can or should Japan play? Before answering this question, however, I wish to address another contemporary issue, that of the relationship between humanity, and science and technology.

SCIENCE, TECHNOLOGY AND HUMANITY

In the second half of the twentieth century, the development of science and technology has substantially influenced human society. In 1945, on 6 and 9 August, atomic bombs were dropped on Hiroshima and Nagasaki to decisively end a war that had become truly global. With the end of the war, the political and economic map of the world was redrawn, and the world economy started its remarkable upward spiral. Much of this was due to science and technology.

In the late 1950s, however, C.P. Snow, the British philosopher and scientist, in a book entitled *The Two Cultures and the Scientific Revolu-*

tion,[2] issued an ominous warning concerning science and technology. He predicted that if a fatal confrontation determining the future direction of human society and culture should arise, it would not take place between the ideologies of capitalism and socialism. Rather, a new culture based on science and technology would emerge which would be independent of the culture of human society constructed by people who have nothing to do with science and technology. As a result, Snow foresaw the two cultures forming the future of the world without any dialogue or interaction with one another. At almost the same time, S.S. Osowski, a Polish sociologist, made a prescient remark at an international sociological conference to the effect that communications and transportation resulting from the advance of science and technology would promote changes such as increased urbanization and a shifting of social classes, irrespective of ideology.[3] This has proved an accurate prediction of the historical developments that followed.

Though nuclear arms seem to be the key to the security of mankind, no country or international organization has ever reached a satisfactory solution to the questions posed by Snow and Osowski. Even after Hiroshima and Nagasaki, members of the nuclear arms club, including the US and the Soviet Union, have continued production of these weapons based on a doctrine of peace through deterrence established before the possibility of a nuclear holocaust. In 1987, however, the US and the Soviet Union discussed nuclear disarmament for the first time, and concluded the INF treaty. Before that, the Independent International Commission for Peace and Security organized in 1983 under the chairmanship of Olaf Palme, the late Swedish Prime Minister, proposed the new concept of 'common security' to the UN General Assembly on Disarmament. At Hiroshima, the Second World Conference of Mayors for Peace through Inter-City Solidarity was held in the summer of 1989. Among the participants were more than a hundred mayors from about thirty countries, including the US and the Soviet Union. Their joint proposal called for increased solidarity among local governments, pressing for peace in advance of central governments. As seen through these various activities, human beings harbour a strong desire for real security. However, up to now no conclusive answers have been reached on the problems of political systems and ideologies and on the fundamental relationship between science and technology and humanity.

From another perspective, the Club of Rome, formerly chaired by the late Mr Peccei of Italy, issued a 1972 report entitled *The Limits to Growth*, which warned that if industrialization maintains its present course the relentless processes of resource depletion, environmental degradation, overpopulation and food shortages will continue to the point that the evolution of mankind may come to a standstill early in the twenty-first century.[4] In the 1980s the global environmental problem emerged as the most serious of these four threats. Numerous warnings have been issued that exhaust gases and liquid and solid wastes are destroying the earth's environment and threatening the existence of humankind. This is further proof of the difficulty of uniting the two forms of culture envisaged by Snow.

It may be correct to observe that science and technology are responsible for Japan's stable and rapid industrialization. In the 1950s, the leaders of Japanese enterprises stressed a new approach, that of research and development within their own companies, as a path to industrial recovery. As a result, private enterprises have been responsible for three-quarters of the funding for research and development in Japan, while the government has paid for only one-quarter. In addition, enterprises have been active in linking the fruits of their research with the products they sell in the market-place. All told, we can safely say that the activities of enterprises in the postwar period have promoted science and technology.

On the other hand, we see little social-science research and education in Japanese universities concerned with the international and domestic problems that have resulted from such technological progress. Among these problems are how to harness science and technology for the development of the Third World, and how to prevent the global spread of environmental destruction. Within Japan, one of the problems involved in creating a harmonious society is how to disperse the population from the megalopolis centring upon Tokyo, where 30 million people, or one-quarter of the total population, now live. It is undeniable that science and technology are geared to economic pursuits in a society where business comes first. The fields of the social sciences and the humanities have, in contrast, been neglected in spite of their potential for solving such problems.

DEMOCRACY AND FREEDOM

The third topic I wish to address is that of democracy, freedom and related problems. Over the past four decades since the war, the US and the Soviet Union have competed in a struggle to establish their respective ideologies. Noticeable changes have occurred however, due to Gorbachev's policy of *perestroika*, and the breakdown of Cold War structures. These changes include, among others, the emergence of new governments in Eastern Europe, and the economic and political reforms now taking place in the Soviet Union. The influence and expansion of free markets can now be seen in that part of the world as well. Furthermore, it is important to note that developments in science and technology are bringing about similar changes in the two blocs despite the existence of different and contradictory ideologies.

In this new situation, how should Japan assess its own society and political system? Japan is committed to freedom and democracy in the fields of economics, politics, education and ideology. However, Japan has two characteristics which are not shared by the US or European countries. One is its position as a latecomer among the developed countries. The other is its location on the periphery of Asia and its differing cultural and social heritage. For these reasons, the subject of democracy and freedom in Japan is not a simple one. One key to understanding Japanese democracy is its origins in the American Occupation. It was the Occupation authorities which ordered the abrogation of the old Constitution and drew up the new version. It was also the Occupation authorities which directed the dissolution of the *zaibatsu* (financial cliques), which implemented land reforms and revived the labour unions, while preserving the Emperor as a symbol of the nation.

It should be noted that this democratization of Japan was far different from the Glorious Revolution of Britain, the French Revolution, or the founding of the United States. It was guided from the top by outsiders, as contrasted with the democratic revolutions in the West that arose from inside and were powered by those at the bottom of society. The nature of this reform, 'from the top and from the outside', also applies to some degree to the Meiji Restoration, in which the Japanese elites themselves, instead of the Occupation forces, were the driving force behind the creation of a modern nation state. However, on both of these occasions Japan was an underdeveloped country and was influenced to a considerable extent by the technical knowledge and ideology of the West.

In the flood of colonial independence movements in the years immediately after the war, as many as one hundred newly independent countries sprang up from the 1940s through the 1950s. It may have been inevitable, but these new nations contained various immature sectors, leading to nationalistic movements, counter-revolutions, or *coups d'état* bringing repeated turmoil to many parts of the globe. Even today, there are problems relating to the establishment of so many newly independent states in Asia, Africa and Latin America. The North now faces the problem of creating a process whereby developed countries of the North extend as much assistance and co-operation as possible to developing countries in the South, corresponding to their needs and helping to further global democracy.

Japan, as mentioned earlier, launched its social and economic reorganization from its earlier status as a developing country physically separated from the West. It had an extremely centralized administrative system already in place. This system consisted of the General Headquarters of the Occupation forces in Tokyo, which held supreme power, and the Japanese central government, with its entrenched bureaucracy (a legacy of the prewar era which survived Occupation attempts to uproot militaristic elements). The political system to emerge has, since the 1950s, concentrated on economic growth, employing a strong and efficient leadership. As

Professor Ezra Vogel sums up in *Japan as Number One,* Japan's political, business and bureaucratic networks operate as an integrated organism.[5] Decisions at the centre are accepted by a well-educated population, who are ready to carry out such directives. Enterprises and government bodies each have internal solidarity, resembling a fictitious family relationship. The strength of Japan's competitive power in the international marketplace comes from such social structures.

Nevertheless, Japan is under constant and increasing international pressure to reform its economic and social structures and participate in the world economy as a responsible partner. This would mean a departure from postwar policies centring solely on narrow concerns of national interest. Japan can no longer ignore the international demands being made upon it.

We in Japan should consider a liberalization which allows for the greater participation of those who are 'inside' and those who stand 'outside' an organization. In other words, a structure lacking in the familial organization characteristic of Japan. In this regard, the social system of the Soviet Union needs to be addressed. The socialism of the Soviet Union, based on Marxist Leninism, espoused the original aim of establishing socialist democracy. The policy of *perestroika* pursued by Gorbachev recognizes that the freedoms of economy, speech, ideology and politics are also indispensable for establishing democracy. Marx stated that absolute truth exists in socialism, the theory by which Party autocracy was justified. What is now under discussion and is being implemented in Eastern Europe is free economic activity, though on a limited scale, and the promotion of foreign trade.

In July of 1989, while on a visit to Budapest, I was made aware that there was a movement towards these kinds of policies. A non-communist Prime Minister was elected in Warsaw in August of that year, and we have subsequently witnessed the reunification of Germany. We cannot yet conclude at this stage whether democracy supported by freedom will progress further in the Soviet Union and Eastern Europe, or whether the changes are no more than a short-term expansion of freedom. However, Gorbachev's call for *perestroika* has undeniably cast doubt on the Soviet Union's socialist model.

Democracy and freedom, previously the monopoly of the US and Western European nations, have thus developed into universal principles. In this context, what position shall Japan take regarding democracy and freedom, the fundamental principles of society? The ruling and opposition parties, the bureaucracy, and the Japanese people as a whole are all confronted with this question.

CULTURAL ISSUES

In Japan too, social, political and economic change is very much a part of the national agenda. This, I think, is typified by the challenge posed to the judiciary by the Recruit Scandal and its implications for both the LDP and the administrative processes. Likewise, the extent to which the media can maintain its independence and authority when reporting scandals involving political corruption remains problematic. A free press and an independent judiciary are essential to the democratic functioning of society, and Japan must ensure that these basic democratic principles are strengthened.

In the Upper House election of June 1989, in which heated debates centred on the introduction of a consumption tax and other matters, the Liberal Democratic Party lost its longstanding majority. Interestingly, those who delivered this victory to the opposition parties were the female candidates who ran in the election and won large numbers of seats. Though women are guaranteed equal rights under the Constitution, they do not actually enjoy opportunities to act and speak freely at home, or in society at large. Their role remains peripheral in government, universities, and large companies. Despite such an impressive victory for women in the election, it is still difficult, therefore, to judge whether the present move-ment towards real equality between the sexes is temporary or the first sign of a new historical trend.

Regarding external affairs, can the Japanese people break away from the slavish admiration of the West and deal with the development, welfare and security needs of the developing nations of the South? The idea that increased Overseas Development Aid for developing countries will solve everything is now long out of date. The touchstone for Japan from now on is whether it can co-operate with people of other countries, developing and developed alike, on a person-to-person basis.

In the circumstances, the ultimate issue is culture. Japan and the Japan-ese people are now interacting with foreign governments and people within and without Japan on the basis of equality, freedom and democracy. When we focus on the cultural aspect of this phenomenon, is this the result of the waves of Westernization that have swept Japan repeatedly since the Meiji era, or the effect of external pressure via economics and politics? It is true that in the past Japan has tended to reconstruct its society and culture through Westernization and external pressure. If Japanese society is to renovate itself thoroughly, however, Japan's indigenous culture must be spurred by social changes and external forces to create a new culture firmly based on inherited culture.

The American scholars, Kent Calder and Roy Hofeinz, in their interest-ing book entitled *The East Asia Edge*,[6] expressed the opinion that Con-fucianism has played a positive role in the changing societies of Korea, Taiwan, Hongkong, Singapore and Japan, and has promoted the economic

development of these countries. Until recently, Confucianism has functioned to maintain conservative and sometimes reactionary attitudes in
China and Japan, encouraging devotion to the group and assuring the
domination of the weak by the powerful, the elderly and men. The reason
this ancient Chinese ideology is being re-examined today is that people
have come to re-evaluate the benefits of its pragmatism in the pursuit of
concrete and individual solutions to problems such as encouraging esteem
for learning and education, intellectualism, and moral training, as well as
promoting domestic responsibility, legitimizing the state, and guiding its
administration. I have introduced this reconsideration of Confucianism into
the discussion since, like Buddhism and other forms of Asian culture, it will
assist us in coming to an understanding of who we really are, now that
Japan and the world are at a historical turning point.

Finally, in conclusion, I wish to call the reader's attention to three
points.

First, I have argued that we can regard Japan as a society that, at least
since 1945, has pursued economic growth solely from the perspective of
national interest. Given the economic power Japan now wields and its position
within the global economy, however, we can no longer proceed on the
basis of narrow self-interest alone. Rather, Japan must now confront its
responsibilities in ensuring the development and stability of the world
economy.

Second, I have pointed out that not only the economy but also national
security depend largely on science and technology, and that various
problems are apparent when this is examined from the human and social
points of view. Thus, Japan should thoroughly review its goals from the
standpoint of the benefit of the individual and the society.

Third, Japan should never ignore the remarks, even if critical, from
foreign quarters about the nature of Japanese society. Profound consideration of Japan's culture is called for if Japan wishes eventually to become a
society where universal values prevail. I believe that dialogue and interaction between the cultures of the East and the West are necessary for this
purpose.

NOTES

1 The Maekawa Report, which was influential in promoting the internationalization of the Japanese economy, was published in 1986. The report gains its name
   from the Chairman of the committee which issued the Report, Maekawa
   Haruo, late President of the Bank of Japan.
2 C.P. Snow, *The Two Cultures and The Scientific Revolution*, (New York:
   Mentor), 1964. This was originally delivered as a public lecture at Cambridge
   University.
3 S.S. Osowski's statement is included in A. Inkels' 'Social stratification and
   mobility in the Soviet Union' in Seymour M. Lipset and Reinhardt Bendix (eds)

Class, Status and Power: Social Stratification in Comparative Perspective, London: Routledge & Kegan Paul, pp. 609–22.

4   The late A. Peccei formed the *Club of Rome* which published *The Limits to Growth*, D.L. Meadows, J. Randers and W.W. Behrems (eds), London: Pan, 1974.
5   Ezra Vogel, *Japan as Number One* Boston: Harvard, 1979.
6   R. Hofeinz and K.E. Calder, *The East Asia Edge*, New York: Basic Books, 1982.

Chapter 17

The internationalization of Japan

Katō Shūichi

INTRODUCTION

'Internationalization'

Key concepts in any meaningful discussion should be precise. By the word 'internationalization' I refer to a country's closer relations with foreign partners, or integration into the international community, whose members share some common values. The definition of 'internationalization' as the international administration of a certain area, or different outside powers' intervention in a regional conflict, is thus too narrow to cover the wide range of issues we wish to discuss here. The word '*kokusai*' (international) or '*kokusaika*' (internationalization), as it is currently used in Japan, on the other hand, is too vague to be a useful conceptual tool. '*kokusai-jin*' (internationalized person) often means nothing more than a Japanese who speaks English, while '*kokusai* taxi' (International Taxi-Cab Company) seems to imply just 'nice' taxi-cabs, which has nothing to do with the driver's linguistic ability.

Encouraged over the past decade by the government, '*kokusaika*' has become the latest in a series of all-embracing slogans. As was the case with *jiyū* (freedom) in the early Meiji era,[1] *kokusaika* has come to mean all things to all men. Following a well-established political tradition of employing euphemism, as in calling Japan's surrender in the last war *shūsen* (the end of the war) rather than *haisen* (defeat in the war) or the Occupation army *shinchūgun* (the stationed army) instead of *shinryakugun* (the invading army), *kokusai* is often trotted out as a cosmetic expression for something else – 'international responsibility' – not concessions made under American pressure, for example.

In discussing our topic, it is important to distinguish 'internationalization' as a given reality, and 'internationalization' as a goal to be attained. The former is the fact of Japan's economic, and technological, ties with the rest of the world; the latter, the aspiration for a stronger sense of belonging to the international community at large.

Internationalization *de facto*: economic aspects

Japan's economic expansion since the 1960s has been inseparable from its ever-increasing interdependence with the world outside – in terms of trade, investment, technology and labour. And the same factors in Japanese society that contributed to its remarkable 'economic success' also created friction, fear and resentment abroad. Japan imports food, energy and raw materials from outside, and exports manufactured goods, such as cars and electronics, to the international market. Through this pattern of trade, the natural resources of the Third World have been remorselessly exploited; and some industrial sectors in North America and Europe have been seriously threatened by the Japanese export drive. These occurrences of 'trade friction' have all too often developed into 'Japan bashing'.

It is true that Japanese investments abroad have created employment for the local population. But the purchase of real estate, such as the Rockefeller Center in New York, understandably produced alarming reactions in the United States. Although only a small fraction of American land and buildings is owned by Japanese firms, the Rockefeller Center is not just a building, but a symbol of the city's dynamism and wealth. Technological interdependence is an accepted reality for all industrial powers. Given trade friction, however, even that could lead to severe tension between two countries, as in the case of the American–Japanese FSX project to produce a new fighter support aircraft. The Japanese government has so far imposed stiff restrictions on the inflow of immigrants from Asian countries. Due to Japan's sustained industrial expansion, however, recruitment of domestic labour has recently become so difficult in certain sectors that the use of foreign labour has become inevitable. In the last decade, the number of legal and illegal immigrants has dramatically increased. This is a major challenge to a society which has little recent experience in properly handling foreign workers.

Moreover, certain conflicts are aggravated by the cultural traditions of Japan, which still preserves much of the legacy from its centuries of closure and isolation. The government and public opinion alike, are now increasingly aware that Japan's remorseless export-led economic success may itself be threatened by the failure to break free of the cocoon of cultural and social isolation. Hence the slogan of 'internationalization'. Here the word does not refer to any real situation, or facts, but designates, however vaguely, a goal to be achieved: the nation's desire for smoother communication and for better cultural exchange. On the other hand, the same economic success which has contributed to the recovery of self-confidence among the Japanese people has also spurred a revival of nationalism, a subject to which we will return later. It has not been mere coincidence that nationalism has gained ground in the last decade, at the same time that *kokusaika* has entered into everyday usage.

POLITICO-MILITARY DEPENDENCE ON THE US

An important factor in Japan's foreign relations has been, and continues to
be, its politico-military dependence on the United States. That exclusive
dependence since the Occupation years certainly helped the country's
economic recovery and further expansion – through the post-war American aid programme, benefits from the Korean War, and American
domestic market – leaving, however, little room for Japan to pursue its own
diplomacy. Under this pressure, Japan officially recognized the Taiwan
government instead of Beijing, and did not venture to resume diplomatic
relations with mainland China until American policy radically changed in
1971. During the Cold War period, Tokyo followed Washington so faith-
fully that no peace treaty was signed with the USSR. In Asia, Japan
profited from the Korean War, and later contributed much to South
Korean economic development, completely ignoring the existence of the
north. As for Europe, cultural influences and more recent trade and investment apart, political co-operation hardly existed. The overwhelming
American presence, especially that in the Cold War context, thus hindered
Japan's development of multilateral, international relations. The more
dependent on the US, the more isolated in the world. The reverse was also
true. Moreover, Japan's dependence did not remove friction with America,
either. The US–Japan Security Treaty meant for the US a guarantee of
Japan's security, the 'burden' of which should naturally be shared by Japan
in proportion to its wealth; for Japan, it meant also a tribute paid to
American military interests, through which American concessions could be
expected in other fields. Relationships between the two countries in the
framework of this treaty could not operate for long without producing
irritation on both sides.

Now the global Cold War is coming to a close. And if the Soviet 'threat'
had to be considered as immutable, then it is only logical to regard the
détente with the Soviets in the same way. No longer convincing is the
argument that, regardless of *détente* in Europe, military tensions persist in
the north-western part of the Pacific. Protection of Japan by American
nuclear forces is obviously less necessary in this situation. Indeed,
economic and technological competition among the industrial powers is
becoming more serious than the military. To such a situation the Japanese
government is reacting rather slowly; but this cannot be said of Japanese
companies. Mitsubishi Heavy Industry, the largest supplier of arms in
Japan, is said to have already decided to shift its main activities from the
military to the civilian field.[2]

TRADITIONAL VALUES

Japan is a group-oriented society, whose traditional values still resist openness towards the outside world. One of these traditional values is a sort of

double standard governing people's attitudes towards insiders and outsiders. That feature is salient, of course, in any self-sufficient, relatively isolated village community. However, unlike European, and most Asian, countries, pre-modern Japan was for a long time isolated from other nations: without wars, without intensive trade, without foreign immigrants. Probably as a result of that history, many of the values and customs in village life were transferred to modern Japan. Even today a great many company employees are inclined to identify themselves with their group, constantly emphasizing a sharp distinction between the insiders and outsiders. Many people in this country even go so far as to divide all human beings into two major categories: Japanese and non-Japanese. Cosmopolitans are rare, and cosmopolitan ideas and values are unwelcome.

Second, in the course of Japan's long history, people have been always reluctant to subscribe to any absolute value or any universal principle that transcends their own community. Kamakura Buddhism was perhaps the sole exception. True devotion to the 'divine' Emperor was often absolute in prewar Japan. But the Emperor was regarded as coterminous with the Japanese nation, and by no means anything beyond the national community. Japanese society today is committed to basic human rights at the legal level, but hesitates to recognize them in practice. Just to quote two examples: when Kim Daejun, the South Korean opposition leader, was kidnapped by South Korean agents on Japanese territory, the government handled the case without proper respect for Kim's human rights. When Vietnamese 'boat people' were helpless at sea, Japanese society failed to demonstrate a strong concern. Such an ambiguous attitude towards principles such as human rights, is part of long-standing tradition.

Third, within the group, consensus of opinion is highly valued. Minority opinions are not respected; instead, those who hold them are put under collective pressure to conform to the majority's standards. Such a practice inside Japan certainly does not help in coping with international relations, where a great variety of opinions always prevails. Thus, some cultural traditions hamper the 'internationalization' of Japan. Will this 'culture' change? Certainly, but not overnight.

Neo-nationalism

What I call 'neo-nationalism' is a sort of popular sentiment, widely felt at different levels of society, which has not yet crystallized into any political philosophy or coherent programme. 'Japan's past was after all not that bad', or 'now everything in Japan goes well', or 'in this and in that, Japanese performance is far superior to other people's'. Such sentiments could not have been uttered say thirty years ago, yet now they are commonplace: phrases of arrogance and revived nationalism.

It may not be difficult to explain this 'nationalistic' tide in the 1980s.

First, as a reaction to the Occupation years, where everything Japanese was regarded negatively, another extreme is now prevalent; namely, that everything Japanese must be good: a pendulum movement. Second, Japan's 'economic success' has been the major source for the recovery of self-confidence, and even arrogance. Third, the Nakasone government during the 1980s encouraged, and catered to, rising nationalistic feelings among the voters, and the mass media largely followed suit. To some extent the masses have been manipulated into neo-nationalism.

Some manifestations of this trend are worth noting. In 1986 Prime Minister Nakasone said in substance that the 'intelligence level' of the Japanese people was higher than that of Americans due to Japan's homogeneous population, in contrast to the mixture of different ethnic and racial groups in America, notably the blacks and Puerto-Ricans.[3]

Moreover, the Minister of Education in his Cabinet, Fujiō Masayuki, openly argued that the Tokyo war crimes trial had not been justified, that nobody knew the truth in the case of the Japanese army's complicity in the Nanking Massacre (1937), and that the annexation of Korea to Japan (1910) was no act of aggression, but only the consequence of an agreement between the two countries.[4] In other words, he proposed a radical revision, or rather a reconstruction, of Japan's recent history. In the same vein, the government attempted to delete the word 'aggression' and replace it with 'advance' in school textbooks describing the Japanese army's actions in China during the 1930s.[5] More recently, the Ministry of Education has imposed its policy on schools, making them hoist the rising sun flag, and sing the 'national anthem' of 'Long Live the Emperor' on ceremonial occasions. For many, the flag and the song remain symbols of Japan's militaristic past.

As for Shintoism, General Tōjō and other war leaders were quietly enshrined at the Yasukuni Shinto shrine, where visits of reverence by Cabinet members are now a regular occurrence. Without drawing much attention from the public, the reorganization of Shinto shrines also has been in progress, integrating regional deities into the centralized shrine system with royal ancestors at the top of the hierarchy. The *daijōsai*, a Shinto ceremony for the Emperor's succession, was held in autumn 1990, only to reaffirm the Emperor as a descendant of deities. There is some criticism of all this by a few intellectuals, journalists and small groups of citizens. But more vocal than this is the overwhelming chorus of the many politicians, business leaders, professors, columnists and popular writers of neo-nationalism. A question is posed: where is Japan heading?

PROSPECTS FOR THE FUTURE

Does 'internationalization' really mean an open-minded Japan beyond economic-technological interactions? Obstacles to that, as we have observed, are twofold: first, traditional values, which will remain by and large unchanged for the foreseeable future; second, the inertia of nearly a half-century-long dependence on the US, which will likely be modified due to the ending of the Cold War. There are also other factors which may promote a change: a large number of Japanese who have lived abroad, either as students, or as business representatives; and an urgent need for 'openness' in employment for the sake of economic efficiency.

Yet the experience of living abroad does not necessarily bring about fundamental changes in society. For example, students trained at foreign universities still face difficulties in finding good jobs on return to Japan. Even if they are employed by corporations, they are often assigned to work as interpreters. For any influence on the structure and policy of the company at large, their presence is not enough. Their assigned posts must be important in the firms. According to a recent study among trade representatives stationed abroad,[6] the 'openness' in attitude towards foreigners is proportional to the number of years of experience living in foreign countries. If Japanese companies keep these employees in the same posts long enough – say, for five years – then it will probably contribute to the 'internationalization' of Japan, too. However, the same study points out that 'internationalization' in lifestyle is more marked among the business people assigned to jobs abroad in the 1960s than those so assigned in the 1970s and 1980s. During the same period, the number of Japanese working abroad dramatically increased. In other words, the more people living abroad, the less 'internationalization'. One reason for this may be that only the strongly motivated elite went to foreign countries during the 1960s; while those working abroad in the 1970s and 1980s are no longer the elite, and are less motivated. Another reason may be that a bigger Japanese colony can, and does, provide more and more Japanese facilities, such as schools, shops, TV programmes and newspapers all in the Japanese language, so that the whole colony can become almost completely isolated from the rest of the society, except in business and other transactions. It is now possible, for example, to live for three years in New York without uttering a single word of English.

Despite all these limitations, however, some students and business representatives are certainly open in their attitudes towards different cultures, and are in that sense being 'internationalized'. Even tourists might be better than nothing in that respect. Organized group tourism usually fails to produce anything meaningful. But half of Japanese tourists are travelling abroad alone or in pairs, so some of them may find a new way to approach the world. Most Japanese companies seem intent upon recruiting their future cadres from the Japanese male population, excluding women and foreigners. But the recent shortage of competent employees in skilled advanced technology, and in some rapidly developing industries, has compelled many companies to adopt a new employment policy of recruiting anyone competent and willing, regardless of sex or nationality. That trend will probably continue in the decades to come. There will be no other choice, indeed, for efficiency and competitiveness. And the presence of women and foreigners at the workplace will not fail to move people towards openness, equality and cultural pluralism.

We have observed what inhibits or promotes the 'internationalization of the Japanese mind', so to speak. The balance between the two processes will decide Japan's future. Unhappy, for Japan as well as for the rest of the world, if Japanese industrial power develops without a strong sense of responsibility for mankind at large. Happy, potentially, if an internationally minded Japan finds a way to use its skill and wealth, not for the destruction, but for the saving of all the lives and resources of our small earth.

NOTES

1   By the year 1882, at the height of the *Jiyū Minken* Movement, a great many things were epitomized by the word '*jiyū*'. Not only was the newspaper of the movement called *Jiyū Shimbun*, but also pills (*jiyū gan*), restaurants (*jiyū tei*) public baths (*jiyū no yu*), handkerchiefs (*jiyū tenugui*), and cosmetic powders (*jiyū oshiroi*), were called '*jiyū*'. Quoted by Ishida Takeshi, *Nihon no Seiji to Kotoba*, (Japanese Politics and Language) I, Tokyo: Daigaku Shuppankai, 1989, pp. 36–7.
2   *The Asahi Shimbun*, 12 June, 1990.
3   Statement made in a meeting of Liberal Democratic Party deputies, 22 September 1986. American reactions were so strong that Prime Minister Nakasone was later forced to apologize.
4   Masayukio Fujiō, 'Hogen Daijin Ōi ni Hoeru' (The Outspoken Minister has More to Say) *Bungeishunjū*, October 1986.
5   Chinese and Korean embassies in Tokyo protested; the government had to revise its position over the textbook issue.
6   Sawada Akio and Kadowaki Atsushi (eds), *Nihonjin no Kokusaika* (Internationalization of the Japanese), Tokyo: Nihonkeizai Shimbunsha, 1990.

Index

All references are to Japan and Japanese institutions, unless otherwise stated.

Castles, S. 212, 241
Centre for Education Research and
    Innovation (CERI) 281
Centre for Financial Industry
    Information Systems (FIISC) 286
children: educated abroad 2, 40, 65;
    living overseas 280–81; returnees 40,
    67–8, 95, 240, 280; *see also*
    education
China: cultural and social exchange
    194–5; nineteenth century 106–8;
    promotion of labour migration 235
Chinese residents 246; in Kanagawa
    200–201; racial discrimination 239;
    support for illegal Chinese workers
    236
Churchill, Sir Winston Spencer 21, 174
Clean Government Party (CGP) 178,
    183
closing of Japan 39–40
Club of Rome 303
Coates, Bryan 10
Cold War: as basis for economic
    stability 57; as basis for European
    stability 56; benefits to Japan 36;
    collapse of 32, 36, 304
collaboration, Britain and United States
    21–6, 29–30
Communist Party 175, 178
Communist trade unions 263–4
computer privacy 286–7, 288–9
Confucianism 46, 307–8
Conquest, R.C. 7, 131–48
Conservative Party (British) 26–8
construction industry: labour shortages
    216–17; trade unions 255–6, 264;
    unskilled migrant workers 256
consumerism 38, 45
Corn Laws 7
corporate culture 66–7
corporate philanthropy 67
Cowling, M. 23
Crowe, Sir Eyre 20
cultural exchange 85–91; with Chinese
    194–5; corporate initiatives 89–90;
    Japan Exchange and Teaching (JET)
    Programme 10, 94, 275; local
    community level 193; private
    initiatives 89–90; public opinion
    79–81
cultural exclusiveness 41, 64, 249–50,
    315

culture 307–8; American 32–3, 37–8,
    42–6, 118; American interest in 48,
    66; and Americanization 37–8;
    corporate 66–7; traditional values
    312–14
currency reserves 145–6
current account surplus 131

Daewoo Motors 155, 165
data protection 3, 11, 284–98
Delors, Jacques 27
democracy 104–15, 304–6; grafted
    174–7; introduced by Occupation
    forces 37, 46, 114, 175–7, 301, 305
Democratic Socialist Party (DSP) 178,
    183
developing countries *see* aid to
    developing countries
diplomatic initiative 42
discrimination *see* racial discrimination
dollar standard 119

ecological problems 45, 49–50, 58–9,
    303–4
economic exchange programmes 197–9
economic growth and voting trends
    184–6
Economic Planning Agency 72, 81
economic policy 119–30; British 28
economic protectionism 41, 47
economic union, European 27–8, 121
economy, historical development 301–2
Edo (Tokyo) 174
Edogawa Union 258, 263
education: Centre for Educational
    Research and Innovation (CERI)
    281; closed system 271; foreign
    students in Japan 68–9, 88, 275–9;
    foreign teachers in Japan 275, 279;
    internationalization of 68, 92–3,
    98–9, 269–82; Japan Exchange and
    Teaching (JET) Programme 10, 94,
    275; Japanese children abroad 2, 40,
    65; Japanese students abroad 93,
    275–7, 315; Japanese studies 88;
    Japanese teachers sent abroad 275,
    279–80; Korean residents 280–1;
    language teaching *see* language
    teaching; migrant workers 281;
    Ministry of 85, 94, 269; National
    Council on Educational Reform 269,
    281; returnee children 40, 67–8, 95,